Mission Creep

Mission Creep

The Militarization of US Foreign Policy?

Gordon Adams and
Shoon Murray

Editors

Georgetown University Press / Washington, DC

Library of Congress Cataloging-in-Publication Data

Mission creep : the militarization of US foreign policy? / Gordon Adams
and Shoon Murray, editors.
       pages   cm
Includes bibliographical references and index.
ISBN 978-1-62616-114-6 (hardcover : alk. paper) — ISBN 978-1-62616-093-4 (pbk. : alk. paper)
            — ISBN 978-1-62616-094-1 (ebook)
1. United States—Foreign relations—21st century. 2. United States—Military relations
    3. United States—Military policy. 4. United States. Department of Defense.
 5. United States. Department of State. 6. Interagency coordination—United States.
7. Civil-military relations—United States. I. Adams, Gordon, 1941– , author, editor of compilation.
      II. Murray, Shoon Kathleen, 1961– , author, editor of compilation.
            JZ1480.M567 2014
            327'73—dc23
            2014011282

Cover Design by Connie Gabbert Design and Illustration LLC

♾ This book is printed on acid-free paper meeting the requirements
of the American National Standard for Permanence in Paper for
Printed Library Materials.

15 14 13   9 8 7 6 5 4 3 2 First printing
Printed in the United States of America

Contents

Illustrations

Acronyms and Abbreviations

ACP	Andean Counterdrug Program
ACSA	Acquisition and Cross-Servicing Agreements
ADT	Agribusiness Development Teams
AECA	Arms Export Control Act
AFRICOM	US Africa Command
AFS	Allied Forces Support
AOR	area of responsibility
AQAP	Al-Qaeda in the Arabian Peninsula
AQN ExOrd	Al-Qaeda Network Execute Order
ASCs	Armed Service Committees
AUMF	Authorization for Use of Military Force
BBG	Broadcasting Board of Governors
CCIF	Combatant Commanders' Initiative Fund
CD	counter-drug (DOD term for counternarcotics)
CENTCOM	US Central Command
CERP	Commander's Emergency Response Program
CIA	Central Intelligence Agency
CIF	Commander-in-Chief's Initiative Fund (renamed CCIF)
CJTF-HOA	Combined Joint Task Force—Horn of Africa
CN	counternarcotics
COCOM	combatant command
COIN	counterinsurgency
COM	chief of mission
CPI	Committee on Public Information
CT	counterterrorism
CTFP	Counterterrorism Fellowship Program
CTPT	Counterterrorism Pursuit Teams
CTR	Cooperative Threat Reduction Program
DATT	defense attaché
DoD	Department of Defense
DOS	Department of State
DSCA	Defense Security Cooperation Agency
EPIC	Enhanced International Peacekeeping Capability Education and Training Program
ESF	Economic Support Fund

EUCOM	US European Command
FAA	Foreign Assistance Act of 1961, as amended
FMF	Foreign Military Financing
FMS	Foreign Military Sales
FSN	Foreign Service Nationals
GAO	Government Accountability Office
GSCF	Global Security Contingency Fund
GWOT	Global War on Terror
HAC	House Appropriations Committee
HAC-D	House Defense Appropriations Subcommittee
HAC-SFO	House State, Foreign Operations, and Related Programs Subcommittee
HAP	Humanitarian Assistance Program
HASC	House Armed Services Committee
HCA	humanitarian and civic action
HFAC	House Committee on Foreign Affairs
HPSCI	House Permanent Select Committee on Intelligence
IMET	International Military Education and Training
IMF	International Monetary Fund
INCLE	International Narcotics Control and Law Enforcement
IO	information operations
JCET	Joint Combined Exercise Training
JCS	Joint Chiefs of Staff
JSOC	Joint Special Operations Command
JSSR	Justice and Security Sector Reform
LE	law enforcement
MCC	Millennium Challenge Corporation
MIST	Military Information Support Operations
MLE	Military Liaison Elements
MNNA	Major Non-NATO Ally
MoD	Ministry of Defense
MODA	Ministry of Defense civilian advisors program
MSP	mission strategic plan
NADR	Nonproliferation, Anti-terrorism, Demining, and Related Programs
NDAA	National Defense Authorization Act
NGO	nongovernmental organization
NORTHCOM	US Northern Command
NSC	National Security Council
NSS	National Security Staff

ODC	Office of Defense Cooperation
OFDA	Office of Foreign Disaster Assistance
OHDACA	Overseas, Humanitarian, Disaster Assistance and Civic Action
OMB	Office of Management and Budget
OWI	Office of War Information
PACOM	US Pacific Command
PAO	Public Affairs Officer
PCCF	Pakistan Counterinsurgency Capability Fund
PCF	Pakistan Counterinsurgency Fund
PDO	public diplomacy officer
PEPFAR	President's Emergency Plan for AIDS Relief
PfP	Partnership for Peace
PKO	Peacekeeping Operations
POLAD	political adviser
PPBS	Planning, Programming, and Budgeting System
PPG	Presidential Policy Guidance
PRT	Provincial Reconstruction Teams
psyops	psychological operations
QDDR	Quadrennial Diplomacy and Development Review
QDR	Quadrennial Defense Review
RFE	Radio Free Europe
RL	Radio Liberty
SAC	Senate Appropriations Committee
SAC-D	Senate Defense Appropriations Subcommittee
SACEUR	Supreme Allied Commander Europe
SAC-SFO	Senate State, Foreign Operations, and Related Programs Subcommittee
SAO	Security Assistance Organization
SASC	Senate Armed Services Committee
SDO	senior defense official
SFRC	Senate Foreign Relations Committee
SOCOM	US Special Operations Command
SOF	Special Operations Forces
SOUTHCOM	US Southern Command
SSCI	Senate Select Committee on Intelligence
SSR	Security Sector Reform
TMA	traditional military activities
USAID	United States Agency for International Development
USC	United States Code

USIA	United States Information Agency
USTR	United States Trade Representative
VOA	Voice of America
WIF	Warsaw Initiative Funds

Acknowledgments

We owe thanks to many people for their insights and assistance: Louis Goodman, Dana Priest, Cathy Downes, James Goldgeier, Jordon Tama, Eric Fillinger, Erin Quinn, Uri Lerner, Mary Kaszynski, Eric Loui, Nathan Levine, Russell Rumbaugh, Rebecca Williams, Paul Clayman, Ann Richards, Matthew Leatherman, Michael Miklaucic, Chuck Call, Carl LeVan, Annabel Hertz, David Glaudemans, John Cappel, Karen Saunders, Greg LeRoy, and Donald Jacobs.

PART I

THE INSTITUTIONAL AND POLITICAL CONTEXT

Chapter 1

An Introduction to Mission Creep

Gordon Adams and Shoon Murray

Overall, even outside Iraq and Afghanistan, the United States military has become more involved in a range of activities that in the past were perceived to be the exclusive province of civilian agencies and organizations. This has led to concern among many organizations ... about what's seen as a creeping "militarization" of some aspects of America's foreign policy. This is not an entirely unreasonable sentiment.

—Secretary of Defense Robert Gates, July 15, 2008,
speech to the US Global Leadership Campaign, Washington, DC

Introduction

Over the past seven decades and, at an accelerating pace since the terrorist attacks on September 11, 2001 (hereafter 9/11), the Department of Defense has expanded its activities and programs into areas that go beyond core military operations. The Pentagon's "mission creep" has been the result of a gradual accretion of responsibilities, authorities, and funding. It has been accommodated, and sometimes accelerated, by the choices made by senior policy officials and congressional representatives, and by the weaknesses and culture of the civilian foreign policy institutions themselves. The trajectory is toward a growing imbalance of resources and authority over national security and foreign policy between the Defense Department and the civilian tools of American statecraft.

In 2008, seven years into America's global war on terrorism, the swift migration of traditionally civilian tasks to the Pentagon provoked even the secretary of defense and the chairman of the Joint Chiefs of Staff (JCS)—in a surprising role-reversal given normal turf conflicts in Washington—to warn about "creeping militarization" (Gates 2008). Secretary Robert Gates observed that "America's civilian institutions of diplomacy and development have been chronically undermanned and underfunded for far too long—relative to what we traditionally spend on the military" (Gates 2008). Admiral Mike Mullen echoed the same concern. The JCS chairman alluded to a troubling political dynamic: Because the military is seen by the political leadership as more capable, it is increasingly used in noncombat missions, and given more resources, thereby leading to an even greater weakness in civilian agencies over time. Then the military is again asked to do more, and the dynamic continues. "I believe we should be more willing to break this cycle, and say when armed forces may not always be the best choice to take the lead," Mullen concluded (quoted in Shanker 2009).

President Barack Obama, responding to such concerns, has sought to integrate the foreign policy/national security toolkit. His administration has emphasized the importance of approaching global issues from the perspective of the "3Ds: Diplomacy, Development and Defense" and using the "whole-of-government" to deal with them. Despite this rhetoric, however, the administration has not righted the balance. These efforts have been weakly funded, leaving a growing institutional and budgetary imbalance in place. Indeed, it is telling that retired three- and four-star generals and admirals continue to lobby Congress about the need to give resources to the State Department and the US Agency for International Development (USAID).[1]

The military's mission creep is not new and it is not a secret. It has been the subject of news articles, conferences (including one that formed the basis for this book), think-tank reports, government studies, petitions to Congress, and congressional hearings. Still, there has been no empirical study examining this trend across different issue areas of policy and over time. This book fills that gap.

Warning Signs of Mission Creep after 9/11

Why were Gates and Mullen, and so many others, concerned about the weakening of the civilian tools of government? What signs did people see that the military services and the Pentagon were increasingly expanding into civilian space after 9/11? What had changed?

Most striking, the military expanded its development, governance, and humanitarian assistance programs around the world—activities such as drilling wells, building roads, constructing schools and clinics, advising national and local governments, and supplying mobile services of optometrists, dentists, doctors, and veterinarians overseas.[2] The examples are plentiful: Army National Guardsmen drilling wells in Djibouti; the US Army Corps of Engineers building school houses in Azerbaijan; and US Navy Seabees building a postnatal care facility in Cambodia, to cite a few (Redente 2008; Ward 2008; Burk 2012). Many development practitioners became suspicious of such increased military activity in their area of expertise and a public debate ensued in Washington about DoD's proper role in overseas developmental assistance. Joe Biden, then chairman of the Senate Foreign Relations Committee, described the trend that had raised concerns in a 2008 hearing on the topic: "Between 2002 and 2005, the share of U.S. official development assistance channeled through the Pentagon budget surged from 5.6 percent in 2002 to 21.7 percent in 2005, rising to $5.5 billion. Much of this increase has gone towards activities in Iraq and Afghanistan. But it still points to an expanding military role in what were traditionally civilian programs" (US Senate 2008).

The Pentagon even incorporated nation-building activities into its military doctrine. For example, the 2005 DoD Directive 3000.05 made "stability operations" a "core U.S. military mission," defining these as "various military missions, tasks, and activities . . . to maintain or reestablish a safe and secure environment, provide essential governmental services, emergency infrastructure reconstruction, and humanitarian relief" (US Department of Defense 2005a). It is a remarkable development that the Pentagon would give marching orders for the services and commands to consider noncombat tasks on par with warfighting. The individual services then reflected the changed priorities in their own guidance documents.[3]

For many, the US Africa Command (AFRICOM), stood up in 2008, came to symbolize this broader perspective on military responsibilities. It was expected that the command would do little fighting but much training and development, that it would focus more on prevention than on warfighting, and that it would even incorporate civilians from the State Department into the leadership of the command. Tasks such as "reconstruction efforts," "turning the tide on HIV/AIDS and malaria," and "fostering respect for the rule of law, civilian control of the military, and budget transparency" were included in AFRICOM's theater strategy (Reveron 2010, 87). The Combined Joint Task Force for the Horn of Africa (CJTF-HOA) based at Camp Lemonnier in Djibouti, the military's primary forward presence in Africa, focused most of its activities on civil affairs projects such as humanitarian assistance, medical care, and building infrastructure.[4]

Because of its expanded focus on stabilization and reconstruction operations, DoD requested and was provided new authorities, programs, and funding. Programs such as the Global Train and Equip (known as "Section 1206") or the Commander's Emergency Response Program (CERP) allowed the generals and admirals who oversee US military activities abroad (known as the geographic combatant commanders) greater flexibility to distribute security and developmental assistance. As a consequence, the State Department, which at one time had sole authority over foreign military aid and training programs, lost ground. As shown in Figure 1.1, the share of overall US security assistance administered through the DoD rose from about 25 percent to almost 70 percent in the post–9/11 era, although it started to come down in 2012. (See Serafino, Chapter 7, for an alternative analysis that excludes war-related programs.)

Media reports also warned of the military's increasing involvement in public information campaigns abroad. Headlines in the *New York Times*, *Washington Post*, and *USA Today* read: "Hearts and Minds: Pentagon Readies for Efforts to Sway Sentiment Abroad," "The Military's Information Is Vast and Often Secretive," and "Pentagon Launches Foreign News Websites."[5] Most stories were about information campaigns and "psychological operations" that the military ran during the Iraq War. But a more lasting institutional change also occurred. The Special Operation Command (SOCOM) has taken on a public diplomacy role, working with the geographic combatant commanders; it has created military-run web sites and other informational material to reach foreign audiences and has sent out small teams to embassies around the world to do "information operations" (Rumbaugh and Leatherman 2012; Carlson, Chapter 8).

Even the civilian agency closest to the Pentagon as a "hard power" tool—the Central Intelligence Agency—has seen DoD expanding directly into its turf since 9/11, both in intelligence gathering and analysis and in covert operations. The Pentagon's Special Operations Command (SOCOM)—not the CIA—was given the lead role to synchronize the "global war on terror." Early on, SOCOM sent out teams to conduct its own intelligence, sometimes without the knowledge of the ambassador (Murray and Quinton, Chapter 9). The Joint Special Operations Command (JSOC), a component of SOCOM, has been deeply involved in the "shadow war" to hunt down and capture or kill al-Qaeda operatives in Afghanistan and elsewhere (Mazzetti 2013a; Kibbe, Chapter 11).

Basic appropriation levels point out the striking disparity in resources and personnel between the military and civilian institutions of statecraft. At more than $600 billion a year, the defense budget is twelve times the size of the total budgets available to the civilian foreign policy institutions (see Figure 1.2). The Defense Department workforce is more than a hundred times larger than the State Department and USAID combined (see Adams, Chapter 2). If the Reserves and National Guard are included, the personnel ratio is more than 155 to 1. Such a profound asymmetry between the military and nonmilitary

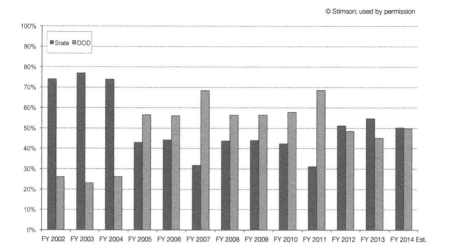

Figure 1.1
State and Defense Department Shares of Security Assistance FY, 2002–14

Sources: Defense and State Congressional Budget Justification materials; OMB Public Database; National Defense Authorization Acts.

agencies, as David Kilcullen observed, is not normal for other Western democracies. The "typical size ratio between armed forces and diplomatic/aid agencies for other Western democracies," he wrote in 2009, "is on the order of 8–10:1" (Kilcullen 2009, 50). To bring home the US disparity in resources, Kilcullen used the now-famous fact that there are "substantially more people employed as musicians in Defense bands than in the entire foreign service" (Kilcullen 2007).

Putting Post–9/11 Mission Creep into Historical and Political Context

The historical origins of this institutional imbalance are rooted in decisions made at the beginning of the Cold War. The National Security Act of 1947, the Truman Doctrine (1947), the creation of the North Atlantic Treaty Organization (NATO) alliance (1949), White House policy memorandum NSC-68 (1950), and the Korean War (1950–53) all played major roles in the creation of foreign policy and national security institutions that had not previously existed: a large, permanent standing Army, a unified civilian establishment to oversee all the military services, a standing intelligence service, and a national

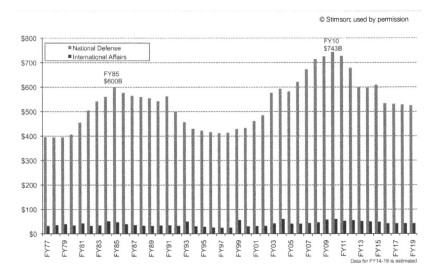

Figure 1.2
National Defense and International Affairs Discretionary Budget Authority

Constant 2013 dollars (billions)
Source: OMB Historical Tables 5-6, 5-1, and 10-1.

security coordination process in the White House—the National Security Council (Gaddis 1972; LaFeber 1973; Ambrose and Brinkley 2010).

Over the succeeding decades, defense budgets and capabilities rapidly surpassed those of the civilian agencies and the Defense Department grew more sophisticated in its strategic, program, and resource planning (Whittaker, Smith, and McKune 2011). From the war in Korea, which left a larger Army in place than before 1950, to Vietnam, to the 1990s, defense resources reached a high level of stability averaging roughly $400 billion in constant 2013 dollars. During the Cold War, the logic of the confrontation with the Soviet Union became a military logic[6]; the comparisons between the two superpowers were military comparisons. Defense budgets and capabilities grew as a direct consequence. Even after the end of the Cold War, US defense budgets remained high, and with the terrorist attacks of 9/11 and the invasions and occupations of Afghanistan and Iraq, the annual average defense budget between FY 2001 and FY 2010 rose to $615 billion in constant 2013 dollars (see Figure 1.2 above).

From an institutional perspective, the Defense Department had enormous capacity to raise funds, attract talented planners, recruit forces, and provide long-term training and career mobility. Defense budgets were spent heavily on weapons systems manufactured and forces deployed in the United States, creating close links between the services and American industry, leading to President Dwight Eisenhower's warning about the risks of "unwarranted influence" by the military-industrial complex. US global military presence was rationalized into regional combatant commands (Watson 2010). The Defense Department created a miniature State Department in 1977, the Office of the Undersecretary of Defense for Policy, to handle strategic planning, policy development, and international negotiations on military issues.

As this evolution of the military institutions proceeded, the services and the Office of the Secretary of Defense created and institutionalized programs and activities beyond the core missions of deterrence and military combat.[7] To be sure, the military has long been involved in noncombat tasks, such as disaster relief, engineering projects, medical readiness exercises, and humanitarian and civic assistance (Graham 1993). But the scope and prioritization of these noncombat activities changed over time.

Starting in the 1980s, for example, the military extended its activities into counternarcotics operations and the Congress formalized authority for the ongoing military practice of conducting humanitarian activities (Serafino, Chapter 7).

The 1990s saw an even more significant expansion in the noncombat tasks assigned to the military. The United States has a long tradition of deploying military assets to deliver humanitarian assistance in response to earthquakes, tsunamis, hurricanes, and other natural disasters, but these deployments increased after the Cold War (Cobble, Gaffney, and Gorenburg 2003). Troops were sent to provide humanitarian assistance to the Kurds in Northern Iraq, to Somalia, to parts of the former Soviet Union, and became involved in stabilization and reconstruction efforts in Bosnia, Haiti, and Kosovo.

US policymakers and military leaders were initially cautious about the "mission creep" involved in these operations. They saw such missions as secondary "military operations other than war" (MOOTW). The deployments were meant to be brief: US leaders remained reticent to take on the complex roles of long-term institution building and development (Zinni and Koltz 2006; Priest 2003).

Eventually the Clinton administration came to believe that US policy and programs for postconflict reconstruction needed to be more formalized to produce sustained results, including an active role for the military in the promotion of the administration's strategy of engagement abroad. While the initial US troop commitment to the NATO-led Implementation Force (IFOR) in Bosnia and Herzegovina did not extend to law enforcement activities, the US troops committed to the subsequent NATO Stabilization Force (SFOR) became more involved in restoring public services, economic reconstruction, and internal governance issues (Dobbins et al. 2003, 96–97). The Kosovo mandate expanded even further to include "ensuring public safety" and "co-ordinating closely" with the "work of the international civil presence" (Dobbins et al. 2003, 115).

By the end of the 1990s, the United States and the international community had contended with a disintegrated Soviet Union, the failed state in Somalia, the restoration of democracy in Haiti, and the genocidal disintegration of Yugoslavia. The US military was building security cooperation in central Europe through the Partnership for Peace (PfP), which incorporated a military socialization and training prerequisite for former Warsaw Pact countries to be considered for inclusion in NATO. The White House had labeled the military's role in regional engagement strategies as an "essential" part of the National Security Strategy and the secretary of defense had encouraged the geographic combatant commanders to take a broader and more preventative approach—to "shape the environment" in their designated regional "areas of responsibility" (Priest 2003; Zinni and Koltz 2006; Murray and Quainton, Chapter 9).

These trends accelerated after 9/11, even though ironically the George W. Bush administration came into office determined to halt and reverse the expansion of military activities into "nation building." The shock of the 9/11 attacks, the subsequent prioritization of counterterrorism as the new organizing principle of US foreign policy, and the decision to invade Iraq created new rationales and circumstances that led the Bush administration to abandon such reservations. The unexpected counterinsurgencies in Iraq and Afghanistan, in particular, transformed US policymakers' attitudes about the use of the military for nation-building, stabilization, and reconstruction. Faced with a high risk of failure, US policymakers and military leaders rediscovered—in the words of Gen. David Petraeus—"the age-old counterinsurgency tenet: Eighty percent is political, twenty percent is military" (Hodge 2011, 156). The US government embraced nation building and an active role for the military in a manner not seen since the Vietnam War (Hodge 2011).

The civilian side of the US government could not mobilize for governance reform, humanitarian assistance, and the rebuilding of infrastructure in Iraq and Afghanistan with the same speed or apparent competence. The Bush administration had not anticipated the need for a postconflict stabilization and reconstruction effort, and long-term underinvestment in the State Department and US Agency for International Development (USAID) during the 1990s had left these agencies unprepared to meet the surge in demand for stability in conflict situations or in fragile states. Consequently, the Pentagon, with its "can do" attitude and surge capacity, took on new nation-building, governance, economic development, and humanitarian assistance roles.

The military's role in stabilization and reconstruction extended well beyond these two combat zones. As part of the broader confrontation with terrorist organizations, new priority was given to stabilization and institution building in weak states. The al-Qaeda attacks, organized from training camps in Afghanistan, gave meaning to the idea that conditions within a weak state could threaten the national security of the United States. The military's so-called "phase zero" (precombat) operations in Africa and elsewhere were intended to "shape the environment" so that stable institutions could be built and extremism and violence did not develop (Ploch 2011).

DoD's Directive 3000.05 embodied this change in thinking and missions. The directive committed the military to operations "across the spectrum from peace to conflict to establish or maintain order in States and regions," giving them "priority comparable to combat operations." The long-term goal of such operations is to "help develop indigenous capacity for securing essential services, a viable market economy, rule of law, democratic institutions, and a robust civil society." The mission was broadly defined to include "develop[ing] representative governmental institutions" and "ensuring security, developing local governance structures, promoting bottom-up economic activity, rebuilding infrastructure, and building indigenous capacity for such tasks." Recognizing that these were or should be core missions for civilian institutions, the DoD directive argued that the military must be "prepared to perform all tasks necessary to establish or maintain order when civilians cannot do so" (US Department of Defense 2005a). This mission expansion reflected the military's experience in Iraq and Afghanistan and the prevailing view that civilian institutions such as State and USAID were not capable of carrying out these tasks.[8]

As part of this stabilization mission, the military also expanded its role in security assistance and cooperation programs during the Iraq and Afghanistan wars. Traditionally, US security assistance programs were the responsibility of the State Department, under the Foreign Assistance Act of 1961 and the Arms Export Control Act of 1976, reflecting the reality that equipping and training another country's military is a decision with foreign policy consequences that can affect diplomatic relationships with the United States, the American image abroad, and the balance of power in a region. As the wars in Iraq and Afghanistan and the conflict with terrorist organizations proceeded, however, DoD began to develop its own security assistance programs, under its own authorities and funded through its own budget, including supporting foreign governments' military budgets, training Afghan and Iraqi security and police forces, and creating a new, global security assistance program to support counterterrorism training and equipping. As shown in Figure 1.1, by 2011 DoD was directly providing close to 70 percent of US security assistance overseas.[9] Though the US military has always played a central role in the shaping and implementing of US security assistance programs, this new agenda expanded the military's funding and direct authority over these programs and expanded their coverage to a wider set of security-related activities (Adams and Williams 2011; Serafino et al. 2008; Serafino 2011a, and Chapter 7). Even though the DoD share drops as the US draws down from two wars, it remains high (estimated at 50 percent in FY 2014) and the precedent has been established.

By contrast, the civilian foreign policy institutions have lagged consistently behind in this evolution. Resources for personnel, diplomacy, and foreign assistance rose during the 1950s as an integral part of the Cold War strategy, but then declined over the succeeding decades. As this book documents, the United States developed a fragmented architecture of institutions on the civilian side of the foreign policy toolkit after World War II (Adams, Chapter 2). The broad decline in resources and institutional capabilities on the civilian side left these institutions ill-equipped to respond to a rising demand for reconstruction and stabilization efforts in Iraq and Afghanistan and broader efforts to strengthen weak states. As a result, DoD was given more responsibility for these counterinsurgency and counterterrorism missions, leading some military leaders to worry about where the capacity of the civilian institutions had gone.

Today DoD and the military services have extensive operations and responsibility in the broader areas of foreign policy strategy planning[10]; military diplomacy (Priest 2003; Reveron 2004; Murray and Quainton, Chapter 9); relationships with foreign security forces of all kinds and the wider security sectors of other countries (Reveron 2010; Reveron, Chapter 4); economic assistance and governance advising (Van Buren 2011; Hodge 2011; Anderson and Veillette, Chapter 6); public diplomacy and strategic communications (Defense Science Board 2011; Rumbaugh and Leatherman 2012; Carlson, Chapter 8); and human intelligence and covert operations (Miller 2006; Kibbe, Chapter 11).[11]

Defining Militarization

Should this "militarization" trend and institutional imbalance cause concern? Does it raise questions about civil-military relations in the United States? In some striking ways, this institutional trend raises issues not dealt with by the standard literature in civil-military relations, which simply does not focus on such institutional processes. Instead, the existing literature tends to focus on the nature and extent of civilian control over the military, and the existence and importance of a "gap" between the military culture and that of civilian society and leadership.[12] As Samuel Huntington put it, "The principal focus of civil-military relations is the relation of the officer corps to the state" (Huntington 1957, 3). For Huntington, and for most scholars of civil-military relations, this personal and political relationship at the top of the military hierarchy is the central problem of the relationship between the civilian state and its military.[13] This is not without reason, given that, in world history, the seizure of state power by the military has occurred frequently, with severe consequences for democracy and long-term state effectiveness (Finer 1988; Perlmutter 1977).

For Huntington, the core mission of the military is "the management of violence"; the rest of the military tasks are "auxiliary vocations" (Huntington 1957, 11–12). The best relationship between the two forces—military and civilian leadership—is what he calls "objective civilian control," with the military strictly and thoroughly professional, focused on war preparations and conduct (Ibid., 89–97). "Subjective control," he argues, civilianizes the military, making the armed forces resemble and become immersed in the activities of the rest of the state. For Huntington, "[t]he military profession is expert and limited. Its members have specialized competence within their field and lack that competence outside their field. The relation of the profession to the state is based upon this natural division of labor" (Ibid., 70).

This definition of desirable and undesirable civil-military relations seems almost quaint, given the institutional trends this book discusses. Clearly, as the military has extended its reach into noncombat missions, it has, in many ways, transgressed the line Huntington has drawn. But a coup has not taken place, not in any formal sense. The active-duty military can, with reason, say civilian control continues to be effective.[14]

This book investigates a more subtle, less studied, and more critical aspect of the US civil-military relationship—an institutional evolution that, rather than leading to military officers being at the apex of the political system, has brought about a growing institutional imbalance at the heart of the foreign policy and national security policy process. This imbalance, many of the chapters in this book suggest, could be said to be gradually "militarizing" American statecraft and global engagement.

"Militarization" as used in this volume has a more complex definition than that commonly used in discussions of civil-military relations. We do not suggest that this institutional trend involves generals or admirals directly challenging civilian control over policy. The trend is more subtle, involving a gradual seeping in of military perspectives and priorities into the broader foreign policy and national security strategies and policies of the United States. Most directly, the trend is reflected in an increasing reliance by policymakers on military instruments as they shape, decide on, and implement foreign policy and national security policy choices. Over time, the military becomes a leading face of how the United States engages the world.[15]

Put another way, militarization means a growing trend to view decisions on national security strategy, policies, and policy implementation from a military perspective. Strategic planning comes to be seen as coterminous with Department of Defense strategic planning. Foreign policy issues and security challenges discussed at the senior policymaker level are framed as military challenges, most readily susceptible to policy solutions and programs for which military capabilities are seen as the appropriate response. Over time, this means a growing reliance on the military for the execution of a widening range of foreign and national security programs and building capabilities in the US military that go well beyond traditional military core competence.

The trend is gradual, relatively uncontested, and appears even normal and necessary to some who have contributed to this book. "Mission creep" has not always been a conscious, deliberate act, but often a gradual evolution: decision by decision, event by event, program by program.[16] Over time, these expanded missions, programs, authorities, and the budgets that support them have become institutionalized in the structure, doctrine, and training of the military services. Ultimately, the institutionalization of the military perspective and these missions and responsibilities has become a self-fulfilling prophecy for policymakers. There is a waning consciousness among policymakers that they are drawing the military into noncore activities: the military begins to look like the only available entity able and competent to take on the particular task at hand. Policy discourse defines the issues as susceptible to a solution using military capabilities (the "if all you have is a hammer, every problem looks like a nail" dilemma).

Over time, this perspective has rebalanced the national security institutions toward military capabilities and a military view of what our national security and foreign policy challenges are. This trend does not risk a coup in any formal sense, but a creeping evolution where military purposes and missions dominate US national security strategy and operations in the field.[17] Policy leaders simply assume that military, not civilian, institutions are the most effective instrument for executing a growing range of missions and goals of American statecraft.[18] As that view has taken root, the civilian institutions have lost ground, leading to a growing imbalance of authority and capability, and a subordination of the civilian organizations at State and USAID to the leadership of the Defense Department and the military.[19]

The concept of civil-military relations can be broadened to reflect this subtle trend. There are four dimensions at play in this concept. The first is the traditional issue posed by the civil-military relations literature: To what extent and in what ways does civilian authority exercise control over the military in the state? Is that relationship stable? What ensures that stability and what can make the relationship less stable? Second, what are the cultural differences between the military and the surrounding society? What is the impact of those cultural differences on the stability of the civil-military relationship?

The other two dimensions come closer to the heart of the concerns in this book. The first of these explores the extent to which the military plays a dominant role in defining overall strategic views and goals and sets the context for foreign and national security policy. Is the military the lead institution in carrying out strategic planning? Does the military define the direction and details of policy, as the United States defines its overseas engagement? Do policymakers come to see policies within a military perspective—as military or security challenges, as opposed to diplomatic, political, or economic challenges? Does the language in policy discussions reflect military perspectives and issues?[20]

The last dimension is the subject of much of this book. It involves policy execution and implementation. To what extent do policymakers draw on military capabilities to deal with foreign and national security policy challenges and problems? Over time, does the military expand its missions and capabilities to incorporate tasks not traditionally seen as part of the core competence of the military? What tasks and missions—economic, diplomatic, political, public diplomacy—may be involved in such mission expansion?

This evolution in the institutional balance may be completely unintentional, which is why the trend can be distinguished from the traditional civil-military relations literature's concern with the stability of the relationship and the risks of a military takeover. But the trend is not without potential consequences. In the conclusion to this book, we elaborate on the possible downside of the trend. Briefly, the incremental decision to rely on the military for executing missions that are not core competencies risks faulty execution of these missions precisely because they are not core to military capabilities. The experience of the US military as nation-builders in Iraq and Afghanistan suggests this may be the case, to the actual detriment of US national security as the military is seen to fail at executing such unfamiliar tasks. Second, the assumption that the military is the default competence for such missions risks turning the view that civilian foreign policy organizations are not competent for these missions into a self-fulfilling prophecy, further weakening the civilian instruments of statecraft and exacerbating the institutional imbalance. Finally, the growing reliance on the military instrument of national power risks blowback, as other countries come to see the United States as a country that pursues its objectives primarily with military power. The consequences of this perception could risk harm to the ability of the United States to achieve its foreign policy and national security objectives.

Book Overview

The book is divided into three parts. The first section provides different interpretations about the historical and institutional context behind the military's mission creep. Gordon Adams, in Chapter 2, shows that the growing institutional imbalance seen after 9/11 is rooted not only in the expansion of DoD budgets, roles, and missions, but also in long-term institutional and cultural trends within the civilian institutions. Adams explores the greater degree of unity of the military compared to the civilian foreign policy institutions, and compares domestic constituencies, organizational cultures, adeptness at planning, and reputations for competence in the White House and the Congress. He explores the troubling dynamic wherein the military is seen as more capable, so it is used in new missions, thereby leading to even greater weakness in civilian agencies.

James Dobbins, in Chapter 3, links the post–9/11 mission creep by the military to mistakes made by policymakers in Iraq and Afghanistan. The United States did not deploy enough troops at the start of these conflicts to secure the environment, which allowed organized resistance to emerge. The US military then became the dominant provider of postconflict stabilization and reconstruction efforts in these countries because of the active counterinsurgency. This overreliance on the military for nation building in turn created a duplication of expertise among DoD, State, and USAID and fostered confusion about the proper roles of military and civilian institutions. Consequently, the Iraq and Afghanistan model of postconflict stabilization and reconstruction, in Dobbins's view, is not the one to emulate. The model seen in the Balkans during the 1990s—where the State Department handled economic assistance and governance programs in the targeted country, while the Department of Defense focused on security—is a more appropriate approach than the DoD-centered reconstruction model seen in Afghanistan and Iraq during the 2000s.

In Chapter 4, Derek S. Reveron argues that the mission creep documented in this book is not unintentional and it is not worrisome. It is part of a larger transformation wherein the US military has moved from being an agent of confrontation to becoming an agent of global cooperation. The military's increasing involvement in development, humanitarian assistance, and diplomacy since the 1990s—its focus on security assistance to build capacity and stability in other countries—represents a maturing of US military strategy and a "civilizing" of the military. The United States no longer seeks to dominate or coerce other countries; rather, it strives to enable partner countries to combat challenges that threaten their stability. Reveron also argues that the Pentagon embraces the whole-of-government approach and that its assumption of traditionally civilian tasks does not upset civil-military relations.

In Chapter 5, Charles Cushman explains why Congress favors DoD over State and why it is unlikely to be the source of any effort to rebalance the military and civilian branches of the foreign policy community. The Defense Department, with its dominant budget, hundreds of domestic bases and installations, and thousands of supplier factories and offices in so many congressional districts, has a far greater electoral and political footprint than the State Department. State, with its limited domestic spending and its orientation to the outside world, has little leverage to incentivize members of Congress to become foreign policy experts or to defend civilian foreign policy and assistance institutions and their budgets. Foreign affairs work does little if anything to improve a member's electoral prospects, and may take time from other issues that have a more powerful electoral impact. Institutionally, the Armed Services Committees are far more influential than their peer committees on foreign affairs/relations. Members seeking reelection and institutional power, therefore, are less inclined to engage on foreign affairs issues than they are on defense issues and policies.

The second section of the book empirically investigates the extent to which US military leaders and programs in the Department of Defense have increased their influence and activity across a range of policy domains: development, security assistance, public diplomacy, state diplomacy, policy debates, and covert operations.

Connie Veillette and G. William Anderson investigate DoD's role in development assistance in Chapter 6. The authors discuss how USAID, created in 1961, had been in charge of postconflict environments until the Iraq War convinced military and civilian leaders of the need for the US military to again take on a reconstruction mission. The military stepped in, the authors observe, because USAID had been enfeebled in the 1990s. They describe the current array of authorities, activities, and environments in which the Department of Defense is engaging and then tease out where DoD adds value for development, and where it should follow a civilian lead or disengage completely.

In Chapter 7, Nina M. Serafino delves into the history of institutional authority and management of military security cooperation over time. Serafino documents the original division of labor between the State Department and DoD after World War II, the initial expansion of DoD authorities in the 1980s (largely in response to its new counternarcotics role), and the more recent expansion of DoD authorities after 9/11. In contrast to the data shown in Figure 1.1, Serafino takes out those programs directly related to the wars in Iraq and Afghanistan, to assess whether these expansions in authority are likely permanent or tied to specific conflicts. She finds that even as Congress grants the DoD increased authorities over security assistance programs, it still believes that appropriate civilian oversight, centered in the Secretary of State, remains important. Many of DoD's increased authorities require State concurrence.

Brian E. Carlson looks at the issue of public diplomacy in Chapter 8. He describes how civilian institutions were weakened after the Cold War, when the United States Information Agency was reduced and folded into the State Department. The military—with a new view of the strategic environment after 9/11—then took on strategic communications because it saw the civilian side as incapable of doing the job. He observes that the military now has resources for communication efforts that dwarf and overwhelm those at State, and this disparity is unlikely to be reversed.

Shoon Murray and Anthony Quainton, in Chapter 9, explore the effects of the increased activities of geographic combatant commanders on traditional diplomacy. They investigate whether combatant commanders complement or rival the traditional role of State Department diplomats by asking more than two dozen ambassadors about their experiences and perspectives. Most ambassadors, they find, speak favorably about the working relationship with their respective combatant commander, finding them cooperative, not competitive or displacing. Although the top military leadership respects ambassadorial authority and civilian control over policy, Murray and Quainton still find that the military possesses a subtle agenda-setting power due to resource disparities and that the commanders wield regional diplomatic influence even though it doesn't impinge directly on that of individual ambassadors.

In Chapter 10, Sharon Weiner analyzes *New York Times* coverage of public statements made by the service chiefs of staff from 1947–2009 and shows a clear increase in the willingness of the military to offer advice on policy issues that go beyond military strategy and operations. Weiner argues that this is a consequence of changes in the decision-making structure of the Joint Chiefs of Staff and the power of the chairman of the Joint Chiefs, who has increasingly entered policy arenas traditionally the domain of civilian decision makers.

Jennifer Kibbe, in Chapter 11, describes the unprecedented expansion of the military's Special Operations Forces (SOF) after 9/11 as they competed with the CIA's paramilitary operatives for the prestige and resources that went with leading the fight against terrorism, a fight that would spread far beyond Washington's wars in Afghanistan and Iraq. Kibbe argues that congressional reform is necessary to maintain adequate oversight and accountability as the military takes on an enhanced role in covert operations outside of combat zones.

The third section of this book considers the costs and consequences of using the US military in such a wide-ranging set of missions as part of US global engagement.

Edward Marks, in Chapter 12, argues that the US Department of State has lost its traditional role of foreign policy gatekeeper and has not yet attained the goal of effective whole-of-government coordinator for US global efforts, in part because of competition from the combatant commands. He argues that the geographic combatant commands have set up a parallel foreign policy establishment in countries that now give foreign leaders two sets of contact to the US government. He proposes ideas for reducing the role of the combatant commands and for replicating the embassy's Country Team model within Washington to make State an operational coordinator.

Finally, Gordon Adams, in the conclusion, highlights three negative consequences of creeping militarization for US foreign and national security policy and global relations: ineffective or failed policies implemented by military institutions carrying out programs and activities that are not their core competence; weakened civilian foreign policy institutions as a result of default recourse to the DoD for policy implementation; and international blowback against a foreign policy increasingly delivered by the military. He ends with a brief summary and discussion of the policy recommendations offered by the other authors in the book.

Notes

1. In 2012, more than eighty retired senior military leaders sent a letter to Congress asking them not to cut the International Affairs budget that provides resources to the civilian diplomacy and development agencies. In 2013, twenty retired three- and four-star generals and admirals went to Congress to petition for an increase in the International Affairs budget. Gen. James Mattis, then commander of US Central Command, is reported to have said, "If you don't fund the State Department fully, then I need to buy more ammunition ultimately." See US Global Leadership Council website, www.usglc.org/2013/03/08/the-military-understands-smart-power/.

2. For example, a 2012 exercise called Beyond the Horizon involved "the deployment of 1,800 U.S. service members" into Guatemala and Honduras "resulting in the completion of 18 engineer projects, including schools and clinics in 12 communities, and 6 MEDRETEs [Medical Readiness Exercises] that provided care to 33,330 patients and treated 27,800 animals for veterinary support" (Kelly 2013, 28).

3. The Navy's 2007 maritime strategy "upgraded humanitarian assistance and disaster relief as a core capability on par with power projection and sea control." (Reveron 2010, 3). The Army's operations manual elevated "the mission of stabilizing war-torn nations, making it equal in importance to defeating adversaries on the battlefield" (Gordon 2008).

4. GAO 2010b as cited in Anderson and Veillette, Chapter 6.

5. For a thorough listing of articles, see Rumbaugh and Leatherman 2012.

6. Freeman (2011, 422) argues that the expansion of the military role in the Cold War confrontation "reinforced the tendency for Americans to equate national security with military postures and programs."

7. Huntington notes that, as early as the 1940s and 1950s, military personnel were stepping into civilian functions because "no ready source of civilians with administrative and diplomatic skills was available. Consequently, the military were called upon to fill the vacuum" (Huntington 1957, 359).

8. Cathy Downes argues that this assumption of mission in Iraq led to a distortion of how it was performed. She argues that in Iraq "critical questions concerning security, disarmament and development have been influenced disproportionately by military perspectives and considerations. In many cases, this has had a militarizing effect upon priorities and approaches for rebuilding Iraqi civil society" (Downes 2010, 373). The result can be schools and clinics that are not sustainable by the local or national governments.

9. Note that a significant share of this was security assistance provided for Iraqi and Afghan security forces, which would lead this share to decline in the future as such support shrinks. It is relevant here, however, because of the precedent it has created for direct DoD provision of security assistance.

10. Between the Office of the Secretary and the Joint Staff, the Defense Department and the services produce an abundance of strategic and military planning documents that influence the overall direction of the department's program planning and budgeting, as well as the development of doctrine and planning in the military services. See, for example, US Department of Defense (2010a), US Department of Defense (2012c), and US Joint Chiefs of Staff (2011). Until 2009, no other foreign policy agency engaged in a formal strategic planning process. In 2010, the State Department and USAID released the report of its first ever Quadrennial Diplomacy and Development Review. However, the QDDR did not examine or set strategic goals for the civilian institutions. Instead, it focused on the institutional capacity of the two institutions. There is, as yet, no statutory requirement to repeat the exercise and no institutionalized bureaucracy to carry it out, unlike the QDR at DoD. See US Department of State (2010a).

11. This mission expansion goes well beyond these areas. For examples of the military's growing role in health care, see Pincus (2011a, 3). On the military's growing role in alternative energy policy, see Davenport and Dreazen (2011, 23–27). For an example in the rapidly growing area of cyber defense and offense, see Nakashima (2012, 1). For an excellent source of general background on the expansion of military missions, see Serafino et al. (2008).

12. Two of the landmark studies are by Finer (1988) and Huntington (1957). More recent literature includes Feaver and Kohn (2001), Nielsen and Snider (2009), and Owens (2011).

13. This same focus is the major preoccupation of many of the chapters in Nielsen and Snider (2009).

14. This does not mean that the civil-military relationship has not been tested. Bacevich (2007) describes episodes in which the US military resisted decisions by civilian authorities. A fascinating piece that links mission expansion to an actual coup is a fictional narrative, rooted in fact, written by Air Force Lt. Col. Charles Dunlap (1992, 2), as he describes the origins of his fictional coup: "Faced with intractable national problems on one hand and an energetic and capable military on the other, it can be all too seductive to start viewing the military as a cost-effective solution." His coup is the result of a series of small, institutional,

and program decisions (mostly real in the 1970–90 time period) that consistently move greater responsibilities for domestic needs to the military: law enforcement, health care for the poor, military schools, environmental cleanup, infrastructure engineering and repair, and domestic disaster relief. Gradually, the military sought a greater voice in overall policymaking. Each step was taken without awareness of the pattern being created, but was the result of domestic discontent: "Americans ... compared the military's principled competence with the chicanery and ineptitude of many elected officials, and found the latter wanting" (Dunlap 1992, 4).

15. Amb. Charles W. Freeman Jr., former US ambassador to Saudi Arabia, has noted: "The disparity in military versus civilian capabilities demonstrably skews US foreign policy towards military responses to international events. Most of the challenges before the United States, however, are not amenable to military solutions" (Freeman 2011, 414).

16. Cathy Downes describes this as an "almost subliminal form of militarism" where the military has influence on matters outside military affairs and "the influence exercised is unintentional" (Downes 2010, 371).

17. Olson describes the trend this way: "It is, in effect, a slow motion coup in which increasingly military officers and military counsel dominates strategic thinking and significant parts of the political agenda, in a reversal of Clausewitz's dictum that war is an extension of politics" (Olson 2012, 1). Owens agrees that the risk of a formal military seizure of power is not the issue: "[T]he low likelihood of a coup in the United States does not mean that military actors cannot still find other ways to undermine balanced civil-military relations" (Owens 2011, 17). Kohn's description is similar: "What I have detected is no conspiracy but repeated efforts on the part of the armed forces to frustrate or evade civilian authority when that opposition seems likely to preclude outcomes the military dislikes" Kohn (2002, 9).

18. This claim across a broad range of noncore competencies is well expressed in Reveron's (2010, 42) book on security assistance: "Military leaders typically command more attention than civilian leaders do, and they see themselves as policy actors .... In addition to influence, military leaders also command more capabilities than leaders from other government departments and are consistently viewed by presidential administrations as capable of 'getting the job done' ... The military continues to respond to this funding preference by retooling its force to conduct noncombat operations and to formulate and implement national security policy."

19. Huntington defined this as a question of "horizontal" control: "Horizontal civilian control is exercised against the military to the extent that they are confined within a limited scope by the parallel activities of civilian agencies or groups roughly at the same level of authority in the government" (Huntington 1957, 88).

20. There is a growing literature on the role of the military in shaping the general US national security strategy and the political culture of the United States. These studies generally focus on competing military and civilian perspectives on Cold War strategy and national security policy choices or on the interactions of senior policymakers. See, for example, several books by Andrew Bacevich (2006, 2010). See, also, Risa Brooks (2008), and Kohn (2002, 2009). In a more journalistic vein, see Ungar (2012), Maddow (2012), Glain (2011), and Woodward (2003, 2004, 2007, and 2011). See, also, the particularly interesting post by William J. Olson (2012), of the National Defense University.

Chapter 2

The Institutional Imbalance of American Statecraft

Gordon Adams

> It is important . . . that the habits of thinking in a free country should inspire caution in those entrusted with its administration, to confine themselves within their respective constitutional spheres, avoiding in the exercise of the powers of one department to encroach upon another. The spirit of encroachment tends to consolidate the powers of all the departments in one, and thus to create, whatever the form of government, a real despotism.
>
> —*President George Washington, Farewell Address, 1796*

Over the past seventy years, the Defense Department and the military services have increasingly become "full service" institutions, with broad and deep involvement in strategic planning, diplomacy, public diplomacy, economic development and reconstruction, and many other areas of policy (Adams and Murray, Chapter 1). Today, DoD is simply larger, better financed, and has a much broader array of capabilities than the civilian foreign policy institutions, principally the State Department and USAID. The evolution of US strategic purposes in the Cold War, rooted in a military confrontation with the Soviet Union, played an important role in the emergence of a serious imbalance between the military and the civilian institutions of American statecraft. But the imbalance is not purely a result of the larger size and budgetary endowment of the Defense Department; it also grows out of cultural and institutional weaknesses and realities internal to the civilian foreign policy institutions.

This chapter argues that the imbalance between the military and civilian institutions of American statecraft is the result of a combination of factors.

One is the difference in sheer size and in the coherence of the two sets of institutions. A second is the measurable difference in the constituencies in the Congress, the economy, and American society that support the institutions and their missions. A third is the distinct differences in the organizational culture of the military and that of diplomacy and foreign assistance. A fourth is the difference between the two when it comes to planning capacity for strategy and resources. These multiple differences have in turn affected the way the two sets of institutions are dealt with in the White House and in the Congress.

There is little research focusing on this institutional imbalance and virtually no analytical writing on the evolution of the civilian institutions or the consequences of this trend for civilian foreign policy institutional evolution and capacity.[1] This is a critical research gap. Merely reassigning programs and authorities from one set of institutions to the other will fail, unless these deeper organizational and cultural differences are understood.

Institutional and Structural Size and Coherence

The disparity in size and institutional coherence between the military and civilian institutions is a significant source of the imbalance and the trend toward the militarization of American statecraft. At nearly $600 billion a year in fiscal year 2013, the defense budget is twelve times the size of the budget available to the civilian foreign policy institutions. The Defense Department work force is more than a hundred times as large as that of the State Department and USAID. DoD employs over 1.5 million active duty forces, another million in the Reserves and National Guard, and nearly 770,000 civilians, nearly 28 percent of the federal civil service (Office of Personnel Management 2012; US Department of Defense 2012b).[2] At 68,000, the Special Operations forces of the Pentagon are larger than the personnel of the civilian foreign policy agencies. The State Department, by contrast, employs roughly 19,000 Foreign Service officers and civil servants, while USAID's total employment is slightly over 2,000.[3] The Defense Department's overseas presence also dwarfs that of State/USAID. DoD has more than 660 overseas bases and permanent installations in 40 countries, while the State Department/USAID have 250 embassies, consulates, and missions spread across 196 countries (US Department of Defense 2012a). In 2008, for example, for every single USAID employee deployed overseas, there were 23 State Department employees, and 600 DoD military and civilian personnel (Adams et al. 2010).[4]

In sheer size and capabilities, the US military not only dwarfs the civilian foreign policy institutions, it is exponentially more significantly endowed than of the military forces of any other country, making it a powerful tool for

US policy officials. It is the world's only truly global military force: it could, if needed, deploy to any country, fly in any airspace, sail to any port. It has the only global logistics, infrastructure, transportation, communications, and intelligence. Neither the civilian institutions, nor any other country, have equivalent capacity, resources, flexibility, or readiness.[5]

The capability "gap" alone is a critical source of the institutional imbalance. But it is reinforced by a significant difference in institutional coherence, one rarely mentioned in research and writing on foreign policy institutions. Despite decades of analysis of the divisions, differences, and conflicts among the military services and much scholarly and policy attention to the difficulties the secretary of defense has imposing central discipline on the defense bureaucracy, DoD has had significantly greater institutional unity and coherence than the civilian foreign policy institutions. Huntington's observation is astute: "a group which is structurally united possesses great advantages in dealing with a group which is structurally disunited" (Huntington 1957, 87).

This disparity in institutional coherence began in the 1940s and has grown over time. The secretary of defense and the Defense Department can think, plan, strategize and speak with a significantly more unified voice in national security policy deliberations than the civilian institutions. When the DoD was created, the military services retained considerable autonomy over resource and force planning and there was at best only a limited capacity in the Office of the Secretary to control strategic or resource planning across the services (Hitch 1965). Nonetheless all significant military capabilities were grouped under one institutional roof, an important first step, and the secretary could begin to play a role as the single voice on defense policy.

Faced with the reality that greater organizational unity was needed, the central authority of the secretary and the chairman of the Joint Chiefs of Staff was strengthened in 1958. The true revolution in central authority, however, was the arrival of Secretary of Defense Robert McNamara, whose reforms constituted a quantum leap in centralized management of the military services and the empowerment of his office. The Planning, Programming and Budgeting System (PPBS) McNamara created cemented a central role for the secretary in defense planning, budgeting, and management. It allowed the secretary greater access to and control over force and budget planning with respect to all military capabilities.[6] Today, for all the internal institutional politics of the Defense Department, the secretary is its most important voice and leader and the chairman of the Joint Chiefs of Staff is the first among equals among the military service chiefs (Locher 2004).

By contrast, the secretary of state does not have the same broad authority over all the civilian institutions involved in US foreign policy. She does not have the capacity to carry out coherent strategic, program, or budgetary planning for all of the institutions that play a foreign policy role. Nor does she have substantive authority over all the nonmilitary ways in which the United States engages overseas: trade, finance, diplomacy, economic and security assistance, or exchanges. This is one of the most important and fundamental sources of the institutional imbalance between the military and civilian institutions. While the military instrument was being unified after World War II, US civilian engagement underwent an institutional "diaspora" that grew directly out of the way the civilian foreign policy institutions and programs evolved after World War II and reflects the institutional culture of the State Department itself.

Before World War II, US foreign relations had essentially two features: diplomacy toward other nations and US involvement in international trade and financial matters—missions that were already divided between the State Department and the Treasury Department.[7] However, the agenda of US global engagement broadened substantially after the war. The trade and financial missions expanded as the US emerged as the dominant global economy and new institutions like the International Monetary Fund (IMF), the International Bank for Reconstruction and Development, and the General Agreement on Tariffs and Trade were created, largely under American leadership. The responsibility for US involvement in the expanded set of international financial institutions, however, remained largely with the Treasury Department, while leadership in trade negotiations was removed from State in the 1960s and ultimately given to the White House when the Office of the US Trade Representative (USTR) was created in 1962.

Beyond finance and trade, other new missions became part of American foreign policy, including foreign economic assistance, security assistance, public diplomacy, and arms control negotiations. None of these missions had much precedent in US foreign operations and none had a clear institutional home. As each mission began to grow it was housed, fully or in part, in some other institution than the State Department, which did not assert strong claims for leadership in these areas of policy that had not been elements of traditional US diplomacy.

The institutional diaspora that occurred—with other or even new agencies being responsible for planning, budgeting, and implementing these missions—has been a major obstacle to the ability of the State Department to oversee and direct the civilian elements of overseas US engagement, and an important source of State's declining role relative to DoD. The patchwork quilt of departments and agencies has weakened the coherence of US foreign relations, sapped the secretary of state's influence in interagency discussions, and hamstrung the secretary's ability to make a coherent, strategic case for foreign affairs budgets to the Congress.

State has always been the home of the elite Foreign Service, whose members represent the United States, negotiate on its behalf, report back to Washington, DC, and advise the president on foreign policy matters. Rather than expand the State Department's mission to accommodate the growing agenda of US statecraft, the Foreign Service resisted this evolution, reflecting cultural characteristics discussed below.[8]

In the realm of economic assistance, the Marshall Plan (European Recovery Program) was the first such decision. Although it was designed at the State Department, it was soon lodged in an independent institutional home as the Economic Cooperation Administration.[9] Over time, responsibility for US international economic engagement was distributed to several institutions, each with its own agenda, budget, and relationship with the Congress. The Export-Import Bank, supporting the financing of US exports, remained an independent agency. The US Agency for International Development, created in 1961, was intentionally separated from State, so as to focus on long-term development and be (ostensibly) free of direct ties to near-term US policy objectives. The Peace Corps was created in 1961, similarly free of a formal connection to US foreign policy goals as shaped at State.

The Treasury Department's role in such assistance also expanded over the years. To its IMF and World Bank responsibilities, it has added budgetary and planning control over the US role in the regional development banks (the Inter-American, African, Asian Development Banks and Funds, and the European Bank for Reconstruction and Development). Treasury was also given responsibility for US debt forgiveness to low-income countries (HIPC, for Heavily Indebted Poor Countries) and directly administers its own technical assistance program providing advice on financial and budgetary practices to developing countries and the former Soviet Union.

This diaspora of foreign economic assistance programs has continued to the present day. President George W. Bush created two innovative foreign assistance programs: the Millennium Challenge Corporation (MCC) and the President's Emergency Program for AIDS Relief (PEPFAR). The former was established as a separate institution by statute, while the latter was located at the State Department, but is headed by a coordinator who has substantial budgetary and planning autonomy, including the coordination of HIV/AIDS programs in other federal agencies.[10]

With regard to economic assistance programs, State has direct responsibility and control over Economic Support Funds (ESF) and economic assistance to Central Europe and the former Soviet Union countries. ESF, a roughly $5 billion program, provides economic assistance closely linked to US foreign policy objectives and only secondarily to development objectives. State, however, lacks the internal capacity to implement programs with economic goals, which is not a core competence of the Foreign Service. Hence, to add to the institutional complexity, State has the policy lead over ESF decisions with respect to countries and overall funding levels, but implementation is largely the responsibility of USAID.

The management of security assistance programs is even more complex.[11] State has direct authority over budgets and country selection for the traditional security assistance portfolio, namely Foreign Military Financing (FMF), Foreign Military Sales (FMS), and International Military Education and Training (IMET).

However, lacking military expertise and appropriate personnel, State shares responsibility for the development of security assistance programs with the combatant commands and the military services, while implementation is the responsibility of a DoD agency—the Defense Security Cooperation Agency (DSCA)—and the military services. In addition, as noted below, DoD has also developed its own direct portfolio of security cooperation programs.

Authority over US public diplomacy (exchange programs, overseas cultural centers, and international broadcasting) has also been dispersed over the years. Some public diplomacy programs and activities (such as exchanges) have been inside State, then outside, then back inside. From 1953 to 1999, the United States Information Agency (USIA) had responsibility for public diplomacy including the Voice of America. In 1999, it was absorbed into the State Department in a reversal of the diaspora trend. However, at the same time, international broadcasting operations (largely the Voice of America) were spun off from USIA and merged into yet another independent agency—the Broadcasting Board of Governors—whose responsibilities now also include funding and oversight of surrogate broadcasting (see Carlson, Chapter 8).[12]

As noted, the Defense Department itself has been part of this foreign policy diaspora. Its global deployments and operations overlap substantially with State Department and even USAID operations, including such missions as development assistance, governance advice, diplomacy, and public diplomacy. Nor is DoD the only federal agency with an expanding international agenda and presence. As the array of issues on the US foreign policy agenda has grown, most of the other federal agencies have created international programs and operate out of US embassies abroad. This trend has included a sizable contingent from the Department of Justice and FBI, dealing with international crime and terrorism, growing activity by the Department of Health and Human Services and the Centers for Disease Control and Prevention, and an expanding overseas presence from the Department of Homeland Security.[13]

The Secretary of State has no authoritative oversight responsibility or internal capacity to coordinate this broad inventory of international funding, programs, and policies among the civilian agencies. In 2005, a State Department office to coordinate budget planning for foreign assistance programs was created. It has authority only over State and USAID programs, and even that relationship is an uneasy one (Adams and Williams 2010, 32–65).

The reality of this institutional diaspora makes it virtually impossible for the secretary of state to provide the same kind of strategic direction to US civilian engagement, build integrated programs, or manage budgetary trade-offs among agencies and policy priorities the secretary of defense can provide at DoD. She cannot coordinate these instruments and programs abroad, deploy or redeploy capabilities, or respond quickly to crisis and opportunity. While diplomats suggest that coordination works better in the field than it does in Washington, making integration work in the field depends greatly on the ability of the ambassador to coordinate at the mission level (Marks, Chapter 12). This ability is not routinely found in every embassy, nor has such coordination been successfully transplanted back to Washington, DC. Over time, this has led to a weakening of the civilian side of the institutional balance with DoD.

This institutional weakness is exacerbated by internal structural realities at State that make coordination of policy and programs even more challenging. The regional bureaus are at the apex of the department, in terms of prestige, influence, and institutional authority, but uneven structural changes over decades have left the department somewhat fractured internally. Functional bureaus and offices, intended to deal with policy and program issues that cut across regions, are undervalued in an institution driven by regional and country bureaus and offices. The leadership role played at State by the Foreign Service has led to an undervaluing of the department's sizable civil service staff, who are frequently the actual managers of State Department programs. Repeated efforts to reform the human resources and structural challenges inside State have generally fallen short of changing this reality. These internal challenges further weakened the capacity of the State Department to balance the capabilities of DoD.[14]

Constituencies

The budgets and capabilities of US government organizations are substantially strengthened by their linkages within American society, its economy, and its political culture. The network that exists between an agency and the society, economy, and politics of the country can create a constituency that reinforces the agency's mission and capabilities. The linkages can be both direct, between the agency and its stakeholders, and indirect, through the Congress. The differences between the military and civilian institutions along this dimension are one of the most significant sources of the institutional imbalance and mission creep at DoD. The military and civilian agencies are at opposite extremes with respect to their domestic networks and constituency inside the United States.[15]

The Defense Department and the military services have a significant domestic presence, providing an ample local, regional, and congressional constituency, which the civilian foreign policy agencies do not have.[16] The Department of Defense, its contractors, and its supporters in the Congress are not reluctant to mobilize this national constituency on behalf of their needs.[17] As noted, employment in the Defense Department is a large proportion of total US government employment. In addition, there are over a million National Guard and military reservists, more than 2 million military retirees (plus their spouses and dependents), and over 20 million military veterans.

This directly employed and retiree population is based at more than 2,500 defense installations—bases, offices, depots, and headquarters—scattered across the country, with some kind of economic impact in every location. While the number of defense installations has shrunk since the mid-1980s, as the military has shrunk and bases have been closed, the military presence is notable in Alabama, Alaska, Arizona, California, Hawaii, Missouri, New Jersey, Texas, and Virginia, in particular. Moreover, this same constituency is organized into active-duty, veterans, and retiree organizations with strong grass roots and a presence in Washington such as the Military Officers Association of America, the Reserve Officers Association, the National Guard Association, the Navy League, the Association of the US Army, and the Air Force Association.

Contracting is another vehicle for constituency development. Over time, the impact of defense spending on US economic activity has declined, with the share of defense spending in the gross domestic product falling from an average of 9.4 percent in the 1950s to 3.8 percent in the first decade of the 21st Century.[18] Nevertheless, defense funds that buy weapons, other products, and services constitute more than 40 percent of the defense budget in any given year, a market of more than $300 billion. DoD buys 75 percent of all goods and services purchased by the federal government. While the prime contracting firms doing business with DoD have become more geographically concentrated, the local economic impact of these firms can be significant.[19] Dollars for prime contracts continue to flow into the economies of such states as California, Virginia, Texas, Maryland, and Connecticut, among others.[20] Moreover, this economic impact expands as the prime contractors subcontract work out to the thousands of technology and parts suppliers and vendors supplying metal parts, materials, wiring, electronics, communications, information, and other gear and services, reaching widely into the broader economy.

This broad constituency for DoD and the military is actively engaged in the business and politics of defense budgets and policy.[21] Contractors mobilize local work forces and communities and encourage them to engage in direct grass roots lobbying aimed at the appropriate members of Congress. The industrial community serving the defense market is also organized into national-level organizations such as the Aerospace Industries Association, the Electronics Industries Association, and the National Defense Industrial Association.

When it comes to constituency development there could hardly be a more striking contrast than with the civilian foreign policy agencies. Few of the civilian foreign policy institutions have as direct a penetration into American society and the economy. The much smaller federal employment base of these institutions is largely concentrated in the Washington, DC, area (roughly 13,000 State Department employees, for example) or deployed overseas. Aside from a finance center in South Carolina and twenty-five passport offices in major cities, State Department and USAID installations are not scattered widely across the country.

The local and national constituency for diplomacy outside of Washington, DC, is relatively small, concentrated in groups and national organizations with an interest in foreign affairs: World Affairs Councils, the Chicago Council on Global Affairs, the Pacific Council on International Policy, the Council on Foreign Relations in New York, for example. There are few "trade associations" linked to diplomacy, the most prominent being the relatively new (1995) US Global Leadership Campaign, founded with the explicit purpose of supporting the budget for all civilian foreign policy agencies, whose members include corporations, as well as retired military officers and diplomats and former senior policy officials.

USAID and the other foreign economic assistance organizations have their own constituency, albeit a small one. The bulk of foreign economic assistance dollars are spent in the United States, buying goods and services and paying consultants and contractors. The funding is small, however, less than a tenth of what DoD spends annually, with a relatively small footprint in the American economy. The bulk of development assistance consultants and contractors, for example, are in the Washington, DC, area or overseas. These firms, and the nongovernmental organizations that support foreign assistance, are smaller and less geographically dispersed than DoD contractors. There are several national-level organizations based in Washington, DC, supporting USAID, principally Interaction (1984), a coalition of 165 American and international nonprofits, consulting groups, and nongovernmental organizations, many with grass roots membership, who support the agency and advocate for foreign assistance dollars. These organizations have generally supported the autonomy of USAID and the other foreign assistance agencies, which reinforces the institutional diaspora of the civilian institutions.

The same can be said for the foreign policy agencies responsible for trade, investment, and financial programs and policies. This constituency is more elite than grass roots, but includes, for example, the major exporting companies in energy and commercial aircraft; foreign investors in technology, hotels, and tourism; and oil and engineering infrastructure firms that use and support the funding for the Export-Import Bank, Overseas Private Investment Corporation, and Trade and Development Agency. Exporting firms support an open trade policy and trade negotiations, and are also organized into such associations as the National Foreign Trade Council (1914) with three hundred corporate members. While these businesses clearly constitute a constituency for overseas engagement, their work also reinforces the institutional diaspora on the civilian side of the government.

In sum, defense programs, budgets, and policies have a substantial constituency inside the United States, consistent with the size and geographic dispersal of the defense institutions, bases, and DoD's contractors. The civilian foreign policy and foreign assistance agencies do not have the same domestic constituency, making it more difficult to win public and congressional support for institutional needs and foreign policy programs.

Organizational Culture

Institutional resources, coherence, and constituency are major sources of the institutional imbalance. Differences in organizational culture, which are rarely included in research on foreign policy institutions, also play an important role.[22] Institutional culture means their different values, customs and operating norms, and the behavioral consequences of the training and operational experience they provide for their employees.[23] There are important differences between the military and civilian institutional cultures, particularly DoD and the State Department, that make an important contribution to the institutional balance, the way the agencies participate in the interagency policy process, and the militarization of statecraft. One analyst of the cultural differences put it this way:

> These two cultures are as alien as life forms from two competing planets, the warrior from Mars and the diplomats from Venus. Similar in many respects – professionalism, dedication and competence – Martians and Venutians often have an antagonistic relationship. They are generally polar opposites in character, in approach to problem solving, and in worldview. (Rife 1998, 3)[24]

The uniformed military is at the center of the DoD culture. While generalizations are risky, the culture of the military services and the military personnel system value hierarchy, discipline, and organization. As Colonel Rife described it, the military culture values "competence, efficiency, achievement ... [people who are] mission/task oriented ... 'give me a mission and get out of my way' types."[25]

The military system rewards personnel who are organized and disciplined, and prepared to range across multiple tasks. Military training focuses on strategy, warfighting skills, and technical know-how. At the outset, there is relatively little attention to a specific country or region where combat might take place. The core military skill is prevailing over adversaries, at sea, in the air, or on land. The military career process assigns its officers across a broad variety of job categories, including combat command, program management, resource planning, policymaking, even relations on Capitol Hill, valuing the experience obtained in each assignment. It provides systematic, career-long training opportunities. A career military officer might rise through onboard posts in the Navy, company-regiment-battalion responsibilities in the Army, or air wing positions in the Air Force, followed by a base management slot or a program acquisition position, as they move up the promotion ladder. Senior officers might be detailed to defense strategy and policy offices, the Joint Staff, and such external responsibilities as the National Security Council, or to the office of a member of Congress.

As a result, in the senior military ranks, one finds officers with this combination of experiences. They might have worn both uniforms and civilian dress, know how the equipment works, understand the planning and budget processes, what their counterparts in the other services and the Pentagon civilians do, and how the senior appointed officials and members of Congress do their jobs. They arrive at the senior level with a sense of discipline and hierarchy and a "can do" attitude. Once a decision is made on doctrine, programs, policies, or budgets, military members and the military system are organized, responsive, and ready to execute.

In addition, the Department of Defense is organized to execute across a wide spectrum of activities. Its 2.2 million military and civilian personnel function as a virtual government, with functions ranging across the entire spectrum of public sector activities, from program management, to strategic planning, to administration, to finance and accounting, to field and hospital medicine, to education and training, to basic and applied research. For almost every aspect of governmental responsibility and many functions in society, there is likely to be an equivalent somewhere in DoD.

The diplomatic culture at the State Department is a sharp contrast. To cite, again, the perceptive analysis by Colonel Rife, the diplomatic community, whose core culture is that of the Foreign Service, is from Venus. The diplomatic culture values competence, intellectual ability, and individual achievement; they "believe in intuition and psychology. Planning is not a core value to most Venutians [sic] . . . they prefer a more fluid approach that is event driven" (Ibid., 7). Diplomats are more "feeling" than "thinking" oriented. They see the world in terms of "endless possibilities," and prefer to keep decisions open to evolve with events (Ibid., 11). Rife quotes Ambassador Robert Beecroft, summing it up: "The military wants a roadmap before they start the journey, the foreign service officer gets in the car, starts driving, and then says, 'OK—who has the compass?'" (Ibid., 13). There is no judgment implied here; the cultures are simply different. But in response to the challenges of the first decade of the 21st century, this difference has been important in the way the military and civilian institutions respond. They also make a difference in the way in which the two sets of institutions have developed internally.

While similarly hierarchical in structure, the Foreign Service culture emphasizes skills in negotiation, political analysis, and report writing in comparatively narrow stovepipes of responsibility. The culture and training tend not to include skills in program management, strategic planning, or administration.[26] Organizationally, these latter functions are largely carried out by State Department civil servants. Training programs for the Foreign Service focus on culture and language, reporting and negotiation, and policy analysis. Training of this kind takes place only at the start of a career or with a change in country, with little or no further training opportunities or requirements as a Foreign Service career develops.[27] Career paths take place along fairly circumscribed stovepipes, usually called "cones"—management, consular, political, economic, and public diplomacy. The political cone has the most prestige, taking a career Foreign Service Officer overseas with regularity, an ambassadorship being the ultimate rank. Career paths based solely in the United States are less valued, as are interagency assignments (to USAID, for example), management, and strategic and resource planning. Such assignments are unlikely to be career enhancing.[28]

Foreign Service Officers who are part of USAID have greater management responsibilities, but their professional orientation is largely external to the United States. They, and the other civilian foreign assistance professionals, receive greater management training, as they are directly involved in shaping and implementing assistance programs overseas or are overseeing private contractors, who are implementing programs. Training and mobility in the foreign assistance culture, however, focus on activities in countries and regions outside the United States, and on the technical dimensions of economic assistance—agriculture, water supply, education, humanitarian aid, economic planning, or governance. International knowledge—of other governments and international organizations—takes precedence in career advancement over an understanding of domestic policymaking, budgeting, or US political processes. And as with the traditional diplomatic corps, foreign assistance career paths are oriented toward overseas missions.

The diaspora of foreign assistance agencies away from State is reinforced by another cultural feature of the development community. The dominant value of "economic development" is powerful, leading to a resistance to linking development work with other foreign policy and national security strategy goals being pursued by the State Department. Development professionals are often wary of the link between their work and the broader foreign policy goals of the United States. Development, itself, separate from other strategic goals, is viewed as a long-term US interest, rather than focusing on assistance to countries of strategic importance in the pursuit of more immediate political or security needs.[29] This aspect of foreign assistance culture can make it difficult to persuade policy officials at State, the White House, or Congress that foreign assistance investments pay appreciable dividends for US national security. It tends to sideline development professionals in the policy process, and poses problems for obtaining foreign assistance funding.

These marked differences in personnel and in organizational culture have real consequences for the balance between the military and civilian institutions. Senior-level policymakers tend to see the military institutions as organized, disciplined, and capable of taking on a task it will perform efficiently and effectively. In the interagency process, diplomatic institutions are seen as important for negotiating and advising policy, but not for planning and management, or program delivery. Inside the State Department, planning and management are not a central value, reinforcing this disparity in the way the institutions are viewed. As Derek Reveron has put it:

> Military leaders typically command more attention than civilian leaders do, and they see themselves as policy actors .... In addition to influence, military leaders also command more capabilities than leaders from other government departments and are consistently viewed by presidential administrations as capable of "getting the job done" (Reveron 2010, 42).

Strategic and Budgetary Planning

The cultural difference between the military and civilian institutions is apparent when it comes to strategic thinking, planning, and budgeting. Here, the culture of the State Department contributes noticeably to the imbalance in the department's impact on national security policymaking and implementation.

As noted above, the Department of Defense gained considerable institutional coherence with the introduction of the Planning, Programming, and Budgeting System (PPBS) in the 1960s.[30] Although the PPBS system was initially resisted by the services, in reality it fit well within a culture where combat and campaign planning was already the norm.[31] The addition in the early 1990s of a statutory requirement for a quadrennial review of strategy was not a stretch for an institution already steeped in planning culture.[32]

Strategic thinking and planning for forces and resources became a norm for the military and the Defense Department during the Cold War. The adversary was clearly defined and his military capabilities known. The objective was military "containment" of the Soviet Union, with a force that could deter, defend, and prevail if conflict occurred. However overstated that threat might be, the technological and military requirements could be defined. The first and most significant PPBS exercise was to shape and project US strategic nuclear forces, across services, in response to a defined requirement (Gordon, McNichol, and Jack 2009).

The strategy and planning exercise for the military and DoD necessarily focused on the long term: deterrence and containment were long-term strategic goals and recruiting, training, and equipping the force—DoD "outputs"—took much longer than one or two years to deliver.[33] While the effectiveness of PPBS has been debated (and it was eroded by the decision to plan funding for the wars in Iraq and Afghanistan outside the PPBS process), the basic DoD commitment to a multiyear, structured planning process and culture remains largely intact.[34] Even if predictions turn out to be wrong, the simple act of forecasting forces the military to focus on the relationship between means and ends over time.

Moreover, despite the criticisms of DoD management (especially financial management), the outputs and even many of the outcomes of military planning can largely be measured.[35] DoD can measure the forces, equipment, and training funded by the defense budget. Force size and organization, equipment acquired, training provided, sailing, flying, driving days and hours, and readiness can all be quantified. The cost, quantity, and performance of equipment can be evaluated, and become a subject of frequent political argument as a result. Even the outcome of military operations can be observed and, to some degree, measured, as well as disputed.[36]

The unique strategic and resource planning process at DoD gives defense plans an unusual degree of transparency, clarity, and consistency, and facilitates the justification of these plans, and the budgets that support them, to OMB and the Congress. It provides major political "heft" to the defense budget request that the civilian foreign policy agencies lack.[37] They do not have an equivalent planning culture or process. The requirement for an overall report from the White House on national security strategy is relatively recent (1986).[38] There is no statutory requirement for a State Department strategic plan equivalent to the QDR.[39] In 2009, for the first time, Secretary of State Hillary Clinton undertook a top-down strategic planning process, the Quadrennial Diplomacy and Development Review (QDDR), modeled after the Defense Department's QDR, covering both State and USAID. This first effort was not the same as the QDR or linked to a PPBS-type process, however. The secretary provided no strategic guidance at the start of the QDDR and the focus of the effort was on "capabilities," not foreign policy goals. The QDDR process was ad hoc, not institutionalized in the two agencies. And the outcome was some restructuring of processes and offices at State and USAID, but not a set of planning guidelines that might influence resource planning in either agency.

Strategic and resource planning at State has been an institutional challenge for decades. The output of diplomacy does not lend itself to the same kind of measurement as the outputs of the Defense Department. International events and diplomatic relations are notoriously difficult to forecast. The secretary's span of control over other civilian foreign affairs agencies is limited. The Foreign Service culture has not encouraged training in strategic planning, program management, or budgeting. Budgets in the foreign policy world are, as a result, planned year by year, not over a longer term.

Until 2005, the department did not have a formal budget office or process at the level of the secretary of state. Budgets for State Department personnel and administration were prepared by the under secretary of state for management, while foreign assistance budgets were prepared separately by relevant regional and functional bureaus. There was no review process at State for the budgets of other foreign affairs agencies. In 2005, building on a small staff for the secretary, Condoleezza Rice created the position of director of foreign assistance (known as "F") to coordinate budget planning for foreign assistance programs. While F is clearly a step toward a more institutionalized planning process, its authority and range of coverage is limited. F does not have statutory standing; it oversees foreign assistance programs, but not State Department operations and management; and it has responsibility only for State and USAID programs, not those of other agencies involved in foreign assistance.[40]

Measuring the outputs and outcomes of civilian foreign policy is also uneven and more difficult than for the military. Some outputs can be measured—diplomats trained, dollars provided for particular countries. Some diplomacy output measures would be trivial; the number of demarches, cables, and diplomatic facilities tells us little about the success or failure of statecraft. Even significant outputs—treaties, for example—take years to negotiate and the outcome of those treaties may take even longer to observe, often in non-events, such as the nonproliferation of nuclear weapons.

Much of the outcome of diplomacy is difficult to measure or is disputed: maintenance of good relations, promotion of national interests, effectiveness and longevity of international organizations. Does the apparent failure of economic assistance over decades to Egypt constitute a negative performance outcome or is it a consequence of events over which the US has no control? Is a decade of peace with Israel the appropriate performance measurement for the assistance program to Egypt? Does the deferral of the North Korean nuclear program as a result of the 1994 Agreed Framework constitute success, or did the North Koreans simply end-run the terms of the agreement, thereby making it a performance failure? Was negotiating the Kyoto Protocol on climate change a success, while deferring its ratification by the Senate a failure? The goals of diplomacy are often so broad—democracy and economic freedom in the Muslim world, or strengthened alliances and partnerships—that the outcome is difficult to measure, especially in the near term. Moreover, because many other countries and international organizations, as well as international events, will affect these goals and events, it is often difficult to draw causal links between US diplomatic activity and the outcomes.

Outputs are more numerically measurable with respect to foreign economic assistance—dollars spent, wells drilled, schools and health clinics built. Outcomes—development itself—are also measurable, but establishing a link with bilateral US assistance programs is often problematic, making it challenging to justify the funding to the Congress. US foreign assistance agencies regularly cite success stories. But was South Korea's economic growth the result of US aid, or of decades of foreign investment and internal savings? Is the slow development of African economies due to assistance failures or a more complex mixture of internal culture, health, infrastructure, education, commodity prices, debt, and weak or corrupt governance?

The civilian foreign policy agencies are still a long way from having the strategic and resource planning processes available to the Defense Department. The civilian agencies' planning processes are poorly institutionalized, their strategic and resource planning staffs are small, and they lack coherence as a group of institutions. Outputs and outcomes are more intractable. As a result, defense agencies can prepare, present, and defend an apparently more credible, long-term strategy and plan and display results more persuasively than the civilian institutions. This reality exacerbates the funding gap and incentivizes policymakers to call on the military institutions to execute additional missions, and thus advance the process of militarizing US foreign policy.

The Impact of the Imbalance on the White House and Congress

The imbalance between DoD and the civilian foreign policy institutions clearly has an impact on how the two sets of institutions are dealt with in the White House, both in crisis and in longer-term planning. DoD and the military bring to the table significant assets: an institutional capacity to act quickly, a constituency of public support, a "can-do" operational culture, long-term strategic and planning capabilities, and the capacity to measure and demonstrate results. The civilian foreign policy institutions are hampered by fewer resources, internal and interagency coordination challenges, a small public constituency, a culture of negotiation, deliberation and deferral, a much smaller operational capability, an absence of strategic planning, and difficulty demonstrating results.

While both sets of institutions and cultures have value in the policy process, the White House generally likes to act quickly and with impact. Some secretaries of state, such as Henry Kissinger, command personal influence that can outweigh the institutional imbalance.[41] But the ability to deliver plays an important role in shaping how a national security issue is defined and which agency is asked to execute policy.

The White House offices are also organized in a way that both recognizes and perpetuates DoD's influence. The National Security Council is organized with a specific office dedicated to defense issues, but more than one for the diplomatic, regional, and assistance issues. Functional offices at the NSC operate on an interagency basis, with both DoD and State participating. At the NSC Principals Committee meetings, there are two military participants—the Office of the Secretary of Defense, and the Joint Chiefs of Staff. The secretary of state participates, but a representative from USAID is not usually at the table, unless specifically invited.[42]

On the resource side, the White House Office of Management and Budget is deeply involved in the DoD planning process, well before the defense budget arrives at the White House, through a process known as the "joint review." This process, which is unique to DoD, permits OMB budget examiners to meet with military service budget offices as they prepare the initial stage of the PPBS process—programming—in the preparation of the services' Program Objective Memorandums (POMs). Once the services have reported their POMs to the secretary of defense, OMB participates directly in the DoD meetings that prepare the program and budget decisions at the Pentagon. OMB also conducts its own internal review of DoD budget issues, so that by the time DoD transmits its budget numbers formally to OMB, there are no surprises for the White House, and the few remaining issues can be resolved at a senior, even presidential level.

OMB does not conduct a joint review with State/USAID or the other civilian foreign policy agencies, although it may be invited to some of the hearings State's Office of the Director of Foreign Assistance (F) conducts to review its budgets. OMB is the only executive branch organization where the budgets of all of the foreign affairs agencies come together, but it provides minimal strategic or program integration of those requests.[43]

The consequence of this disparity in capabilities and treatment is that the views, preferences, and operational capabilities of the military weigh heavily in the White House decision-making process. The Defense Department can deliver capability; the State Department faces a greater challenge.

The civilian/military institutional imbalance is reflected in the Congress, as well. The authorizing committees for the two sets of institutions are strikingly different in composition and impact in the congressional process (Cushman, Chapter 5).[44] The Armed Services Committees in the two chambers legislate authorities and programs for the Defense Department every year, hold high-visibility hearings, and over the years have played a significant role in legislating what scholars call "structural" provisions with respect to the defense institutions.[45] In particular, these committees legislate the authorities that have expanded the military's role into missions beyond deterrence and combat.[46]

In contrast, the House and Senate Foreign Affairs/Relations committees, while prestigious, have significantly less legislative impact. On the foreign assistance side, in particular, while the committees have been able to pass legislation authorizing specific new foreign assistance programs, such as the Support for East European Democracy (SEED) and the Freedom Support Act (FSA, for the former Soviet Union states), the foreign relations authorizers have not passed a bill authorizing US foreign assistance programs overall since 1986, leaving it to the Appropriations Committees to waive the need for authorization to provide appropriated funds.[47]

As for its treatment of budgets, the congressional process tends to fund the military budget request fully while diplomatic and foreign assistance budget requests are often a residual category in the budget process. The congressional budget committees set ceilings for budget "functions." The "function" for national defense consists largely of the Department of Defense (plus nuclear weapons programs at the Department of Energy), while the International Affairs function covers the many budgets in the foreign policy institutional diaspora. From 1990 to 2002, when overall discretionary spending was limited by statutory caps, there were also subcaps (1991–93 and again for 1996–99) that provided a specific funding level for "national defense." "International affairs" funds, on the other hand, were included in the overall cap for "non-defense discretionary" spending. This disparity of treatment meant that defense would generally be fully funded, while international affairs funds had to be weighed against the budget requests for domestic agencies. Given the weak constituency for foreign affairs, the Budget Committee has typically reduced international affairs funds below the administration's budget request, using the excess funds to support domestic programs, at little political cost to legislators.

Once the Budget Committee has set the overall funding ceilings, the budgets for the two sets of agencies arrive at the appropriations committee, where DoD also fares better than the civilian agencies. Allocations by the appropriations committee chair to the appropriations subcommittees generally provide full funding for defense, while the allocations for international affairs are frequently below the requested level, even below the level set in the Budget Committee. Both DoD and the foreign affairs agencies have dedicated appropriations subcommittees.[48] The impact of the ample constituency for defense is seen in the appropriations process, through "earmarks" and member requests for programs with local impacts. Civilian foreign policy agencies do not have comparable constituency support. Reinforced by the general congressional skepticism about State Department and USAID planning and management capabilities, diplomacy and foreign assistance programs have never been popular in Congress.

The civil/military institutional imbalance in the executive branch is reflected and sometimes magnified in the Congress. The military organization, with plans, heft, and coherence, and a large budget request with a significant domestic constituency, stands in sharp contrast to a dispersed set of agencies with less funding and the absence of a domestic constituency.

Conclusion

Over time, the Defense Department and the military services have been asked to develop the capability to provide a growing number of missions and functions that are not core to military combat or deterrence. This has led to a growing imbalance in the resources and capabilities of the major institutions of American statecraft. As this chapter demonstrates, this imbalance and the reliance on the military is not a new trend, nor is it solely the result of a national security strategy that focused on a military confrontation with the Soviet Union or the unintended consequences of the decision to invade Iraq. This chapter argues that the trend has its origins in the way the institutions of American statecraft have developed, their size, coherence, constituencies, and culture. History plays an important role. The Cold War clearly emphasized the capabilities of the Defense Department and incentivized its growth. But DoD and the services also benefited from the reality that they became a large, institutionalized presence inside the United States, creating a strong constituency for their programs and budgets. History also played a role in the evolving weaknesses of the civilian institutions, especially a series of decisions that dispersed responsibility for civilian foreign policy across a variety of agencies and programs the State Department does not coordinate or plan.

Culture has also played a significant role in the imbalance and the militarization process. The military provides a focused, planned, coordinated, "can-do" opportunity to the White House. The State Department culture is slower and less operationally driven. The impact of this difference was strikingly apparent in the invasions and occupations of Iraq and Afghanistan, on which Reveron (Chapter 4) focuses in this book. State and USAID were both blocked from the task, and slow to rise to the challenge, leaving the responsibility with the military.

It is not obvious how this trend might be reversed. The weaknesses of the State Department and USAID can become a self-fulfilling prophecy; each slow response, lack of capacity or resources, or absence of a long-term plan further reinforces the sense policymakers have that the civilian institutions are not capable of providing the strategic leadership and operational capabilities they require. This, in turn, reinforces the policymakers' tendency to call upon DoD for rapid response and planning, exacerbating the disparity in resources and capabilities. Removing these capabilities from DoD and returning them or grafting them on to the State Department, without cultural and institutional changes at State, runs the risk of failure. As the conclusion to this book suggests, however, not examining and correcting this imbalance poses serious risks for the long-term success of American statecraft.

Notes

1. Glain (2011) deals largely with the strategic perspectives of senior policymakers. Reveron (2010) focuses on security cooperation policies and programs, but not on the institutional trends in depth. Priest (2003) deals with the diplomatic activities of regional commanders, but not the broader institutional relationships.

2. In addition, DoD contracting for services, alone, employed the equivalent of 767,000 workers as of 2009 (Government Accountability Office 2011, 13).

3. The State Department also employs over 30,000 non-Americans overseas, known as "Foreign Service Nationals." There are no data available on DoD employment of non-Americans overseas or on the number of State/USAID services contracting personnel, though that is likely to be small.

4. The military/civilian number would be 356, if one subtracted active-duty personnel then in Iraq, Afghanistan, and counterterror operations. All figures derived from the

US Office of Personnel Management, with the exception of military personnel taken from DoD's Statistical Information Analysis Division, available at siadapp.dmdc.osd.mil/person nel/MILITARY/miltop.htm. Reveron (2010, 4, 87) notes that the Combatant Command for Africa, AFRICOM, has 1,200 people on its staff; the State Department's Africa Bureau has 80; the military has 2,000 people deployed in East Africa; State/USAID have only a few hundred. And, he notes, the Navy has more construction personnel than the entire Foreign Service. Owens underlines the impact of this disparity: "Unfortunately, the power of a the- ater combatant commander, which exceeds that of just about every civilian in government except the president and secretary of defense, makes it tempting for him to go beyond im- plementing policy to presuming to make it" (Owens 2011, 74).

5. As Owens puts it: "Of course, when it comes to the influence of the military, the fact is that the size, budget, available manpower, and attitude of the American defense estab- lishment enable the military to take on challenges that are not within the capacity of other government agencies" (Owens 2011, 79).

6. On the origins and development of the PPBS system, see Enthoven and Smith (1971), Hitch (1965), and Gordon, McNichol, and Jack (2009).

7. In addition to these major functions, trade policy responsibility was scattered be- tween Treasury and Commerce, while the Export-Import Bank for trade promotion was created in 1934 largely to ensure that US exports to the Soviet Union would be guaranteed.

8. Much of the following discussion is drawn from Adams and Williams (2010, 8–92).

9. Economist Tom Schelling described this decision as "a Congressional vote of 'no confidence' in the executive talents of the State Department" (Schelling 1968, 7).

10. Suggestive of the dilemmas created by the "diaspora," USAID implements the MCC "threshold" country agreements, but not its larger "compacts," and also implements a number of global health programs, beyond those it executes for PEPFAR.

11. This and the later discussion of security assistance programs draw substantially on Adams and Williams (2011) and Serafino (2011a).

12. Surrogate radios provide news-like services prepared by nationals of the serviced countries, such as Radio Free Europe/Radio Liberty, Radio Sawa, Radio Free Asia, and Radio and Television Marti.

13. For an early inventory of the international efforts of other federal agencies, see US Senate (1998).

14. There have been a number of reform studies focusing on the State Department. The most recent include Stimson Center/American Academy of Diplomacy (2008), Advisory Committee on Transformational Diplomacy (2008), and the HELP Commission (2007). For incisive discussions of the department's internal issues, see Rubin (1985) and Schake (2012).

15. This is an important, if commonly underestimated, source of the difference in civil- military relations when the US is compared with other countries, most of which have par- liamentary systems of government, with substantially more disciplined legislative bodies. A disciplined party majority translated into government can provide considerable autonomy for defense and foreign policy decisions in a country like the United Kingdom, compared with the more dispersed political authority characteristic of the American system.

16. The terms frequently used to describe this relationship—"military industrial com- plex," or "iron triangle"—capture some of the essence of the relationship, though they may ascribe more effective control over policy and resources at all times than is the case.

17. There is substantial literature on the politics of defense lobbying, going back to the well-known Eisenhower farewell address, warning of the consequences of this relation- ship. See Adams (1981), among many such studies. William Olson (2012) notes: "Power in Washington is a function of manpower and money ... DOD has developed into the largest

lobbying organization in the country, working Congress and the Executive Branch not so much with finesse as with sheer weight of numbers." For a discussion of the role of constituencies in national security budget decision making, see Adams and Williams (2010, 221–44).

18. "National Defense" (budget function 050) as a proportion of US GDP, from US Department of Defense (2012b Table 7, 264–66).

19. Major prime contractors like Boeing continue to be important employers in St. Louis, Missouri; Long Beach, California (both former McDonnell Douglas facilities); and Seattle, Washington. Lockheed Martin is economically important to Georgia and Texas, while General Dynamics is significant to the local economy of eastern Connecticut and San Diego, California, among others.

20. See www.statemaster.com/graph/mil_def_con_exp-military-defense-contracts -expenditures for state-by-state data.

21. See, for example, the major 2012 campaign against allowing automatic cuts (sequester) to impact the defense budget, led by the Aerospace Industries Association at www.aia -aerospace.org/.

22. On the role of institutional culture in the national security agencies, see George and Rishikof (2011).

23. George and Rishikof define organizational culture as "a system of shared meaning or values that the organization's membership holds and that distinguish it from other groups" (George and Rishikof 2011, 4). Huntington describes the impact of cultural differences on the institutional balance having been established during World War II, when the civilian institutions left the economic aspects of the war to the military, out of disinterest: "This was due primarily to the lack of interest in the nonmilitary aspects of the war by the civilian branches of the government, and the absence of civilian institutions equipped to perform these functions. As a result, the War Department assumed the job of mobilization planning. The civilians imposed a civilian war function on a military agency. In this sense, the national mobilization planning of the War Department in the thirties was a forerunner of the vast civilian abdication of function which was to take place during and after World War II" (Huntington 1957, 309).

24. The Myers-Briggs data is based on interviews done by Ted Strickler (1985).

25. On the Myers-Briggs Type Inventory, he reports, military personnel are 30 percent introverted, sensing, thinking, and judging, as opposed to 6 percent of the US population as a whole (Rife 1985, 10).

26. Schake writes: "State has a terrible reputation on Capitol Hill for pulling rabbits out of its budgetary hat instead of carefully costing and tracking programs in ways that would build congressional confidence in its ability to manage larger budgets" (Schake 2012, 11). Ted Strickler, who retired from the Foreign Service, writes: "While recognizing the need for true management skills in senior leadership positions, the Foreign Service has never been able to take the necessary actions to insure that these skills are developed and tested throughout an officer's career . . . . [T]he Foreign Service fills its senior managerial positions with ambassadors . . . based on the assumption that success in managing policy will equate to success in managing resources . . . . Management functions are viewed with considerable disdain by most FSO's" (Strickler 1985, 43–44, 52).

27. Strickler calls this an "aversion to formal training as an important part of career development" (Strickler 1985, 51).

28. There is little interest in changing this culture, according to Schake: "The Foreign Service is content to replicate itself rather than evolve, and has been permitted to" (Schake 2012, 36).

29. This orientation is reflected in the proposal to establish an independent cabinet-level department for economic development. See Modernizing Foreign Assistance Network (2008).

30. For a detailed description of the PPBS process (now known as PPBES with the addition of "Execution" to the name), see Keehan and Land (2010).

31. For a discussion of the early years of PPBS and the services' reactions, see Gordon, McNichol, and Jack (2009), and Hitch (1965).

32. For the most recent QDR, the fifth since the requirement was created, see US Department of Defense (2014).

33. A ready division for the Army, air wing for the Air Force, or battle group for the Navy takes years to assemble, has a long, predictable and measurable cycle between preparation, deployment, downtime and new preparation, and has costs over that time that can be predicted with reasonable accuracy. Military hardware takes a long time to develop (well over ten years for major equipment) and production can run for many years.

34. See, for example, Business Executives for National Security (2001, 20–21), based on two papers by Tom Davis, "Framing the Problem of PPBS" and "Changing PPBS," unpublished, 2000.

35. See, for example, Government Accountability Office (2012b).

36. This is not always the case. The Cold War military was designed to deter attack, defend the nation and its allies, and prevail in conflicts. These desired outcomes were a nonevent in the Cold War—success meant no Soviet attack, or no expansion of Soviet influence. Proving the negative, however, is not simple; other factors such as internal weakness or lack of intention could explain the absence of Soviet military action and the outcome.

37. Other agencies have tried, with mixed success, to emulate the PPBS system, notably the Departments of Energy and Homeland Security. See, for example, US Department of Energy (2003).

38. The first and probably most comprehensive such strategy document was NSC 68, "United States Objectives and Programs for National Security" (US National Security Council 1950). President Nixon and Henry Kissinger undertook a similar effort known as NSSM 3 in 1970.

39. In 1993, the Government Performance and Results Act required all federal agencies to develop a strategic plan. State and USAID drafted several plans consistent with this requirement. However, it sets no priorities and has not been integrated into any overall program or resource planning at State. The last such report, covering the years 2007–12, was released in May 2007. See US Department of State (2007).

40. In the 1960s, economist Thomas Schelling examined the applicability of PPBS to foreign policy programs and budgeting. He urged that recipient countries be the focus of such a planning effort, but argued that the diaspora of organizations and the difficulties of measuring outputs and outcomes would make such an effort difficult (Schelling, 1968, 26–36).

41. One might argue that Henry Kissinger was such a secretary of state, but his influence stemmed from his relationship with the president as National Security Advisor, rather than representing the strength of the State Department.

42. For a detailed discussion of NSS structure and practices, see Whittaker, Smith, and McKune (2011).

43. For the difference in OMB treatment of the defense and foreign policy agencies, see Gordon Adams, "The Office of Management and Budget: The President's Policy Tool," in George and Rishikof (2011, 55–78).

44. The literature on Congress and foreign and national security policymaking is relatively thin and somewhat dated. See, particularly, the following pieces in Lindsay and Ripley (1993), particularly Lindsay and Ripley, "How Congress Influences Foreign and Defense Policy," 17–35; James M. McCormick, "Decision Making in the Foreign Affairs and Foreign Relations Committees," 115–53; and Christopher J. Deering, "Decision Making in the Armed Services Committees," 155–82. Though dated, the general conclusions and analyses of these three pieces continue to reflect congressional realities.

45. One of the most significant such structural legislative actions was the passage of the Goldwater-Nichols Act in 1986, which made the chairman of the Joint Chiefs of Staff the principal military adviser to the president, enhanced the role of the combatant commanders, and required "joint" service as a prerequisite for promotion to flag officer. See Locher (2004).

46. The authorities that allowed the military to engage in development-oriented reconstruction and governance assistance in Iraq and Afghanistan (the Commander's Emergency Response Program, CERP), to educate foreign militaries' counterterrorism personnel (Counter Terrorism Fellowship Program), to reimburse other countries for material support to US counterterrorism operations (Coalition Support Funds), to provide global security sector assistance jointly with State (Global Security Contingency Fund) and to provide counterterrorism assistance to countries around the globe (the Section 1206 program) were all legislated by the Armed Services committees. See Adams and Williams (2011) and Serafino (2011a).

47. The two foreign relations/affairs committees did pass legislation in 2008 authorizing the State Department's office of the Coordinator for Reconstruction and Stabilization and the creation of a civilian corps for reconstruction operations, but the program has been weakly funded, limiting its activities. See Serafino (2012c).

48. Until 2005–07, State operations (personnel and administration) and foreign assistance funds were divided between two appropriations subcommittees, forcing a trade-off between State's operating funds and the funds for Commerce and Justice. This division was ended in 2005 and 2007, when State operations were folded into the existing Foreign Operations subcommittee, creating a single subcommittee for State and Foreign Operations. Defense budgets are considered in three subcommittees, but two of them—Defense Appropriations, and Military Construction and Veterans Affairs—focus almost entirely on defense-related funding. The third—Energy and Water—covers the budget for nuclear weapons programs of the National Nuclear Security Administration (NNSA—Department of Energy), which generally has significant political support.

Chapter 3

Civil-Military Roles in Postconflict Stabilization and Reconstruction

James Dobbins

Since the end of the Cold War, the United States has repeatedly faced serious challenges posed by failing states, humanitarian crises, and transnational security threats. These events have repeatedly prompted the White House to commit US military forces to peacekeeping, stabilization, or regime change missions. Once committed, the United States and its coalition partners have often inherited responsibility for a wider range of tasks, including the restoration of government institutions and processes, ensuring social order, and overseeing the reconstruction or development of a country's economy.

These interventions offer lessons about how best to allocate responsibilities, funding, and capabilities among the national security institutions when the decision is made to go forward. Those lessons suggest that in future civil-military roles in postconflict reconstruction (as opposed to large-scale counterinsurgency operations), the Balkans model of the 1990s—where the State Department handled interagency involvement within the targeted country, while the Department of Defense focused on security—is more appropriate than the DoD-centered reconstruction model seen in Afghanistan and Iraq.[1]

Modern American generals are fond of asserting that there is no military solution to the challenges they face. This is often a sign that they are losing, and they are usually losing not because of an inadequacy of civilian capacity but rather of military capacity. Establishing and maintaining a secure environment in the immediate aftermath of war is primarily a military task, albeit one with significant civilian components. The United States made many mistakes in the aftermath of its invasions of Afghanistan and Iraq, but the most decisive was the failure to deploy forces adequate to secure the territory and protect the populations it had just overrun.

As a result of this decisive failure, both these missions soon shifted from postconflict stabilization and reconstruction to counterinsurgency, a far more difficult challenge, and one for which the US government was even less prepared. Eventually, the United States greatly expanded its commitment of both military and civilian assets to both countries. Not surprisingly, the Defense Department proved better at surging resources than did the much smaller civilian agencies like State and USAID. Consequently, some functions that a decade earlier in Bosnia and Kosovo had been handled by civilian agencies transitioned to DoD in Iraq and Afghanistan. Police training is one example of a formerly civilian responsibility that was picked up by the US military. (Indeed, in the Balkans in the late 1990s, even military training had been overseen by State, not the Defense Department.)

These shifts have created a well-founded impression that State and USAID have lost ground to DoD and the US military in the allocation of resources and responsibilities for areas in conflict. In wartime, indeed, such a shift is exactly what one would expect. Stabilization and reconstruction are not wartime missions, however. They are postwar missions, ones that, if done properly, prevent the renewal of conflict. There is a major military role in such operations for the provision of security, but many of the other nonsecurity functions that have migrated from State and USAID to Defense should transition back to those civilian agencies with the end of US military engagement.

There is much to be learned from the wars in Iraq and Afghanistan, and the United States should not shed the hard-won expertise in counterinsurgency operations, as it did after Vietnam, but neither should these conflicts provide the model for civil-military relations elsewhere, in circumstances where American forces are not themselves engaged in major combat operations. The institutional balance needs to be corrected, making the military responsible for security issues and the civilian institutions responsible for governance and reconstruction. This means greater restraint in the missions given the military and significant action to strengthen and centralize civilian leadership and capability in the State Department.

Botched Stabilization

Observing the American occupation of Iraq, one might be forgiven for thinking it the first time that the United States had embarked upon such an enterprise. One unanticipated challenge after another occasioned one improvised response after another. This was, however, not the first but the seventh occasion in little more than a decade that the United States had helped liberate a society and then tried to rebuild it, beginning with Kuwait in 1991, and then Somalia, Haiti, Bosnia, Kosovo, Afghanistan, and finally Iraq.

Six of those seven societies are predominantly Muslim. Thus, by 2003, there was no country in the world more experienced in nation building than the United States, and no Western army with more modern experience operating with a Muslim society. How, one might ask, could the United States perform this mission so frequently, yet do it so poorly? The answer was that neither the American military nor any of the relevant civilian agencies regarded postconflict stabilization and reconstruction as a core function, to be adequately funded, regularly practiced, and routinely executed. Instead, the US government tended to treat each of these successive missions as if it were the first encountered, sending new people with new ideas to face what should have been familiar challenges. Worse yet, it treated each successive mission as if it were the last. No agency was taking steps to harvest and sustain the expertise gained. No one was establishing an evolving doctrine for the conduct of these operations or building a cadre of experts available to go from one mission to the next.

There were certainly improvements in American performance of these missions through the 1990s, as the same people in the same administration repeatedly grappled with similar problems. During his eight years in office, President Clinton oversaw four successive efforts at stabilization and postconflict reconstruction. Beginning with a dismal failure in Somalia, followed by a largely wasted effort in Haiti, his administration was eventually able to achieve more enduring results in Bosnia and Kosovo. None of these efforts was perfect, but each successive operation was better conceived, more abundantly resourced, and more competently conducted than its predecessor.

The Clinton administration derived three large policy lessons from its experience: first, employ overwhelming force; second, accept responsibility for the provision of public security; and third, engage neighboring and regional states, particularly those behaving most irresponsibly.

Deploy Overwhelming Force

In Somalia, President George H. W. Bush had originally sent a large American force to do a limited task, protecting humanitarian food and medicine shipments. Bill Clinton reduced that American presence from 20,000 soldiers and marines to 2,000, and gave this residual force the mission of supporting a UN-led grass-roots democratization campaign that was bound to antagonize every warlord in the country. Capabilities plummeted even as ambitions soared. The reduced American force was soon challenged. The encounter, chronicled in the book and movie "Black Hawk Down" resulted in a firestorm of domestic criticism and caused the administration to withdraw American troops from Somalia.

From then on, the Clinton administration embraced the "Powell Doctrine" of decisive force, choosing to super-size each of its subsequent interventions, going in heavy and then scaling back once a secure environment had been established and potential adversaries had been deterred from mounting violent resistance.

Provide Public Security

In Somalia, Haiti, and Kosovo, the United States arrived to find local security forces incompetent, abusive, or entirely nonexistent. Building new institutions and reforming existing ones took several years. In the interim, responsibility for public security devolved on the United States and its coalition partners. The US military resisted this mission, but to no avail. By 1999, when they went into Kosovo, US and NATO military authorities accepted that responsibility for public safety would be a military responsibility until international and local police could be mobilized in sufficient numbers.

In Haiti, Bosnia, and Kosovo, civilian agencies were able to deploy international police in large numbers relatively quickly, so that military responsibility for routine policing was short lived. In Iraq and Afghanistan, much larger societies, the Bush administration made no attempt to deploy civilian international police; nevertheless, even a limited effort in this regard would have been helpful.

Engage Neighboring States

Adjoining states played a major role in fomenting the conflicts in Somalia, Bosnia, and Kosovo. This problem was largely ignored in Somalia, but faced squarely in Bosnia. The presidents of Serbia and Croatia, both of whom bore heavy responsibility for the ethnic cleansing that NATO was trying to stop, were invited by the United States to the peace conference in Dayton, Ohio. Both men were given privileged places in that process, and continued to be engaged in the subsequent peace implementation. Both men won subsequent elections in their own countries, their domestic stature having been enhanced by this elevated international role. Had Washington treated them as pariahs, the war in Bosnia might still be under way.

By 1999, that same Serbian leader, Slobodan Milosevic, had actually been indicted by the international tribunal in The Hague for genocide and other war crimes. Yet NATO and the Clinton administration still negotiated with his regime to end the air campaign and the conflict in Kosovo.

Unlearning Lessons

Each of these large lessons was rejected by a successor administration initially determined to avoid nation building altogether, and subsequently insistent on doing it entirely differently, and in particular more economically.

Ironically, the Powell Doctrine of overwhelming force had been embraced by the Clinton administration only after General Colin Powell left office in 1993, and then was abandoned by its successor as soon as Powell returned to office in 2001. Secretary of Defense Donald Rumsfeld's views were diametrically opposed. Rumsfeld argued in speeches and op-ed articles that by flooding Bosnia and Kosovo with military manpower and economic assistance, these societies had been turned into permanent wards of the international community. The Bush administration, he explained, by stinting on such commitments, would ensure that Afghanistan and Iraq more quickly become self-sufficient. This minimalist approach to nation building proved vastly more expensive than the "decisive force" model that preceded it. By making minimal initial efforts at stabilization in Afghanistan and Iraq, and then reinforcing only once challenged, the administration failed to deter the emergence of organized resistance in either country. The Rumsfeld vision of "defense transformation" proved well suited to conventional combat against vastly inferior adversaries, but turned out to be a much more expensive approach to postconflict stabilization and reconstruction than the then-out-of-fashion Powell Doctrine.

During the 2000 presidential campaign, Condoleezza Rice spoke dismissively of stability operations, declaring "we don't need to have the 82nd Airborne escorting kids to kindergarten" (Gordon 2000). Consistent with this view, the Bush administration, having overthrown the Taliban and installed a new government in Kabul, determined that American troops would do no peacekeeping and that peacekeepers from other countries would not be allowed to venture beyond the Kabul city limits. Public security throughout the rest of the country was to be left entirely to the Afghans, even though Afghanistan had no army and no police force. A year later, President Bush was asking his advisers irritably why the reconstruction that had occurred was limited largely to the capital.

The same attitude toward public security informed US plans for postwar Iraq. Washington assumed that Iraqi police and military would continue to maintain public order once Saddam's regime was removed. The fact that this had proved impossible not just in Afghanistan a year earlier, but also in Somalia, Haiti, and Kosovo, was ignored. In the weeks leading up to the invasion, the Pentagon leadership cut the number of military police proposed by US military authorities for the operation, while the White House cut even more drastically the number of international civilian police proposed by experts in the State Department. The White House also directed that any civilian police sent to Iraq should be unarmed. For the next several years, as Iraq descended into civil war, American authorities declined to collect data on the number of Iraqis getting killed. Secretary Rumsfeld maintained that such statistics were not a relevant indicator of the success or failure of the American military mission. Only with the arrival of Gen. David Petraeus in 2007 did the number of civilian casualties become the chief metric for measuring the progress of this campaign.

America's quick success in overthrowing the Taliban and replacing it with a broadly based successor regime owed much to the assistance received from nearby states, to include such long-term opponents of the Taliban as Iran, Russia, and India. Yet no sooner had the Karzai government been installed than Washington rebuffed offers of further assistance from Iran, and relaxed the pressure on Pakistan to sever its remaining ties with violent extremist groups. The broad regional strategy, so critical to both Washington's initial military victory and political achievement, was effectively abandoned.

A regional strategy was not even attempted with respect to Iraq. The invasion was conducted not just against the advice of several of Washington's most important allies, but also contrary to the wishes of most regional states. With the exception of Kuwait, none of Iraq's neighbors supported the intervention. Even Kuwait cannot have been enthusiastic about the announced American intention to make Iraq a democratic model for the region in the hopes of inspiring similar changes in the form of government of all its neighbors. Not surprisingly, neighborly interference quickly became a significant factor in stoking Iraq's sectarian passions.

In his second term, President Bush worked hard to recover from these early mistakes. In the process his administration embraced the mission of postconflict stabilization with the fervor of a new convert. The president issued a new directive setting out an interagency structure for managing such operations. Condoleezza Rice recanted her earlier dismissal of nation building. The State Department established an Office of Reconstruction and Stabilization charged with establishing a doctrine for the civilian conduct of such missions and with building a cadre of experts ready to man them. The Defense Department issued a directive making stability operations a core function of the American military.

In Iraq, more forces and money were committed, public security was embraced as the heart of a new counterinsurgency strategy, and efforts were made to better engage neighboring states, not even excepting Iran. The lessons of the 1990s had been relearned and Iraq pulled back from the abyss.

Both the Clinton and Bush administrations began poorly and gradually improved their management of nation-building operations. President Obama's election offered every prospect of seeing this pattern repeated, as a new administration of a different party took office intent on doing things differently from its predecessor. Fortunately, and rather remarkably, Obama chose to keep Robert Gates as secretary of defense, Gen. David Petraeus at Central Command, and Lt. Gen. Douglas Lute, along with a team of professional military, diplomatic, and intelligence officers, in the White House, advising him and organizing the interagency management of both wars. The result was a degree of continuity that left some Democrats uneasy but ensured that lessons from the past two decades would continue to be applied at least as long as American forces remained engaged in Iraq and Afghanistan.

The Shifting Civil-Military Balance

One may debate the wisdom of invading Afghanistan or Iraq, but having done so, the United States assumed the practical as well as moral obligation of ensuring that the regimes it installed were better than those it had toppled. In this regard, the initial deficiencies, in both cases, were not the paucity of civilian resources devoted to the tasks of stabilization and reconstruction, but of military resources. In both cases, the United States deployed too few soldiers to secure the territory they had overrun, and those troops that were available lacked suitable training, tactics, and doctrine.

The resultant setbacks in Iraq and Afghanistan caused significant changes in the way the United States approached these missions. Additional troops were sent, first to Iraq and then to Afghanistan. The US military was given a good deal of money for development and humanitarian-type activities (the Commander's Emergency Response Program, or CERP). They had more flexibility in the use of these funds than any of the civilian agencies. American commanders also acquired a good deal of civilian expertise through details of personnel from other agencies and contracting with individuals and private organizations. State, USAID, and to a lesser extent domestic agencies also shifted resources toward these two operations. The State Department began to elaborate a doctrine for the conduct of reconstruction and stabilization operations and to build a cadre of experts to help carry them out. These various initiatives have greatly increased civilian capacity, albeit at the cost of substantial overlap among the major US agencies involved.

The hardest-fought interagency battles are usually over who pays for what. Issues of this nature can seldom be resolved in the field, no matter what's delegated to a local supreme authority, for no local proconsul can exercise real control over anyone's budget except his own. Indeed, only with great difficulty can these funding disputes be overcome in Washington. The president has sufficient authority to adjudicate policy differences among agencies, but even he cannot normally shift money from one department to another, nor can he compel agencies to perform activities for which they lack congressional authorization. In recent years, workarounds have been employed to deal with this lack of flexibility. Congress has granted limited permission to shift money from Defense to State, and authorities from State to Defense. The result has been a better alignment of resources and strategy, but at the cost of large-scale duplication of functions and capabilities, and substantial confusion over roles and missions.

Whether further institutional adjustments are needed (as opposed to more money and people) is a matter of some debate. Experience of the past twenty years suggests that the main problem is not inadequate civilian capacity in the field, but rather Washington's failure to retain acquired expertise, formulate realistically resourced plans, and successfully integrate the various elements of American power and international influence. If this is an accurate diagnosis, prescriptions for change should be directed primarily to fixing the interagency problem in Washington, and only secondarily in the field.

Promoting Continuity of Expertise

The Obama administration picked up where its predecessor had left off in the conduct of operations in both Iraq and Afghanistan, retaining senior officials and key staffers in both the White House and Defense Department, and thereby avoiding the abrupt drop-off in competence that had plagued both of its immediate predecessors. In addition to keeping Bob Gates, Obama appointed other senior DoD officials committed to building on the lessons learned over the preceding eight years rather than relearning them. This was, unfortunately, an aberration rather than the norm. One cannot and should not count on future presidents to behave likewise.

Gyrations in governing capacity reflect not just the characteristics of different chief executives but the nature of the American spoils system, which replaces thousands of senior and mid-level officials every eight years or so. The US military, intelligence, and law enforcement agencies are largely insulated from these periodic purges, on the grounds that domestic and external security are too important to be politicized or run by amateurs. Yet State, USAID, the civilian elements of the Defense Department, and the entire national security apparatus within the White House are afforded no such protection from the spoils system. If civilian expertise is essential to success in stability operations, counterinsurgency, and irregular warfare, then there is a case for treating these repositories of that expertise similarly to the nation's military, intelligence, and law enforcement establishments. Senior positions in the national security bureaucracy should not become civil service sinecures, but presidents should be encouraged to choose a higher proportion of such officials in State, Defense, and the National Security Council Staff from career professionals.

Establishing an Enduring Division of Labor

In the 1990s, the division of labor among national security agencies was pretty clear-cut. The Congress did not like nation building, and reinforced the American military's own aversion to taking on functions associated with it. Thus in the Balkans, US and NATO forces confined themselves almost exclusively to peacekeeping, fairly narrowly defined, leaving civilian agencies to work the underlying political, social, and bureaucratic changes that would make the interventions worthwhile. It was thus State, not Defense, that organized military training, rebuilt police forces, and arranged protection for local leaders. It was USAID that built schools, dug wells, and improved roads.

In the Bush administration's first foray into nation building, this division was turned on its head. In 2002, American forces did no peacekeeping in Afghanistan, but they did train the local military and police, protect Hamid Karzai, build schools, and dig wells. Thus one administration where the American military sought to do nothing but peacekeeping was succeeded by another administration where the military was charged with doing everything except peacekeeping. In 2003, this redistribution of portfolios was taken to an even further extreme, when DoD was given responsibility for overseeing all civilian as well as military activity in Iraq, to include organizing elections, promoting a free press, encouraging civil society, writing a constitution, and expanding the economy.

Beyond the immediate confusion occasioned by these changes, the longer-term effect was to promote large-scale duplication in expertise and activity, create deep uncertainty about agency roles and missions, and thereby diminish the incentive of all the agencies to make long-term investments in these areas of overlap. Why spend now to make your agency better at a given task ten or twenty years hence if there is no reason to be confident that your agency will retain the function? Why work to change bureaucratic culture if the need for new capabilities is not to endure? A lot of supplemental money went into deploying civilian expertise in Afghanistan and Iraq, but little regular funding was devoted to long-term development of such institutional capacity.

There is debate over where such capacity ought to be located. Congress, based upon its record of funding, would seem to prefer DoD. The secretary of defense has argued that civilian capacity ought to be centered in State and

USAID. Several others have suggested either creating a new agency especially to handle the reconstruction in conflict or postconflict environments, and/or beefing up the Executive Office of the President.

In order to evaluate these proposals, it helps to have some understanding of the various levels of responsibility within the executive branch.

- First there is the responsibility to set national policy and ensure that all agencies adhere to it.
- The second level of decision making involves the integration of various agency programs to maximize achievement of national policy in a given country. This is normally a State Department function. In normal times the ambassador, through his country team, ensures that the activities of all agencies operating within a given country are doing so consistent with the president's policies. In conflict or postconflict environments, this function is usually fulfilled by either the local chief of mission or a Washington-based special envoy located in the State Department.
- The third level of responsibility is for program execution. This is performed abroad by a large range of agencies.

Only the president and his staff can execute the first of these responsibilities. Cabinet agencies with independent budgets, responsible to different congressional oversight committees, cannot be effectively subordinated one to another.

The second level of responsibility, for coordinating program design and execution in a given country, could in theory be transferred from State to Defense. This was tried in Iraq in 2003. The experiment was not deemed a success. Setting up and managing branch offices of the US government all over the world is a core mission of the State Department. Creating such a capacity in DoD would be difficult and expensive. Creating yet a new agency to perform such a function in conflict and postconflict areas would simply introduce a third major bureaucratic player, alongside State and Defense. The new agency would not likely be given authority over military operations or the conduct of diplomacy, so instead of two lead agencies in the field, one would have three.

It is in the area of program execution that most of the current confusion regarding roles and missions resides, as key functions such as police training are continually passed back and forth from one agency to another. This is the area where some rationalization would be most useful, ideally in the form of legislation laying out a more enduring division of labor among agencies. (See Chapter 6 by Anderson and Veillette for ideas about the proper allocation of development and humanitarian assistance tasks between civilian agencies and the Pentagon.)

Thus responsibility for setting national policy and keeping all agencies on task should continue to be lodged in the White House. Responsibility for ensuring the integration, within a given country, of all nonmilitary activities in support of that policy should continue to be exercised by the State Department. Responsibility for conducting those activities should be allocated among a number of agencies based on some judgment of their comparative advantage. To the extent that other agencies do not have an obvious comparative advantage, reconstruction and development programs should be assigned to USAID. This division of labor should be established in law, leaving the president some leeway to reassign functions, but not to the wholesale degree experienced over the past decade.

Bolstering State Department Authority and USAID Capacity

The three layers of responsibility laid out above describe how the executive branch is designed to function, and how it does so most of the time. To the extent that it fails to function satisfactorily, the fault can lie at one or more of these levels. In 2003, for instance, the president and his staff failed to exercise their responsibility for setting national policy regarding the occupation of Iraq, and ensuring that all agencies adhered to it. Instead, responsibility for interagency coordination was delegated to the secretary of defense and then to the Coalition Provisional Authority administrator in Iraq, neither of whom had the experienced staff or the authority needed to adequately perform the function. This abdication of responsibility should not be repeated.

Often the State Department is in a weak position to design and oversee implementation of a multiagency strategy for the achievement of national objectives in a given country because it lacks control over the funding. A strong ambassador or special envoy can prevent another agency from doing something stupid with its money, but he cannot make it do something smart. If, on the other hand, State controls the funding, it can always find an agency to conduct the desired program. In conflict and postconflict environments, therefore, the Congress should provide the funding for all nonmilitary activities to State, with the intention that State, via the resident ambassador or Washington-based special envoy, should design and oversee a range of USAID, Treasury, Agriculture, Drug Enforcement, and other agency activities in support of national policy. This is how reconstruction funding was handled in the Balkans in the late 1990s. The amounts provided by Congress were commensurate with the needs, as was the leeway granted to State regarding their disbursement. Many agencies were involved in rebuilding postwar Bosnia and Kosovo, but the money and the direction came from State.

USAID today is a shadow of the organization that could send over a thousand officers to Vietnam in support of the rural pacification. This decline has been accompanied by an increased reliance upon private contractors and a declining ability to guide and oversee their work. The cause of USAID's diminishment has been the number of functions that have been stripped out of it and allocated elsewhere. Police training and refugee assistance went long ago to State. Significant economic assistance funding has gone to the Millennium Development Challenge Corporation. Combating AIDS in Africa has gone to a new office overseen by the State Department. The Office of Reconstruction and Stabilization, recently reorganized into the Bureau of Conflict and Stabilization Operations, has been located in the State Department. In Iraq, most heavy infrastructure development was done (badly) by the Army Corps of Engineers. (Adams, in Chapter 2, underscores the difficulties the diaspora of foreign policy organizations poses for successful coordination of civilian tasks for such missions.)

USAID could be brought back to its former size and capacity without adding a person to the US payroll or a dollar to the US budget by returning these functions, staffs, and budgets to that agency. To signify the agency's enlarged responsibilities, reconstruction might usefully be added to development in its title. But Congress should continue to provide the funding for all nonmilitary activities in postconflict environments to State, allowing that agency to design the overall approach to civilian implementation, and dole out the money to the agencies best able to meet the resultant demands.

These proposals actually describe how responsibilities for stabilization and reconstruction were allocated in the Balkans in the late 1990s. The president set policy and his staff kept all agencies on task. The Defense Department confined itself to essentially military tasks and resisted efforts to expand its mission. Funding for nonmilitary activities went to State, which allocated money to USAID, Treasury, Justice, and other agencies to carry out specified functions. The Bosnia and Kosovo operations were far from perfect, but they are the most successful such American-led efforts of the past twenty years. The machinery employed then and described here may not be ideal, but it does represent a good place to start.

Conclusion: Civil-Military Relations Beyond Iraq and Afghanistan

Secretary of Defense Leon Panetta promulgated a revised defense strategy in January 2012 that says the US military force structure will not be sized in the future around long-term stabilization operations. The experience in both Afghanistan and Iraq demonstrated that the failure to adequately man a stability operation in its early stages allows violent resistance to emerge that will eventually call for much greater resources to tamp down. The solution to this dilemma proposed by President Obama is not to invade and occupy any more large countries. This is, of course, precisely what George W. Bush promised not to do during the 2000 presidential campaign, only subsequently to do just the opposite, not once, but twice during his first term in office.

The results of those two interventions admittedly discourage any near future repetition, and President Obama is no doubt sincere in his intention to avoid such commitments. Yet a collapse of North Korea, a war with Iran, a total collapse in Syria, or contingencies we cannot now even imagine, just as no one envisaged invading Iraq in early 2001, or bombing Libya in early 2011, may eventually compel a different course, perhaps earlier than we can currently anticipate.

Recognizing these possibilities, President Obama has promised that the rundown in American capacity to conduct large-scale stability or counterinsurgency operations will be made reversible in order that the United States not replicate the mistake it made in the wake of the Vietnam War by shedding the expertise and forgetting the lessons learned in that conflict. Despite this pledge, budgetary pressures will make it difficult to fund capabilities for which the administration and the Congress see little immediate need.

The US-led interventions of the 1990s took place in relatively small societies, under comparatively permissive environments, and in circumstances where the United States was only one of many well-heeled donors. The missions entailed stabilization and reconstruction, not counterinsurgency. Other than in Somalia, American troops engaged in no fighting and suffered no casualties. US civilian agencies proved able to handle all the basically civil tasks with the military's role largely confined to peacekeeping narrowly defined. By contrast, Afghanistan and Iraq are each eight to fifteen times more populous than Bosnia or Kosovo, the United States has been by far the dominant external contributor to each, and pervasive combat operations have been the norm. In these circumstances, there was no possibility of US civilian agencies quickly surging the level of civilian capacity needed to fill the governance gaps left by the overthrown regimes. Such capacity had in large measure to be contracted for on the open market, and the contracting was to be done by whichever agency had the necessary funds, which often turned out to be DoD.

Building up State and USAID capacity to the point where those agencies could handle the full panoply of civilian responsibilities for two simultaneous American-dominated combat operations in two widely separated countries is probably never going to happen. Only the Defense Department will be allowed to maintain large standby forces and have expansive contingency funding. Congress is unlikely to award any civilian agency similar capacity. But large ground wars are not the most likely contingencies the United States will face in the coming years. More likely are smaller-scale nation-building missions, either in postconflict environments where the United States is only one of many donors, or in support of partner governments wrestling with internal disorder. In these circumstances, it makes sense to return to the ultimately successful division of labor worked out in the 1990s, rather than retain the much more military-centric, DoD-dominated arrangements that emerged over the next decade. Moving to a more civilian-centric model for handling American engagement in conflict and postconflict environments around the globe means retaining and strengthening the relevant capabilities in State and USAID, even as the Defense Department and the US military scale back their manpower and resource commitments in this area.

At the same time, it must be emphasized that without adequate security most other lines of endeavor will prove futile, and that in a conflict or immediate postconflict environment, only the military can provide such security. Thus no improvement in civilian capacity will relieve the United States of the need to deploy appropriately trained and sufficiently numerous military forces in those instances where it chooses to intervene.

Note

1. The analysis in this chapter is drawn from a number of previous works, for example, Dobbins et al. 2003; Dobbins et al. 2007; Dobbins 2008; Dobbins et al. 2009.

Chapter 4

From Confrontation to Cooperation
Weak States, Demanding Allies, and the US Military

Derek S. Reveron

US forces will conduct a sustainable pace of presence operations abroad, including rotational deployments and bilateral and multilateral training exercises. These activities reinforce deterrence, help to build the capacity and competence of US, allied, and partner forces for internal and external defense, strengthen alliance cohesion, and increase US influence (US Department of Defense 2012c).

Reaffirmed by the 2014 defense review, the US military has been gradually shifting from a force designed for confrontation to one intended to promote international cooperation to strengthen sovereignty challenged by subnational, transnational, and traditional threats. To be sure, the US military retains a technical and doctrinal advantage as a warfighting entity. However, over the past two decades, the military has been incorporating new organizations, doctrine, and training to prioritize efforts to prevent war by building partnership capacity and supporting its partners' implementation of their foreign policies. This is based both in national strategy that seeks to dissuade or deter conflicts in Asia, and also in US diplomatic efforts that attempt to bolster the security capacity of almost every country in the world.

This shift in focus has raised concerns about the "militarization of US foreign policy," which began in the 1990s with the recognition that combatant commanders are as much policy entrepreneurs as they are war fighters (Reveron 2004). Generals like Tony Zinni or Wesley Clark epitomized the new breed of warrior-diplomat who directly engaged with foreign heads of state

(Priest 2003). Far from rogue generals, these military leaders were directed by President Bill Clinton to engage with the world and promote security by assisting partners and assuring allies in a security environment freed from the Cold War dynamic. At the same time international engagement became a core function of the military, President Clinton's secretary of state, Madeleine Albright, also tapped the nonwarfighting potential of the US military by deploying forces in stability operations and conducting humanitarian assistance operations. By using organic medical, logistics, and engineering capabilities, the military offered the president a solution to the global demand for US international assistance. As the military became valued for these activities and the role it played in implementing US foreign policy, critics contended that these operations undermined traditional diplomacy and development efforts. Further, critics within defense circles assumed that an emphasis on helping weak states jeopardized American military dominance and preparation for major war.[1]

In response to these perceived misuses of the military, President George W. Bush and his secretary of defense, Donald Rumsfeld, intended to refocus the military on preparation for war with major powers. A rising China provided the raison d'être; the April 2001 collision between a US reconnaissance aircraft and a Chinese fighter seemed to buttress the Bush administration's efforts to reset the military's role in national security and focus on a rising regional power. In contrast to President Clinton's foreign policy, nation building would fall outside the military's scope; the military's role would be limited to deterring war and preparing to win wars. So-called activist generals were restrained by strict guidance to limit engagements for explicit national security purposes. Emphasizing this point, Secretary Rumsfeld took away the title commander-in-chief and substituted it with combatant commander and "engagement" was recast as "security cooperation" to focus efforts on improving security.

Just eight months into his presidency, however, the terrorist attack on September 11, 2001, stunted President Bush's efforts to ignore the challenge of weak states and the importance of state-building activities. Instead of refocusing the military as a defensive bulwark to a rising China, President Bush's eight years in office produced comprehensive systems for stability operations, counterinsurgency, and security force assistance.

Outside of combat zones, partnership and engagement became key components of a grand strategy that sought to confront challenges at their roots and stabilize partners. Further, combating terrorism required unprecedented levels of international cooperation to share information, target terrorists, and provide governments the tools they need to confront national threats before they become regional. In short, the White House shifted its defense policy from a "suit of armor" against a rising peer competitor to an "immune system" that would protect the United States from threats without borders by reducing security deficits and promoting sovereignty.[2] In practice, this meant that what happened in Somalia impacted US national security.

President Barack Obama continued what had become since the 1990s an American tradition of prioritizing weak states in national security thinking. His speech in Cairo illustrated the connection between American national security and subnational and transnational threats: "We have learned from recent experience that when a financial system weakens in one country, prosperity is hurt everywhere. When a new flu infects one human being, all are at risk. When one nation pursues a nuclear weapon, the risk of nuclear attack rises for all nations. When violent extremists operate in one stretch of mountains, people are endangered across an ocean" (Obama 2009). These points were manifest in key national security documents such as the National Security Strategy and the National Military Strategy. Consequently, President Obama retained the interdependence of national security assumption, President Bush's secretary of defense (Robert Gates), and robust security assistance programs. By training and equipping other militaries, the goal is to reduce American military presence internationally and allow others to provide for their own security. For example, with every Joint Strike Fighter plane Japan deploys, there is one less that the United States needs in Asia. This has positive benefits not only for the US defense budget, but also for international security marred by states at risk (e.g., Mexico, Philippines, and Nigeria), developed countries with security dilemmas (e.g., Japan, South Korea, and Singapore), and developed countries that lack the military capabilities to implement their foreign policies (e.g., France in Mali or the United Kingdom in Libya).

Changed Security Landscape and the Priority of Weak States

At least since the early 1990s, state failure and weak states were identified as risks to international peace and security.[3] For example, the 2002 National Security Strategy highlighted that "the events of September 11, 2001 taught us that weak states, like Afghanistan, can pose as great a danger to our national interests as strong states" (White House 2002: v). This view continued throughout the 2000s when policymakers saw a direct connection between weak states and international terrorism (Hagel 2004). For former Secretary of Defense Robert Gates:

> The recent past vividly demonstrated the consequences of failing to address adequately the dangers posed by insurgencies and failing states.

Terrorist networks can find sanctuary within the borders of a weak nation and strength within the chaos of social breakdown. The most likely catastrophic threats to the U.S. homeland, for example, that of a U.S. city being poisoned or reduced to rubble by a terrorist attack, are more likely to emanate from failing states than from aggressor states (Gates 2009a).

Former Secretary of State Condoleezza Rice made a similar point: "it is clear that managing the problems of state failure and ungoverned spaces will be a feature of U.S. foreign policy for the foreseeable future—whether we like it or not" (Rice 2008). Secretary of State Hillary Clinton continued this tradition, with her statement that "[i]n today's world, we face challenges that have no respect for borders" (Clinton 2009). There is a realization within US policy-making circles that subnational challenges can create regional crises and that weak states pose an acute risk to US national security (Krasner and Pascual 2005). To bolster weak states challenged by internal or transnational actors, the United States deployed forces to countries such as the Philippines, Colombia, Uganda, and Pakistan and bolstered security commitments with almost every country in the world. Seldom engaged in direct combat operations, US forces are enabling partner countries to combat challenges that threaten their stability.

Prioritizing weak or failing states represents an important shift in strategic thinking. Historically, countering a peer competitor such as the Soviet Union or economic interests such as threats to oil trade routes drove US foreign policy decisions and military deployments. Security assistance is now a key pillar of US military strategy, which places American officers and noncommissioned officers in more than 150 countries to train, mentor, and professionalize other militaries. The impetus for the change is based on the belief that capacity building sets the conditions for conflict prevention, and there is a global need for capable military partners to serve in peacekeeping operations, control their own territory, and promote regional stability.

To formalize these activities, President Bush issued National Security Presidential Directive 44 in 2005, which directed the United States to "work with other countries and organizations to anticipate state failure, avoid it whenever possible, and respond quickly and effectively when necessary to promote peace, security, development, democratic practices, market economies, and the rule of law" (White House 2005). Consequently, the Bush administration stepped up Clinton-era programs in Africa, Asia, and Latin America. All of a sudden, the Defense Department found itself building militaries in Liberia, Georgia, Rwanda, Yemen, the Trans-Sahara, East Africa, and the Philippines, providing disaster relief in Indonesia, Pakistan, and the US

Gulf Coast, and leading reconstruction efforts in Iraq and Afghanistan. Previously, the institutional military saw these operations as distractions from its core function of fighting and winning the nation's wars. However, with the inadequacies of international institutions, long-time partners, and other US government agencies, the military embraced the mission to bridge the gap between national ends, ways, and means.

While they are executing foreign policy, military officers have gradually learned that they cannot completely rely on international organizations, nongovernmental organizations, or other US government departments to provide the capabilities for noncombat operations. Instead, they learned that the military needs to incorporate capabilities expected in civilian organizations. Secretary of Defense Robert Gates observed, "One of the most important lessons of the wars in Iraq and Afghanistan is that military success is not sufficient to win: economic development, institution building and the rule of law, promoting internal reconciliation, good governance, providing basic services ... along with security, are essential ingredients for long-term success" (Gates 2007b). With few institutional alternatives to ensuring national success, the president increasingly places the military in the nonwarfighting roles of promoting development, assisting institutional reform, and facilitating restoration of social harmony after conflict; the president does so out of necessity, however, rather than because of the military's experience.

Old Allies, New Friends, and Partners

Even as the United States placed new emphasis on the stabilization of weak states, it also answered security demands from wealthy and stable partners. Under mutual defense treaties, the United States has assumed an obligation to assist its treaty partners in the event of an armed attack. Originally driven by US security concerns of an expansionist Soviet Union, the treaties have evolved to support broader global concerns and operations. Today, many countries need partnership with the United States to sustain their security forces and enable their foreign policy objectives and US presidents continue to reaffirm that partnership is a large part of US grand strategy. Through these arrangements, the United States formally pledges to protect the sovereignty of twenty-seven NATO countries and five Asian countries.

After the Cold War, there seemed to be little relevance to these treaties and security arrangements, let alone a rationale for invoking or expanding them. Yet, the opposite occurred. NATO increased its membership three times: from sixteen to nineteen in 1999; to twenty-six in 2006; and to twenty-eight in 2009. At the same time, NATO changed from its traditional mission of territorial defense to one of global security engagement. With each expansion, new members required training and equipping to NATO standards. With each new operation, member countries continue to require access to US intelligence, critical technology, and global logistics. The benefits to US partners are obvious, but in return the United States gains forward operating locations, financial subsidy through host nation support programs that total in the billions, and access to other countries' intelligence and unique capabilities.

In addition to formal treaties of alliance, an additional dozen countries are offered protection under the US security umbrella either by law, such as the *Taiwan Relations Act,* or by policy, such as United States' support for Israel.[4] These protections include provisions to train and equip their militaries. Another dozen countries are offered special security provisions through Major Non-NATO Ally (MNNA) status. MNNA does not confer a mutual defense relationship; instead the largely symbolic act implies a close working relationship with another country's defense forces.[5] It is more akin to a preferred buyer's program, allowing countries like Morocco, Kuwait, and Pakistan access to advanced weapons systems. With weapons purchases also come long-term training and maintenance contracts. From a US perspective, it has a comparative advantage in defense exports; and strategically, programs like these are intended to overcome the free-rider problem the United States faces with its partners.[6] Given the diplomatic nature of these security partnerships, the Department of State's Bureau of Political-Military Affairs focuses on these activities, regulates the defense trade and arms transfers to reinforce the military capabilities of friends, allies, and coalition partners, and ensures that the transfer of US-origin defense equipment and technology supports US national security interests. At the country level, US ambassadors exert critical control over security assistance to ensure military diplomacy is aligned with embassy plans. This is certainly visible in the Asia-Pacific region as diplomats deepen the economic and security relationships with new partners such as India, Myanmar, and Vietnam.

Not Just for Weak States

Discussion of security assistance often centers on dependencies that seek US assistance to confront terrorism, insurgency, and illicit trafficking. Yet, as the preceding section suggests, security assistance is not just for weak states. As France learned during its 2013 intervention in Mali, it had limited ability to sustain its military 2,000 miles from French territory. To support its foreign policy agenda of confronting an Islamist insurgency in Mali, France needed the US Air Force to fly its ground forces and to refuel its attack aircraft. As the operation continued, the United States provided intelligence for French and African forces as they shifted to stability operations.

A shared counterterrorism concern certainly explains US support of France's intervention in Mali; however, enabling French intervention in Mali is illustrative of the role the United States plays in supporting developed countries that need US security assistance to implement their foreign policies. On a grand scale, this was visible in Afghanistan, where fifty countries with forces serving there relied on the United States for food, fuel, and intelligence. This was also the case for European countries in the Balkans, Australian forces in East Timor, and British forces in West Africa. These examples highlight that the foreign policy goals of many developed countries exceed their military capacity, which requires them to rely on the US military for assistance. As developed countries' defense budgets fall further, reliance on the United States is going to increase. This remains a decades-old frustration on both sides of the Atlantic. The NATO secretary general, Anders Fogh Rasmussen, said, "There is a lower limit on how little we can spend on defense, while living up to our responsibilities" (Fidler 2013). Pragmatically, the United States would like its partners to do more, but shared challenges and partners' limited budgets will reinforce the importance of American logistics, combat experience, and intelligence capacity.

Military Diplomacy

The military's emergence in once civilian-only domains is based on four interrelated ideas (Reveron 2010). First, weak states have largely supplanted peer competitors as the focus of concern for strategic thinkers. The United States is more concerned that Pakistan will fail than that Russia will invade Western Europe. Thus, Paul Collier argues that the role for advanced militaries of the world is "to supply the global public good of peace in territories that otherwise have the potential for nightmare" (Collier 2007, 125).

Second, long-time allies, friends, and partners request US assistance for training, equipment, and professionalization. Australia and Singapore want increased security cooperation with the United States to ensure its interests are protected against future threats. US diplomacy actively includes a security component as the Department of State manages US relations with other states. Far from preparation for major war, these activities rely on a unique blend of charitable American political culture, latent civil-military capacity, and ambitious military officers who see the strategic landscape characterized by challenges to human security, weak states, and transnational actors.

Third, the Defense Department has a distinct advantage over the foreign assistance agencies in both size and resources, which is most evident in staff size. For example, Africa Command headquarters is composed of about 1,500 military personnel and the State Department's Africa Bureau has only about 80. Or, in East Africa, the US military has over 700 personnel, who are primarily noncombat personnel focused on engineering and construction projects, medical and veterinary care, and various forms of military training. In contrast, US Foreign Service and development officers in the region number in only the hundreds.[7] In fact, the disparity is by design as ambassadors are directed to minimize Foreign Service presence in countries, but there is no corresponding guidance for combatant commands to minimize their presence (it is important to note that the ambassador can and does limit military presence through the country clearance process).[8]

Finally, changes in the US foreign assistance bureaucracy has turned development specialists into contract managers who rely on NGOs to deliver services. In both personnel and budget, USAID is a pale comparison to what it was during the Cold War. From 1990 to 2005, the agency lost 40 percent of its staff and ceased to have a planning division and a budget office (Steinberg 2012, 161). As the deputy administrator for USAID Donald Steinberg noted in 2012, the development space has become more crowded with not only military-led development projects, but also dozens of separate US government agencies promoting development. However, this is an opportunity, "since it means greater resources, greater expertise, and greater capacity to contribute" (Ibid., 158). Outside of the military, the government has few options to send direct assistance. But as Bill Anderson and Connie Veillette (Chapter 6) write in this book, "Identifying where DoD adds value to development depends on several factors and often differs by country or region."

Driven by national security strategy objectives, military diplomacy, with a primary mission of developing relationships and partnerships with other militaries or their governments, is increasingly common. Reflecting on his command, Gen. Tony Zinni remarked, "As my experiences throughout the region in general and with [Pakistan's former president] Musharraf in particular illustrate, I did not intend to sit back and say, 'Hey, my job is purely military. When you're ready to send me in, coach, that's when I go in.' When I assumed command of CENTCOM [Central Command] and had the ability to choose between fighting fires or preventing them, I chose prevention" (Quoted in Reveron 2007a). Yet, it is the goal of conflict prevention that raised the profile of combatant commanders and provoked ire and fears of militarization.

Military commanders have learned that they need to be more than a 911 force responding to crises. And when a crisis occurs, the United States needs international partners to be successful. If a common foundation does not exist between the United States and its partners prior to a crisis, then motivations will be questioned and action will be more difficult. Many leaders have found that it is much better to consult with allies and partners between crises, not only after one begins. One commander told me that his role was to "build trust and reliability."[9] To gain entry into partners' military establishments, US commanders host regional conferences, build allies' capabilities, and enhance the education of military leaders. All of this is done under the auspices of or in partnership with the US ambassador in the partner country. (See Murray and Quainton, Chapter 9, for a discussion of the relationship between combatant commanders and ambassadors.)

Military leaders also have common experiences and common frames of reference that facilitate dialogue and relationships less hindered by political realities. Often, these foreign military leaders attended US military schools and developed their own networks of US officers as their careers progressed. To be sure, these activities are fundamentally different from warfighting. Engagement is about managing relationships, not command and control; it is about cooperation, not fighting; and it is about partnership, not dominance. Success often relies on fully comprehending the influence of warrior-diplomats, these leaders' penchant for intercultural communication, and the role of the military in our partners' societies.

With this in mind, there is concern that the development and diplomacy space is being militarized. Ambassador Edward Marks writes in this book (Chapter 12) that geographic commands militate against effective "whole-of-government" engagement programs and prevent a coherent foreign policy. Consequently, Ambassador Marks thinks combatant commands should be dismantled and the Department of State should reassert its authority for diplomacy. With ongoing budget cuts, this point echoes in national security debates. However, this overlooks the important role security assistance plays in embassy country plans and the security challenges that countries seek assistance to control.[10] US combatant commands respond to US ambassadors' requests for security assistance to advance US national interests.

Security Assistance

The overall goals of security assistance include: creating favorable military balances of power (e.g., selling weapons and training to Saudi Arabia to balance Iran); advancing areas of mutual defense or security arrangements (e.g., collaborating with Japan on missile defense technology); building allied and friendly military capabilities for self-defense and multinational operations (e.g., Georgia was the third-largest troop contributor in Iraq in 2008); and preventing crisis and conflict (e.g., facilitating Colombia's counterterrorism campaign against the decades-old FARC [Revolutionary Armed Forces of Colombia] insurgency).

Traditionally, the Department of Defense implements these international military assistance programs funded through the Department of State. Financed under Title 22 (account 150), the international assistance budget was $32.9 billion in FY 2014 (see Table 4.1). Excluded from normal assistance are those activities funded by supplemental budgets that largely benefit Iraq and Afghanistan (see Serafino, Chapter 7). Fifteen different programs are included in the account 150, but only six programs can be considered security related. These include Foreign Military Financing (FMF), International Military Education and Training (IMET), International Narcotics Control and Law Enforcement (INCLE), peacekeeping operations (PKO), the Andean Counterdrug Program (ACP), and Nonproliferation, Anti-terrorism, Demining, and Related Programs (NADR). While security assistance programs are substantial, nonsecurity assistance programs exceed them by at least a two-to-one ratio. And there are substantial differences across regions, too. In Africa, for example, public health programs dominate US assistance. In the Near East, however, the opposite is true because of military assistance to Egypt and Israel. And in Asia, traditional development activities and trade account for the preponderance of US foreign policy. Overall, however, nonsecurity assistance consumes the lion's share of US international assistance.

Though the United States has security assistance programs with about 150 countries, it does privilege several nations over the rest (see Table 4.2). Historically, Israel has been the largest recipient of security assistance, and Egypt benefited from its recognition of Israel, the Camp David Accords, and control of the Suez Canal.[11] Because of its proximity to the United States and challenges with drug-trafficking organizations, Mexico is a top recipient of security assistance. Yet, the history of American military interventions in Mexico

Table 4.1
US International Assistance (Account 150), by Region,
Fiscal Year 2014 ($ in thousands)

Region	Nonsecurity Assistance	Security Assistance	Total
Total	25,230,172	7,644,384	32,874,556
Africa	6,242,497	358,019	6,600,516
East Asia and the Pacific	618,665	149,615	768,280
Europe and Eurasia	383,945	179,073	563,018
Near East	1,792,896	5,069,097	6,861,993
South and Central Asia	1,496,286	648,354	2,144,640
Western Hemisphere	977,323	554,527	1,531,850

Data Source: Department of State, Congressional Budget Justification, FOREIGN ASSISTANCE SUMMARY TABLES Fiscal Year 2014, Table 3b: Country / Account Summary* FY 2014 Request http://www.state.gov/documents/organization/208292.pdf.

Table 4.2
Top Recipients of US International Assistance (Account 150)
Fiscal Year 2014 Request

Overall	Nonsecurity Assistance	Security Assistance
Israel	Nigeria	Israel
Egypt	Tanzania	Egypt
Pakistan	Kenya	Pakistan
Afghanistan	Afghanistan	Jordan
Nigeria	Pakistan	Afghanistan
Jordan	Uganda	Colombia
Kenya	South Africa	Mexico
South Africa	Ethiopia	West Bank and Gaza
West Bank and Gaza	West Bank and Gaza	Lebanon
Ethiopia	Mozambique	Philippines

Data Source: Derived from Department of State, Congressional Budget Justification, FOREIGN ASSISTANCE SUMMARY TABLES Fiscal Year 2014, Table 3b: Country / Account Summary* FY 2014 Request http://www.state.gov/documents/organization/208292.pdf.

has required some effort to build trust and reassure the Mexican government that the United States seeks to strengthen it and not undermine it.[12] Not all countries welcome the United States with open arms.

One reason the United States concentrates assistance on just a few countries is to promote particular countries as regional leaders. In practice, this means that Jordan hosts an international special operations exercise, peace operations training center, and an international police-training center. Or in Latin America, Colombia provides helicopter training for regional militaries and El Salvador hosts a regional peacekeeping institute attracting military personnel from countries throughout the Western Hemisphere. Through the significant US investment in Afghanistan's military and police-training infrastructure, it is possible that Afghanistan could host regional training if the insurgency subsides to acceptable levels. This approach not only strengthens key partners, but it also reduces the need for American presence and the negative attention it sometimes generates.

Conclusion: Changing Role of the Military

With national security focused on weak states and persistent security concerns among stable allies like South Korea, the US military has changed over the last twenty-five years from a force of confrontation to one of cooperation. The military has learned that partnership is better than clientelism and is adapting its command structure from one optimized for waging major combat to one focused on conflict prevention. These changes are reflected in the continued evolution of language to describe how to guarantee national security. President Roosevelt's *War Department* gave rise to President Truman's *Department of Defense*. While no formal name change is expected, it is better to think of today's Defense Department as the *Cooperative Security Department* as this emphasizes how much effort is now expended on supporting other countries' militaries from Afghanistan to Yemen. There is still a tremendous warfighting capability in the US military, but coalition warfare is the norm and developing compatible warfighting partners is a key goal of this cooperative strategy. In some sense, this turns the idea of militarization of foreign policy on its head; combatant commands are being demilitarized and valued for their ability to impart military capabilities to US partners. The US support of the 2011 European operations against Libya and the 2013 French intervention in Mali is illustrative of this phenomenon.

While the Defense Department's capacity certainly explains why international assistance missions increasingly have a military face, it is essential to understand that the new security landscape cannot be navigated by a single bureaucratic entity. The last twenty-five years illustrate that the changes to national security do not easily divide activities between war and peace. A problem like an insurgency is simultaneously military, economic, social, and political. When drug traffickers use submarines to ship cocaine and use the profits to finance an insurgency, we clearly need new ways to think about the military's role in foreign policy. Solutions often require unity of effort of the US government, industry, NGOs, and international partners. Yet, the dangers of operating in combat zones place those in uniform in nonwarfighting roles. Exacerbating these challenges is the difference in timelines; villages can be cleared faster than a police force can be trained and fielded, a judicial system can be developed, and commerce can be normalized. Through experience, the Defense Department learned that military personnel can build a school, but it needs the Department of State to identify where the school should be built, USAID to train teachers, and NGOs to provide school supplies. And none of this works if the partner government does not take an active part in and drive the cooperation through shared goals. The military also knows that it is better at achieving quick victories than it is resolving underlying conditions that produce instability.

To be sure, the military has been out front in adapting to the new security landscape. Through its organic medical, construction, and logistics capabilities, military personnel perform development missions, which often occur alongside NGOs, USAID, and international partners. The military's size and resources often overwhelm the civilian agencies of government, but it has realized that it must coordinate its activities with USAID and is driven by foreign policy developed by the Department of State.

The new model of security assistance is a far cry from what the military practiced in most of the 20th century. Then, military activism meant installing US-friendly governments through the power of the bayonet. While there are Cold War legacy programs that persist, the new security assistance programs, by and large, do not resemble those of an earlier era that focused on promoting insurgency to overthrow unfriendly governments or training and arming friendly regimes to repress dissent. With congressional oversight, Leahy vetting procedures to screen foreign military units for human rights abuses, nongovernmental organization cooperation, and the importance of soft power, the hard lessons have been learned and reinforced by challenges in Iraq and Afghanistan. These new programs represent a maturity developed over the last several decades.[13] Reinforced by the current structure of the international system and technological advances, the United States does not need partners in the same way as it did in the past—where they provided direct benefits through coaling stations, maintenance facilities, or large bases. While the number of forward bases is still substantial, the numbers of forward-deployed forces are greatly reduced. More importantly, the nature of the presence has changed; the United States aspires to create true partners that can confront their own threats to internal stability (e.g., assistance to the Philippines) or alleviate security dilemmas (e.g., rise of China). It also seeks to foster independence by training and equipping militaries to support the global demand for peacekeepers.[14] The United States certainly gets increased access to countries around the world through these programs, but the United States does not abuse these relationships or ignore seemingly insignificant states. Instead, it seeks to create partners where sovereignty is respected and all parties derive benefits.

Notes

1. As evidenced in how the United States fought in Afghanistan in 2001 and Iraq in 2003, nonwarfighting missions did not compromise the military's ability to engage in major combat operations. If anything, stability operations in Bosnia and Kosovo provided a glimpse of what the military faced after major combat ceased in Afghanistan and Iraq. Unfortunately, those lessons were largely ignored.

2. The notable exception to this approach was Iraq. Because of the nature of the Iraq intervention and the subsequent loss of life, the war and ensuing doctrine of counterinsurgency came to symbolize a new era of US militarism in foreign policy. See Bacevich (2006).

3. Ted Robert Gurr cofounded the State Failure Project that became the Political Instability Task Force.

4. Congress enacted the Taiwan Relations Act "to resist any resort to force or other forms of coercion that would jeopardize the security, or the social or economic system, of the people on Taiwan" (Taiwan Relations Act 1979).

5. Title 10 US Code Section 2350a authorizes the secretary of defense, with the concurrence of the secretary of state, to designate MNNAs for purposes of participating with the Department of Defense (DoD) in cooperative research and development programs. MNNA status does not entail the same mutual defense and security guarantees afforded to NATO members. Status makes a nation eligible to get priority delivery of excess defense articles, buy depleted uranium ammunition, have US-owned War Reserve Stockpiles on its territory, enter into agreements with the US government for the cooperative furnishing of training on a bilateral or multilateral basis under reciprocal financial arrangements, use US-provided Foreign Military Financing for commercial leasing of certain defense articles, makes a country eligible for loans of materials, supplies, and equipment for cooperative R&D projects and testing and evaluation, and makes a country eligible for expedited processing of export licenses of commercial satellites, their technologies, components, and systems.

6. US military spending is the highest in the world at about 4.5 percent of GDP; most European countries spend just under 2 percent. Only six countries meet the NATO target of 2 percent of GDP to support defense.

7. See US Africa Command Public Affairs Office (2011), US Department of State (2009), US Department of Defense, Personnel and Procurement Statistics (2011), and US Africa Command Combined Joint Task Force—Horn of Africa (2012).

8. Author interview with serving US ambassador. See also Murray and Quainton in Chapter 9.

9. Author interview with a combatant commander.

10. This was noted in the 1997 QDR, Section III, "DoD's role in shaping the international environment is closely integrated with our diplomatic efforts" (US Department of Defense 1997).

11. It is uncertain how the Arab Awakening and long-term challenges of US-Israel relations may be changing this.

12. The Marine Corps hymn remembers past invasions of Mexico: "From the Halls of Montezuma."

13. First enacted in 1997, the Leahy vetting procedures reflect Congress's concern that American tax dollars were spent on training foreign security forces that subsequently committed gross violations of human rights. The current version of the Leahy Amendment in the National Defense Authorization Act states the following: "None of the funds made available by this Act may be used to support any training program involving a unit of the security forces of a foreign country if the Secretary of Defense has received credible information from the Department of State that the unit has committed a gross violation of human rights, unless all necessary corrective steps have been taken" (Department of Defense Appropriations Act 2010). Additionally, the Department of State provides guidance for the implementation of both the State and DoD practice for Leahy. "A Guide to the Vetting Process," 24 April 2007, provides procedures to embassy personnel for how Leahy is applied. The policy states, "Although the Leahy amendment only mentions 'unit,' it is State and DoD policy to vet individuals for individual training. Because there is no human rights history to vet for newly formed units, individual members of a new unit must be vetted the first time the unit is nominated to receive assistance."

14. See Global Peacekeeping Operations Initiative (GPOI) at the Department of State, http://www.state.gov/t/pm/ppa/gpoi/.

Chapter 5

Congress and the Politics of Defense and Foreign Policy Making

Big Barriers to Balance

Charles B. Cushman Jr.

Noted political scientist Richard Fenno famously summarizes the goals of members of Congress as a three-point plan: Winning reelection, gaining influence in the institution, and making good policy (Fenno 1978, 215). Fenno's three congressional goals go a long way toward understanding why Congress is not very good at articulating its foreign policy and defense goals, funding foreign affairs and defense strategically, and overseeing policy execution in a useful manner. The pursuit of Fenno's three goals pushes Congress to pay more attention to defense than to foreign policy, exacerbating a century-long shift of power over US foreign policy making away from the State Department and other civilian capabilities, and toward the Pentagon.

Applying the lessons of congressional research to the topic of imbalance between foreign and defense policy in contemporary US practice makes it clear that Congress has *no* incentives to press for a more balanced national security policy; the incentives—electoral, influence building, and good policy—conspire to reinforce the imbalance.

Most members of Congress derive limited electoral benefits from working on foreign affairs—unlike defense, which is enormously helpful for members with bases and contractors in their districts. The difference between foreign and defense policy is more pronounced today, as Congress has evolved into a fiercely partisan, polarized institution far more interested in its representative role—to the detriment of its legislative, policymaking role.[1] Foreign affairs expertise also does not offer a path to power in either the House of Representatives or the Senate, whereas a seat on the Armed Services Committee does bring greater influence in the chamber. And since Congress has become more polarized, in partisan and ideological terms, over the past three decades, it has become difficult to build consensus on what "good policy" means; this impacts foreign policy far more than it does defense since so few legislators have any foreign affairs experience to help guide their peers in policy formulation.

In this chapter, I explore how Congress fulfills its constitutional responsibilities for foreign and defense policy, and the barriers to doing so in a balanced way, using Fenno's three goals to organize, and prioritize, the discussion.

Part One: The Electoral Connection and Foreign and Defense Policy

What does reelection—Fenno's first goal—have to do with the imbalance between foreign and defense policymaking in Congress? Congress places two institutional demands on its members: in addition to being a *legislative* body tasked with national policymaking, Congress is simultaneously a *representative* body—members of the House and Senate serve their particular constituents. Over the past thirty years, Congress has shifted away from a "two Congress" institution (one that balanced lawmaking and constituency service) into more of a "one Congress" place (where constituency service is the main focus of members' work)—and the representative role is now predominant. This shift happened because it helps members get reelected; and working on defense policy helps with reelection more than foreign policy does.

Of necessity, members of Congress focus first on reelection: you must stay in Congress if you hope to work on Fenno's second and third goals.[2] Only after reelection can a member work on influence building or long-term policy work. Since the early 1970s, two interconnected trends have combined to make members of Congress focus heavily on the representative role: easy travel and the emergence of candidate-centered politics. Before the advent of the jet age, which has made it easy for most members of Congress to return to their districts nearly every weekend, Congress stayed in session longer, and members lived and worked in Washington (Davidson and Oleszek 2004, 140–41).

Staying connected to constituents is an important task for most members. It has become vital since the advent in the late 1960s of primaries as the default mechanism for selecting candidates. Before reformers in both parties pushed to open the candidate-selection process to the voters, party leaders chose their candidates in closed-door meetings, and the party supplied the campaign staff (and most of the campaign cash) needed to run for office. Moving to primaries, coupled with significant campaign finance legislation in the

1970s, which restricted party usage of campaign cash, has led to congressional elections that are candidate-centered rather than party-centered (Herrnson 2012, 7–19).[3] Candidates and office-holders are now responsible for their own campaigns—organizing support, getting out their voters, and communicating with the public (Herrnson 2001, 97–123). Staying present in a candidate-centered politics requires the officeholders to be back in their districts regularly to meet with constituents and demonstrate continuing connections to their voters.[4]

These changes are two key contributors to the dramatic increase in partisan polarization over the past four decades. The Democratic and Republican Parties have become more ideologically coherent and more distant from each other. The Cold War foreign policy consensus kept some of that polarization out of national security policy until 1991, but since then, the rift visible in domestic policy is also apparent in national security policy.

Political parties have been part of the American political scene since the 1820s, and they are not going anywhere. Party leaders were far more powerful in the nineteenth century than today, and primary elections have eroded their control of electoral choices, but parties still shape American politics in key ways.[5]

Perhaps the most central way is in organizing like-minded voters and members. The two major parties are less alike today than they have been since the end of Reconstruction (1877); polarization is way up in recent decades, making it harder for the two parties to find any areas of consensus, which they were able to do during the 1930s–60s. Figure 5.1 indicates the degree of polarization between the two parties, using a standard score developed by Poole and Rosenthal and generally accepted by political scientists who study congressional politics.[6]

Some ideological overlap of the two parties was once a feature of Congress. Part of why the parties have become more polarized is that they have sorted themselves ideologically. The Democratic Party's mid-1960s embrace of civil rights legislation and the emergence of the conservative movement within the Republican Party have combined to create more ideologically distinct parties. Since the 1960s we have a seen a migration of conservatives into the Republican Party, with a similar movement of liberals and moderates into the Democratic Party (Sinclair 2006, 3–142). This sorting is reflected in the membership of Congress; in the Senate, the change has been stark. In 1982, there were thirty-eight members whose "conservative-liberal" scores fell between the most liberal Republican senator, Lowell Weicker (CT), and the most conservative Democrat, Edward Zorinsky (NE). By 2002 the gap had narrowed: most liberal GOP senator Lincoln Chafee (RI) and most conservative Democrat Zell Miller (GA) only had seven members between them.

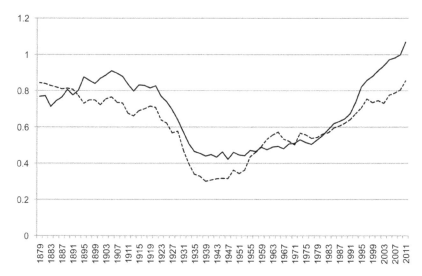

Figure 5.1
Polarization in House and Senate, 1879–Present

Note: Solid line is House, dotted line is Senate. The vertical axis is distance between the mean party ideological scores in the chamber for Democrats and Republicans. Source: http://voteview.com /political_polarization.asp.

In 2010, the overlap disappeared: most conservative Democrat Ben Nelson (NE) was to the left of least conservative Republican George Voinovich (OH) (Brownstein 2011).[7] Without some ability of members of both parties to work with like-minded members of the other party, it becomes extremely difficult for the Senate to find the sixty votes that are now de facto required to move any legislation (Koger 2010). Figure 5.2 shows the declining overlap between members of the two parties in the two chambers: little common ground exists now in either chamber of Congress.

Political polarization is not just a feature of Congress; a similar trend is visible in American life. Voters have been moving to districts that better reflect their own views, sorting themselves over the past three decades into more Democratic and Republican districts (Bishop 2008). Redistricting further reinforces polarization; both parties have become experts in designing congressional districts to protect their incumbents (Draper 2012).[8]

The net effect of all these trends is a Congress that cannot come to consensus on much policy, as we will see in section three.[9]

But it is also a Congress that no longer devotes much energy to its national lawmaker role: spending *more* time in their districts means spending *less* time in Washington. Over the past decade, Congress has not left itself much time

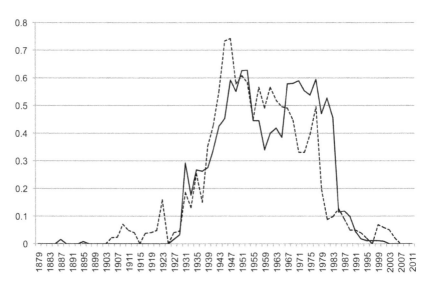

Figure 5.2
End of Ideological Overlap in House and Senate

Note: Solid line is House, dotted line is Senate. The vertical axis is degree of overlap between
Democrats and Republicans. Source: http://voteview.com/political_polarization.asp.

to do legislative work. Congresses in 2001–07 worked three days in Washington every week, then returned home; Congresses of 2007–11 worked four days
a week in Washington, and returned to their districts for long weekends. Congress also took regular recesses of one or more weeks to allow all members
extra time in their districts. The 112th Congress experimented with a model
of three five-day weeks followed by a full week back home; the 112th Congress
has also observed the regular, longer district work periods, as well.[10] These
schedules maximize district work time for the individual members, at the expense of time for legislating in Washington. Table 5.1 displays the decline in
legislative days in each session of several Congresses since 1979; the first session of the 111th Congress did meet more days—coming right after the 2008
presidential election, and facing major issues demanding action (economic
stimulus bills, health care reform, and financial regulations), that Congress
had much more work to do.

The switch to candidate-centered politics and easy, fast travel also played
into a sea change in how members perceived their positions in the institution
of Congress. Starting with the "Watergate babies" of 1974, candidates have
run *against* Congress—promising to go to Washington to help clean up the

Table 5.1
Decline in Total Legislative Days, 1979–2010

Year	Congress/Session	House	Senate
1979	96th/1	173	166
1980	96th/2	152	166
1989	101st/1	147	136
1990	101st/2	134	138
1999	106th/1	138	138
2000	106th/2	136	136
2009	111th/1	159	159
2010	111th/2	127	127

Data Source: Days in Session Calendars, Library of Congress, 1979–2010, http://thomas.loc.gov/home/ds/index.html.

cesspool (Sinclair 2006). The 1994 Republican takeover of Congress was fueled by a similar disgust with the status quo in Washington. Many freshmen legislators refused to identify with the institution; they came to Washington to fix the mess because someone had to do it, not because public service was a good thing itself (Mann and Ornstein 2006).This anti-institutional orientation is unlikely to foster any desire on the part of individual members to concentrate on the long, difficult work of legislation. The total legislative workload and output of Congress has declined significantly over the past several decades, as Table 5.2 indicates. The 111th Congress passed less than half as many laws as the 86th Congress did (1959–60).

Campaigning against Congress and refusing to buy into institutional norms has gotten many members elected to Congress over the past forty-plus years. It feeds the members' desire to work in their districts more than in

Table 5.2
Legislative Workload of Congress, 86th–111th Congresses

Years	Congress	Bills Introduced	Laws Passed
1959–60	86th	18,261	800
1969–70	91st	26,303	695
1979–80	96th	12,583	613
1989–90	101st	10,333	650
1999–2000	106th	9,158	580
2009–10	111th	10,621	383

Data Sources: Data for 86th–106th Congresses: Norman Ornstein, Thomas Mann, and Michael Malbin, *Vital Statistics on Congress*, Tables 6-1, 6-2, 6-4 (Washington, DC: Brookings Institution, 2008, 124–25, 127); Data for 111th Congress: Library of Congress, Bills Introduced, 111th Congress, http://thomas .loc.gov/home/bills_res.html.

Washington, and it has transformed Congress into a body that worries much more about its representative role, at the expense of legislating.[11]

With less time available in Washington to work on legislation, Congress has to focus only on high-return topics: those that most help members frame their cases for reelection. Paradoxically, this does not necessarily lead to major legislation, or to timely completion of the bills that fund the government.

In the past two decades, Congress has worked on fewer major policy reforms (welfare in 1995, education in 2001, and health care in 2009–10 come to mind) than in previous periods, but that has not translated into better focus on the annual appropriations process. Congress last passed all twelve of these bills on time in 1995, and in recent years Congress completed the annual appropriations cycle after the new fiscal year already started, through the expedient passing of a catch-all "omnibus" bill that combines languishing bills into one gigantic package. Failing to follow its own rules, and to move legislation from committees to the floor, to conference between the two chambers, has been a feature of Congress since the mid-1990s, and this decline in "regular order" makes getting anything done significantly more difficult (Dean 2007, 25–70).[12]

The end of the Cold War did not affect one procedural artifact that keeps the House and Senate Armed Services Committees (HASC/SASC) more powerful than their foreign policy counterparts. The Armed Services Committees bring their version of the annual National Defense Authorization Act (NDAA) to the floor every year, around mid-June. Because the HASC and SASC bring their bills to the floor every year, the leaders of both chambers treat the NDAA much the way they plan for floor action on appropriations bills: they block out time for NDAA, and build the rest of their legislative calendars around the defense bill.

Congress passes the NDAA every year, as it has since 1961. This fact underscores a key difference in how members perceive the relative value of working on defense or foreign policy. Who wins elections to Congress on foreign policy issues? Almost nobody! While foreign affairs and defense policy can play major roles in presidential campaigns, these issues are much less salient in congressional elections.[13] But members whose districts include military bases or defense industry have a clear electoral incentive to work on defense policy since it connects directly to the well-being of their constituents. Foreign aid bills generate a much more limited incentive—they usually only garner support from interests (industry as well as advocacy groups) that expect to benefit from increased overseas markets for their commodities or products. The coalitions are not as large or as energetic as those that support the annual defense bills (Milner and Tingley 2010, 200–32). That spending can help targeted businesses back home, but the foreign aid budget is so much smaller than the defense budget that it is only of limited electoral benefit for any member to become a strong advocate for a big foreign affairs budget.[14]

The Appropriations Committees send their twelve bills to the floor over the course of the late spring and summer every year. The national defense appropriations bill usually follows NDAA to the floor, and passes both chambers. (For fiscal 2012, the final defense appropriations bill was rolled into an omnibus after each chamber passed its versions of the bill [Status of Appropriations Legislation for Fiscal Year 2012]). This is the only pair of authorizing and appropriating bills that gets floor time every year—this institutionalized process maintains the power of the HASC/SASC and their counterparts on the defense appropriations subcommittees: no other committee is guaranteed such regular, expected access to precious floor time to work on their bills. They get that access because their bills have significant electoral impact on their members. The electoral impact gets them the access; but it is their consistent success in passing the NDAA and the spending bill every year that gives these committees power.

Part Two: Gaining Influence in Congress

As members of Congress build careers in Washington (remember, not all do: many come to Congress only for a few terms; others serve in marginal districts that demand full attention to surviving the next reelection, with no time left over for other goals) it is natural to look for ways to play a more influential role in Congress, and in national policymaking.

Here again the nature of the business puts a barrier in the way of developing a more balanced national security policy: a better route to power is working on defense policy, *not* foreign policy.

Just as defense policy offers more useful electoral options for more members, influence in the institution also tips in that direction. It is easier to develop power within Congress through a seat on the HASC or SASC than it is to try it through one on the House Foreign Affairs Committee (HFAC) or the Senate Foreign Relations Committee (SFRC). It is also more prestigious in either chamber to sit on the Defense Appropriations Subcommittee (HAC-D and SAC-D) than it is to sit on the State, Foreign Operations, and Related Programs Subcommittee (HAC-SFO and SAC-SFO).

As Gordon Adams demonstrates clearly in Chapter 2 on the imbalance between DoD and the civilian agencies, defense is a vastly larger enterprise than foreign policy. Budget is policy; it is also *power*. HASC/SASC and HAC-D/

SAC-D members have an easier time getting attention for their issues and time for their legislative proposals. (A glance back at Figure 1-2 in Chapter 1 indicates how much more defense spending there is.)

HASC and SASC members, and HAC-D and SAC-D members, are responsible for oversight of more than half of federal discretionary spending, whereas the foreign affairs committees and the appropriations' foreign operations subcommittees control only a tiny slice of the budget pie.

Also, since the United States has spent so much, for so long, on defense, Congress and successive administrations have looked to DoD for solutions to deal with a crisis; neither Congress nor the executive branch think about State or other agencies in crisis response. Recent Obama administration documents, including Secretary of State Hillary Clinton's *Quadrennial Diplomacy and Development Review*, have called for changing the resource equation so it is slightly less unfavorable for the State Department, and includes budget requests for building capabilities outside DoD, but there is a long way to go to develop anything like balance (US Department of State 2010).

Foreign policy is definitely not as good a path to influence in the institution as defense policy is. Though many policy analysts would dearly like to differ (including me), budget *is* policy—and the relative power and influence of any agency, and the legislators overseeing those agencies, are strongly correlated with the size of their slice of the budget pie. The massive scale differential between defense and foreign affairs spending indicates the relative importance placed on the two policy areas throughout most of the post–World War II period.[15] During the Cold War, the Senate Foreign Relations Committee (SFRC) was considered by many senators and scholars to be among the most prestigious venues in Congress, generally higher in esteem than the Armed Services Committee (Smith and Deering 1990, 87, 101).[16] Until the late 1970s, the SFRC operated under a broadly bipartisan agenda that allowed it to set the tone on foreign policy issues in the Senate, which is the more influential chamber since only it has the powers of treaty ratification and confirmation of appointees to high-level administration positions. But after the 1978 midterm elections, which saw several key conservatives (including Richard Lugar of Indiana and Jesse Helms of North Carolina) joining the SFRC, the minority party chose to hire its own staff and to offer a new alternative to the prevailing approach of the SFRC. This move strengthened the Republicans on the committee, but severely weakened the committee in the chamber—so much so that SASC chose to vote out a negative report on the SALT II treaty even though it was not in their jurisdiction. Since the late 1970s, SFRC has not had the influence it once had, and now SASC is more prestigious and more capable of shaping foreign policy in the Senate (Johnson 2006). While the SASC is still deemed to be the fourth-most-desirable assignment (after Finance,

Appropriations, and Rules and Administration), Foreign Relations has dropped in relative merit, from most prestigious to eleventh (Stewart 2012, 43, 45).

A similar pattern shows up in assessments of the House Armed Services and Foreign Affairs Committees. While Foreign Affairs was thought to be a valuable assignment, by the end of the Vietnam War and the Watergate scandal, it dropped relative to HASC, which rose from sixth- to fourth-most-prestigious assignment; Foreign Affairs dropped from fourth to seventh—effectively trading places with HASC (Groseclose and Stewart 1998, 453–74).[17]

These assessments of the committees' relative prestige track with their records on the floor. HASC and SASC can point to a record going back to 1961 of legislative success: they bring their NDAA to the floor every year. HAC-D and SAC-D usually get their national defense appropriations bill passed on its own, too. Neither Senate Foreign Relations nor House Foreign Affairs can point to such success. Congress reorganized the State Department and its relationship with USAID, and it successfully reauthorized State Department structure in 2003, but several recent efforts to reform, streamline, and better focus US foreign aid programs have failed to reach enactment because the House and Senate could not agree on final versions of the bills (Epstein 2011). Congress has not updated the Foreign Assistance Act of 1961 since 1985, and has instead handled authorization of new monies and programs in stand-alone laws, or by waiving authorization requirements in the annual appropriations acts (Rennack, Mages, and Chesser 2011).

On the appropriations front, financing of the foreign affairs bill has been episodic: in eleven of the past fifteen years, State Department funding has had to be rolled into an omnibus appropriations act because the two chambers could not produce a stand-alone State Department bill; this leaves the State Department and the foreign aid program at the mercy of stopgap, continuing resolutions, which freeze funding at the current level until the next fiscal year's appropriations bill is completed (King 2010, 6–7). Defense spending was part of an omnibus in only three of those years.[18]

Even the contentious issue of national intelligence is better managed by Congress, the two intelligence committees having successfully produced an intelligence authorization act in 2009, 2010, and 2011—despite disadvantages (the intelligence committees are smaller and have fewer staff, and the complexity of the US intelligence community makes their oversight job more complicated, as Jennifer Kibbe explains so clearly in Chapter 11).[19]

In sum, members who want to pursue influence in Congress will prefer to focus on defense topics rather than foreign policy.

Part Three: Congress and Policy Choice

"Good public policy" means something different to each player in any policy debate, but there was once a broadly held (if rarely observed faithfully) principle that "politics stops at the water's edge" (US Senate 2012b). If that principle held only partially during most of the Cold War, no such restraint is true of policy debates since 1991.

The end of the Cold War also meant the end of the Cold War consensus, and that has led to a change in the way US political leaders talk about defense and foreign policy. Defense topics are no longer accorded special status, and now are treated like most domestic policies—as distributive decisions about providing benefits to constituents in their districts (Rundquist and Carsey 2002).[20] The patterns were always the same—programs, jobs, and resources being apportioned around the country. But the Cold War strategic consensus helped blunt the "pork barrel" approach we see in domestic policy. For foreign policy, the end of the Cold War has stripped it of a broad context—leaving foreign policy decisions prone to episodic attention, and partisan or ideological infighting.

What is the interaction of congressional politics and national security policymaking? Political realities do not affect each of the three types of national security policy (crisis, strategic, and structural policy) equally, and the disparate impacts make it hard for Congress to alter the defense–foreign policy imbalance (Ripley and Franklin 1990, 184–210). Since Congress usually plays no role in crisis policy formulation, this analysis focuses on strategic and structural policy.[21]

Congress and Strategic Policy

Strategic policy sets the direction, purposes, and goals of US foreign and defense policy. In strategic policy, the executive branch tends to dominate, setting the government's broad goals and aligning US national capacities in support of those goals, usually with the participation of senior leaders in Congress (chamber leaders and committee chairs). Early in the Cold War, DoD was the focus of much policymaking and investment as the United States for the first time maintained large peacetime military forces. Since the mid-1950s, DoD has eclipsed State as the key agency for formulating US national security strategy, and that pattern replicated itself in the committees in Congress, as we will see below. Congress has been broadly acquiescent, if not supportive, of DoD's policy preeminence (Adams and Williams 2010). In the 1960s and 1970s, Democratic leaders in Congress were certainly shy of appearing "soft on defense" in the wake of the McCarthy era, and the policy failures of the Vietnam era reinforced that caution—leading to a freer hand for the White House in setting national security strategy (Halberstam 1993; Goldstein 2008). Congressional Republicans may well face a similarly difficult position with respect to strategic decision making today. Congressional leaders quickly granted President George W. Bush broad authority to make war, conduct surveillance, and manage wartime captives without much oversight; their willingness to cede so much initiative to the White House makes it harder today for Congress to force a showdown with the Obama administration over operations like US involvement in Libya, or drone strikes in the Middle East, Afghanistan, and Pakistan.

Congressional committees have three tools to use in shaping the strategy and structure of the US national security apparatus: they pass and oversee the execution of laws; they pay for the programs they want through appropriations; and they organize the executive branch agencies to accomplish US national security strategy. Most of this focuses on structure.

The primary strategic tool the committees have is their authorizing bills, which are Congress's main instrument for setting policy. The Armed Service Committees have institutionalized congressional attention to defense policy by bringing their bill to the floor every year; while there are regular disagreements about specific policy options (in 2012, for example, HASC proposed a ban on same-sex marriage ceremonies on military bases, which SASC did not support), the two defense committees work out their differences and bring their chambers a bill. That bill gives Congress a regular, expected opportunity to weigh in on how the Pentagon manages itself.

The same cannot be said for the SFRC and HFAC. Their efforts to shape strategic policy are not as successful. They have lost prestige in the past three decades; their recommendations are less respected. And they have not been able to complete a comprehensive review of foreign aid authorities, or a reform of foreign aid programs, since 1985. Despite several attempts to do so, and despite many professional calls for comprehensive reauthorization, the House and Senate committees have not been able to resolve their differences and produce a final bill.

These two committees' members are farther apart ideologically than are the ASC members, making a bipartisan approach difficult. Using *National Journal's* 2012 ratings of all House and Senate members, for example, we see in Table 5.3 that the gap in "liberalism" score between the Republicans and Democrats on the foreign policy committees is wider than that between the members on HASC and SASC. These scores indicate that the ASC members in both chambers are less ideologically different than the members of the

Table 5.3

Ideological Differences on Defense and Foreign Policy Committees

House			Senate		
HFAC Democrats	HFAC Republicans	**Gap:**	SFRC Democrats	SFRC Republicans	**Gap:**
75.9	27.1	**48.8**	76.9	18.2	**58.7**
HASC Democrats	HASC Republicans	**Gap:**	SASC Democrats	SASC Republicans	**Gap:**
69	27.9	**41.1**	67.7	25.4	**42.3**

Source: http://www.nationaljournal.com/voteratings2011/searchable-vote-ratings-tables-house 20120223 and http://www.nationaljournal.com/voteratings2011/searchable-vote-ratings-tables -senate-20120223.

foreign policy committees, with SFRC being composed of the most liberal set of Democratic members of the four committees—and the most conservative Republicans.

The generally more prodefense Democrats and Republicans on HASC and SASC all support defense spending and defense programs in their districts, easing compromise; the relatively more liberal Democrats and fairly conservative Republicans on the foreign policy committees see the world differently, and have lost their ability to forge bipartisan responses that can earn the support of their chambers (Fowler and Hill 2006).

Congress has a say in defense strategy, which they do by making policy determinations in the annual NDAA and through oversight. Congress has been less successful in shaping foreign policy since it has been unable to forge a workable consensus.

Congress and Structural Policy

Congress emerged during the Cold War as an effective partner in making *structural* decisions—building and resourcing DoD, State, the intelligence community, and the rest of the national security establishment with the specific force levels and equipment needed to pursue US strategic goals.

HASC and SASC make extensive use of the oversight power to shape the structures of the defense establishment. Their annual NDAA legislation comes to the floor of each chamber after a long series of hearings, which feature considerable participation by DoD officials. In addition to hearings, the committees have required DoD to submit reams of reports to Congress, detailing progress on congressional interest items. Since 1995, the HASC has also demanded each service chief to provide lists of unfunded priorities, outside the already enormous official defense budget proposal (Meckstroth 2010).[22] The two committees make it clear that Congress is intimately interested in everything DoD does. The committees have also played a key role in the structure and functioning of the defense establishment, having created it in 1947, and having adjusted it regularly throughout the Cold War. Congress can be credited with forcing the Defense Department to focus more on special forces (by creating the US Special Operations Command and granting it special budget protections), as well as championing the concept of interservice jointness (Cushman 2006, 157–75).

Jointness is almost entirely a congressional product. Starting after World War I, Congress discussed ways to improve Army-Navy cooperation, and Congress forced the Army to incubate air power, from the creation of the Army Air Corps in 1926 to the establishment of the US Air Force in 1947. Congress meshed the differing proposals of the War and Navy Departments into a unified Defense Department in 1947. Congressional attention to jointness culminated in the 1980s with the passage of the landmark 1986 Goldwater-Nichols Defense Reform Act. Without sustained attention to the issue by the Armed Service Committees it is doubtful that the services would ever have worked on improving joint operations on their own (Ibid.; Hammond 1961; Locher 2004).

The foreign policy committees oversee a smaller and much more contentious segment of the executive branch. Congress over the years saw fit to create many foreign aid programs that do not fall within the State Department; they also made the main development agency, USAID, independent of the department. The end of the Cold War saw a congressionally driven reorganization of the foreign policy architecture, which absorbed tasks of the abolished Arms Control and Disarmament Agency and the US Information Agency into State in the Foreign Affairs Agencies Consolidation Act of 1998; the same act allowed the president to shut down USAID (a step not yet taken). Since 2001, though, the trend has been to establish more programs rather than strengthening existing ones (examples include the President's Emergency Plan for AIDS Relief, and the Millennium Challenge Corporation). Congressional action aimed at unifying these many foreign aid programs have failed to gain momentum (Graham-Silverman 2009, 1303). The foreign policy committees have not been able to produce an authorization bill, nor have they managed to bring specific reform legislation to the floor.

The policy committees wield two of Congress's three key powers for shaping executive branch activity: oversight and organization. The Appropriations Committees control the third tool, the purse. A brief review of how the committees use these tools—and how the oversight and appropriations committees interact—suggests that SASC and HASC are much more effective at defending their turf than are the foreign policy committees, with clear implications for any future balancing of the US national security toolkit.

The appropriations process shows that the ASCs are more effective at defending their policy goals than are the foreign policy committees. HASC and SASC produce an annual review of policy and approval of programs in their NDAA; HAC and SAC do not slavishly follow the lead of that bill, but the defense subcommittees do significant consultation with the ASCs, whose larger staff have significant professional experience in defense policy and program management. The HAC-SFO and SAC-SFO subcommittees do not have as easy a time divining policy guidance from their oversight committee counterparts—in the absence of a comprehensive foreign aid reform, the Appropriations Committees fund the individual programs without a broader policy context to judge them. Foreign affairs appropriations bills include language that "deems" all programs to have been authorized, in the absence of a recent bill to guide their spending decisions (McCormick 1993, 145–46). Defense spending tracks reasonably well with the program oversight provided by the Armed Services Committees, while foreign aid and the budget for State lack a similar supporting framework.

Structural policy decision making looks like domestic policymaking: another realm for logrolling, negotiating, and pork, just like everything else Congress does. The more that the ASCs see their job as providing constituency benefits (via a strong national defense), the two committees will act like the rest of the constituency committees (Agriculture, Transportation and Infrastructure, Interior, Science), and the rest of Congress is adept at that work (Deering 1993, 155–82).

Foreign policy is not quite as lucky. SFRC and HFAC conduct substantial hearings on key issues, and the committee staffs regularly publish important and relevant documents that focus on current issues.[23] But this kind of structural oversight is episodic. And in the absence of updated foreign aid authorization, the programs, functions, and structure of the State Department and the various aid agencies will not change dramatically—or strategically.

Oversight is also provided through the appropriations process. Appropriations Committee staff are excellent and professional, with deep expertise, but their focus is on tracking the spending of the individual programs they monitor. Appropriators are interested in comparing performance against stated program goals, and they are diligent in tracking changes in program structure and spending over time.[24] This is important work, but it is not grounded in a broader strategic approach—House rules forbid the inclusion of policy legislation in appropriations bills.

To sum up, the Cold War's end killed the consensus about national security policy that had enabled Congress to work with the president to generate consistent strategic national security policy that drove a coherent structural (spending) program. Some shared consensus still links defense policymakers on the ASCs and their appropriations subcommittee counterparts, but the decades-long rise of partisan, ideological polarization in the foreign policy committees has made for difficult and intense strategic battles in Congress, which limit what the foreign affairs committees can do. The ASCs and HAC-D/SAC-D thus have two advantages over their foreign policy counterparts—the bulk of their work looks like domestic distributive politics, so everyone else in Congress fully understands what they are doing; *and* they are more unified internally.

The result of all this? Defense authorization and spending are institutionalized as part of the fabric of the legislative year, so they are easy to do, whereas major foreign policy is tough, if Congress can do it at all.

Summary: Don't Count on Balance from Congress

Congress faces significant incentives that militate strongly *against* balance in the US foreign policy toolkit. The status quo—heavily defense-centric (with a large helping of homeland security on the side)—is unlikely to change due to any congressional actions. Congress did agree to President Bush's requests in 2002–09 to increase spending on foreign operations dramatically—but they were also dramatically increasing defense spending, and adding a whole new category of defense-related spending on homeland security. It is hard to imagine Congress making such foreign operations investments absent that broader context.

Defense policy, with its huge budget, numerous bases, and industry connections in so many districts, has a far more powerful electoral impact than foreign affairs ever will. The smaller footprint of the State Department makes it hard to incentivize many members of Congress to devote effort to becoming foreign policy experts, knowing that such work cannot ever add to one's electoral prospects, and may interfere with the ability to devote time and energy to other issues that do have a more powerful electoral impact. Defense appropriators and Armed Services Committees are far more influential, and far more esteemed, than their peers on State, Foreign Operations Appropriations, and Foreign Affairs/Relations. They control a larger portion of the federal budget, and the particular manner that Congress approaches defense authorizing means that Congress devotes significantly more of its scant time for floor action to defense policy. Foreign policy is an afterthought and not the source of any reputation or influence in the Congress.

Defense policymaking in Congress since the end of the Cold War is more like "regular" policymaking than it was before the fall of the Soviet Union. Congress can apply its well-honed skills at tradeoffs, logrolling, and pork to defense. Foreign policy does not offer much reward for such a thing to happen—the stakes are so low with State's relatively tiny budget that defense policy would still be more useful to members than is foreign affairs.

The weakness of SFRC and HFAC in producing necessary foreign aid reauthorization legislation is stark enough in light of SASC/HASC's ability to generate annual authorizations for DoD; it becomes more obvious when compared to the success of the much smaller intelligence committees not only in producing recent authorizations but in *institutionalizing* the process by getting their bills done every year for three years.

Fenno's insight into how members of Congress think helps us to understand why it is so difficult for Congress to pursue balance in foreign and defense policy: reelection favors defense focus; influence in the institution sits more with SASC/HASC and HAC-D/SAC-D members than SFRC/HFAC or HAC-SFO/SAC-SFO members; and wide differences on policy goals within the foreign policy committees all militate against Congress achieving such a balance.

Conclusion

What could Congress do to produce support for a more balanced foreign policy for the United States? In the short term, the outlook is not good. Congress is focused on being a representative not a legislative body, and foreign policy simply does not resonate with voters—so Congress sees little upside to developing further expertise on the topic.

Defense is a bigger piece of the federal budget pie, and members of Congress earn electoral support for protecting bases and defense jobs in their districts. That will not change as long as the scale differential between foreign and defense policy spending is so enormous.

But might Congress exercise its policy responsibilities more effectively? A major global crisis could make foreign policy more important for a while (witness the recent financial meltdown for a sense of how that could work), as long as the most effective response to the crisis is diplomatic or developmental, rather than military force. Current budget stresses could force Congress to make significant cuts in defense spending—any diminution of the differential between defense and foreign policy spending cannot but help the relative importance of foreign affairs in many members' eyes.

In the end, Congress is likely to leave things as they are, unless significant events, or a president intent on forcing a debate, makes them change. As *Washington Post* reporter and blogger Ezra Klein wrote,

> [t]he president can't raise taxes. Congress can. The president can't spend money on infrastructure. Congress can. The president can't lift the sequester. Congress can. Even in foreign affairs, where the president

is considered to have much more autonomy, *much of his power is on loan from a Congress that chooses not to get particularly involved* (Klein 2012, emphasis added).

A president willing to use the power and prestige of the bully pulpit to force a rethinking and rebalancing of the US approach to national security might be the only way for Congress to have the political cover to shift toward a more balanced foreign and defense policy mix. Nothing will come of any hope that such a balance might organically emerge from Congress; only shocks and pressure from outside that body will help force it to rethink its current approach to foreign affairs and defense policy.

Notes

1. Roger Davidson and Walter Oleszek (2004) outline the idea of the "two Congresses" (the national legislative body, and the assembly of locally elected representatives of their constituents).

2. David Mayhew (1974) explains the primacy of reelection most effectively.

3. See also Jason Johnson (2012, 2–6), for a discussion of the implications of the switch from party- to candidate-based campaigning.

4. See Dennis Johnson (2007) for a description of modern campaigning.

5. Many congressional scholars have wrestled with the power of parties in shaping the way Congress works; despite some interesting counterarguments [such as Keith Krehbiel's (1991)], the consensus continues to point to a central role for parties, especially in the House. For a good historical review, see Barbara Sinclair (2006).

6. Keith Poole and Howard Rosenthal's measures trace the difference between the parties by tracking the number of times a majority of Democrats votes against a majority of Republicans (Poole and Rosenthal 2012). Their partisanship scores are the standard measures and are used heavily by scholars who work on congressional politics.

7. The accompanying chart by Peter Bell, Scott Bland, and Ryan Morris (2011) shows Senate centrists are in decline, depicting the polarization of the Senate graphically.

8. Gerrymandering is a main feature of the argument made by Thomas Mann and Norman Ornstein (2006 and 2012) in their two most recent books on Congress.

9. Sean Theriault (2008) provides a comprehensive summary of the various contributing factors to the current state of political polarization.

10. The 112th Congress met for 175 (House) and 170 (Senate) legislative days in its first session; the second session has not concluded as of this writing. The total days bucks the trend, which makes some sense given that the House flipped from Democratic to Republican control in the 2010 midterm elections, meaning that the new majority in the House had a large agenda of legislative ideas that the previous Congress declined to consider. Days calculated from Library of Congress, Days in Session Calendar, 112th Congress, http://thomas.loc.gov/home/ds/s1121.html and http://thomas.loc.gov/home/ds/h1121.html.

11. Davidson and Oleszek (2004) suggest that this shift helps to explain why Congress, the institution, is so unpopular, but individual members still earn high approval ratings from their own constituents. Gallup released poll results placing congressional approval at 10 percent, its lowest score ever in a Gallup survey (Frank Newport 2012). Yet reelection

rates have remained in the nineties for the past decade or more (Davidson and Oleszek 2004, 60).

12. Mann and Ornstein (2006) also touch on this issue.

13. Recent polling of American voters on what they perceive as key national priorities consistently shows that only around 5 percent think that foreign policy is a key issue; economic questions and national security and terrorism reliably lead the survey responses. For a good overview of this phenomenon, see Daniel Drezner (2012). Survey results are collected together at http://pollingreport.com/prioriti.htm. Benjamin Page and Marshall Bouton (2006) point out that the low salience of this issue effectively gives members of Congress permission to vote their own consciences on foreign policy topics since they do not fear electoral reprisals; the low level of voter involvement in foreign policy topics also allows members to project their own views on the topic onto their voters, further justifying their actions while separating foreign policy from any electoral impact.

14. One other area where a small number of members can gain electoral advantages is by pursuing international policies driven by large groupings of ethnic voters, such as Arab-Americans in Dearborn, Michigan; Irish-Americans around Boston, Massachusetts; Cuban-Americans in Miami, Florida; or Jewish-Americans in many of the congressional districts representing New York City. With a large enough concentration of ethnic voters, some members find it smart politics to court that constituency by advancing foreign policy proposals that community supports.

15. Forrest Maltzman (1997, 165–66) reinforces the influence of HASC/SASC's work relative to the foreign policy committees by noting that HASC and SASC are the outliers in his measurements of committee salience, drawing far more attention than their relative prestige ranking might indicate.

16. Steven Smith and Christopher Deering identify three types of committees (prestige, which the power committees in each chamber possess; policy, which focuses on issues; and constituency, which provides benefits back to members' districts), and find that HASC and SASC are regarded as a mix of policy and constituency, while SFRC and HFAC are policy committees.

17. See particularly Table 5: House Committee Values in Different Eras for a summary view of their findings.

18. Library of Congress, *Status of Appropriations Bills, FY 1998 through 2013*, http://thomas.loc.gov/home/thomas.php.

19. The intelligence committees successfully worked for passage of annual authorization every year 1978–2005, then again since 2010; the two committees are working to institutionalize an annual congressional consideration and passage of their bill, much as HASC and SASC have done with the NDAA. See Richard Grimmett (2012). For an extensive overview of recent intelligence oversight issues, see Amy Zegart 2011a.

20. *Distributive* policy decisions are those that send federal benefits to individuals, groups, and industries. The specific policy decisions do not generally place the various recipients in competition with one another, nor do these decisions usually get much public notice. Some examples of domestic distributive policies include agriculture subsidies, Army Corps of Engineers water management and development projects, and veterans' benefits. Defense and foreign policy *structural* policy decisions follow the same patterns of decision making: subcommittees and committees are the key players in both policy types, working closely with affected agencies and industries to devise the plans that Congress legislates. Randall Ripley and Grace Franklin (1990) offer a detailed breakdown of policy types

and an in-depth discussion of the players, their interactions, and their relative influence over policy choice.

21. Crisis policy generally requires quick, decisive action—two things Congress cannot do simultaneously most of the time. Congressional leaders may be informed or consulted during a crisis, but the White House and involved agencies usually manage the response, looking to Congress after the fact to pass any necessary follow-up legislation (Ripley and Franklin 1990, 175–81).

22. This practice has not been followed since 2012: the service chiefs reported no unfunded priorities, as directed by the secretary of defense.

23. A recent example is *The Gulf Security Architecture: Partnership with the Gulf Cooperation Council* (2012).

24. Discussion with former professional committee staff members, Defense Acquisition University, Kettering, Ohio, September 21, 2012.

PART II

OBSERVING THE MILITARIZATION TREND

Chapter 6

Soldiers in Sandals

G. William Anderson and Connie Veillette

Introduction

The nature of demands on the US military has changed considerably since the end of the Cold War when threats and adversaries were more well-defined. In the decade following the terrorist attacks on September 11, 2001, the military has been forced to adapt to new threat environments and ways of operating. In response, the Pentagon has sought and obtained authorities and funding to conduct activities normally associated with the work of civilian agencies. As discussed in this chapter, some Department of Defense (DoD) programs and activities have crossed into the development space of US Agency for International Development (USAID) and other US civilian economic assistance agencies.

There has been a significant shift in Pentagon thinking since the problems encountered after military operations in Iraq showed the importance of post-conflict reconstruction. Since then, the DoD has prioritized its role in the prevention of, and recovery from, conflict separate from the work of civilian agencies. The expanded mission involves soldiers conducting civilian assistance projects, from digging wells to building schools to helping farmers. DoD personnel conduct these types of activities not just in countries where troops are deployed on military missions, but also in countries at peace.

Many nongovernmental aid organizations lament the so-called militarization of foreign assistance as an area where DoD lacks the necessary expertise to be effective whereas military operatives argue that deployed forces must have an expanded set of tools to allow them to operate in complex environments. Instead of joining this debate, it may be more useful to understand the criticism and the defense of an expanded role in order to identify where and when it makes sense for DoD to engage in traditionally civilian-led assistance programs.

Part of this process is to also understand the interagency dynamic of the numerous US government agencies operating in the same space. While the Obama administration has adopted a whole-of-government approach, a number of studies and anecdotal evidence point to overlap and duplication of effort and the difficulties in achieving effective coordination and even policy coherence. Yet, by looking at several examples where there have seemingly been positive outcomes, one can conclude the obvious—that a well-functioning interagency process is a necessary component but one that can be quite elusive in practice. Determining the appropriate DoD role may hinge on identifying where and in what areas a DoD role is appropriate, where it should follow a civilian lead, or where it should disengage completely. To this end, the chapter attempts to identify current challenges and lessons learned. Key to this endeavor is understanding that civilian and military objectives vary considerably in a visibility versus viability framework.[1]

Scope and Definitions

This chapter is limited to an examination of DoD's role in development. The activities covered here are not those related to building the capacity of foreign militaries—which Nina Serafino focuses on in Chapter 7—but rather are those devoted to economic assistance of a nonmilitary nature.[2] We begin with the facts—the current array of authorities, activities, and environments in which the Defense Department is engaging. We then turn to the objectives of both civilian and defense approaches as well as how each has been criticized.

The important contribution we are trying to make is to tease out where DoD adds value for development. That is, despite the problems and criticisms, there may be areas where it just makes sense for the US military to dig a well. Or, DoD's work with a nation's coast guard or border guards may complement the work of other US development agencies in improving governance. If we can identify added value, then it may be possible to set some parameters around what DoD does, and how and where it does it. Implicit in this framework is the possibility that there are areas in which DoD should not be engaged.

Critical for understanding the role of DoD is examining the different terminologies used by military and civilian agencies. When the State Department and the US Agency for International Development speak of *development*, it is in terms of the often long-term endeavor to promote economic growth and strengthen institutions of government and civil society. This nomenclature is used with countries in conflict, postconflict, or at peace. In conflict and postconflict countries, the Pentagon speaks in terms of *stability operations* to prevent conflict and instability. These entail not just the rebuilding of security forces, but also support for judicial systems, rebuilding the private sector, constructing infrastructure, and developing representative government institutions.

Stability operations also include humanitarian assistance in countries both in conflict and at peace. Humanitarian aid encompasses disaster response and preparedness but also includes development activities such as building schools, water and sanitation projects, and constructing infrastructure like roads and bridges.

The Shift in DoD Aid Has Largely Occurred since 2001

The Pentagon has significantly shifted its thinking with regard to its role in preventing and recovering from conflict but there is conflicting evidence as to its permanence as a new core DoD mission.

The Pentagon has long had congressional authorities to assist foreign nations through Titles 22 and 10 of the US Code.[3] After 9/11 and the commitments of troops to Afghanistan and Iraq, policymakers began to rely on the military as a source of additional funding for civilian programs. The imperative of security interests in those two countries drove policymakers to make decisions about which agency should manage assistance programs based on which one had the funds, resources, and manpower, rather than on which had the expertise.

This was not a surprising turn of events. Soldiers in the field argued for the need to engage with local populations in ways that would improve the security environment. At the same time, staffing and resources for civilian agencies had been depleted, and some would argue that even with adequate staffing, these agencies were not capable of operating in conflict environments. Underinvestment in civilian international assistance programs and agencies since the end of the Cold War had left the US Agency for International Development, for example, with a much smaller cadre of development experts. When funding for foreign assistance programs began to climb after 2001, the agency was ill prepared to assert its leadership.

The sea change in the Pentagon's thinking became embodied in DoD's Directive 3000.05 issued in 2005. It states that postconflict stability operations are a "core U.S. military mission . . . that shall be given priority comparable to combat operations." Activities include: rebuilding security forces, correctional facilities, and judicial systems necessary to secure the environment;

reviving or building the private sector including encouraging citizen-driven, bottom-up economic activity, and constructing necessary infrastructure; and developing representative governmental institutions (US Department of Defense 2005a).

There has been a fair amount of debate as to DoD's intentions. Will stability operations remain a core mission, or will it eventually defer to civilian agencies once the latter's capacity is rebuilt? The expansion of DoD activities was justified by then Secretary Gates: "And until our government decides to plus up our civilian agencies like the Agency for International Development, Army soldiers can expect to be tasked with reviving public services, rebuilding infrastructure, and promoting good governance. All these so-called 'nontraditional' capabilities have moved into the mainstream of military thinking, planning and strategy—where they must stay" (Gates 2007a). This quote implies both that it will be temporary (until civilian agencies are adequately funded) and permanent (as remaining central to military thinking, planning, and strategy). Even when the Pentagon spoke of its new authorities as being temporary, it was seeking to make them permanent in annual National Defense Authorization Acts.

Environments in Which DoD Operates

Today there are generally three environments in which DoD manages assistance programs—postdisaster, conflict and postconflict, and countries at peace.

Countries Recovering from Man-Made or Natural Disasters

DoD's immense sea and airlift and other logistical capabilities have proven critical in major disasters and complex emergencies ranging from the 2004–05 Asian Tsunami, the 2005 earthquake and 2010 floods in Pakistan, and the 2010 Haiti earthquake. DoD works with USAID's Office of Disaster Assistance in a civilian-led response.

Countries in Conflict or Recovering from Conflict

The US military has a long history of reconstruction work in countries recovering from conflict dating back at least to World War II. From then until the early 1960s, the number of government agencies involved in reconstruction activities expanded significantly. The 1961 Foreign Assistance Act streamlined the growing network of programs and agencies by creating the US Agency for International Development. Until recently, DoD largely confined itself to disaster response and humanitarian assistance often at the direction of the secretary of state and the USAID administrator.

The postconflict problems confronted in Iraq helped to convince both military and civilian policymakers of the need for US military units to once again take on a reconstruction mission. The Commander's Emergency Response Program (CERP) got its start in 2003 using Iraqi funds but was later authorized by Congress in 2004. Between then and 2010, about $3.8 billion has been appropriated for use in Iraq and Afghanistan. Other authorities soon followed. (See Serafino, Chapter 7, for a complete list.)

Countries at Peace

DoD activities in countries at peace are the most controversial when critics speak of a militarization of aid. Under the heading of stability operations as a result of Directive 3000.05, DoD now takes a more proactive stance with regard to countries that are susceptible to political instability or that may provide a friendly environment for foreign terrorists. While many DoD programs in countries at peace are aimed at professionalizing host-country security forces, the mandate includes a considerable level of development activities— governance in the form of justice and security sector reform (JSSR); health in the form of building clinics and the provision of health services and training; and economic growth in the form of constructing schools, digging wells, and providing technical assistance to farmers. These activities have caused the most consternation in the development community for a number of reasons that are discussed later in this chapter.

DoD Aid Accounts, Authorities, and Activities

The Pentagon has a number of general authorities allowing it to engage in humanitarian assistance and to implement military-to-military programs. These are outlined below. With the exception of humanitarian assistance, all represent new or expanded authorities since 2001.

Humanitarian Assistance

The Pentagon's broader definition of humanitarian assistance includes both disaster response and development. For most of the high-profile disasters for which DoD help is requested (that are also few and far between), DoD contributions are under the direction of USAID's Office of Foreign Disaster Assistance. But DoD also has two accounts for which it receives its own appropriation. Together, these are often referred to as DoD's Humanitarian

Assistance Program (HAP): the Overseas Humanitarian, Disaster, and Civic AID program (OHDACA); and the Humanitarian and Civic Assistance program (HCA).[4]

Specific activities include disaster preparedness, reconstruction, digging or improving water wells and other sanitation and drinking water projects, repairing or building rudimentary infrastructure such as roads or bridges, and renovating public facilities such as schools, hospitals, clinics, and orphanages (GAO 2012, 5–6, 10). According to the Government Accountability Office (GAO), funding for these two programs totaled $403 million from fiscal years 2005 through 2010, exclusive of programs in Iraq and Afghanistan. Funds for both programs are minor when compared to civilian programs but have steadily increased in recent years (Epstein and Lawson 2012, 24). ODHACA obligations increased from $45.2 million in fiscal year 2005 to $72.5 million in fiscal year 2010. HCA funding went from $8.5 million in 2005 to $14.9 million in 2010 (GAO 2012, 6).

Commander's Emergency Response Program (CERP)

Conceived in postinvasion Iraq and expanded to Afghanistan in 2004, CERP allows military commanders to initiate projects for a wide berth of activities. According to DoD documents, the criteria for project selection are those that can be executed quickly, that employ and benefit the local population, and that are highly visible (Center for Army Lessons Learned 2008). CERP funds may be used for agriculture and irrigation, economic, financial and management improvements, electricity, food production and distribution, health care, education, telecommunications, transportation, rule of law and governance, and water and sanitation.

CERP was authorized in the 2004 National Defense Authorization Act with initial funding of $180 million, reaching $1.7 billion in 2008. Funding has since declined each year as military operations in Afghanistan and Iraq wind down. Projects are generally less than $500,000 although more expensive projects can be funded but require additional paperwork and approval through the chain of command. CERP was originally designed for use in Iraq and Afghanistan, but was expanded to the Philippines in 2008 legislation. In Afghanistan and Iraq, CERP funds have been used for Provincial Reconstruction Teams (PRTs) and Agribusiness Development Teams (ADTs).

Agribusiness Development Teams

ADTs were first deployed in Afghanistan in 2008 with the understanding that agriculture is an important sector for economic development in rural-based economies. The creation of ADTs also recognized that civilian agencies "were not resourced for the massive amount of work necessary in these areas as well as for the security they required."[5] Teams are composed of Army and Air National Guard soldiers who have agricultural experience in their civilian careers.

The goals are to increase agriculture jobs and income around productivity, agribusiness, and infrastructure, and to increase citizens' confidence in government by increasing, for example, Afghanistan's Ministry of Agriculture, Irrigation and Livestock capacity to deliver services, and to promote Afghan commodities for export. Activities are in the areas of horticulture, irrigation, storage and distribution, animal husbandry, and agribusiness. Consistent with CERP guidelines, ADT projects are small, costing less than $500,000 per project.

Provincial Reconstruction Teams

PRTs were first used in Afghanistan in 2002 with a mix of military and civilian personnel tasked with carrying out quick impact projects. The underlying goal was to build goodwill among the population and to enhance a more secure environment for US military operations. In 2005, PRTs were introduced in Iraq. In both countries, the teams use CERP funds and their few civilian specialists are reportedly dominated by military personnel.

HIV/AIDS

Since at least the mid-2000s, DoD has provided HIV/AIDS treatment and prevention assistance to foreign militaries. DoD receives funds from the President's Emergency Plan for AIDS Relief ($477.3 million from 2005–10) but also has its own budget line-item for its Defense Health Program for HIV/AIDS (funded at $27.3 million over the same period) (GAO 2012).

Combined Joint Task Force—Horn of Africa (CJTF-HOA)

Created after 2001, the CJTF-HOA mission is to support military operations in Somalia, strengthen East African nation militaries, conduct crisis response, and support US military, diplomatic, and civilian personnel throughout East Africa.[6] As of 2010, it had 1,650 personnel. Sixty percent of its budget is designated for quick and short-term civilian projects to undermine potential sources of support for terrorists (GAO 2010b). Small civilian affairs teams of five to six people are deployed to carry out activities such as medical and veterinary care, school renovations, training, and infrastructure building or repair. Project proposals are to be reviewed by USAID, the US embassies, and AFRICOM.

Global Security Contingency Fund

This joint State-DOD program was authorized by the fiscal year 2012 National Defense Authorization Act for urgent security and governance priorities. The Global Security Contingency Fund (GSCF) is a State Department account with the secretary of state as the lead, but requires the secretary of defense's concurrence even for types of projects, such as justice sector and rule of law, that would normally be funded and implemented by the State Department and USAID. The program is to be jointly funded by the two departments. Appropriations bills for fiscal year 2012 provided for transfers of $50 million from the State Department and $200 million from DOD (Serafino 2012b, 7).

Combatant Commanders' Initiative Fund

Authorized by 10 USC 166A, the Combatant Commanders' Initiative Fund (CCIF) was originally established in 1991 to fund the combatant commands to do short-term projects centered around unforeseen contingency needs critical to combat readiness and national security interests. The CCIF was expanded in the fiscal year 2007 National Defense Authorization Act to encompass urgent humanitarian relief and reconstruction assistance outside of Iraq and Afghanistan. It is a relatively small program, funded at between $25 million and $63 million annually since 2002.

Competing Objectives: Visibility versus Viability and Short versus Long Term

DoD, USAID, and State approach their development work from different perspectives. Despite the steady blurring of lines between civilian and military assistance, the rationale for each is quite different. They both support broad US foreign policy goals, but differ in many other respects.

All US foreign assistance programs, regardless of implementing agency, aspire to have both visibility (as in promoting goodwill toward the United States) and viability (as in having sustainable economic outcomes), but civilian programs generally put more emphasis on viability while military programs prioritize visibility. It is not surprising that the military would place greater importance on winning hearts and minds through highly visible projects, particularly in conflict zones where securing the environment through the cooperation of local populations is essential.

Civilian agencies are interested in promoting long-term economic growth that comes from sustained and sustainable development efforts. When done right, they are sensitive to cultural factors and respect country ownership and implementation of aid effectiveness principles as encompassed in Paris/Accra/Busan agendas.[7] They are concerned with transferring skills in order to build the capacity of institutions (economic, political, educational). At its most basic level, this is a "teach a man to fish" approach. The premise is that countries achieving sustained growth will be more stable, probably more democratic, and a lot more pleasant to live with among the community of nations.

The visibility-viability dynamic can become complicated, however, when highly visible projects don't outlast the period of military engagement. In nonconflict areas, the nonviability of project design can even create tensions when goodwill alone doesn't keep the well from drying up or mobilize qualified teachers for new schools.

According to DoD, humanitarian assistance is designed to shape the military environment and enable crisis response by averting humanitarian crises, promoting democratic development and regional stability, enabling countries to recover from conflict, and minimizing the potential development or escalation of crises through early intervention. Additionally, OHDACA assistance is meant to improve DoD visibility, access, and influence while reinforcing security and stability, to build collaborative relationships with civil society, and to generate positive public relations and goodwill toward DoD.[8]

The objectives of HCA are to promote the security interests of the United States and the host country, to improve the operational readiness skills of members of the US armed forces, to improve "DOD visibility, access and influence while building and/or reinforcing security and stability," to strengthen disaster preparedness capacity, to improve relationships with civil society, and to assist the civilian population.[9] DoD guidance includes the approval of the US ambassador or secretary of state. HCA activities are similar to OHDACA but also include the provision of medical, dental, surgical, and veterinary care in rural or underserved areas. DoD hopes that such programs will help to develop similar capabilities of local militaries and to secure access and influence in geographic areas of interest.

The visibility rationale for DoD programs determines the types of projects chosen and how they are implemented. While the stated objectives of each DoD program differ, they are all animated by the need to enhance security and stability and to address threats. In some cases, this is an immediate need where US troops are conducting military operations. In others, it represents the new Pentagon approach to preempt the growth of insurgent or terrorist elements that can create instability. Their interlocutors are their military counterparts in partner nations who are concerned with security rather than the civilian officials who are responsible for economics and public policies.

Critics of DoD programs cite the emphasis on visibility rather than viability, and the Pentagon's lack of development experience. DoD programs are meant to be visible, conducted by soldiers in uniform, in order to build good will among local populations. The desire for visibility can drive decisions on what types of projects are initiated with less regard for their viability over time. The goal of "quick impact" can result in a just as quick evaporation of benefits to the people military units are seeking to serve. Providing a veterinary clinic in a remote area will have immediate visibility and benefits to rural families, but without regular clinics or indigenous facilities to provide ongoing veterinary services (or income to access the existing services), positive effects will be fleeting. The same can be said for health, water, and agriculture programs.

On the planning front, USAID field staff report problems in working with the US military. These include a ponderous DoD bureaucracy for project approvals; the labor-intensive collaboration to keep DoD from making cultural or political missteps; and lack of attention to project sustainability (such as refurbishing education or health facilities without regard to staffing) and the evaluation of impact. In addition, no comprehensive database on projects by DoD and other assistance agencies exists, and information sharing is complicated by use of different terminology to describe similar assistance efforts. Thus effective coordination is often difficult, and duplication of efforts in areas like education and health is possible (GAO 2012a).[10]

Cultural missteps by DoD in Humanitarian Assistance Program (HAP) activities may be the most troubling issue because they suggest that DoD staff may not have the understanding of cultural, economic, political, and other factors that determine whether HAP projects can succeed in reaching their objectives. GAO found that personnel lacked an understanding of cultural factors that affects project implementation, and the workings of the interagency process at US embassies resulted in some projects not being a good fit within a larger strategic framework.

The GAO reported specific missteps in DoD humanitarian activities:

- CJTF-HOA planned a medical clinic in a remote village, but gave insufficient notice for the nomads who lived in the village to travel back to participate.
- CJTF-HOA distributed used clothing to villagers during Ramadan, which offended the Muslim population (GAO 2010c, 40).
- A team from AFRICOM proposed a well project without considering how its location could affect clan relationships or pastoral travel routes (GAO 2010c, 21).

- DoD built a hospice care center for HIV/AIDS patients in Ukraine that did not consider cultural sensitivities and was received negatively by the local community.
- In Uganda, the military built a library without any planning for its staffing or access to books (GAO 2012a, 37–38).

The CERP program has been one of the most visible and controversial DoD assistance programs. CERP was designed for quick impact and to win the hearts and minds of local populations.[11] The projects funded are largely driven by security imperatives even while they may outwardly look like development projects.

Its focus on sectors like transport, energy, water and sanitation, health, and education has seemed to duplicate what USAID and other civilian agencies should have been doing. Moreover, the Iraq and Afghanistan Special Inspectors General (SIGIR and SIGAR) and the GAO have criticized CERP for basic gaps in project management, oversight, monitoring, and evaluation; inadequate coordination with USAID and State; "little or no training" of DoD staff responsible for CERP contracts; absence of maintenance plans (for infrastructure projects); and lack of "sufficient documentation to substantiate payments" to contractors.[12]

In both Iraq and Afghanistan, lack of command unity constrained the ability of military and civilian leadership in-country to achieve unity of purpose and of effort. In Iraq, the senior US military officer in the field was not in charge of civilian staff and programs, and the US ambassador had little influence on activities of US combat forces (Special Inspector General for Iraq Reconstruction 2009, 341). This state of affairs needlessly complicated both civilian and military efforts to support common objectives.

Congress has also expressed concern that DoD's initial focus on small projects has expanded to large projects like power plants that should be funded elsewhere. The fiscal year 2010 Defense Appropriations bill included report language noting that the committee was "deeply concerned that CERP has grown from an incisive counterinsurgency tool to an alternative U.S. development program with few limits and little management" (US House 2009d). DoD recognizes the expansion. The Pentagon's handbook on CERP notes that "CERP has evolved . . . to conduct the multiple development-related tasks in stability operations that have been traditionally performed by the U.S., foreign, or indigenous professional civilian personnel or agencies" (Center for Army Lessons Learned 2008, 1–2).

Another current issue is whether DoD will expand its work with police and other security forces under GSCF authority beyond Afghanistan and Iraq.[13] Such an expansion would mean that DoD would be competing with civilian agencies like State's Bureau for International Narcotics and Law Enforcement (INL) and the Justice Department, potentially resulting in confusion over which US government agency has the lead in working with law enforcement in developing countries.

In addition to these accounts and authorities, the Department of Defense conducts programs that help develop military and civilian capacity in the justice and security sector. A principal objective of DoD's cooperation is to help build professional militaries that are accountable to civilian authorities, respect international human rights standards, and have an appropriate relationship to local populations. If DoD can help develop local militaries in developing countries that reflect these characteristics, the thinking goes, it will make a significant contribution to comprehensive Justice and Security Sector Reform (JSSR) efforts that are aimed at rule of law and governance improvements.

In the 2009 interagency guidelines for JSSR programs, DoD's primary role is described as "supporting the reform, restructuring, or re-establishment of the armed forces and the defense sector across the operational spectrum."[14]

However, DoD's work with local militaries is just one ingredient of a successful approach. Without long-term capacity development of governmental and nongovernmental institutions at both national and local levels that are seen to act legitimately in making decisions and providing services, key conflict drivers will not be addressed effectively (Brinkerhoff 2011). This argues for a development assistance provider like USAID that will be engaged over the long term. Moreover, the lack of thorough monitoring and evaluation of the full range of security cooperation programs complicates interagency relationships in this and other areas of DoD development assistance (Adams and Williams 2011, 20; GAO 2010a).

The Interagency Dynamic

The Obama administration has adopted a whole-of-government approach to foreign assistance in which the expertise of various government agencies can be utilized. This approach carries with it many challenges with regard to leadership and coordination.

The Interagency Context for DoD's Role in Foreign Assistance

In recent years, many scholars and task forces have analyzed the shortcomings of US interagency cooperation in national security and foreign policy. Former defense secretary Robert Gates commented in 2010 that "the United States' interagency tool kit is still a hodgepodge of jury-rigged (sic) arrangements constrained by a dated and complex patchwork of authorities, persistent shortfalls in resources, and unwieldy processes" (Gates 2010, 3).

Among the principal problems hampering interagency cooperation are (1) lack of common strategic and program planning processes among civilian foreign affairs agencies and DoD; (2) continuing weakness of civilian agencies and turf sensitivity; (3) lack of mutual awareness and understanding among DoD and civilian agencies of what each agency brings to the table; and (4) scarcity of staff trained for combined activities with the lack of personnel incentives for interagency assignments (Serafino 2012a, 9–12). The State Department has taken recent steps, including instituting a multiyear Integrated Country Strategy (ICS) involving all US government agencies operating at post, including DoD.[15] But these steps at the country team level do not yet extend to joint programming and evaluation systems.

The majority of DoD's work in developing regional security cooperation and contingency plans and exercises takes place in the regional combatant commands (COCOMs). Each of these regional commands develops theater campaign, security cooperation, and, in conjunction with DoD field staff, country security cooperation plans as well as contingency plans for possible events and joint military operations. The Special Operations Command (SOCOM) has a global responsibility and deploys US Special Operations Forces (SOF) around the world, often through the regional commands.

Since 2001, the number of interagency representatives assigned to DoD regional commands has increased substantially yet their influence is not uniformly felt. Interagency representatives, such as state political advisors (POLADs) or USAID senior development advisors, generally participate in development of the various plans and strategies developed at their commands. But they often do not have decision-making power from their home bureaus or authority to make commitments on behalf of their assistant secretaries (State) or assistant administrators (USAID). DoD staffing at each of its regional command headquarters usually surpasses a thousand plus varying numbers of other military branch personnel assigned to the COCOM's service components. These military personnel are available for deployment in each COCOM's geographic area.

While DoD staff outnumber non-DoD civilians at the COCOMs, they are often dwarfed at the country level by State, USAID, and other US government staff. DoD representation generally consists of a handful of field staff who work as part of the country team under the US ambassador or chief of mission (COM). USAID presence in most developing countries alone is several times the number of DOD staff, including American and local, or foreign service nationals (FSN), staff with deep knowledge of the country and subject expertise. In over eighty countries where USAID has fully-staffed missions,

USAID staff include ten to thirty American staff and several times that number of FSNs. Except in cases like Iraq, Afghanistan, Colombia, Philippines, and a few others, DoD long-term field staff numbers are limited to a Defense attaché (DATT), a small Office of Security Cooperation (OSC), and a small number of FSN staff. Many DoD field staff have little education and training in development program planning, management, and evaluation and limited knowledge of the country's historical, cultural, political, and economic context (GAO 2012a, 37).

The diversity in planning processes, degrees of responsibility, and in-country development knowledge and experience for DoD, State, and USAID at regional and country levels poses significant challenges for effective interagency collaboration. Although DoD regional commands carry out their regional planning at COCOM headquarters, State regional bureaus in Washington define US regional diplomatic plans and priorities. Similarly, USAID regional missions in the field fashion regional plans and priorities. In addition, DoD's planning and budgeting calendars and implementation systems for development activities are quite different from those of USAID and other US civilian assistance agencies. (See Marks, Chapter 12, on the parallel foreign policy presence of DoD and State abroad.)

The Interagency Context for Disaster Response

In disaster response and preparedness, DoD uses funding under its HAP program and its general operations and maintenance budget for transportation of relief supplies and people. Since the early years of the George W. Bush administration, standing policy designates USAID's Office of Foreign Disaster Assistance (OFDA) as the lead federal agency for disaster response with support, when needed, by DoD and its regional commands. When DoD airlift, sealift, and other assets are needed for response to major disasters, such as the 2010 Haitian earthquake and the 2011 Pakistan floods, DoD's assistance is requested by OFDA with State Department coordination.

Recent DoD guidance for HAP programs directs DoD field staff to consult with USAID early in the development of such activities and to "seek concurrence from the USAID Mission Director prior to the Chief of Mission . . . for approval."[16]

If refugees become an additional factor in a disaster situation, the Department of State's Bureau of Population, Refugees, and Migration (PRM) becomes involved. Sometimes COCOM commanders wish to "lean forward" in disaster situations and take action, such as sending a plane with relief supplies and a Civil Affairs team to respond. However, of the annual average of ninety declared disasters, OFDA requests DoD assistance on average in less than 10 percent of those situations. Therefore, one of the jobs of OFDA advisers permanently stationed in each of the regional commands is to determine early the need for DoD assistance in a declared disaster. OFDA also works to clarify US government roles and responsibilities in natural disasters by delivering annually over eighty Joint Humanitarian Operations Courses (JHOC) to DoD personnel stationed at all COCOMs and functional DoD entities, such as the Transportation Command, which is responsible for all DoD air, land, and sea transportation in peace and war.

A relatively recent addition to disaster preparedness has been transnational planning for a potential pandemic influenza outbreak, such as recent strains of avian influenza. USAID is the lead US government agency for the US pandemic response preparedness program. OFDA and USAID staff have worked closely with AFRICOM and in close coordination with USAID's Human Pandemic Influenza Program in Africa to develop an AFRICOM Pandemic Response Program "aimed at assisting African militaries to develop influenza pandemic response plans that are integrated into their countries' overall national response plans" (U.S. Africa Command 2012b).

Success Stories and Lessons Learned

Despite the criticisms of DoD aid programs, there are success stories that can be used to identify when and if continued military engagement is merited. One of the overarching criticisms of military programs is that the Pentagon is not adequately evaluating or reporting on its activities, or when it is, does not report them in the same evaluation framework used by civilian agencies. This seriously undermines attempts to judge the value that DoD brings to the equation. Nonetheless, we believe that the examples we offer below provide some insights on the question.

In *conflict-prone* or *postconflict* situations where US forces are not engaged in combat, DoD field personnel have made valuable contributions in specific situations that have employed DoD's comparative advantages. Where such collaboration has succeeded, DoD's role has usually been identified through early, meticulous interagency coordination. In other situations, additional DoD resources have complemented existing civilian programs.

For example, in Kenya, at the US ambassador's request, CJTF-HOA Civil Affairs teams rehabilitated or reconstructed fourteen schools in Rift Valley Province following postelection violence in December 2007 (Lee and Farrell 2011). USAID and State directed DoD teams to the specific province and communities where schools needed rehabilitation or reconstruction. USAID helped DoD choose appropriate locations and resolve issues on hiring local people at construction sites to provide additional employment.[17]

In Sri Lanka, following the end of that nation's long civil conflict, US Pacific Command (PACOM) Civil Affairs teams helped fill USAID funding gaps for livelihoods and health assistance programs by repairing culverts, bridges, schools, and hospitals in conflict-affected areas.

In South Sudan, DoD staff participated in the development of the USAID Transition Strategy for the new country. USAID personnel saw DoD military assistance as a potential complement to their objective of mitigating conflicts. They hoped that DoD security cooperation would help strengthen Government of South Sudan (GOSS) security institutions and build the professionalism of GOSS military units to prevent their involvement in local conflicts (USAID 2011, 23, 31).

In the Philippines, the PACOM Joint Special Operations Task Force-Philippines (JSOTF-P), in coordination with the US Mission Interagency Mindanao Working Group, works with the armed forces of the Philippines "in a strictly non-combat role to defeat terrorists, eliminate safe havens and create the conditions necessary for peace, stability and prosperity in the southern Philippines" (mainly Mindanao and nearby island chains). On the development side, the JSOTF-P, in partnership with the armed forces of the Philippines, assists conflict-affected communities through medical, dental, veterinary, and community infrastructure projects. Between 2007 and 2011, more than $24 million in DoD funds supported 220 community assistance projects in these areas. The JSOTF-P community assistance programs complement USAID's larger Growth with Equity in Mindanao (GEM) program that has been working to resolve issues of the Muslim population in Mindanao since the 1990s.[18]

With regard to *development* activities, recent interagency initiatives have brought these earlier efforts by DoD and USAID in Mindanao into sharper relief. Under the leadership of the US ambassador to the Philippines, a whole-of-government partnership with the government of the Philippines has developed in the areas of sustainable economic growth, effective governance, and long-term peace and stability. The principal US government partners have been State, USAID, DoD, and Commerce, but the interagency effort is planned to extend to other US government agencies represented at post. DoD's role in this joint US-Philippines effort in Mindanao is seen as essential to achieving the long-term goals of the Mindanao Strategy.

In Djibouti, CJTF-HOA agreed to focus its HAP projects on health clinic construction and rehabilitation to help fill a gap in USAID's funding for its successful Maternal and Child Health program. This action maintained a USAID and US government commitment to the government of Djibouti.[19]

Disaster preparedness and *risk reduction* involve strengthening the capacity of local institutions and communities at all levels to identify, prevent, prepare for, mitigate, and respond to disasters with their own resources. USAID/OFDA traditionally allocates up to 10 percent of its annual budget for preparedness investments in all regions and currently has two regional programs active in Latin America and in South Asia. At least three DoD regional commands—PACOM, SOUTHCOM, and AFRICOM—contribute to disaster preparedness in coordination with USAID and OFDA. The USAID/SOUTHCOM relationship and the OFDA/SOUTHCOM relationship in particular are considered the most mature because of the annual threat of hurricanes in the Caribbean. AFRICOM has developed a Disaster Planning and Preparedness Program (DP3) in lockstep with USAID/OFDA in which "the focus of this program is the civilian agencies responsible for disaster planning and preparedness and the civil-military interface where military assets will be used to support civil response plans."[20]

In Africa, DoD has worked for some years with other international partners to *build military capacity* to deploy forces for regional peacekeeping efforts, including supporting the health of soldiers. One of the groups in developing countries most vulnerable to HIV/AIDS infection has long been local militaries. Therefore, strengthening prevention efforts in partner country military services complements the work of USAID, the Centers for Disease Control (CDC), State's Office of the Global AIDS Coordinator (OGAC), and other US government agencies that implement the President's Emergency Plan for AIDS Relief (PEPFAR). DoD representatives are part of the US government interagency committees that coordinate the allocation of PEPFAR resources and program implementation. Since USAID is prevented by statute from working with local militaries, it is important that DoD, through its regional commands and field staff, can address HIV/AIDS prevention in partner country defense institutions.

Do these examples mean that roles and responsibilities between DoD and civilian agencies are always clear, or that all US government agencies know what each other is doing? Or that in all country teams, effective interagency coordination, collaboration, and joint planning structures and procedures exist? To these questions, the answer is clearly "no." However, the lessons of these and other interagency programs provide guidance for improving the quality of US government interagency collaboration for other country and regional settings.

Where Does DoD Add Value?

Identifying where DoD adds value to development depends on several factors and often differs by country or region. These include: (1) relative US foreign policy and national security priorities; (2) the type of country situation and particularly the level of conflict; (3) country team procedures and structures that support interagency collaboration; (4) numbers and capabilities of DoD country staff, both American and Foreign Service Nationals; and (5) the development sector or problem for which DoD is providing assistance relative to related efforts by USAID, Millennium Challenge Corporation (MCC), State, and other civilian agencies.

From this discussion, we can identify cases where the Department of Defense adds value to the efforts of civilian agencies. However, success in each of these areas depends on effective interagency coordination. We would further argue that civilian agencies should lead in each programming area.

Disaster Response

DoD has a comparative advantage in responding to natural and man-made disasters because of its enormous sea and airlift capacity. It would be foolishly costly for civilian agencies to build or maintain similar capacity. With its human capital, established regional commands, and logistical capabilities for airlift and sealift, DoD offers substantial assets to complement the efforts of other US government agencies. In disaster response, the respective roles of US government actors have remained relatively clear and constant in recent years. In severe natural catastrophes, such as earthquakes, flooding, volcanoes, and tsunamis, DoD can play a major role, especially when several countries are affected.

Conflict Zones

The US military often operates in conflict environments in which civilian agencies have difficulty operating. The type of country situation and level of conflict should determine the roles and responsibilities of DoD, State Department, USAID, and other US interagency partners, and especially who has the lead for the US government. Because of security concerns for civilian personnel, it may be necessary for DoD to carry out some reconstruction and development activities in conflict and even postconflict settings.

Civilian agencies are accustomed to working in poor and dysfunctional environments. They are much less prepared to work in combat zones. By contrast, working in combat zones is the nature of the military's work. Few would argue with giving commanders on the ground the resources and flexibility to enhance the security of US troops in hostile environs. In some cases, digging a needed well may help US troops to operate more safely and effectively.

However, transferring the skills to dig and maintain wells is what is needed for development sustainability. This is the long-term approach used by civilian aid agencies and suggests that even in these difficult environments, some guidance from civilian agencies is necessary so that short-term security imperatives can lend themselves to longer-term development. This is particularly important given the assumption that conflict will abate and civilian agencies will be left to carry on development activities.

The complementarity of the military and civilian side—the military's capacity to operate in insecure environments and civilian agencies' knowledge of how to support sustainable development—needs to be planned and implemented in a more integrated manner. This may require changes to CERP and similar DoD program authorities to improve effectiveness, accountability, and outcomes in tandem with civilian programs.

Augment and Complement Civilian Programs

DoD funds can augment and complement, and therefore extend the reach of, civilian programs. When closely coordinated with USAID, State, and other US government actors, DoD's humanitarian assistance programs can make significant contributions. HAP projects and funding can help fill gaps in USAID or other agency funding. They can use DoD capabilities in infrastructure rehabilitation or construction, for example, as a component of broader conflict-mitigation efforts.

Working with DoD field staff to integrate individual HAP projects into US government long-term development sector strategies in education, health, water, and rural infrastructure is possible although difficult. There are clearly positive examples of successful collaboration between USAID and DoD. On the other hand, a number of difficulties and risks exist, as explored by GAO reports and other studies (GAO 2010c; Bradbury and Kleinman 2009, 63–69). Ensuring that DoD HAP projects do no harm may also require robust engagement and direct pressure by USAID mission directors or ambassadors to maintain focus on agreed-upon objectives.

The area of justice and security is an additional sector in which DoD may add value. Because of the importance of a secure and stable environment, governance, and rule of law for development outcomes, DoD programs can complement State and USAID JSSR programs by inculcating a respect for civilian leadership in countries prone to a larger military role. Just as there is no development without security, there is no security without development.[21]

Special Circumstances

DoD programs can work with some actors, like foreign security forces, that civilian agencies are either prohibited from or have difficulty reaching, such as the DoD HIV/AIDS prevention efforts with foreign militaries. DoD's concern is to help partner country militaries maintain the health of their personnel and families so that local militaries can manage their countries' own security challenges or deploy as regional peacekeepers. In doing so, DoD helps to prevent the spread of HIV to the civilian population and lightens the burden on civilian disease treatment and prevention programs.

Principles to Guide DoD Involvement in Development and Disaster Assistance

Our discussion has shown that DoD has comparative advantages, relevant capabilities, and adds value in some development and disaster situations. However, DoD is not the appropriate primary actor in most such situations. How should US government policymakers decide on whether and how DoD should be asked to deliver assistance in a specific regional or country context? We propose the following four questions to help determine DoD's role in any specific mission.

1. Is the particular regional or country setting one in which DoD generally has a comparative advantage?

DoD generally has a comparative advantage for operating in active conflict situations in which US combat forces are engaged because of its ability to protect itself. It has less of a comparative advantage in conflict-prone and post-conflict situations and in countries at peace. In these settings, DoD should contribute as a subordinate actor to US civilian foreign affairs and development agencies like State and USAID. For DoD to lead in relief, reconstruction, and development assistance, active conflict should make it impossible for US civilian agency personnel and their implementing partners to carry out US-funded reconstruction and development programs in relatively safe conditions.

2. Is the regional or country setting one in which the required types or modes of assistance include those for which DoD brings added value?

The main assistance program areas where DoD provides or should provide added value include airlift/sealift and providing security for disaster situations; strengthening pandemic response capabilities in partner nation militaries; disaster preparedness and risk reduction; professionalizing local militaries; strengthening border and maritime security; providing HIV/AIDS prevention and treatment for local militaries; and providing relief and reconstruction assistance in active conflict areas.

3. What are the primary US national objectives and interests in the regional or country setting—national security, diplomatic and foreign policy, development and humanitarian, or a mixture of all three? If a mixture of security, development, and diplomatic interests, should DoD or civilian agencies take the lead?

DoD's strategies, resources, organizational culture, and values are directly focused on addressing threats and thus on national security. If the primary focus of US policy in an international setting is diplomatic, development, or humanitarian, DoD should act in support of the US civilian lead agency. However, DoD may have a significant subordinate role to play under civilian leadership in such situations. Even if the primary US objective is national security, the chief of mission should take the lead role for all US agency activity except in the case of US forces engaged in combat who report directly to their COCOM commander.

4. When DoD is tasked to provide development or disaster assistance, how can unity of command, purpose, and effort be assured? For the designated US government lead actor, who will define clearly US government roles and responsibilities and enforce this decision?

Ideally, unity of command, purpose, and effort should characterize any US international effort, including those involving development and disaster assistance. However, in conflict situations where US combat forces are engaged, such as Iraq and Afghanistan, two parallel chains of command tend to exist—one for US military forces and one for US civilian personnel. Under current practice, these two chains of command must be linked by the US ambassador and the US military commander (SIGIR 2009, 341). US national security policy does not seem to allow for a unified US chain of command in such situations. This reduces the likelihood of unity of purpose and effort by DoD and US civilian agencies in conflict situations involving US combat forces and raises questions regarding a unified US government posture when engaged in multinational efforts in such situations. Lessons from the US experience in Iraq and Afghanistan should lead over time to greater unity of purpose, effort, and command.

In conflict-prone and postconflict situations, civilian leadership under the US ambassador or chief of mission should take the lead with all other agencies, including DoD, supporting the US chief of mission.

Conclusions

DoD has a significant role to play in providing development and disaster assistance in certain situations. Its role can be direct, indirect, or both. DoD's role depends on the regional or country setting, level of conflict, and the relevance of DOD capabilities, resources, and field assets. In the past decade, DoD has taken on new tasks and responsibilities in disaster relief, stabilization, and reconstruction in postconflict situations and development assistance. DoD development and disaster assistance has been funded under a varied set of old and new statutory authorities. Given the experience of this past decade and the current fiscal environment, how much of this broader development role should DoD retain?

Based on our analysis, DoD's capabilities, resources, and field assets can best be utilized where it has a comparative advantage over civilian agencies. These situations are limited to settings in which civilian agencies have difficulty operating or are prohibited from engaging. In other situations, DoD can help to extend the reach of civilian programs, both through access and as an additional source of funding.

All of these areas depend, however, on more effective interagency coordination at headquarters, regional commands, and in the field. In most areas, a civilian agency with development expertise should be in charge. Even in active conflict zones, consultation with USAID and State is necessary to ensure that DoD planning focused on short-term security imperatives will do no harm and can be adjusted, if necessary, to support longer-term development objectives.

In all but a few cases, DoD's development or disaster assistance efforts should support and unfold under the direction of US civilian foreign affairs and foreign assistance agencies, mainly State and USAID.

Notes

1. We are grateful to Andrew Natsios, former USAID administrator, for suggesting the visibility-versus-viability framework for understanding the sometimes-competing objectives of foreign assistance. "Opposed Development: Concept and Implications," panel at the United States Institute of Peace, June 16, 2010. Cited by Johnson, Ramachandran, and Walz (2011).

2. The Pentagon has expanded its role with its own funding to train and equip foreign militaries. These capacity-building activities are in addition to the Foreign Military Financing and International Military Education and Training programs (funded by the State Department) that the Pentagon implements. Even these military-to-military programs can have a development aspect since it can be argued that professionalizing militaries, strengthening security forces, and stabilizing the security environment are necessary components to economic growth.

3. Title 10 USC 401, 402, 404, and 407 authorize DoD activities relating to humanitarian and civic assistance. Title 10 USC 2557 and 2561 authorize nonlethal excess DoD supplies for humanitarian relief and the transport of relief supplies.

4. OHDACA is authorized by section 2461 and HCA by section 401 of Title 10 of the US Code.

5. Agribusiness Development Teams Tactics, Techniques, and Procedures, Agribusiness Development Team Handbook, November 2009.

6. CJTF-HOA operates in seven countries (Djibouti, Eritrea, Ethiopia, Kenya, Seychelles, Somalia, and Sudan) plus eleven "areas of interest" countries (Burundi, Chad, Comoros, Democratic Republic of Congo, Madagascar, Mauritius, Mozambique, Rwanda, Tanzania, Uganda, and Yemen). Combined Joint Task Force—Horn of Africa, www.hoa.africom.mil.

7. The 2005 Paris Declaration on Aid Effectiveness and the 2008 Accra Agenda for Action laid out an action plan for aid donors and aid-recipient countries for increasing country ownership of aid flows. The Busan (Korea) High-Level Forum in November 2011 shifted the discussion by the international community from "aid effectiveness" to "development effectiveness."

8. Defense Security Cooperation Agency, http://www.dsca.mil/hama_cd/hap/default .htm.

9. Ibid, 32.

10. GAO 2012a, 20, 30, 33, 37. In taking a random sample, the GAO report found that one-year evaluation reports were not completed for 90 percent of DoD projects carried out from FY 2005–09.

11. The report accompanying the Senate National Defense Authorization Act (NDAA) for 2013 states: "The committee notes that a primary purpose of CERP is to enhance force protection for U.S. troops by enabling commanders to fund projects that directly address the humanitarian and reconstruction needs of the Afghan people, particularly in less secure areas of the country, thereby gaining the support of the local populace." See US Senate 2012a, 112–173, 235.

12. See Special Inspector General for Iraq Reconstruction (SIGIR) 2006; GAO 2009; Special Inspector General for Afghanistan Reconstruction (SIGAR) 2011; and Johnson, Ramachandran, and Walz 2012.

13. Current authority is to assist "security forces responsible for conducting border and maritime security, internal security, and counter-terrorism operations, as well as the government agencies responsible for such forces." See Serafino 2012b, 11.

14. "Security Sector Reform," Department of State, Department of Defense, and US Agency for International Development (Washington, DC: 2009): 3, http://www.state.gov /documents/organization/115810.pdf.

15. State Department unclassified cable no. 124737, "Introducing New Strategic Planning and Budgeting Processes," December 17, 2011: Paragraph 6.

16. "Policy Guidance of DOD Overseas Humanitarian Assistance Program (HAP)," Cable from Secretary of Defense, Washington, DC, Paragraph 3.C., November 8, 2009. See also GAO 2012a.

17. Phone interview with Maureen Farrell and Jessica Lee, April 28, 2012, who carried out the assessments of the civil-military operations in Kenya's Rift Valley discussed in their 2011 *Prism* article (see Lee and Farrell 2011). At the time they wrote the article, Jessica Lee was a member of the Social Science Research Center in US Africa Command (Knowledge Development). Maureen Farrell was a member of the Sociocultural Research and Advisory Team in Combined Joint Task Force—Horn of Africa (CJTF-HOA).

18. Joint Special Operations Task Force-Philippines Fact Sheet, July, 2011, http://jsotf-p .blogspot.com/2011/09/type-your-summary-here_20.html.

19. E-mail from USAID/Djibouti Representative Stephanie Funk, April 27, 2012.

20. "U.S. Africa Command Disaster Planning and Preparedness Program (DP3)" USAFRICOM fact sheet. Given to G. William Anderson by the USAID/OFDA senior humanitarian assistance advisor/civ-mil at AFRICOM on the AFRICOM Disaster Preparedness program in 2012.

21. US Global Leadership Coalition (USGLC) Hi-Level Panel on new US Global Development Policy (Washington, DC: Federal News Service Transcript, September 28, 2010), 4, http://www.usglc.org/2010/09/28/the-administrations-new-global-development -policy-a-roundtable-discussion/.

Chapter 7

Foreign Assistance in Camouflage?

Measuring the Military Security Cooperation Role

Nina M. Serafino*

There is a widespread perception that the US military has sought and acquired a markedly expanded role abroad since 2001, undermining the secretary of state's authority over foreign assistance and fostering a "militarization" of foreign policy. Whether that perception is valid, and the degre to which it may be so, depends largely on the lens through which one looks at the military role.

The most common lens is the increase in the number of provisions under which the Department of Defense (DoD) assists or interacts with foreign militaries and security forces under Title 10 (Armed Forces) of the US Code (USC) or the annual National Defense Authorization Act (NDAA). (These provisions of law are generally referred to as "authorities.") There are, however, other quantitative measures of DoD assistance and interaction as well: levels of funding, number of countries assisted, and the number of foreign troops or security personnel trained.[1]

While quantitative indicators may suffice to measure whether there has been an expansion of DoD's foreign assistance and foreign assistance–like activities, and thus its role in foreign policy, judging whether DoD has seized an inappropriate role in foreign policy is not a simple counting exercise. Judgments must draw on the historical and current context for DoD authorities,

*Nina M. Serafino is a Specialist in International Security Affairs at the Congressional Research Service. The views expressed in this chapter are those of the author, and do not represent a position of the Congressional Research Service or of the Library of Congress. The author does not necessarily endorse the conclusions of the other contributors or the book as a whole. She thanks two American University students for their help with this work: Erin Quinn for compiling the data used in the tables, and Erin Loui for checking it.

including the formal (legal) and informal (bureaucratic) division of labor between DoD and the Department of State, as well as the political factors determining this division of labor, in particular the role of Congress in setting the legal framework and providing funding for activities.

The purpose of this chapter is to examine possible measures for activities that DoD refers to as security cooperation and to provide historical context for understanding the division of labor between DoD and the State Department and the congressional role. To that end it first discusses the DoD–State Department division of labor and the evolution of State and DoD authorities and activities, then examines available quantitative measures, and finally discusses the current status of DoD authorities and civilian control, influence, and oversight. Unlike Chapter 6 by G. William Anderson and Connie Veillette, which discusses humanitarian and development-type DoD programs, this chapter deals primarily with the new DoD authorities to train and equip foreign military forces, also known as "building partner capacity."

The Development of the Statutory and de Facto Division of Labor between the Departments of State and Defense

As the law-making branch of the US government and the decision maker on US budgets, Congress can be the starting and end point for much of the civilian oversight of US activities and operations abroad. To a large extent, Congress determines the division of labor between the State Department, DoD, and other agencies for those efforts. It decides which activities and operations will be conducted, and influences the choice of recipient countries, organizations, or groups. It appropriates funds to the chosen agency's budget accounts, and may set conditions and limitations on the amounts to be spent. Through its committees, principally the armed services, foreign affairs, and appropriations committees, Congress then oversees the conduct of those activities and makes adjustments as it sees fit.

Statutory Framework

The framework for the statutory division of labor between the Departments of State and Defense on military assistance developed soon after World War II, as the United States began its massive foreign assistance programs. In the first division of labor under the Mutual Defense Assistance Act of 1949,[2] the forerunner to current military assistance programs, Congress assigned responsibility for assistance provided by that act, including assistance to foreign military forces, to the secretary of state. Subsequent legislation placed responsibility for foreign assistance, including military assistance, in the White House. When responsibility for foreign assistance shifted to the Department of State under the Mutual Security Act of 1954, President Eisenhower bestowed the responsibility for military assistance on the secretary of state through an executive order in 1955. Writing to then–secretary of state John Foster Dulles of his decision, President Eisenhower stated: "[T]he Secretary of State, under the President, must be the official responsible for the development and control of foreign policy and all relations with foreign governments, to include policies affecting mutual security" (Eisenhower 1955).[3]

Congress's passage of the Foreign Assistance Act (FAA) of 1961 placed this responsibility in statute. The secretary of state is given responsibility for the "continuous supervision and general direction" of all assistance authorized by the act, with specific reference to "military assistance."[4] In 1976, when the International Military Education and Training (IMET) program was added to the FAA and authorization for arms sales was moved to the Arms Export Control Act, Congress removed the limit on the exercise of this responsibility to assistance provided under the act. New language charged the secretary of state with responsibility for continuous supervision and general direction of economic and military assistance, specifically including military education and training and civic action, without regard to the authority under which it is provided. Under the FAA, the secretary of state is also responsible "for determining whether there shall be a military assistance (including civic action) or a military education and training program for a country and the value thereof, to the end that such programs are effectively integrated both at home and abroad and the foreign policy of the United States is best served thereby." The secretary of defense is charged with responsibility for administering military assistance.[5]

Congress appropriated funds for development and military assistance programs under the new foreign aid regime to the president, as was the practice under the prior Mutual Security Appropriations Act. In line with general practice, the president then delegated authority over the funds appropriated to him. At least for the first year of the new foreign aid regime, the president allocated to DoD the military assistance funds appropriated by the Foreign Assistance and Related Agencies Appropriations Act of 1962.[6] At some point, funding for major military foreign assistance programs—the Foreign Military Financing (FMF) train and equip account and later the IMET education and training account—was placed under the State Department budget. (In an anomaly from this arrangement, during the Vietnam War, Congress established the Military Assistance Support Fund, authorized under the NDAA and funded in DoD appropriations acts, to aid coalition partners.) Within two decades of the adoption of the new foreign aid regime under the FAA, Congress began providing DoD with its own authority through laws amending Title 10 (Armed Services) of the US Code and through provisions under the annual National Defense Authorization Act to assist foreign military forces, as well as funds in the DoD budget, to carry out new DoD programs.

State Department–DoD Division of Labor

While the FAA requirement that the secretary of state provide general direction for and continuous supervision of military assistance programs remains in law, in practice the exercise of that oversight function varies according to differing interpretations of what constitutes military "assistance." For FAA Title 22 programs, the State Department is in the lead, through US embassies abroad and the regional State Department bureaus in Washington, DC, with substantial DoD contributions to program planning, administration, and implementation. The Defense Security Cooperation Agency's (DSCA) security cooperation organizations (SCOs) stationed at US embassies and reporting to both the US ambassador and the commander of each Geographic Combatant Command play a considerable role in planning and implementation.[7] For programs under DoD Title 10 and NDAA statutes, some of which are described as "foreign assistance-related" and others as integral parts of DoD operations rather than as assistance per se, the secretary of state, State Department personnel, ambassadors, and other personnel at US embassies can play an important role. The State Department may influence DoD activities through the civilians it assigns to the geographic combatant commands that direct military activities and operations in their areas of responsibility. The State Department has long assigned political advisers (more often known as "POLADs") to top military commanders abroad, and in 2010 offered to provide ambassador-ranked personnel to serve as deputy civilian commanders in combatant commands "where such appointments effectively advance our national interests" and to detail mid- to senior-level State and USAID personnel to those commands as available (US Department of State 2010, 54). In 2005, USAID created an Office of Military Affairs (now the Office of Civilian-Military Cooperation) to provide advice to the military commands and personnel carrying out humanitarian programs abroad.

Terminology

The evolution of the DoD role has been accompanied by a change in terminology from the blanket term "military assistance" to "security assistance" and variations thereof. There are no standard FAA, DoD, or governmentwide definitions for the terms "military assistance" or "security assistance," and the use of terminology has been inconsistent among and within agencies. The FAA continues to use "military assistance" for all activities in which the military plays a role encompassed under the act. DoD has long used the term security assistance for the same activities, but only recently, in its February 2009 budget request for FY 2010, did the Department of State change the heading for the categories of assistance accounts to train, equip, and educate foreign militaries—FMF, IMET, and Peacekeeping Operations (PKO)—from "military assistance" to "international security assistance." In recent years, authorities to train and equip foreign military and security forces have been referred to as Building Partnership Capacity (BPC) programs, initially at DoD and subsequently at State. Further muddling the picture, DoD sometimes uses the terms security assistance and "security force assistance" for its own training and equipping activities, including them under the broader rubric of "security cooperation," which encompasses training exercises, humanitarian and civic assistance, and educational programs, as well as conferences and other military-to-military contacts.

The debate over the "militarization" of foreign policy draws examples from the full range of security cooperation activities. These encompass the new DoD authorities that overlap with the traditional State Department authorities to educate, train, and equip foreign forces (FMF, IMET[8]) and the newer State Department PKO programs, usually implemented by the DSCA.[9] They also include activities that DoD has traditionally carried out under its own authorities.

Development of DoD Authorities

Despite the perception that DoD authorities to assist foreign forces are a post–9/11 phenomenon, the expansion of DoD authorities began in the 1980s. The pre–9/11 statutes provided authority for a variety of activities. The post–9/11 authorities largely concerned the conflicts in Afghanistan and Iraq, or counterterrorism.

The Growth of Pre–9/11 Authorities and Programs

The pre–9/11 authorities covered a variety of activities, among them counternarcotics, where Congress provided a role for the military where civilian resources were lacking, and humanitarian and civic assistance, where Congress provided conditions and guidance for long-standing military activities.

- In 1980, in what appears to be the first of these DoD foreign assistance authorities, Congress passed the Acquisition and Cross-Servicing Agreements (ACSC) statute authorizing DoD to provide logistics support, supplies, and services to specified foreign military forces and international organizations.[10]
- Congress formalized a DoD role in counternarcotics (CN) with the first of three general DoD counterdrug authorities in 1981, authorizing the US military to assist US federal law enforcement personnel abroad by operating equipment and providing transportation (Title 10 Section 374). Two other CN authorities followed, which have never been made permanent law: "Section 1004" in 1990 permitting DoD to support foreign law enforcement agencies in a wide variety of ways, and "Section 1033" in 1997 to provide additional support for CN activities in specified countries.[11] The CN authorities enacted into law a new military mission, and one that initially troubled some defense officials as *posse comitatus* restrictions in US law had long been seen as a barrier to the use of military forces in the exercise of law enforcement functions. Nevertheless, Congress established a bright line between support for and performance of law enforcement activities, and has regularly extended and expanded these temporary authorities, as well as separate CN authorities for individual countries.
- Authority for military humanitarian and civic action (HCA) programs was set in statute in 1986 to regulate an ongoing DoD activity, not to mandate a new military activity. Permitted uses now include medical and veterinary visits and small-scale construction, although these have changed over time. A second authority provided in 1992 primarily to transport humanitarian assistance apparently has also been used recently for civic action programs. HCA programs are funded through DoD's Overseas Humanitarian, Disaster, and Civic Action Account (OHDACA) and from the DoD operations and maintenance account.[12]
- Similarly, the 1991 adoption of the Joint Combined Exchange Training (JCET) program authorized Special Operations Forces (SOF) to train with foreign military and other security forces, although the primary purpose is to train US SOF.[13]
- Before "building partnership capacity" became a term of art in the late 2000s, DoD's Warsaw Initiative Fund (WIF), established soon after NATO created its Partnership for Peace (PfP) program in 1994, provided an account to support programs to train military forces of the states of the former Soviet Union and Eastern Europe. Through WIF, DoD funded PfP military activities that drew on multiple existing authorities.[14]

- Counterterrorism provisions were adopted before and after 9/11. In 1998, the 1981 CN statute was altered by grafting onto it the authority to carry out the same military assistance mission for counterterrorism support to law enforcement personnel.[15] The Combating Terrorism Fellowship Program (CTFP), established by law soon after 9/11 in January 2002, was part of a gradual trend of increasing DoD educational authorities, not a dramatic new practice.[16]

Most of the pre–9/11 DoD authorities do not require the secretary of state's approval to conduct activities abroad, but a few do, which results in striking inconsistencies. Among those that require the secretary of state's approval are Title 10 Humanitarian and Civic Assistance (Section 401), DoD assistance to maintain and operate equipment for foreign law enforcement (Section 374), and military-to-military contacts (Section 168). The primary purpose by law of Title 10 Section 401 is to train US troops, as is the primary purpose of Section 2011 authority for special operations forces training exercises with friendly foreign forces, but the former requires the secretary of state's approval (usually exercised through the chief of mission) and the latter does not. Nor do other DoD humanitarian assistance authorities require the secretary of state's approval. Similarly, Congress made the secretary of state's approval necessary for Section 374 anticrime and counterdrug assistance (with counterterrorism later added to Section 374 uses), but not other counterdrug assistance carried out under the Section 1004 and Section 1033 annual national defense authorization acts' authority. The Title 10 Section 168 "Military-to-Military Contacts and Comparable Activities" authority added in 1994, which by its title conveys the impression it is a military and not a foreign assistance function, also calls for secretary of state approval, perhaps because it authorizes exchanges of civilians and payment of expenses for civilian defense personnel in addition to long-standing contact opportunities with foreign military forces.

Post–9/11 Development of DoD Authorities and Programs

For some policymakers, the terrorist attacks on the United States were a game changer, requiring new approaches and laws. The post–9/11 authorities correspond to defense officials' view that assistance to foreign military and security forces is not just a tool of US national security and foreign policy, but in some cases is essential to the safety of US forces abroad. DoD also has argued for its own authorities on the grounds that it needs more flexible, rapid-response resources than are available from the State Department, with their three- to four-year planning and approval cycles, and that it needs larger amounts than

Congress would fund through the State Department budget. A 2008 DoD Directive emphasizes the importance DoD attributes to its security cooperation role. "Security cooperation, which includes DoD-administered security assistance programs, is an important tool of national security and foreign policy and is an integral element of the DoD mission. Security cooperation activities should be planned, programmed, budgeted, and executed with the same high degree of attention and efficiency as other integral DoD activities" (US Department of Defense 2008, 1). The most recent and controversial new authorities were associated with the military operations in Iraq and Afghanistan, as well as authorities for counterterrorism activities. The first of the counterterrorism authorities, the Combating Terrorism Fellowship Program (CTFP), mentioned above, was made law shortly after 9/11 although the program had started earlier.

New DoD laws to support military operations in the war zones provided for:

- Authority and funds to train and equip military and other security forces in Iraq and Afghanistan[17];
- The Commander's Emergency Response Fund (CERP) first established in 2003 to provide "walking-around" money for field commanders in Iraq to carry out humanitarian and reconstruction projects to assist in counterinsurgency efforts, which was later extended to Afghanistan[18];
- Coalition Support Funds (CSF) in 2003 and Support for Allied Forces (AFS) in 2006 (Title 10 USC 127d), to support coalition nations operating in those theaters.[19]

Most of the Afghanistan, Iraq, and related coalition authorities, with CERP the exception, required the "concurrence," that is, the approval, of the secretary of state.

Even as it waged wars in Iraq and Afghanistan, DoD looked beyond those campaigns and asked for broader authorities that could also be used to assist other foreign military forces and US forces also operating elsewhere in the world in the Global War on Terror (GWOT). Some incorporated provisions providing a greater role for the secretary of state.

- In 2005, Congress provided Section 1208 authority and funds to support foreign forces, irregular forces, groups, or individuals supporting or facilitating US SOF counterterrorism operations.[20] (Details of this program are classified.)
- In 2006, the Section 1206 global train and equip authority permitted DoD to provide equipment, supplies, and training to enable foreign national military forces (and later also maritime security forces) to conduct counterterrorism operations, as well as to support military and

stability operations in which the United States participates. In addition to requiring the concurrence of the secretary of state, Section 1206 incorporated a new power-sharing arrangement with the secretaries of defense and state jointly formulating projects.[21]

- For FY 2011, Congress put in statute a Ministry of Defense civilian advisors (MODA) authority, permitting DoD to extend worldwide a program first started in Afghanistan. This program sends senior DoD civilian employees abroad to assist their counterparts in foreign ministries of defense to improve their institutions.[22]

- Also for FY 2011, Congress provided the secretaries of defense and state with authority to jointly develop and carry out infrastructure projects in Afghanistan funded by a new Afghanistan Infrastructure Fund (AIF) in the DoD budget.[23] The AIF drew on the Section 1206 power-sharing arrangement for joint project development. Unlike Section 1206, however, the secretary of state is given responsibility for implementing projects in coordination with the secretary of defense, except when the secretaries jointly determine that the secretary of defense should implement them.

- For those recent DoD authorities for Iraq, Afghanistan, and coalition security assistance requiring the concurrence of the secretary of state, the State Department established procedures for consideration at the highest levels, with the most important requiring the approval of the secretary herself. The secretary's veto power provides for a give-and-take on DoD plans that appears to be a rough equivalent to providing the State Department's "general direction" required by the FAA. DoD's Section 1206 authority contains a unique mechanism for joint DoD-State decision making, with joint DoD-State program formulation and the secretary's concurrence required for new programs. In addition, DoD policy calls for chief of mission approval of Section 1206 proposals. In other cases, DoD statutes or policies require an ambassador's chief of mission approval.

In addition, Congress has funded new programs that use existing authorities to educate foreign military and civilian defense personnel. In FY 2010, DoD established the Defense Institution Reform Initiative (DIRI) to "develop accountable, professional, and transparent defense establishments."[24] The same year, DoD initiated a program for the combatant commands to develop and implement rule of law-based programs with direction provided by the Office of the Secretary of Defense.[25]

Overall, the number of DoD authorities has steadily grown over time, generally expanding the scope of DoD activity under its own statutory authority, as shown in Figure 7.1. In this figure, the red circles indicate State Department authorities; the blue circles, DoD authorities; the purple circle indicates a joint authority. Although the increasing number of post–9/11 DoD authorities is the continuation of a trend that began in the 1980s, the post–9/11 authorities and programs may be viewed as somewhat distinct. DoD officials have argued that the new DoD authorities and programs are different from traditional State Department security assistance programs because they meet "military" or "operational requirements," that is, they are an integral part of or they contribute to US military missions, while the State Department's programs are "political," largely used to respond to foreign militaries' own perceived needs and thus to foster diplomatic relations with foreign states. However, another difference is that the purposes of new DoD authorities— equipping and training foreign military and related personnel—overlap with existing State Department programs to a greater extent than pre–9/11 authorities, which institutionalized or regulated previous military practices or supplemented civilian efforts.

This overlap suggests that a major concern behind the new DoD authorities is securing sufficient funding to meet the perceived demands of the post– 9/11 security environment, in addition to addressing the security gaps DoD views as most critical. The joint DoD–State Department Global Security Contingency Fund (GSCF) authorized on the last day of 2011 to provide resources for urgent security and governance priorities is heralded as a new approach to DoD-State cooperation.[26] It also can be viewed as a compromise to secure funding for State programs. While the GSCF authority puts the secretary of state in the lead, the secretary of defense's concurrence is required even for justice-sector and rule-of-law programs that normally would be funded by the State Department budgets and implemented by State Department and US Agency for International Development (USAID) personnel. Although the GSCF is to be jointly funded by State and DoD, the expectation is that DoD, with its vastly larger budget, will contribute most of the funding.

Other Possible Quantitative Measures

There are other possible quantitative measures of the DoD role. They include DoD and State Department funding levels and measures of foreign troops trained. These are discussed below.

DoD and Department of State Funding Levels

Funding levels have been used as a means to demonstrate an expansion of the DoD role since 9/11. There has been a huge increase in DoD spending for

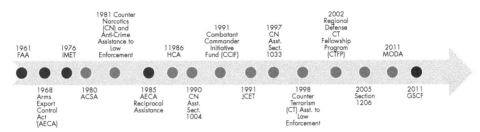

Figure 7.1
Selected Security Assistance and Cooperation Authorities, 1961 Forward

Source: Title 10 USC, Title 22 USC, and National Defense Authorization Acts.

foreign assistance and related activities, in both environments of peace and of hostilities. In these analyses, funding includes various coalition support accounts that are treated as analogous to the State Department's Foreign Military Financing (FMF) and International Military Education and Training (IMET), as well as country-specific assistance for Iraq, Afghanistan, and Pakistan. Some may add CERP as well. DoD security assistance alone outstrips State Department security assistance by these measures. A 2011 Stimson Center report cites a 66 percent growth in State Department security assistance from FY 2002 to FY 2010, compared to a 500 percent growth in DoD security assistance for the same period. Both include funding for activities in Iraq and Afghanistan that have been or are expected to move to the State Department with US military drawdowns (Adams and Williams 2011, 23–24). Figure 1.1 in Chapter 1 uses this same all-inclusive methodology to show that the percentage of overall US security assistance administered through DoD has risen from about 25 percent to more than 60 percent.

To judge the degree to which foreign assistance has been "militarized," however, there are two other possible funding indicators. One is the level of peacetime, "steady-state" DoD funding for a number of security cooperation activities, excluding war-related funding. Another is a comparison of DoD "steady-state" foreign assistance-type funding to similar categories of State Department funding. Unfortunately, the most that can be provided is a snapshot using the categories of DoD activities for which information is publicly available. Because DoD provides limited information categorized by activity, available data at best indicates possible trends and disparities and cannot be extrapolated across all DoD security cooperation accounts.

Measures of Foreign Troops Trained

A third possible measure is a comparison between the number of troops trained under State Department and DoD programs. The annual *State Department Foreign Military Training and DOD Engagement Activities of Interest* report provides a means to count the number of countries and foreign troops and other defense personnel involved in a number of State Department and DoD education and training programs.[27]

Comparisons

Comparing the funding data from Tables 7.1 and 7.2, several points stand out, all pointing to a willingness in Congress to increase State Department spending for certain categories of assistance, such as counterterrorism and foreign military training, where new authorities have been added at DoD.

- Excluding war-related funding, the State Department security assistance and related accounts grew at a faster rate from FY 2001 to FY 2010 than the related DoD categories for which information is publicly available. The State Department accounts grew 65 percent while the DoD accounts grew 22 percent in constant dollars.[28]
- Comparing the most equivalent accounts providing for counternarcotics, counterterrorism, peacekeeping, demining, and some rule-of-law training, the State Department accounts grew 168 percent while the DoD accounts grew 20 percent in constant dollars.[29]
- The available data shows decreases in two DoD accounts—OHDACA demining and DoD nonproliferation—where funding in similar State Department accounts grew considerably.[30]

Often funding is not the entire or most interesting part of the story. The number of countries involved and the number of foreign forces trained or sent to U.S. military schools can show greater variation than funding data.

- For instance, as shown in the Tables 7.1 and 7.2, increases in the State Department's IMET funding and DoD's regional centers funding from FY 2001 to FY 2010 are each a little over 50 percent, but there is a great difference between the numbers of troops trained under IMET and educated at regional centers with that funding. Table 7.3 shows that despite the funding increase, 23 percent fewer troops were trained in 2010 through IMET funding than in 2001. On the other hand, Table 7.3 also shows that the number of students participating in DoD regional centers' programs increased by over 300 percent from FY 2001 to FY 2010.[31]

- Even though Table 7.2 shows that funding has increased only modestly for DoD counterdrug assistance, other measures of the level of effort indicate greater outreach. As seen in Table 7.3, from FY 2001 through FY 2010 the number of countries reached through Section 1004 training increased by 20 percent (although far fewer students were trained). Table 7.3 also shows that Congress added twenty countries to the list of those eligible for Section 1033 assistance during that period (as well as thirteen new countries for FY 2012).

Most interesting is the glimpse that available funding data may give into the growth of the low-cost security cooperation tools through which the combatant commands reach out to large numbers of people.

- As seen in Table 7.2, in FY 2010 Congress provided almost two-thirds more funding to geographic combatant commanders through the CIF/CCIF than it did in FY 2001. This account funds a wide variety of small activities, including attendance at conferences and seminars and training.[32]
- Table 7.2 also shows a 65 percent increase in funding for the Overseas Humanitarian, Disaster, and Civil Assistance (OHDACA) account in FY 2010 over FY 2001. OHDACA provides funding for humanitarian assistance, civic action programs, and disaster relief under six specified authorities.[33] However, the variation in total funding for humanitarian assistance may be quite different because of the limitations discussed below.

There are limitations in interpreting this data.

- DoD funding in programs where US troops perform functions abroad may underrepresent the level of DoD effort compared with the State Department, as DoD funding amounts include only "incremental" costs, a DoD budget term that means the additional costs of performing a mission over the normal costs of personnel and other expenses that are considered normal peacetime expenses for military forces. This understatement is especially true for counternarcotics assistance and some OHDACA activities. As a result, the costs for State Department (and USAID programs) will be higher to the extent that DoD uses military personnel rather than contractors. Most State Department and USAID programs are implemented by contractors, while DoD programs vary.
- Funding levels for categories of assistance most often represented by a specified account are at best approximations, as funding may be drawn from additional accounts, not all of which are easily traceable in the

case of DoD. In FY 2010, for instance, the defense appropriations act (P.L. 111–118) included $16 million in Navy funds for programs such as training and exercises with foreign military forces and humanitarian assistance under the Asia Pacific Regional Initiative Program. (Congress also may provide additional funding for State Department programs under regional or bilateral rather than the global accounts tallied in Table 7.1, but the magnitudes are unlikely to be as great.)

- Many DoD activities are not publicly reported or traceable; for instance, details on Section 1206 programs and funding are not publicly reported even though congressional oversight committees receive extensive data.

Because of the limitations mentioned above, drawing even sketchy conclusions about the absolute amounts and relative magnitude of nonwartime DoD funding would warrant a more extensive probe of DoD costs and outreach than possible from publicly available data. This data does, however, demonstrate two points relevant to the "militarization" debate. First, the State

Table 7.1

State Department Assistance ($ millions, current and constant 2005 dollars)

Program/Account	FY 2001 (Actuals)		FY 2010 (Actuals)		% Increase Constant $
	Current $	Constant $	Current $	Constant $	
Foreign Military Financing (FMF)	3,568.4	3,918.7	5,526.2	4,955.3	26%
International Military Education and Training (IMET)	57.7	63.4	108.0	96.8	53%
International Narcotics and Law Enforcement (INL)	325.0	356.9	2,170.7	1,946.4	445%
Non-Proliferation, Antiterrorism, De-mining, and Related Programs (NADR)	310.9	341.4	754.0	676.1	198%
NADR Nonproliferation	*212.0*	*232.8*	*296.0*	*265.4*	*114%*
NADR Antiterrorism	*57.0*	*62.6*	*296.5*	*265.9*	*425%*
NADR Demining and Small Arms/ Light Weapons Destruction	*41.9*	*46.0*	*161.6*	*144.9*	*315%*
Peacekeeping Operations (PKO)	126.7	139.2	331.5	297.3	114%
TOTALS		4,819.6		7,972.0	65%

Totals may not add due to rounding.

Data source: US Department of State. International Affairs Congressional Budget Justifications for FY2003 and FY2012. ("Actual" amounts are reported with two-year lags.)

Table 7.2
DoD Assistance ($ millions, current and constant 2005 dollars)

Program/ Account	FY2001 Appropriations or Reported Spending		FY2010 Appropriations or Reported Spending		% Increase Constant $	Related State Department Programs
	Current $	Constant $	Current $	Constant $		
CIF/CCIF	25	27.45	50.0 (Excluding additional $12.5 million for Iraq and Afghanistan)	44.84	63%	IMET NADR USAID
Counterdrug (CD)	869 appropriated	954.32	1,158.2 appropriated	1,038.56	9%	INL
Combating Terrorism Fellowship Program Training (CTFP)	0	0	$26.8 ($35m authorized level)	24.03	New since 2001	IMET NADR
Cooperative Threat Reduction (CTR)	443	486.49	424.1	380.29	–22%	NADR
OHDACA	55.9 appropriated	61.39	109.9 appropriated	98.55	61%	USAID NADR (Demining, etc., only)
OHDACA Demining	*10.9*	*12.0*	*3.5*	*3.1*	*–74%*	*NADR Demining*
Regional Centers Training	13.05	14.33	24.37	21.85	52%	IMET
Section 1206 Global Train and Equip	0	0	340.6 (350 authorized)	305.42 (313.9 authorized)	New since 2001	FMF IMET NADR
TOTALS (Excluding OHDACA, except for demining)		1,495.6		1,818.09	22%	

Totals may not add due to rounding.
Data Source: Appropriations in P.L. 111-118, Department of Defense Appropriations Act, 2010, other figures as provided by appropriate offices of the Department of Defense.

Table 7.3

State Department Training Assistance by Number of Countries and Number of Personnel Trained

Program/Account (State Department in Italics; **DoD in Bold**)	Countries		Trainees	
	FY2001	FY2010	FY2001	FY2010
Enhanced International Peacekeeping Capability Program (EIPC)	*11*	*Absorbed by GPOI, below*	*162*	*Absorbed by GPOI, below*
Africa Peacekeeping Training	*5*	*Absorbed by GPOI, below*	*5,421*	*Absorbed by GPOI, below*
GPOI (Includes EPIC and Africa training after 2005)	*0*	*52*	*0*	*12,134*
IMET	*113*	*122*	*9,062*	*6,833*
INL Training	*8*	*5*	*689*	*948*
Section 1004 Training	**20**	**24**	**9,670**	**2,024**
CTFP	**0**	**112**	**0**	**2,529**
Regional Centers	**156**	**150** (plus Palestine Authority)	**2,480**	**13,721**

Totals may not add due to rounding.
Source: US Department of State. *Foreign Military Training and DOD Engagements of Interest,* FY2001–FY2002 and FY2010–FY2011. http://www.state.gov.

Department has received substantial increased funding for accounts that are of particular interest to Congress that overlap with post–9/11 DoD authorities and related funding. Second, DoD has significantly expanded its outreach under pre–9/11 authorities, particularly through educational programs. This expansion raises the question as to whether some pre–9/11 DoD educational programs, that is, the CTFP and regional programs, are similar in purpose to IMET and also belong under State Department authority.

Possible Consequences and Potential for Change

Whether one considers the expansion of the DoD role and activities a "militarization" of foreign policy depends on what is meant by the term. That term can represent a belief that DoD is now setting foreign policy priorities where it did not previously. Or it can mean that DoD is exercising increasing influence over foreign policy. Or it may mean that the face of the US presence abroad is increasingly that of the US military. The answer to this question may differ according to the interpretation of the term "militarization" and may be assessed differently by different analysts. Different interpretations may also result from the time frame considered, as DoD has long carried out programs that overlap with State Department programs. It has also always implemented State Department military assistance programs.

As can be seen by the frequent requirement for secretary of state concurrence in post–9/11 authorities, these "new" authorities do not, per se, generally provide DoD with the power to place military priorities over foreign relations priorities. In some cases, the new mechanisms put in place to provide USAID and State Department input into military decisions may provide a useful civil-military synergy that benefits US interests, although in others they are found wanting. While USAID can influence DoD humanitarian missions and US ambassadors can appeal to the secretary of state to block any unwanted military and security activities, the exercise of these prerogatives depends on personalities, bureaucratic position, and bureaucratic politics. For instance, among other problems with the placement of civilians in geographic combatant commands, some have noted that because of the hierarchical nature of combatant commands the potential influence of USAID personnel is limited if they are not of sufficient rank to personally address command leadership. With the addition of personnel in recent years, the State Department's Bureau of Political Military Affairs (the principal office for overseeing State Department security assistance and coordinating with the military on a range of civilian-military programs, including DoD authorities requiring secretary of state "concurrence") is viewed as better positioned to accomplish its tasks but could be stretched thin if asked to oversee more DoD programs.[34]

On the other hand, the new DoD authorities and increased activities may have opened the door to greater DoD influence on the tenor of US foreign policy, intended or not. This influence may flow from the negotiating power that control over budgets provides to affect outcomes and from differing DoD and State Department priorities. At the embassy level, the lack of civilian personnel—in numbers and perhaps expertise—to think through military activities may mean that the military inadvertently influences relations with that country by undertaking activities that have not been appropriately vetted and may have unintended consequences. Even when an indispensable part of military operations, DoD activities where US military personnel interact with foreign populations, militaries, and governments can have long-term consequences for foreign relations. Concerns remain that those potential consequences necessitate consistent and effective civilian "general direction and continuous supervision" over all such programs, but that the State Department and US ambassadors are not provided with the tools and authority to exercise that responsibility. However, judging the effects of possible greater DoD influence abroad is the subject of case-by-case studies and beyond the scope of this chapter.

Even if case-by-case studies show marked adverse effects, changing the status quo may be difficult. The post–9/11 evolution of DoD authorities for foreign assistance is the result of a mix of political realities and bureaucratic imperatives that differ greatly from some fifty to seventy years ago, when the initial distribution of responsibility and balance of power was established. Some thirty Congresses have come and gone since the 81st Congress established the first framework for US military assistance in 1949. Their political composition, attitudes toward international relations, US military power, and agencies' roles and capabilities, as well as their expertise in military and foreign affairs, have differed markedly. The historical primacy of the State Department as the lead agency in foreign policy was accepted as an established fact in the early post–World War II years of the Truman presidency, and, further, appreciated by army general Eisenhower when he was president. Despite the military triumph of World War II, by the late 1940s the military was viewed as an incoherent collection of individual military services that needed the discipline of civilian control under the new Department of Defense, with funding cut to a minimum.

In 2013, perceptions about the two departments and the political balance of power between them is reversed. Since 9/11, if not before, the military enjoys a considerable popular constituency reflected in Congress's relative reluctance to restrict defense funding. The State Department's functions and the role of foreign assistance, on the other hand, are poorly understood by a skeptical population and thus subject to stricter budget limitations by Congress. These popular perceptions played out in Congress have led to what many analysts have pointed to as gross imbalance between military and civilian resources, including prominent military and defense leaders who urge strong support for diplomacy and development.[35] Still, the potential growth in isolationist sentiments and an ever more constrained budget environment since FY 2010 reinforce what is usually termed an "imbalance" of power.

The popular and congressional disposition toward the military is compounded by the widespread perception among civilian leaders and agencies that the State Department culture and institutional bias is so dominated by its core mission of diplomacy that it is not only incapable of effectively conducting foreign security assistance missions but will short-shrift them in times of budget shortfalls. In this context, DoD's decision to seek its own authorities for "building partnership capacity"—a mission traditionally conducted under State Department funding and authority except in the midst of war—can be viewed as a logical bureaucratic response to the perception this is the only way to ensure that the job is done, and some members of Congress do see a primary role for DoD as important, at least in the current environment.[36] On the other hand, in previous years with a better budget climate, Congress has been willing to grant some increases in funding for the State Department in key areas.

Yet, many of those who favor DoD authorities believe that appropriate civilian oversight, centered in the secretary of state (although most often exercised by others), remains important. As in the early post–World War II years, assistance provided by the US military in peacetime, however it may be labeled and whatever military purposes it serves, will inevitably be perceived outside the United States as a function of US national interest and foreign policy. While foreign policy is made at the White House, US law places responsibility for ensuring the coherence of US foreign policy with one person, the secretary of state, the only US official besides the president whose scope is global, whose perspective must calibrate responses to short-term needs to ensure enduring US interests, and who oversees the major instruments of US peacetime engagement.

There are what some consider significant drawbacks in providing DoD with its own authority and funds for foreign assistance activities. Particularly in an era of shrinking budgets, such activities may be viewed as drawing resources from core defense functions. In addition to the possible de facto lack of accountability to civilian authorities, such authority and funding create a lack of transparency in programs and funding important to US foreign policy interests, as DoD does not provide for its programs the same public detail that State does for its programs. In addition, many fear that DoD may seek exemption for its assistance from important FAA and Arms Export Control Act (AECA) limitations, even though in some cases statutes or DoD policies currently incorporate such restrictions. These include the FAA Section 620M "Leahy Amendment" restrictions on foreign training and equipping of units credibly believed to be responsible for gross violations of human rights (the DoD "Leahy" legislation prohibits training such forces, but permits equipping them as well as other forms of assistance), as well as the multiple AECA requirements regarding a country's eligibility and authorization for assistance.

Conclusion

Despite the growth of DoD authorities from 2005 forward, Congress is not wedded in principle to a wholesale redistribution of responsibilities toward DoD. Congress has sometimes reflected the sentiments of many defense officials, most prominently former Secretary of Defense Robert Gates, who have called for an increase in the budgets and personnel of the State Department and other civilian agencies with foreign affairs roles related to national security.[37] In addition, as noted above, Congress has required the concurrence of the secretary of state for nearly all of the post–9/11 legislation dealing with DoD assistance for security forces in Iraq and Afghanistan and for forces from coalition countries participating in military operations there, as well as for the Ministry of Defense civilian advisors program (P.L.112-81, Section 1081, FY2012 NDAA), and in 2004, it incorporated a specific provision for chief of mission concurrence in the Section 1208 Special Operations Forces support for foreign forces, irregular forces, and groups or individuals supporting operations.[38] (Yet inconsistencies regarding civilian oversight of DoD authorities persist.[39]) It has also transferred to civilian agencies funding previously appropriated in DoD budgets, including stabilization and security assistance[40] and funding for Pakistan Security Forces.[41]

Nevertheless, recent congressional action also reflects continued concern about State Department capacity, as well as budgetary realities, especially of the civilian international affairs budgets.[42] Unless, and until, the balance of civil-military power in Congress shifts considerably, permitting much larger State Department budgets for security and related assistance, the current balance of authority and funding is unlikely to substantially change.

In the absence of larger change, a series of smaller measures may enhance the State and USAID control mechanisms and improve transparency and accountability. Among these measures might be congressional support for training new ambassadors and deputy chiefs of mission to better equip them in decision making regarding security assistance and combatant command security cooperation activities, additional State Department personnel to oversee security assistance and cooperation activities at embassies, and a legislative requirement for secretary of state concurrence (to be delegated as appropriate) on all DoD foreign assistance–like authorities, even those enacted pre–9/11.[43] Another might be to supplement USAID personnel at combatant commands with USAID personnel assigned an oversight role of development-like military activities at the embassies, where they would have a line of communication to the ambassador. Legislation requiring greater disclosure of DoD security assistance and cooperation activities and costs might be enacted. In addition, congressional foreign affairs committees might exercise oversight of the role for the State Department under the Obama administration's April 2013 Presidential Policy Directive (PPD) 23, US Security Sector Assistance Policy, the details of which have not been made public.

Notes

1. A related question is whether the number of US troops involved in training and activities has increased, but such data is not publicly available. In any case, the number of US troops involved may well have shrunk because deployments to Iraq and Afghanistan led to an increasing use of US contractors (perhaps largely retired military) for some activities outside of war zones.

2. The Mutual Defense Act of 1949 provided three types of grant military aid to member states of the North Atlantic Treaty Organization (NATO), which had been established

months earlier, and several other states that did not have the ability to pay for their defense needs. This act provided funds to European countries to enable them to increase the production of military items without disrupting their economic recovery, as well as the direct transfer of military equipment, and assistance in producing and using military equipment and training personnel.

3. Responsibility was transferred on May 9, 1955, by Executive Order 10610.

4. Section 622(c) of the FAA of 1961 as amended.

5. Section 623 of the FAA of 1961, as amended, assigns "primary responsibility" to the secretary of defense for six functions: determining military end-item requirements; procuring military equipment in a manner that permits its integration with service programs; supervising end-item use by recipient countries; supervising the training of foreign military and related civilian personnel; transporting and delivering military end-use items; and within the Department of Defense, performing any other functions necessary to furnish military assistance, education, and training.

6. Letter of September 30, 1961, to Secretary of Defense Robert S. McNamara, Delegation of Authority to Secretary of Defense with Respect to Foreign Assistance, signed by President John F. Kennedy.

7. The DSCA administers and implements the "traditional" State Department military assistance programs, FMF and IMET, and assists with others. DSCA is an agency within the Office of the Secretary of Defense, under the undersecretary for policy. It is funded from both DoD and State Department accounts.

8. FAA of 1961, as amended, Section 541.

9. The DSCA assists with some PKO programs.

10. Title 10 USC Section 2342.

11. NDAA for FY 1991, P.L. 101-510, Section 1004. Support may include maintenance, repair, and upgrading of equipment made available by DoD, provision of vehicles and aircraft, aerial and ground reconnaissance, training of law-enforcement personnel, transport of personnel, linguistic and intelligence services, and the establishment and operation of bases and training facilities. NDAA for FY 1998, P.L. 105-85, Section 1033. This assistance may include equipment, vehicles, boats and aircraft, and maintenance and repair for CN equipment.

12. HCA was codified at Title 10 USC 401 with the restriction that its primary purpose be training for US forces, but HCA has also long been viewed as a tool for training foreign military and security forces and accomplishing other military objectives such as establishing a relationship with local populations. Specified permitted activities are medical, surgical, dental, and veterinary care; construction of rudimentary surface transportation systems; well drilling and construction of basic sanitation facilities; and rudimentary construction and repair of public facilities. Title 10 USC 2561, codified in 1992 with the primary purpose of transporting humanitarian assistance, also permits the use of funds for "other humanitarian purposes," providing an additional and unrestricted authority for civic action. Specified civic action activities are rudimentary construction and renovation of public facilities; digging or improving water wells and other sanitation and drinking water projects; and repair and building of rudimentary infrastructure, including roads and bridges.

13. Title 10 USC 2011.

14. Title 10 USC 168, military-to-military contacts; Title 10 USC 1051, payment of personnel expenses; and Title 10 USC 2010, developing country combined exercises expenses.

15. Omnibus Consolidated and Emergency Supplemental Appropriations, P.L. 105-277, Division B, Title II (Anti-terrorism) Section 201, amending Title 10 USC 374.

16. FY 2002 Defense Appropriations Act, P.L. 107-117, Section 8125, as amended, 10 USC 2249c. The statutory name for the program is Regional Defense Counterterrorism Fellowship Program.

17. Funding to train and equip the "New Iraqi Army" and the "Afghan National Army" was first included in the FY 2004 Emergency Supplemental Appropriations Act, P.L. 108-106, Section 1107, and authority to train and equip Iraqi and Afghan military and other security forces, including police, was first provided in the FY 2005 Ronald W. Reagan NDAA, P.L. 108-375, Section 1202.

18. Congress first funded CERP in the Emergency Supplemental Appropriations Act, FY 2004, P.L. 108-106, Section 1100, and authorized it in the NDAA for FY2005, P.L. 108-375, Section 1201. The delivery of humanitarian assistance by US military forces to foreign populations during war is not entirely new, as during World War II US armed forces delivered some $6 billion in "foodstuffs, fuel and petroleum, clothing, textiles, medical supplies and other equipment . . . until rehabilitation and recovery programs were established" (US House 1959, 1).

19. Congress first provided funding for supplies, services, transportation, including airlift and sealift, and other logistical support to coalition forces supporting military and stability operations in Iraq in the FY 2004 Emergency Supplemental Appropriations Act, P.L. 108-106, Section 1106; subsequently Congress first authorized the reimbursement of certain coalition nations for these types of support to or in connection with US military operations in Iraq, Afghanistan, and the global war on terrorism by the NDAA for FY 2006, P.L. 109-163, Section 1208.

20. NDAA for FY 2008, P.L. 108-375, Section 1208.

21. NDAA for FY 2006, P.L. 109-163, Section 1206.

22. NDAA for FY 2012, P.L. 112-81, Section 1081.

23. NDAA for FY 2011, P.L. 111-383, Section 1217. Authorized projects are water, power, and transportation projects, as well as other projects in support of the counterinsurgency strategy in Afghanistan. The secretary of defense is required to provide thirty days' prior notification to specified congressional committees before obligating or expending funds or transferring them to the secretary of state. The secretary of defense, in coordination with the secretary of state, is also required to submit an annual report to those committees. Specified committees are the House and Senate armed services and appropriations committees, the Senate Foreign Relations Committee, and the House Foreign Affairs Committee.

24. This program draws on three Title 10 authorities: Sections 168 (Military-to-Military Contacts), 1051 (Payment of Personnel Expenses), and 2010 (Developing Countries' Exercise Reimbursement).

25. The rule-of-law programs are carried out by the Defense Institute for International Legal Studies (DIILS). DIILS is a small organization of about thirty people that provides "rule of law training and education focused on human rights, international humanitarian law, and the law of armed conflict," according to its website, with its staff military lawyers traveling to foreign countries "to conduct courses, seminars, and workshops for foreign military officers, legal advisors, and related civilians," as well as resident courses at the DIILS base in Newport, Rhode Island. (http://diils.org/node/145541/about). DIILS activities are funded from DoD and State Department accounts.

26. NDAA for FY 2012, P.L. 112-81, Section 1207.

27. Available online through the State Department website, http:// www.state.gov.

28. The State Department accounts are: Foreign Military Financing (FMF); International Military Education and Training (IMET); International Narcotics Control and Law

Enforcement (INCLE); Nonproliferation, Anti-terrorism, Demining, and Related program (NADR); and Peacekeeping Operations (PKO). The related, although not precisely equivalent, DoD accounts are: Combatant Commander's Initiative Fund (CCIF) (formerly the Commander-in-Chief's Initiative Fund [CIF]); Section 1206 Global Train and Equip; Counter-Drug; Combating Terrorism Fellowship Program (CTFP); Cooperative Threat Reduction Program (CTR): and the five DoD regional centers. (These centers are: Africa Center for Strategic Studies; Asia-Pacific Center for Security Studies; Center for Hemispheric Defense Studies; George C. Marshall European Center for Security Studies; and Near East South Asia Center for Strategic Studies. As of October 2005, the Defense Security Cooperation Agency is the executive agent for the centers, responsible for administrative functions. The Geographic Combatant Commanders have operational control.) OHDACA spending other than demining is excluded from this comparison because it most resembles US Agency for International Development spending rather than any State Department security assistance account.

29. The State Department accounts were NADR, INCLE, and PKO. The DoD accounts were CD, CTFP, CTR, OHDACA demining, and Section 1206. All three State Department accounts funded new programs, for example, NADR and INL both supported the anti-terrorism and anticrime Regional Strategic Initiatives developed since 9/11, and PKO funded the Global Peacekeeping Operations Initiative (GPOI) started in 2005 to train foreign military troops and police forces for peacekeeping operations, a much expanded version of two previous State Department programs. DoD funding also included support for two new programs.

30. Spending for NADR demining activities and the destruction of small arms and light weapons grew 315 percent, while the spending for DoD demining funded under OHDACA decreased 74 percent, and the State Department account is many times larger. Spending for State Department nonproliferation activities grew by 114 percent, while DoD CTR spending decreased by 21 percent, although the State Department account is somewhat smaller. The decrease in CTR resulted from a substantial reduction in CTR funding from FY 2005 to FY 2010, due in part to the near completion of some arms-elimination projects.

31. This difference reflects at least in part the higher costs for IMET education and training, most of which takes place in the United States and involve stays of many months. However, activities at the regional centers bring some students to the centers themselves (most are located in Washington, DC) for coursework over extended periods of time, but also include many regional in-theater programs such as courses, seminars, and conferences.

32. Some CCIF activities are classified and there is no unclassified report regarding the unclassified activities.

33. 10 USC 2557 covers DoD nonlethal excess property, such as medical, school, and office equipment and supplies, construction and disaster-related equipment and tools, and vehicles. 10 USC 2561 and 10 USC 401 are discussed above. 10 USC 407 is for humanitarian demining, 10 USC 402 is for the transport of humanitarian supplies provided by a nongovernmental source, and 10 USC 404 is for disaster assistance.

34. In an October 2008 report, the American Academy of Diplomacy and the Stimson Center recommended a reversal of the post–Cold War decline in the State Department's Bureau of Political-Military Affairs (PM) staff and the hiring of additional staff to manage the State Department's responsibilities for the programs under DoD authorities. While the post–Cold War decline in PM staff has been addressed, oversight of the post–9/11 authorities may require new staff. The American Academy of Diplomacy and the Stimson Center.

A Foreign Affairs Budget for the Future: Fixing the Crisis in Diplomatic Readiness, Washington, DC, October 2008, 23.

35. For instance, see the March 27, 2012, Military Leaders' Letter to Congress, signed by the cochairs of the National Security Advisory Council, Adm. James M. Loy, USCG (Ret.), former commandant of the US Coast Guard, and Gen. Michael W. Hagee, USMC (Ret.), former commandant of the US Marine Corps, as well as eighty other retired flag officers. Cosigners include Gen. Henry H. Shelton, USA (Ret.), and former chairman of the joint chiefs of staff; Gen. Michael V. Hayden, USAF (Ret.), and former director of the Central Intelligence Agency; Gen. Peter J. Schoomaker, USA (Ret.), and former chief of staff, US Army; ten retired regional combatant commanders; and a former commander of US Special Operations Forces. This letter is accessible through the website of the US Global Leadership Coalition, http://www.usglc.org. This letter urged members of Congress to "oppose deep and disproportionate cuts to American's development and diplomacy programs" because they are "critical to America's national security."

36 Explaining its attitude toward the Section 1206 Building Partnership Capacity train and equip authority in 2009, the House Armed Services Committee stated that over time it had come to perceive the need for an authority that responded to a combatant commander's "need to build certain capacities in partner nations to satisfy specific theater security requirements." US Congress, Committee on Armed Services, *Report on National Defense Authorization Act for FY 2010, H.R. 2647*, H. Rept. 111-166. The full quote reads: "In the past, the committee has regarded this and related authorities as part of the foreign assistance family of authorities that has traditionally resided within the Department of State's purview. However, as the committee has observed the execution and growth of this program over time, the committee has come to see a distinction between traditional foreign assistance-related authorities designed to assist a foreign country to meet what it perceives as its own national security requirements within the context of a larger United States foreign policy framework, and this new type of authority, which generally represents the Secretary of Defense's assessment of a combatant commander's need to build certain capacities in partner nations to satisfy specific theater security requirements." The committee further noted that while the "optimal" arrangement for the future might place this authority under the secretary of state, the secretary of defense "must play a primary role in generating requirements." The committee also noted its concern that the Department of State "still lacks the capacity to execute these authorities."

37. For example, for legislation establishing the DoD Pakistan Counterinsurgency Fund in 2009, conferees stated their concern with "providing the Department of Defense with the authority and funding to conduct an assistance program which would traditionally fall under the purview of the Department of State." Supplemental Appropriations Act, 2009, H.R. 2246, H. Rept. 111-151, Conference Report, June 12, 2009.

38. These are the Afghanistan Security Forces Fund and the Iraq Security Forces Fund (P.L. 109-364, Sections 1517 and 1516, respectively, as amended (FY 2007 National Defense Authorization Act [NDAA]), Coalition Support Funds P.L. 110-181, Section 1233, as amended (FY 2008 NDAA), the Pakistan Counterinsurgency Fund (P.L. 111-84, Section 1224, as amended, FY 2010 NDAA), and the Pakistan Frontier Corps (P.L. 110-81. Section 1206, as amended, FY 2008 NDAA).

39. For example, Congress did not add a concurrence requirement to the authority for nonreciprocal exchanges of defense personnel between the United States and foreign countries. P.L. 112-81, Section 1081, FY 2012 NDAA.

40. In 2010, Congress let expire the controversial DoD Section 1207 Stabilization and Security Assistance $100 million transfer authority that supported small-conflict prevention and stabilization efforts, after establishing in 2009 a new USAID Complex Crises Fund (CCF) for similar purposes. (However, reflecting the problems of budgeting for civilian foreign assistance, the initial FY 2010–authorized CCF amount was $50 million, or half the authorized DoD transfer authority.) The original Section 1207 provision in the FY 2006 National Defense Authorization Act (P.L. 109-163) authorized DoD to transfer to the State Department up to $100 million in defense articles, services, training, or other support to use for reconstruction, stabilization, and security activities in FY 2006 and FY 2007. Subsequent legislation extended it through FY 2010. Congressional armed services committees had authorized the funding to carry out conflict prevention and response activities in the annual National Defense Authorization Act and appropriators had inserted the original funding provision into a defense appropriations measure when the George W. Bush administration's request for a civilian crisis response fund went nowhere in State Department legislation. Committee reports stated this authority was intended to be temporary.

41. The DoD Pakistan Counterinsurgency Fund (PCF) was stretched out an extra year, through FY 2011, with conferees on the FY 2010 supplemental appropriations legislation stating that they understood "the near term needs of the Pakistan Security Forces and the lack of capacity within the State Department warrant an exception to traditional lines of authority" (US House 2009c). Although this funding expired at the end of FY 2011, it was renewed for FY 2013 by Section 1228, National Defense Authorization Act for Fiscal Year 2013, P.L. 112-239, but was not renewed for FY 2014.

42. For instance, the new USAID Complex Crises Fund that replaced DoD Section 1207 stabilization and security assistance authority received no FY 2012 funds as Congress tightened the foreign operations budget.

43. This option is in line with State Department plans to emphasize the role of ambassadors in decision making and to provide the tools needed to make them more effective at their posts. See US Department of State 2010, 28–30.

Chapter 8

Who Tells America's Story Abroad?
State's Public Diplomacy or DoD's
Strategic Communication?

Brian E. Carlson

The media center in Fayetteville, N.C., would be the envy of any global communications company.

In state of the art studios, producers prepare the daily mix of music and news for the group's radio stations or spots for friendly television outlets. Writers putting out newspapers and magazines in Baghdad and Kabul converse via teleconferences. Mobile trailers with high-tech gear are parked outside, ready for the next crisis.

The center is not part of a news organization, but a military operation, and those writers and producers are soldiers. The 1,200-strong psychological operations unit based at Fort Bragg turns out what its officers call 'truthful messages' to support the United States government's objectives, though its commander acknowledges that those stories are one-sided and their American sponsorship is hidden.

—*New York Times,* December 11, 2005

Introduction

In December 2005, the *New York Times* launched a series of disclosures such as the one above about a Pentagon contractor in Iraq paying local newspapers to print "good news" articles written by American soldiers. The "Lincoln Group scandal" (named after the contractor) prompted an outcry in Washington. Members of Congress said the practice undermined American credibility, top military and White House officials denied any knowledge of the activity, and President George W. Bush was rumored to be "very troubled" by the matter (Gerth 2005).

But, this was no rogue operation. Nor was it unique.[1] In fact, the US military addresses foreign publics every day. They target not just foreign soldiers, but the general public in foreign countries. And, this happens not only in countries where the United States is engaged in combat; it also happens in independent countries that range from moderately hostile to friendly and allied.

More and more American communication with foreign publics has been funded by and directed by the military side of our government since 2001. Indeed, it is no longer news that the US military has joined the State Department and other government agencies in trying to counter anti-American sentiment and even wage "information operations" in certain parts of the globe.

This chapter describes the background and reasons for the migration of the Department of Defense into traditionally civilian-controlled public diplomacy areas, and the differences between State's view of public diplomacy and DoD's idea of strategic communication. It begins with the history of America's public diplomacy as well as the roots of our military's strategic communication effort. Then it clarifies different terms the military uses to discuss information operations. After providing this background, the chapter discusses how and why the military commitment to strategic communication has grown in recent years; compares the differences in the State Department's and Department of Defense's approaches and resources; and considers what America's international communication looks like from the field—where the foreigners see it. The chapter concludes with concise policy recommendations to rebalance American strategic communication.

The Rise (and Decline) of Public Diplomacy

First of all, where does the idea of public diplomacy come from?

Our Declaration of Independence indicates America has long believed that "a decent respect to the opinions of mankind requires" that we explain ourselves to the world around us. As democracy spread around the world in the nineteenth and twentieth centuries, national governments began more earnestly to communicate their arguments and their policy positions—not just to foreign kings and prime ministers (traditional diplomacy), but to the general public and especially national opinion leaders (public diplomacy) such as journalists, intellectuals, opposition politicians, and academics.

During the twentieth century, the US government repeatedly geared up its public diplomacy in times of war, and then withdrew from the conversation once the conflict ended. During World War I, for example, the United States established the Committee on Public Information (CPI). While the CPI was bent on encouraging patriotism among Americans with an upbeat picture of the US war effort, it also had nine foreign bureaus and conducted information and exchange programs aimed at foreign journalists and other opinion leaders (Jackall and Hirota 2000, 14). As soon as the war was over, the Committee on Public Information was abolished.

With the onset of World War II, Washington created the Office of War Information (OWI), amalgamating several government information services with a goal of shaping both domestic and foreign opinion. The OWI spent significant effort on posters, radio programs, and movies intended for the domestic audience, but it also included a Psychological Warfare Branch that employed radio as well as print products to demoralize enemy soldiers and to discourage enemy civilians. The OWI in 1942 founded the Voice of America (VOA) international radio broadcasts. The first broadcast included the pledge: "Today, and every day from now on, we will be with you from America to talk about the war . . . . The news may be good or bad for us—we will always tell you the truth."[2] The OWI also had storied success in enlisting Hollywood producers and directors to help "win the war." But again, as soon as the war ended, the OWI was abolished. Its foreign functions were transferred to the Department of State in September 1945.

Before long Washington perceived a need to reengage. In 1953, stung by the Korean conflict and the emerging struggle against international communism in Latin America, Asia, and Central Europe, President Dwight D. Eisenhower signed the US Information Agency (USIA) into law. The agency's mission was "to understand, inform and influence foreign publics in promotion of the national interest, and to broaden the dialogue between Americans and U.S. institutions, and their counterparts abroad."[3]

Throughout the Cold War USIA was buoyed by a continuing American national commitment to explain US actions, policies, and values in the face of competing ideologies. The logo on the USIA headquarters building at 1776 Pennsylvania Avenue said it: "Telling America's story to the world."

But, once again, after the East-West contest was resolved in America's favor by the 1989 fall of the Berlin Wall and the 1991 implosion of the Soviet Union, America again disengaged.

First, State Department and USIA budgets were sliced. Hiring and training of new diplomats were reduced below attrition, foreign national employees were let go, libraries, reading rooms, and consulates were closed. International civilian broadcasting was stripped from USIA and made independent of foreign policy with the creation of the Broadcasting Board of Governors in 1994.

Broadcasting

From World War II and throughout the Cold War years, broadcasting was a key component of America's public diplomacy. The Voice of America, much better known to the public than its USIA parent, delivered international news and commentary to audiences worldwide. Its goal was to deliver an interesting and attractive picture of American culture and values along with audience-attracting objective information about American and world current events.

Radio Free Europe (RFE), Radio Liberty (RL), and other "surrogate broadcasters" under the RFE/RL banner served as a free, objective press for countries whose own governments repressed or prevented independent journalism. Surrogate broadcasting enjoyed congressional support and eventually Radio Marti to Cuba, Radio Farda to Iran, and Radio Free Asia were added to the mix.

But amid the 1989 ruins of the Berlin Wall and the 1991 collapse of the Soviet Union, all the broadcasters, as well as USIA, struggled to define their mission and maintain domestic political support.

Some members of Congress believed that American international broadcasting, in order to have credibility with audiences, had to be independent of US foreign policy, "firewalled" from all federal agencies such as the Department of State. By 1999, all broadcasting activities were consolidated under the fully independent Broadcasting Board of Governors. That left American public diplomacy without *any* significant radio or television capability.

In October 1999, USIA was merged into the US Department of State, ending its existence as a small, efficient, single-purpose federal agency. By then, however, USIA was already only a shadow of its former self. Funding, employees, and programs were reduced throughout the 1990s such that the USIA that merged into State was one-third the size of the 1987 USIA in terms of budget and people.

These institutional changes and serial budget cuts help to explain why, after 2003, many perceived that America was "being out-communicated by a guy in a cave" (Morgan 2009, 40). The US government journalists were faithfully providing "objective news and information" on Voice of America, Radio Sawa, and RFE/RL. But nowhere did American public diplomacy have a radio or television capability to refute adversary allegations, to argue the case for American policy, or to offer an alternative to violent extremism's propaganda. American public diplomacy had neither its own broadcast equipment nor the skills and wherewithal to put its story on the airwaves and television screens in key parts of the globe.

With the civilian side so enfeebled, the US military began to develop its own capacity to deliver its message.

The Roots of Military Strategic Communication

So, with that explanation of the roots and decline of public diplomacy, how did the US military get involved in information operations and strategic communication? In particular, how did the military become engaged in information operations directed at foreign public audiences in noncombat areas?

First, let us recall that war has long been conducted for purposes and in ways that do not require actual battle. Military strategists from Sun Tzu to Clausewitz have argued that the ultimate military objective may well be something not found on the battlefield itself.

US military doctrine long recognized both the requirement to inform (public affairs) and the need to influence (information operations, etc.); these two requirements are generally kept separate. In practice, a shorthand develops that public affairs is for the American and allied press and public, while Information Operations (IO) and especially psychological operations (PSYOP) are aimed at adversary forces and publics.

Information Operations deliver selected information to foreign audiences to influence their emotions, motives, objective reasoning, and ultimately the behavior of foreign governments, organizations, groups, and individuals.[4] In the past, the "foreign audiences" were generally conceived to be enemy soldiers. Over time, especially in the twentieth century, the definition broadened to include the civilian population that surrounds, supplies, and supports the enemy combatant.

For the sake of clarity, we need to talk a little about the military's definitions for various information operations.

Psychological Operations

Without delving into a history of psychological operations, there has long been a role for the military in addressing foreign publics. Officially, the purpose of military psychological operations has been to induce or reinforce behavior favorable to US objectives. These operations are an important part of the range of diplomatic, informational, military, and economic activities available to the United States. They can be utilized during both peacetime and conflict.

In practice, psychological operations, now called Military Information Support Operations (MISO), are the delivery of messages via visual, audio, or printed media. The MISO plan could use leaflets, billboards, telephone calls, radio broadcasts, television advertisements or programs, or even loudspeakers. The principal MISO units are the Army's 4th Military Information Support Operations Group and the Air Force's Commando Solo units. MISO tend to be carried out by teams of two to eight people, led by a senior noncommissioned officer or a junior commissioned officer.

Information Operations

Psychological operations are, according to US military doctrine, one component of something larger called information operations (IO). According to the Joint Chiefs of Staff, IO comprises five distinct activities: (1) electronic warfare; (2) computer network operations, including computer network attacks; (3) psychological operations, now renamed military information support operations; (4) military deception; and (5) operational security (US Department of Defense 2010b, 135–36).

In the Pentagon, IO is broadly defined as efforts seeking "to influence, disrupt, corrupt, or usurp adversarial human and automated decision making while protecting [one's] own."[5] In general, information operations tend to be wider in scope than psyops and are most often led or directed by colonels and US Navy captains.

Strategic Communication

And then there is one more, even broader category called strategic communication. (Note: no "s" on the end of "communication.") Strategic communication is the overarching concept, the umbrella that brings together all the military's efforts to communicate with foreign audiences and links them to broad military and national goals. We frequently say that strategic communication is the effort to ensure that America's actions and America's words align with each other and coincide to support our policies and our goals. Strategic communication is generally led by field-grade officers.

When senior military officers and civilians at the Department of Defense talk about "strategic communication," they have in mind the same thing that senior diplomats and political appointees at the State Department talk about under the heading of "public diplomacy." For example, from a Pentagon explanation of strategic communication:

> Focused USG processes and efforts to *understand* and *engage* key audiences to create, strengthen or preserve conditions favorable to *advance national interests* and objectives through the use of coordinated information, themes, plans, programs and actions synchronized with other

elements of national power (US Department of Defense 2005b, emphasis added).

Compare that with a State Department definition of public diplomacy:

Public Diplomacy seeks to *promote the national interest* of the United States through *understanding*, informing and *influencing* foreign audiences [emphasis added].[6]

Both are working to achieve national interests by understanding and engaging as well as influencing foreign audiences.

New Ways to Defeat an Adversary

Generals and admirals, along with their civilian counterparts, concluded that they must employ strategic communication along with traditional military capabilities to win in the post-9/11 environment.

This environment is one of counterinsurgency tactics and small wars. It features un-uniformed enemies who neither defend home territory nor hold life dear. US forces confront adversaries who derive strength, sustenance, and support from civilian populations. Sometimes those populations live in lands far from the traditional battlefield. It is the age of instant, global communication.

Tactics must change. And they have.

The American military is a learning organization. And in the years after September 11, 2001, fueled by a clear and well-funded mandate to defeat terrorism, the US military began to learn a new way to fight. Among the many thought leaders, Gen. David Petraeus is often credited with a new counterinsurgency doctrine that emphasized winning the "hearts and minds" of the civilian population (US Army 2007).[7]

In addition to counterinsurgency tactics, other factors encouraged military thinkers to embrace strategic communication. One is the long-recognized need to prepare the battle space. Since the days of cannon "softening up" the enemy before an attack, West Point wisdom held that a commander does all he can to prepare the battlefield to his advantage before actual conflict. Military thinkers understood the need to prepare the battle space, that is, to understand the topography, the threats and advantages within it, and the ways one might overcome or make use of them.

Commanders began to talk of "information preparation of the battle space." That is, employing all the available tools—political (including diplomatic), informational (including appeals to religious, ethnic, or ideological beliefs), psychological, educational, and economic means—to prepare for military action to defeat the insurgency. Indeed, some commanders argued that if you could prepare the "information battle space" well enough, you might never need to use deadly force, or at least much less of it.

Other factors favoring more strategic communication included the international law of war and the Geneva treaties. Both call on commanders to use the *minimal* amount of force and to cause the least possible destruction necessary to accomplish a military objective. More important may have been the increasing public concern and strategic implications of collateral civilian casualties. Force protection issues only added to the justification for employing information and other nonkinetic means of achieving tactical goals.

Strategic Communication and Public Diplomacy

The 2006 Quadrennial Defense Review declared that "victory in the long war ultimately depends on strategic communication by the United States and its international partners" (US Department of Defense 2006, 91). The Defense Science Board reported in 2008 that strategic communication and public diplomacy "coordinated and executed in association with all aspects of national capacity, can help to prevent and limit conflicts, and greatly enhance responses to global challenges that threaten America's interests and values" (Defense Science Board 2008, ix). The 2009 NATO Summit concluded that strategic communication must be an integral part of both political and military objectives. The 2010 QDR reaffirms that "strategic communication is essential in COIN [counterinsurgency], CT [counterterrorism], and stability operations, where population and stakeholder beliefs and perceptions are crucial to our success, and where adversaries often enjoy the advantage of greater local knowledge and calibrate their activities to achieve sophisticated information objectives" (US Department of Defense 2010a, 25).

The Pentagon defined and redefined strategic communication over the last decade. The State Department vows that public diplomacy is important.

For both State and DoD, strategic communication and public diplomacy are today disciplines that bridge the civilian and military domains. They are intricately enmeshed with political, economic, and military operations. Communication with foreign audiences requires careful planning and forethought; it needs to synchronize with our strategy and national goals; it must reflect our values; and it needs to be pervasive among the leadership. Nevertheless, the State Department and the military approach the task differently.

Public Diplomacy's Three Missions

Public diplomacy has three fundamental missions: present American values, advocate US policy, and shape the host nation environment in our favor.

First, one of the fundamental goals of public diplomacy, certainly since the time of J. William Fulbright[8] and before, has been the presentation and explanation of American ideas and values, the things that make America different as a nation. Some might say the mandate to explain America first appears in the Declaration of Independence when it says, "a decent respect to the opinions of mankind requires" that Americans explain ourselves and the causes that drive us to action.

In today's world, this mission authorizes the exchange programs that bring foreigners here for academic study and professional training, the arts and other exhibits we send abroad, the American centers and libraries in major cities, and support to English language training and American studies in foreign universities.

Second is the fundamental responsibility of public diplomacy to advocate for US policy. In this respect the public diplomacy officers in US embassies abroad are simply counterparts to the political and economic officers—and all are working off the same agenda. While the political counselor is down at the foreign ministry presenting a demarche in support of some US position (be it a draft trade treaty, a sanctions resolution in the United Nations, or a human rights complaint), the public diplomacy officer is making the same case—perhaps in different words—to journalists, academics, union leaders, religious figures, or whoever might help shape the host nation's public opinion.

The third mission is much less visible, but often more important and more effective: shaping the host nation's environment in order to benefit American interests and objectives. This is usually done with a long-term view, and often by drawing on resources from other agencies. In this category might fall a lot of activities such as countering human trafficking, fighting corruption, promoting respect for human rights, anti-money laundering campaigns, countering drug smuggling, etc.

Let me offer an example from my own experience in postcommunist Latvia a few years ago. The issue was corruption. In many ways the corruption in Latvia was a holdover from the Soviet days. People in political and government positions could and did influence government decisions in ways that benefited themselves or their friends—contracts, zoning, tax exemptions, etc.

Now, in 2005 anticorruption was not a specific American value or idea (like democracy or free markets) that the United States wanted to present and explain. Nor was anticorruption a short-term policy issue on which Washington wanted the embassy to advocate and lobby for a government decision.

But clearly corruption was a problem that could affect negatively an ally of the United States, a fellow NATO member, a nation with which we needed to share intelligence, a country that hosts numerous banks and financial organizations linked inextricably with America's banks, corporations, and financial institutions. So the embassy in Riga spent not only State Department money but also Treasury and Justice dollars to conduct judicial training seminars, translate and distribute publications, send key officials on exchange visits to the United States, support nongovernmental organizations like Transparency International, train investigative journalists, and so on.

The anticorruption programs, whether managed by public diplomacy officers or economic officers, were done to cause changes in the host nation. While it was not a specific objective in US policy terms, we believed that those changes would make Latvia a better partner for the United States. So, those are the three core missions given to public diplomacy officers. They are expected to plan and carry out public diplomacy programs:

- Present and explain American culture, history, and ideas;
- Advocate and lobby for US policies and objectives; and
- Shape the host-nation environment to the benefit of US interests.

The Military's Two Missions

Now let us turn to the military side of the modern international communication environment. What does military strategic communication, including information operations and psychological operations, intend to do?

First, information operations, including the subset MISO, have the principal mission of supporting the combatant commander by achieving tactical information goals and countering adversary propaganda. In the first instance, these activities will be aimed at the adversary's soldiers. But they might also be designed to affect the knowledge, perceptions, and actions of the population in the area where the adversary lives and fights.

It is important to appreciate this organic link between information operations carried out by US forces and the commander's core mission. You will not find an approved MISO or other information operation that does not support the commander's mission.

After the attacks on 9/11, the paramount mission of US military units was framed as the Global War on Terror (GWOT). Every military information activity or psyops engagement was designed and approved to contribute to winning the war on terror. Thus, even something apparently so benign as, say, a voter education drive in a sub-Saharan African country, was eventually linked to the war on terror. The links may have gone through a long and tenuous logic chain that involved strengthening host-nation democratic institutions as a means of discouraging the kind of social, economic, and political conditions that lead to social disengagement and the eventual recruitment as foreign fighters, but they would be there in the planning documents.

In practical terms, information operations can range from leaflet drops and business cards telling enemy combatants how to surrender or how to tip off authorities about suspected terrorists, to television advertisements, billboards, and even radio dramas designed to weaken adversary resolve, discourage recruitment, counter enemy propaganda, or suggest alternative ways to achieve political, economic and cultural goals.

The second mission of military strategic communication is not unlike that of public diplomacy: shaping the environment in ways that will make it easier to accomplish American goals. This is where the military concentrates on aligning actions and words, ensuring that what we do is synchronized with what we say we are doing, and with our long-term objectives. Sometimes under a rubric of "building partnership capacity," the targets of this effort are the leaders of partner nations and the general public as well as foreign military personnel and the media. The military objective is visibility, whereas the USAID objective is viability first and foremost (as discussed by Anderson and Veillette, Chapter 6). Whether it is civil and humanitarian affairs teams digging wells, or medical and veterinarian units carrying out vaccination and medical exercises for the benefit of host-nation civilians, or a MISO team funding a women's political rights forum in Yemen, or a voter education caravan in Mali, or establishing a community radio program, the military's shaping activities are intended to leave a better situation than we faced before they began.

As former chairman of the Joint Chiefs of Staff, Adm. Mike Mullen, said, in the fight against violent extremism, "we cannot kill our way to victory." Instead, in places like Afghanistan, we need "better governance, more foreign investment, a viable alternative to the poppy farming, greater cooperation with Pakistan, and more non-military assistance." In other words, Mullen was saying that we need to reshape the environment in Afghanistan.[9]

Let me note that this "environment shaping" is not a concept invented in the Pentagon in the last ten years, either. I remember clearly my boss at the State Department in 1999, ambassador and assistant secretary for Europe, Marc Grossman, telling audiences that the Foreign Service had changed even then, that American diplomacy had changed during his career. "When I joined the State Department," he said, "diplomats were sent abroad to observe and report home. Today, when we send American diplomats abroad, we expect them not simply to report what they see, but to change the outcome in America's favor."

There is, however, an entirely unintended, but perhaps inevitable and unpleasant, consequence to the Defense Department's increasing engagement in military strategic communication, including information operations and psychological operations. The fact is that when the military is the messenger,

American international engagement wears a military uniform. Hard as it is for many Americans to realize, people in other countries often may not regard the military—ours or theirs—as bearers of good tidings, providers of peace, or sources of security and stability. If the United States uses its military to do diplomacy, deliver humanitarian assistance, implement economic development projects, vaccinate the herds, and provide medical treatment to the children, what does that say about the role of the military in any given society? Should the people of Egypt or Afghanistan expect their military to carry out governmental functions too? What conclusions should foreign military officers draw from what they observe?

Differences between State and Defense

While you can trace a long history of US military efforts to communicate with foreign civilian audiences, we really began to notice an increase in military activity around 2004. That was the year when Gen. David Petraeus and the 101st Airborne began to employ classic counterinsurgency methods to build security and stability in Mosul, Iraq. The US military not only engaged in traditional combat operations, but also put priority on nontraditional military tasks: they jump-started the economy, built up local security forces, staged elections for the city council, initiated a program of public works, and launched reconstruction projects. Commanders like Petraeus approached nation building as a central contribution to the military mission. As the *New York Times* observed, the US military was "prepared to *act* while the civilian authority in Baghdad was still getting organized" (Gordon 2003).

And, as the fighting worsened in 2005 and 2006, with traveling suicide bombers and foreign fighters showing up in Iraq and Afghanistan, military commanders began to ask: Where were they coming from? Why wasn't someone doing something about it?

To summarize a lot of conversations, emails, meetings, and conferences, the US military realized that, more than a messaging problem in Iraq or Afghanistan, the United States faced a communication problem around the world. When DoD asked, "Who was doing the counterpropaganda against al-Qaeda, who was addressing Muslim and other disaffected youth around the world, who was offering an alternative vision, who was countering violent extremism?," the answer was unsatisfactory. Many in the Pentagon and elsewhere in the US government concluded that State and other civilian agencies did not take the Global War on Terror seriously enough or lacked the capacity to act. How else to explain the absence of anyone pushing back against terrorist propaganda?

In thinking about the differences between State and Defense approaches to understanding, informing, and influencing foreign audiences, one is tempted to resort to the old "Mars and Venus" analogy (Rife 1998). While there is truth in that analogy, it is more complex than that.

Let us examine some of the key ways they differ: time frames, plans, funds, scope, and authority.

A Matter of Time

First, the military and the diplomats think in different time frames. For the military officer, every challenge is a mission. Missions are meant to be accomplished. Complex missions, such as the war on terrorism, simply must be broken down into discrete and possible tasks. Military personnel are assigned to a command or a ship for eighteen months to two years. They need and want to accomplish tasks within that time. They expect to deploy, fight, and return home. The work of warfighters has generally been thought of as something you get done in a year or two. Until the Iraq and Afghanistan wars, four or five years constituted a long engagement for the US military.

The diplomat, by contrast, has a task with no clear end in sight. Foreign policy never finishes, and it is pretty rare that the secretary of state celebrates anything with a "mission accomplished" photo op. There are, of course, short-term goals such as getting the host nation to join us on a UN vote or to sign a treaty, but they rarely carry the impact or clarity of a surrender ceremony on the deck of a ship, such as the Japanese surrender in 1945. Indeed, most diplomatic success stories are tales of compromise and adaptation, where both we and the opponent have given up something, not clear and simple victory. To paraphrase Arnold Toynbee, foreign policy is just "one damn thing after another."

So when the military asked Washington about the communication plan for deterring the radicalization of youth in countries across North Africa and the Middle East, they did not get a very satisfying answer.

Plans versus Planning

Eisenhower said he did not have much use for plans, but "planning is indispensible." This might also be the difference between the Defense and State Department approaches.

For the military, plans are essential to success. It has long been clear that for any military operation to succeed in a foreign environment, you must ensure that trained troops are in place at the time they are needed, and that—at the right moment—they have all the guns, bullets, trucks, food, communications, air cover, and intelligence information necessary to carry out their mission. The plans take into account the many unchanging physical challenges of time, distance, and logistics as well as possible changes on the ground that may occur before the plan can be implemented. At least for large armies, this kind of precision logistics can be accomplished only through carefully drawn and followed plans. And because plans are so important to success, the military is continually updating and revising the plan until the moment of execution. It is not surprising to find that there is an entire, doctrine-driven career field—planners, or J-5—in the military personnel system.

There is no such job description at the State Department. You may find offices or jobs that have "plans" or "planning" in their title, but no one in the military would recognize what they produce as a real "plan." State, of course, has mission strategic plans (MSPs) for each embassy, and a bureau strategic plan for regional and functional bureaus, but they are long on verbosity and short on specific tasks or benchmarks.[10] They tend to be wish lists rather than a hard-nosed evaluation of how finite resources can be applied to rank-ordered priorities in order to decide on actions that lead to success within a specific time period. Indeed, if the State Department is dismissive of plans, diplomats have even less enthusiasm for measurement and performance evaluation.

There is a good reason for the diplomat's disdain for planning and evaluation. Foreign affairs are an ever-changing calculus of multiple players' interests, objectives, means, and methods. As each actor in the foreign affairs game reacts to events, receives new information, reassesses capabilities, and counts again the loyalty and strength of allies, the other actors all change their own judgments and shift positions. Yes, countries have long-term national interests, and many even have medium-term goals. But how to achieve them, day to day or month to month, is a fluid, intuitive, three-dimensional chess game. It simply does not lend itself to adherence to written plans.

This clash of bureaucratic cultures was evident recently in a hotly contested, rather underdeveloped Middle Eastern country. The American objective was to dampen terrorist recruitment and stop al-Qaeda training activity in remote areas by, among other things, training and operating with friendly-but-unproven host national special forces troops. The US military commander kept coming back to the embassy with a twelve-month plan. His plan foresaw ever-increasing numbers of US military trainers and the steady delivery of more and more weapons and increasingly sophisticated equipment.

The general had it all laid out military style: twenty-five trainers would arrive in September, thirty-five more in October, another fifty in November, and so on. There would be planned deliveries of increasingly lethal, complex, and numerous weapons on a similar schedule. More and more host-nation personnel would be trained and equipped. It was a plan for an inexorable march toward success and mission accomplished.

The American ambassador pushed back hard. Increases in US troops on the ground and weapons and equipment deliveries needed to happen, the ambassador argued, but only when the host government was ready to take delivery and ready to make good use of them. The host government was not fully with us, and they might use some weapons against their own people. They needed a lot of education, not to mention arm-twisting. The attitudes of key host-nation leaders did not change in linear fashion, but rather ebbed and flowed like the tides. The situation on the ground would have to determine the delivery of more US assistance, not some plan cooked up in Tampa.

In the end, the ambassador's view won out, because it was right, and because the military will, in the end, accept the ambassador's authority (as discussed by Murray and Quainton, Chapter 9). But there were some heated and repeated discussions of the issue.

Funding

Any comparison of State funding for public diplomacy, and the military's expenditures on strategic communication activities, quickly turns to a comparison of apples and oranges—or perhaps grapes and watermelons. The two Departments do not count things the same ways. More importantly, while you can easily identify an appropriation for addressing foreign publics through public diplomacy at State, there is no such identifiable counterpart appropriation at Defense (Nakamura 2009, 26).[11]

This is because, at Defense, strategic communication and information operations are woven into the fabric of the military mission. Put simply, a commander in the field is given a mission to accomplish. It is up to that commander whether to purchase and expend more bullets or bombs, or instead to spend some funds on information operations or better audience research. After the fact, the military can sometimes add up the contracts signed and begin to approach a figure for Military Information Support Team (MIST) or other activities, but it never reflects even an approximation of the Defense Department effort.[12]

In addition, many programs and activities in the commander's toolbox are not counted as strategic communication, information operations, or even public affairs in the military accounts. The US military has many programs and ways to wine and dine, transport, entertain, and orient, educate, train, and equip foreigners. Not only foreign military officers but also civilian officials can be given scholarships, travel, and other opportunities. Military teams can build bridges and schools, dig wells, vaccinate cattle and pigs, and treat sick women and children. To give but one example from the field, there are routinely Military Information Support Teams dispatched to work with the public diplomacy office in our embassies in Africa. A public diplomacy operation in a country like Mali might have, in addition to salaries for staff and allocations of various support from Washington for exchange programs, a budget of perhaps $50,000 for discretionary activities—renting a hall for a seminar, hiring a translator, publishing a local newsletter, etc. When a MIST arrives in country, it brings with it a $1 million expense account. Even if this covers the four-person team's lodging and vehicle rental, you can see the way the military effort potentially outstrips the US civilian impact in that country.

On the other hand, the MIST does not go to a country unless the US ambassador asks for it. For a chief of mission, it can be tempting to request and get an infusion of resources, expertise, and funds to address a specific problem set. A couple of years ago, I witnessed an exceptional synchronization of effort between the Public Affairs Officer (PAO) in Yemen and a MIST. The embassy public diplomacy programs dealt with democratic values, religious tolerance, press freedom, trafficking in persons, human rights, and other issues. The MIST, working cheek-by-jowl in the PAO's offices, had enabled the embassy to identify, and quietly collaborate with, some new, indigenous nongovernmental organizations involved in women's political empowerment, governance, and volunteer organizations. In the Yemeni context, that was extraordinary.

Direct versus Indirect

A MIST is likely to get praise and support from State officers, precisely because it is willing to work hand-in-glove with State. Drawn from the Special Operations community, a MIST is trained and accustomed to working quietly and indirectly. It is used to allowing indigenous partners to be the interface with the public and to get the credit. The MIST stays in the background, adapting itself to the local environment, blending in, and listening carefully.

But some parts of the military are impatient with State's deliberate pace and relative passivity. They want more action, and more direct action. In 2006, with the Iraq insurgency at its peak, the military and many in Washington were demanding a global counterpropaganda strategy to reply to and rebut every al-Qaeda broadcast or video. The critics believed that America and its allies were losing the propaganda fight. Calmer heads eventually prevailed, but the military did go forward with a transregional Web initiative that sponsors internet news sites in local languages around the globe.[13] Other IO campaigns have sponsored television advertisements, magazines in local languages, television dramas, billboards, and community radio programs—all carrying an antiterrorism and prodemocratic values message. The State Department has not generally objected to these activities, and often assists with advice and counsel.

The sheer cost of producing television or radio programming, or even of producing and placing advertisements on commercial media in foreign countries, is today far beyond the State Department's public diplomacy budget. Other than individual embassy websites (usually featuring translations of the secretary's and the president's speeches and announcements of embassy activities), the State Department does not field websites aimed at foreign publics in their languages. Aside from a few successful embassy Facebook pages and Twitter accounts, public diplomacy officers do not even dream of such expensive outreach to the general public. The US military, by contrast, not only thinks it must be done, but has the wherewithal to do it.

State's public diplomacy brings a toolbox of proven activities that develop knowledge, understanding, sympathy, and even cooperation. It is a toolbox the military does not have and largely is not equipped to employ. The public diplomacy officer's (PDO) tools are forged in a deep understanding of the host nation's culture, language, and values. They range from information delivery to placing articles in newspapers, from a quiet word with an editor to an op-ed column in the newspaper, from professional seminars to book translation programs, from teacher exchanges to research grants, and from orientation travel to Fulbright scholarships. Public diplomacy tends to work through host-nation organizations and leaders. The good PDOs spend most of their time dissecting the host-country power structure, learning about who are the influential people, perceiving what motivates them, and deciding how to approach and persuade them. Public diplomacy tends to seek allies among the influential people and elites, and it builds coalitions of the like-minded.

Mission Scope: DoD's Massive Presence Distorts the US Profile

Another difference to be bridged in the field is the difference in "mission scope" between State and Defense operators.

Any US embassy has a fairly broad set of policy objectives and issues it needs to address. These are found in the Mission Strategic Plan (which may not be a great plan, but it does list the subjects the embassy intends to address). The issues vary from embassy to embassy, but they range across a broad spectrum. They reflect anything and everything the US government cares about, from political goals to economic, trade, and finance objectives, to human rights, protection and welfare of American citizens, environmental issues, fishing rights, religious freedoms, minerals and petroleum, and obtaining a fair shake for American business.

By contrast, since 2001, the principal mission of the Department of Defense and America's military has been the war on terror. It has been a big task, involving combat in Iraq and Afghanistan, the loss of many American lives, wounded warriors by the tens of thousands, and enormous amounts of American treasure. As the United States grew more sophisticated about terrorism, it began to appreciate the need to address countries around the world, whether as sources of recruits, safe havens for terrorists, funding sources, or sympathizers and supporters. And it is right and proper that DoD do its best to win that war.

But the fact is, when the size and weight of the military mission abroad is juxtaposed with our normal, civilian, foreign policy agenda, the American presence begins to look unbalanced to foreigners. Our national conversation with many countries became monochromatic: all about terrorism. Don't we care about those other subjects anymore? More than one foreign leader has commented, "You Americans don't seem to talk about anything *but* terrorism anymore."

An American ambassador in an African country pointed out to me that his PAO would normally have an annual budget of under $30,000 for all public diplomacy, outreach, staff travel, and other activities on all the mission's priorities. "What happens," he asked rhetorically, "when a four-person MIST team arrives with a million dollars to spend in 179 days?"

The fact is that with State's and the civilian agencies' scant resources spread across a wide array of both bilateral and multilateral issues, the arrival of the US military with deep pockets and a single-minded, laser-like focus on terrorism or political-security subjects can unbalance the relationship. The imbalance may even appear worse than it really is, simply because the steady flow of US visitors from DoD and the regional command, public events, signing of agreements, and donations of equipment grab the local media's attention far more than the dull, day-to-day grind of development work, political negotiations, and economic advocacy.

Let's face it, even where the military's agenda does not dominate American foreign policy, it often appears to do so.

Conclusion: Who Is in Charge?

Former defense secretary Robert M. Gates warned on July 15, 2008, against the risk of a "creeping militarization" of US foreign policy, saying the State Department should lead US engagement with other countries, with the military playing a supporting role. Echoing his generals, Gates said, "We cannot kill or capture our way to victory" in the long-term campaign against terrorism. He argued eloquently that military action should be subordinate to political, economic, and social-cultural efforts to undermine extremism (Gates 2008).

America indeed needs a robust public diplomacy and strategic communication effort. The Department of State is the only agency in Washington whose fundamental job is to understand and manage our relationships with the rest of the world. As Secretary Gates said, the State Department should lead US engagement with other countries. The military should play a supporting role. American public diplomacy should not wear combat boots.

But I am also a realist. We will not be able to shift the balance of federal resources from the Defense Department to the civilian side of the government in the near term, even if there were a national consensus to do so. The fiscal pendulum has been swinging toward the military side since the 1980s at least, and it will not be reversed in much less time.

For a long time in the future, therefore, America's engagement with foreign publics will be—like a New York skyscraper—the product of many skills, abilities, and inputs. Like a skyscraper, many different companies and labor unions will have a hand in the final structure, and they all need to do their best work. But like a skyscraper project, there must be a single architect.

The Bush administration made the correct decision in issuing a Presidential Decision Directive that designated a single individual—one of the six policymaking appointees at State, the under secretary for public diplomacy and public affairs—to lead all US government communication with foreign publics.[14]

Note: "lead" and not "direct." The White House, and for that matter the under secretary, understood that no one at the State Department can give orders to other Cabinet agencies. Each has its own mandate, its own congressional oversight committees, and its own stakeholders. But they all will follow a leader, especially one who is understood to be in sync with the president and the National Security Council.

In 2008, the Defense Science Board wrote, "Strategic communication requires sustained senior leadership . . . that focuses exclusively on global communication and directs all relevant aspects of national capacity. These leaders must have authority as well as responsibility—authorities to establish priorities, assign operational responsibilities, transfer funds, and concur in senior personnel appointments. Importantly, these senior leaders must have direct access to the President on critical communication issues when policies are formulated and implemented" (Defense Science Board 2008, viii).

No new legislation is needed, and no new position needs to be created. All that is required is for the president to nominate an under secretary of state for public diplomacy and public affairs with the requisite knowledge, ability, experience, and stature to lead the US government's efforts to understand, inform, and influence our allies, partners, and adversaries.

That is not easy to do, but it is not impossible. Recently, some sixty former US ambassadors and public diplomacy experts wrote a letter to Secretary of State John Kerry, calling on him to nominate a knowledgeable, experienced professional to lead this important function at the State Department.[15]

Whether it is a foundation, a corporation, an army, or the US government, strategic communication begins at the top. Our public diplomacy does not suffer from too much military involvement; it suffers from an insufficiency of leadership.

Notes

1. With regularity, journalists such as Walter Pineus at the *Washington Post*, Eric Schmidt at the *New York Times*, or freelancers working for *Rolling Stone* exposed cases of the American military's attempts to spin the message and shape foreign public opinion. See Rumbaugh and Leatherman (2012) for a listing of such news stories.

2. See Chris Kern's account of VOA's first broadcast at http://www.chriskern.net/essay /voaFirstBroadcast.html.

3. The mission statement is stated in USIA website archives, available through Electronic Research Collections, the Federal Depository Library at the Richard J. Daley Library, University of Illinois at Chicago. See "USIA Overview Brochure" at http://dosfan.lib.uic .edu/usia/index.html.

4. The Joint Chiefs of Staff "Information Operations," Joint Publication 3-13 (November 27, 2012) defines information operations as "the integrated employment, during military operations, of information-related capabilities in concert with other lines of operation to influence, disrupt, corrupt, or usurp the decision-making of adversaries and potential adversaries while protecting our own." See http://www.fas.org/isp/doddir/dod/jp3_13.pdf.

5. See, for example, "Air Force Basic Doctrine, Organization and Command," October 14, 2011, page 50, http://www.apc.maxwell.af.mil/l004/pubs/afdd1.pdf.

6. This definition is taken from The Planning Group for the Integration of the US Information Agency, June 20, 1997. It is a standard definition that still appears on the State Department website, http://www.state.gov/r/.

7. In his Field Manual for Counter Insurgency Operations, Gen. David Petraeus wrote in 2006 that "the side that learns faster and adapts more rapidly—the better learning organization—usually wins." As the manual points out, an insurgency is "an organized movement aimed at the overthrow of a constituted government through the use of subversion and armed conflict. Stated another way, an insurgency is an organized, protracted politico-military struggle designed to weaken the control and legitimacy of an established government" (US Army 2007). Counterinsurgency, therefore, is the collection of military, paramilitary, political, economic, psychological, and civic actions used to defeat an insurgency. Clearly, General Petraeus came a long way from the days of his predecessors who believed the task of a soldier was simply to defeat an opposing soldier.

8. Senator J. William Fulbright (1905–95) had profound influence on America's foreign policy, and his vision for mutual understanding as a component of American public diplomacy shaped the prestigious exchange program that bears his name.

9. Adm. Michael Mullen, in testimony before the House Armed Services Committee, September 10, 2008. See the report of the event, http://www.cnn.com/2008/POLITICS/09/10/mullen.afghanistan/.

10. See, for example, "FY 2007-2012 Department of State and USAID Strategic Plan" (US Department of State 2007).

11. For the State Department Public Diplomacy budget, see Nakamura, 2009, 26.

12. On June 22, 2011, Walter Pincus wrote in the *Washington Post* that "several years ago, when Congress first paid attention to this subject, it was called Strategic Communication and it was said to have been costing around $900 million" (Pincus 2011b).

13. The websites began with European Command (EUCOM), which established its South East European Times (SETimes.com) website in 1999, serving the Balkan region in nine local languages and English. EUCOM then set up a website for the Maghreb (now run by AFRICOM), called magharebia.com. Other commands became interested in the concept, and in April 2007, the Trans Regional Website Initiative (TRWI) was approved, to synchronize other geographic combatant commands' websites. This history is discussed in Rumbaugh and Leatherman (2012).

14. In April 2006, under the authority of NSPD 1, a new Policy Coordinating Committee for Public Diplomacy and Strategic Communication was established. It was chaired by the under secretary of state for public diplomacy and public affairs, Karen Hughes. It remained in existence until January 2009.

15. This letter was sent to Secretary of State John Kerry in May 2013. It is posted on the Public Diplomacy Council website, http://publicdiplomacycouncil.org/commentaries/06-01-13/more-ambassadors-and-fsos-call-public-diplomacy-professional.

Chapter 9

Combatant Commanders, Ambassadorial Authority, and the Conduct of Diplomacy

Shoon Murray and Anthony Quainton

Introduction

Ambassadors are the president's diplomatic representatives responsible for the holistic execution of US policy in their countries of assignment. The six geographic combatant commanders are four-star generals or admirals responsible for military operations and activities across a large region that includes dozens of countries.[1] This chapter investigates the relationship between these US officials and their subordinates working abroad—one side reporting to the State Department, the other to the Pentagon—in an era when the military is taking on noncombat tasks that were previously the responsibility of civilian agencies.

Some analysts have concluded that the combatant commanders have taken on roles that rival or even displace those of civilian diplomats (Priest 2003; Fettweis 2004; Reveron 2010 43–46; Marks 2010b). This is not a new observation. Award-winning *Washington Post* journalist Dana Priest (2003, 42) pointed to the 1990s as the era when "the military slowly, without public scrutiny or debate, came to surpass its civilian leaders in resources and influence around the world." Whatever imbalance Priest saw during the Clinton administration between the military and civilian presence abroad would only be exacerbated by the surge in money, training, special operations, and new roles taken on by the military post–9/11. As one former diplomat blogged, "The superstars of the U.S. official presence overseas are, let's face it, not the 190 or so ambassadors accredited to conduct bilateral relations, but the four-star geographic combatant commanders of EUCOM [European Command],

CENTCOM [Central Command], PACOM [Pacific Command], SOUTHCOM [Southern Command] and AFRICOM [African Command]" (Loftus 2007).[2]

The main question we focus on is whether ambassadors perceive their role as the principal interlocutor between the US government and a foreign government to have been diminished or usurped as a result of the active engagement of the geographic combatant commanders in developing personal relationships with individual countries' political and military leaders. To answer this question, we interviewed more than two dozen ambassadors, most recently retired; most of our interviewees could speak about experiences in two or three countries.[3]

Our findings were mixed. On the one hand, almost all of the ambassadors spoke favorably about their respective geographic combatant commanders, describing them as cooperative, not as competitive or displacing.[4] Ambassadors did sometimes experience problems lower down the chain of command. Several of our interviewees gave concrete examples of stopping some politically insensitive, ill-conceived, or heavy-handed military plans and activities. Yet, when faced with such disputes, top military officials usually displayed a respect for the authority and opinions of the ambassador. Notably, however, the favorable view held by ambassadors toward their respective geographic combatant commanders often did not extend to Special Operations Forces (SOF) from the Special Operations Command (SOCOM), which is a functional rather than a geographic command. Many of the ambassadors we spoke with were suspicious of SOCOM, perceiving SOF as more free-wheeling and less deferential to ambassadorial authority.

On the other hand, the stories told by ambassadors hinted at more subtle dynamics that arise from the disparity of resources given to the military compared to the State Department. Although the geographic combatant commanders respect the ambassador's authority over bilateral relations with a particular country, they still do engage in regional-level diplomacy, particularly with regard to military-to-military relations. The combatant commanders conceptualize an overall relationship with the region as a whole and this broader view is carried into their bilateral conversations with individual countries. They also have the authority, flexibility, and resources to act on that overview. Consequently, the combatant command priorities can influence the US relationship with a country, pushing it toward a security-oriented direction in ways not initiated by the ambassador or the embassy.

This chapter examines this complex relationship. In the first section, we discuss the growing diplomatic role of commanders in the post–Cold War era; the second points out some basic institutional features about ambassadorial authority. The third section examines whether the personal relationships established between regional combatant commanders and foreign leaders displaces the State Department's lead policy role (Fettweis 2004) or whether the establishment of a deep security relationship with a country inevitably creates a parallel structure alongside the US embassy, thereby diluting the leadership of the ambassador (Marks, Chapter 12). Our fourth section explores the different ways ambassadors perceive and manage the disparity in resources between the Department of Defense and the State Department. Our fifth section describes instances where ambassadors had disputes with military personnel at post and how those disputes were treated by top military officials. Our sixth section describes how several ambassadors and the State Department had to push back encroachments on chief of mission authority by the Special Operations Command in the aftermath of 9/11 and the continued suspicions among ambassadors about that command and its forces. We conclude with a few policy recommendations.

Commanders' Increased Political and Diplomatic Role

The US Department of Defense, as authorized by the president, divides the world into six geographic "areas of responsibility" (AORs) and assigns each to a combatant command (COCOM).[5] These unified commands are led by the four-star generals or admirals known as geographic combatant commanders. While not often household names, these commanders and their forces constitute a powerful presence abroad: they carry out military operations, organize military exercises, train foreign militaries, provide security equipment, conduct intelligence and information campaigns, and provide disaster relief and humanitarian assistance in their designated areas.[6] The combatant commanders oversee well-staffed headquarters, each with more than 1,000 personnel (Priest 2003, 74). They travel aboard their own aircraft, often accompanied by a large entourage, a privilege normally reserved for only the highest levels of the State Department (i.e., the secretary and deputy secretary of state).[7] They meet with military and civilian leaders of countries in their AORs and are able to offer them security and humanitarian assistance and training.[8] After traveling with the combatant commanders in the late 1990s, Priest (2000, A1) described them as "the modern-day equivalent of the Roman Empire's proconsuls—well-funded, semi-autonomous, unconventional centers of American foreign policy."

Commanders themselves acknowledge that their job is more than managing military operations and exercises; it is also diplomatic and political. For example, Gen. Joseph Ralston, who was the supreme allied commander Europe (SACEUR) and the combatant commander for the EUCOM from 2000 to 2003, estimated that "he spent about 70 percent of his time on political-military issues, despite having on-going combat operations in Bosnia,

Kosovo, and Macedonia. . . . Believing his greatest impact was with decision-makers throughout Europe, Ralston devoted up to 80 percent of his political-military time with various national ambassadors to NATO, heads of state, members of parliament, ministers of defense, and chiefs of defense" (Belote 2004, 3). Gen. Anthony Zinni, commander of CENTCOM from 1997 to 2000, reflected that "I was asked to carry out presidential and other diplomatic missions that would normally have fallen to diplomats" (Quoted in Reveron 2010, 43).

Starting in the 1990s, as a component of President Bill Clinton's engagement strategy, combatant commanders were "given the authority to take [their] regional strategies much farther than ever before" (Zinni and Koltz 2006, 195). In 1997, the White House released its National Security Strategy, which articulated an "essential" role for the military in "building coalitions and shaping the international environment" (White House 1997, 11). The combatant commanders were authorized to include activities to "shape the environment" in their Theater Engagement Plans (Priest 2003, 97; Zinni and Koltz 2006, 135). "This was very controversial," General Zinni wrote, "not in the least because it involved us in *more* than military activities and operations" (Zinni and Koltz 2006, 194).[9]

But it was after 9/11, in reaction to the insurgencies in Iraq and Afghanistan, that the military explicitly incorporated "noncombat" or "nontraditional" roles into military doctrine. In 2005, the Pentagon, in Defense Decision Directive 3000.05, officially stated that the mission of conflict prevention and stabilization was on par with warfighting. The commanders were allocated increased resources to assist countries in enhancing their security and stability, which meant more flexibility in distributing security assistance as well as development and humanitarian aid (see Adams and Murray, Chapter 1; Reveron, Chapter 4; Anderson and Veillette, Chapter 6; and Serafino, Chapter 7).

Take the example of Gen. Charles Wald, the deputy commander of EUCOM from 2002 to 2006, who was given responsibility to "mold" Africa at this time (most of Africa was included in EUCOM's AOR before AFRICOM was created).[10] He pursued many projects that "were not exactly military."[11] For example, EUCOM initiated a forum called the "Africa Clearing House" to coordinate US, European, NATO, and nongovernmental organization security and humanitarian assistance efforts. General Wald convened the US ambassadors from the region at conferences, acting as a "surrogate" for the State Department.[12] He invited the Northern African chiefs of defense to EUCOM headquarters in Stuttgart, Germany—"the first time they ever met each other"—and got them to cooperate on the chase and capture of a terrorist leader who was moving between their territories.[13] EUCOM held MEDFLAG exercises (bilateral military exercises focused on medical training) helping thousands of people "that had never seen a doctor"; it organized a regional website called *Magharebia*, an information operation to counter extremist Islamic propaganda; it built HIV/AIDS clinics and trained regional militaries on HIV/AIDS prevention and medical care.[14] One of Wald's personal favorites: EUCOM distributed thousands of pairs of spectacles with self-adjusting lenses; these glasses had a small American flag and the phrase "From the American people" engraved on the side. Wald loved to tell congressional delegations about how "the first thing this person ever saw clearly was a US flag or a US soldier."[15]

It is clear that the geographic combatant commands now engage in a wide variety of activities that were previously the exclusive purview of diplomats—both at the elite level and among foreign populations.

Some Basics about Ambassadorial Authority

In terms of formal authority, an ambassador is the president's personal representative, and, as such, the highest ranking US official residing in the country. When assigned a new post, an ambassador is issued a formal letter signed by the president, charging him or her to oversee all executive branch personnel on official duty in the country except those "under the command of a US area military commander." The ambassador, in other words, is the chief of mission who oversees a Country Team composed of all agencies represented at post. Ambassadors have authority to determine the size of each agency represented on the Country Team.[16] In addition the chief of mission has authority to grant country clearance: that is, the ambassador decides whether a US government employee can come into or stay in the country, including military personnel not directly deployed by the combatant commander. The presidential letter goes on to instruct ambassadors that they and "the area military commander must keep each other currently and fully informed and cooperate on all matters of mutual interest."[17]

Notwithstanding these authorities, an ambassador can be at a disadvantage vis-à-vis the combatant commander. An ambassador has a relatively small staff and few resources. Overall, more than 60 percent of embassy employees work for agencies other than State, and an ambassador has virtually no control over the budgets or resource allocation decisions made in Washington of other agencies with staff under his authority (Dorman 2005; Oakley and Casey 2007). Also, ambassadors, in practice, report to the regional assistant secretary in Washington, although in countries of high foreign policy priority they would also have access to the secretary of state and the deputy secretary of state, and in conflict countries such as Iraq or Afghanistan, to the president and the national security advisor. Last, ambassadors rarely have the same career seniority as the four-star combatant commanders.[18] By contrast, the geographic combatant commanders have the rank equivalent closer to the under secretaries of state, they have access to the secretary of defense and chairman of the Joint Chiefs of Staff, and they have substantial resources and regional responsibilities.

"Face-time" with Foreign Leaders

One piece of evidence used to support the thesis that combatant commanders have veered into (or taken over) the diplomatic lane traditionally driven by the State Department is the amount of time they spend in the field. For example, Christopher Fettweis writes: "The combatant commander has much more 'face time' [than the assistant secretaries at the Department of State] to develop personal relationships with local officials, and therefore often emerges as not only the head military actor *but also the lead U.S. diplomat in his AOR*" (Fettweis 2004, 62–63 emphasis added). Do the personal relationships established between geographic combatant commanders and foreign leaders overshadow American civilian leadership?

It is true that a geographic combatant commander spends more time with foreign leaders in a particular region than the assistant secretary, the counterpart at the State Department with the equivalent regional responsibility. Unlike the assistant secretaries, the military commanders have personal planes. Gen. Carter F. Ham, the commander of US Africa Command from 2011 to 2013, commented that one of his goals was to develop relationships with foreign leaders: "It's hard to develop relationships with Africans when you are sitting in Stuttgart (location of AFRICOM headquarters in Germany). I spend a lot of time in Africa. . . . It is one of the great benefits of coming from the United States. We are well supported by our people and our government and we have the tools to get around and meet people."[19]

But usually a combatant commander will have much less contact with any given foreign leader than the US ambassador. Each combatant commander has numerous countries within his AOR while the civilian representative on the ground, the ambassador, has just one.[20] With more than fifty countries in AFRICOM, General Ham, or any other combatant commander, is not likely to spend that much time with specific leaders in his AOR compared with individual ambassadors. Ambassador Barbara Bodine captures this difference, recalling her response when Gen. Tommy Franks, the combatant commander of US Central Command, shared his plan to heighten "engagement" in Yemen by coming every three months: "Tommy, I don't know how to tell you this, but 24 hours every 3 months is not engagement. Engagement is 24 hours a day, 7 days a week. You have to live here."[21]

Judging from our interviews, a combatant commander typically might visit two or three times during an ambassador's three-year assignment, if he came at all. In most cases he would meet with the minister of defense and high-ranking military officials, but he might also meet with the president or foreign minister. In all such cases that we reviewed, the ambassador would accompany him on these high-level civilian meetings.

True, in strategically important countries, the combatant commander might visit more frequently or start a separate track of discussions with a foreign leader through phone calls. General Zinni traveled to Saudi Arabia fifteen times during his three years as commander of CENTCOM (Priest 2003, 87). Zinni's successor, Gen. Tommy Franks, would occasionally talk on the phone with King Abdullah II of Jordan. As Edward Gnehm, US ambassador in Jordan (2001–04), recalled:

> The King of Jordan is a military man and loves his military. He has an affinity. That can be abused. There were a couple of times when [Gen. Tommy] Franks called the King directly. I asked him to inform me. His staff did so.[22]

As will be illustrated in a later example, Gnehm was not always able to control the agenda or outcome of interactions between the combatant commander and the King of Jordan. We found this direct interaction between the leader of a country and the commander to be the exception.

Ambassadors have the advantage of living in the country and the opportunity to develop deep personal relationships with its leaders. Donald Yamamoto, the US ambassador in Djibouti (2000–03), for example, describes his interaction with President Ismail Omar Guelleh after the United States negotiated the creation of a counterterrorism base in the country for the Combined Joint Task Force in the Horn of Africa (known as CJTF-HOA). "When President Guelleh sees a general, he sees the United States, and if this is a representative of the United States, he wants to deal with him," Yamamoto explains.

> Still, this commander comes and goes; I'm there all the time. And so we talk all the time. The relationship—once the military started coming— was such that I used to go to the president's private villa. We would talk in private about a lot of issues. It's a very personal relationship. But more important he told me what he wanted out of the United States. And so he—Guelleh—would tell the commander "What do you want? We can help you." Then to me he says: "This is what we want in return and I hope you can help us."[23]

As this example shows, the ambassador is likely to have a deeper personal relationship with the civilian leadership of the country, and to act as the liaison between the foreign leader and the US government, including the geo-graphic combatant commander. At the same time, the military relationship can be of great importance to the country's leadership, and shape the tenor of the diplomatic relationship: Yamamoto implies it was the larger strategic relationship which gave impetus for his frequent access to the President of Djibouti.

Significantly, not one of the ambassadors we spoke with felt marginalized or overshadowed by discussions between the combatant commander and the president or prime minister or king of the country where he or she served. Combatant commanders are often important players in US relations with a country; but their personal relationships with foreign leaders did not replace those made by the ambassador. Even so, in some countries, military and se-curity interests drive the relationship with the United States, which height-ens the importance of the combatant commands to the overall diplomatic relationship.

Senior Defense Official in a Strategically Important Country

Even if the four-star combatant commander himself is not a regular pres-ence in most countries, what about the senior defense official (SDO), who, like the ambassador, resides within a country and works with the military there? If there is a significant strategic relationship or a joint military op-eration, does this circumstance diminish the ambassador's ability to serve as the principal interlocutor between the US government and that foreign government?

The experience of Ross Wilson, ambassador to Turkey from 2005 to 2008, provides some insight into this dynamic. The US relationship with Turkey is shaped by Turkey's membership in NATO, and during these years, by Turkey's proximity to Iraq, where the United States was involved in a military conflict. The senior defense official in Turkey during this time was the chief of the Of-fice of Defense Cooperation (ODC), a position held by a two-star general. The ODC chief represents the EUCOM commander and the secretary of de-fense to the leadership in Turkey; he is the point of contact for that govern-ment with the US military.[24] While the ODC chief was an adviser to the US ambassador concerning military affairs, he also had, in Wilson's words, "di-rect reporting lines and sets of responsibilities to EUCOM." What made the relationship difficult, Wilson explained, was the "blurred lines of reporting authority . . . because of the way things come back to Washington."[25]

EUCOM had separate activities, missions, and plans that it pursued in Tur-key, and the challenge for the ambassador was to exercise his authority if a military plan interfered with larger US foreign policy goals. Wilson recalled an example from 2008 when "General [Bantz J.] Craddick [the supreme allied commander Europe and commander of EUCOM] . . . sent a message directing the ODC chief to make a request to the Turkish authorities for facilities to carry out a certain set of actions." The military command potentially wanted to use a Turkish base as a launching point for military activity against another country. The ODC chief told him about the request and Wilson immediately realized that it was "going to be a big deal for Turkey and if the Turks [said] 'no,' there [was] going to be a huge problem with EUCOM, and potentially with Washington." In light of the Turkish Parliament's refusal to allow the use of bases for the invasion of Iraq in 2003, Wilson worried that this request would have a negative impact on US-Turkish relations, and he wanted to double-check that Washington knew about it. So on the one hand, the ODC chief had "an order from a Supreme Allied Commander, a four-star, in his direct line of command," and on the other hand, the ambassador was telling him to wait until there was clearance from civilians in Washington. Wilson talked with the chairman of the Joint Chiefs of Staff and others, and eventually instructions came back that the White House did not know about this plan and did not support it. As this anecdote illustrates, the military commands can have a separate agenda that intersects with politics, and the ambassador has to deal with senior military officials who have a separate line of authority. The ambassador's responsibility is to monitor the activities of agencies operating within the country, including the military, with an eye to consistency with long-term US interests and the president's policy. Notably, the ODC chief cooperated with the ambassador, complying with his request to delay approaching the Turkish military, even though it put him at odds with his superiors in Stuttgart.

During this period, the US military began providing intelligence support to the Turkish military as it attacked the Kurdistan Workers' Party (PKK) in Northern Iraq. On these operational issues the ODC chief was in charge, and he informed the ambassador but not other embassy personnel about these operations. Wilson recalls:

> We worked it out because I respected what he had to do. And he respected my policy guidance. So it ended up working out adequately, but not always for my staff. My staff was not always briefed. And the ODC chief and his people felt quite strongly that the COM [chief of mission] authority did not mean subservience to the State Department personnel at post.[26]

Ambassador Wilson recounted a conflict when his political-military counselor asked the ODC chief for information and the ODC chief refused to give it. But from Wilson's perspective:

I knew what was going on. I had trust that he [the ODC chief] was telling me what was going on. We were talking . . . every day. This was a very hot period. . . . So how that COM authority relates to a section chief [from the embassy] that tries to throw the ambassador's weight around—it doesn't work. You are guaranteed to have problems. I finally told this guy [his political-military counselor] "Don't worry about it. I got it."[27]

These stories illustrate the challenges of working with military officials within a country who represent the agenda of the combatant command and who take charge when a joint military or intelligence operation is at play. Ambassador Edward Marks (Chapter 12) describes the combatant commands as a "separate 'foreign affairs' organization, which interacts directly with foreign governments at the highest levels in parallel with the Department of State and its embassy structure." The examples described here would qualify that description. The ODC chief in Turkey did represent EUCOM and the secretary of defense to the government of Turkey; but he was also a key adviser to the ambassador. The ODC chief did work with the embassy; on several occasions he delayed acting upon a request by the combatant commander or reporting information to EUCOM in order to allow the ambassador time to find out more information or coordinate with Washington. Only when military operations were at play did the ODC chief take leadership.

The Disparity of Resources between DoD and State

While the ambassador has political authority within a country, the military commanders have more money, more manpower, and more equipment at their disposal. This gap is not a recent occurrence—the ratio of funding to the DoD versus the international affairs budget is historically about 12 to 1; but the Global War on Terror exacerbated the situation as Congress allocated more flexible contingency funds to Combatant Commands. As the military began to take on more noncombat missions with the purpose of "shaping the environment" to prevent Islamic extremism, embassies around the world saw increased DoD resources for security assistance, special operations, development projects, and public diplomacy. The question is: Does the disparity in resources between DoD and State affect the ambassador's ability to manage the diplomatic priorities of the United States?

We found a variety of patterns describing how ambassadors manage DoD resources: 1) well-planned collaboration with the combatant commander; 2) ad hoc channeling of available military resources; 3) the ambassador reacting to an agenda set by the COCOM; and 4) embassies being overwhelmed by military personnel and projects or not offering proper supervision and control.

Collaboration

Ambassadors sometimes collaborate with combatant commanders to initiate important projects that they wanted to do in any case.

Barbara Bodine recalled her partnership with CENTCOM commander Anthony Zinni: "Tony Zinni and I had a great relationship . . . . [H]e really wanted to do something with Yemen and he was a strategic thinker . . . . And so he was a great ally . . . . And we were able to come up with some really interesting, good programs. Probably the most notable was the establishment of the Yemeni Coast Guard."[28] The ambassador and the commander both saw that the unmonitored, porous coastline of Yemen represented a security problem that affected the United States. They worked together to create a Yemeni coast guard from scratch. Zinni started by putting Yemen on a list to receive "excess defense articles" from the US Coast Guard, such as patrol boats, and adding Yemenis to various training programs (Zinni and Koltz 2006, 168).

Donald Yamamoto recalls working with the COCOM to bring military-sponsored developmental assistance to Djibouti. As discussed above, the United States negotiated the CJTF-HOA base in 2002 at Camp Lemonnier. President Guelleh wanted assistance (as well as about $30 million in rent annually) in return for permitting the base to be stationed in Djibouti. One day, President Guelleh called Ambassador Yamamoto into his office, and while holding a Koran, asked him whether the Americans could "help us with schools and clinics, help us help my people."[29] Yamamoto and Guelleh then talked to Gen. Tommy Franks (commander of CENTCOM) and Gen. John Abizaid (deputy commander of CENTCOM), and "they all got it." Soon Marines were "helping to paint schools." The military also sponsored medical civil action programs (MEDCAPs) and sent water-drilling teams to villages (*Somaliland Times* 2003; Fitzgerald 2003). "It was great," Yamamoto observed. "And where was USAID? AID was nowhere to be seen. It was the U.S. military, and it was very positive. They were helping with the Three D's [diplomacy, development, and defense]."[30]

The ambassadors in these two cases collaborated with combatant commanders to initiate major projects that utilized the military's resources or capabilities.

Ad Hoc Channeling of Resources

When asked directly about the imbalance in resources, a common response among our State interviewees was resignation. As one senior Foreign Service

official put it: Given that "State can't make the case" in Congress for more resources, it is important to "do what we can through resources given to DoD."[31]
(This is a version of the "imbalance is inevitable and irreversible, so if you
can't beat 'em, join 'em" perspective discussed by Adams in Chapter 13). The
effect of going through DoD has implications, however; security issues inevitably become a larger part of the overall relationship.

Ambassadors were often appreciative of military programs, especially at
posts where resources were scarce. Rust Deming recalls that when posted as
ambassador in Tunisia starting in 2001:

> [T]he military played a very useful role. We had no aid. USAID had
> gone. Peace Corps had gone. We had very few tools. And the military
> at EUCOM had these small programs—$5, $10, $20 million kinds
> of things . . . we welcomed that, them coming down. . . . [W]hen we
> needed some money, some $5 million of a slush fund to fix up a school
> or something, they'd have teams come down to do small group exer-
> cises with the Tunisians and that was a useful link with the Tunisian
> military.[32]

Mary Yates mused that "[a]nytime anybody had a spigot of money, when I was
an ambassador at my two posts [Burundi 1999–2002 and Ghana 2002–05], I
figured out a way to turn it on and use it to sort of advance the goals that we
had. And the military were great about that."[33]

Ambassadors described a situation where the military had more people
and immediately available money than anyone else in the mission, and they
were energetic: new projects would suddenly emerge, externally generated
from outside the Country Team. The challenge for the ambassador is, first, to
identify what is happening, and, second, to integrate these projects with other
mission objectives. This is particularly critical in the development area, where
short-term humanitarian or development projects may be undertaken by the
military that run counter to or do not fully support the development priorities
of USAID. Linda Jewell, ambassador to the Republic of Ecuador (2005–08),
described this dynamic:

> [I]t was really tricky because it [the DoD-sponsored project] wasn't
> necessarily a bad idea, but it was like, "Oh man, if I had this kind of
> money this is not what I would be doing with it" . . . . So I didn't want
> to be the "no, no, no" ambassador who didn't want to do any of these
> things because some of them, if you could nudge them in the right direc-
> tion, they were helpful; but [it] took some doing and it didn't start from
> anything that the Country Team said "you know we really need to be
> doing X." . . . So you were taking these resources that didn't quite fit into

your round hole and smoothing off the edges to the point you [could] squeeze them in and make them fit.[34]

The ambassador maintains the authority to stop ill-conceived plans if she chooses to exercise it; but the availability of these resources also channels the embassy's efforts in certain directions.

Military Agenda-Setting

Now, what if the military-initiated project was something large scale, say, a $99 million Special Operations Training Center to be funded out of a DoD supplemental budget request? This was the situation that Ambassador Edward Gnehm faced in 2003 when Jordanian King Abdullah II began talking with CENTCOM about such a project. The ambassador was initially wary of the idea: building one of the world's largest training centers to simulate urban warfare and train troops in counterinsurgency techniques would necessarily put a spotlight on the US-Jordanian military collaboration. The ambassador was "sensitive to the fact that the Jordanian public was not nearly as happy with the military-to-military relationship as the leadership."[35] The proposed US-funded project did not emerge out of planning through the embassy; it was initiated by CENTCOM and the project was "moving forward rapidly without any sort of policy look at (whether) this was the right thing to do."[36] The political dynamics were such that it was difficult to stop: Jordanian King Abdullah II wanted the counterterrorism center and CENTCOM "salivated over anything it could do to build the relationship with the military in the region."[37] In the end, Gnehm supported the project.[38]

Perhaps facing a similar situation, one ambassador complained to Richard Lugar's Senate staff team sent to interview embassy personnel in 2006 that "his effectiveness in representing the United States to foreign officials was beginning to wane, as more resources are directed to special operations forces and intelligence." The ambassador felt that "foreign officials are 'following the money' in terms of determining which relationships to emphasize" (US Senate 2006b, 12).[39]

Overwhelmed

In some African countries, the influx of military resources and manpower after 9/11, often on temporary duty (TDY) assignments, overwhelmed the embassy staff. The embassy at Addis Ababa in Ethiopia, for example, received military personnel working on civil affairs programs, public diplomacy, AFRICOM units, and at "least four other US command elements." A 2010 inspector general's report warned that "this array of military elements risks swamping an embassy if not carefully controlled" (US Department of State and the Broadcasting Board of Governors 2010, 18). In a few cases, ambassadors had to deny country clearance for military personnel to slow down the inundation.[40]

Sometimes ambassadors did not exercise appropriate control over the military personnel or projects being funded through the Combatant Command. Sen. Richard Lugar's staff members reported in 2006 that:

> In three embassies visited . . . ambassadors appeared overwhelmed by the growing presence of military personnel and insistent requests from combatant commanders. Neither were the ambassadors as knowledgeable on the breadth of military activity in country as they should have been. In one case, an ambassador to a country that is receiving Section 1206 funding had not heard of the program. *In several cases, embassy staff saw their role as limited to a review of choices already made by the "military side of the house"* (US Senate 2006b, 10, emphasis added).[41]

One ambassador we interviewed complained about not being able to control DoD program resources.[42] In this case, there was a US military installation located in a country that had been part of the former Soviet Union; the population was still suspicious of the United States. The colonel who commanded the base had a directive from DoD to "win hearts and minds" by engaging in humanitarian and development activities. As discussed by Anderson and Veillette (Chapter 6) and Carlson (Chapter 8), the military tends to emphasize the "visibility" of humanitarian projects as part of an "information operation"; but this tactic can backfire in a situation where feelings toward the US military are entrenched and negative. In this case, the ambassador reasoned that it made more sense for US military personnel to keep a low profile: military-sponsored good works just attracted attention to their controversial presence in the country. The ambassador was kept informed about the projects through Country Team meetings but felt unable to stop them without going up the line of command, an act that would have poisoned the relationship with the colonel. So the ambassador acquiesced in these ineffective and ill-advised projects.

Often ambassadors are grateful for the availability of resources for projects at their post that come through DoD. But a subtle shift in priorities may be taking place as ambassadors choose to support military-initiated projects or as the geographic combatant commanders bring additional security assistance. The point is not that these projects are damaging, or that the ambassador's authority is being usurped. Ambassadors can usually stop a project if they feel strongly about it. But if the list of discretionary programs that they have to pick from comes disproportionately from DoD's menu, military concerns are likely to flavor the relationship between the United States and the target country. If comparable contingency funds were allocated to ambassadors, the projects pursued would be designed differently. In an era where the US military is the source of billions of dollars in security and development assistance and is engaged in more than a hundred countries, the line between military-to-military relations and broader foreign policy influence can potentially become blurred.[43]

When an Ambassador Says "No"

Who has power is revealed by who wins in a dispute. If an ambassador disagrees with an initiative planned by a Combatant Command, can he or she stop it? Are the ambassador's concerns listened to? What happens when an ambassador says "No"?

A few of the ambassadors that we interviewed did object to actions that were being planned by the military. For example, Ambassador Vicki Huddleston recalled difficult disputes that she had with Gen. Charles Wald, a four-star Air Force general and deputy commander of EUCOM, about the potential use of kinetic strikes against suspected terrorists in Mali.[44] Wald believed, somewhat presciently, that armed Islamists "are going to look for a place where they can do the same thing they did in Afghanistan, Iraq or other places. They have a need to train, equip, organize, recruit . . . they are moving toward Africa" (Tremlett 2004). When EUCOM observed a training camp in Northern Mali in 2003, General Wald began making plans about how to disrupt it. Huddleston recalls that "we had this news from General Wald, a cable or telephone call, saying that they wanted to do a kinetic strike, a TLAM [Tomahawk Land Attack Missile] or some kind of ordnance, not an attack with personnel involved, against what he saw on a video from probably a P3 [Orion reconnaissance aircraft] showing one of the leaders, Mokhtar Belmokhtar, with a bunch of Arabs who he assumed were terrorists."[45] The ambassador disagreed with the proposal for an air strike:

> First of all . . . [y]ou see some people who look like Arabs out in the desert being trained—but you don't know who they are. And secondly . . . the means [are] . . . so imprecise. When you send ordnance from great distance—Who is going to be there when it lands? . . . So we sent them back with an answer that there was no way we are doing this.[46]

In short, the ambassador says she blocked the airstrike because of concerns about incomplete intelligence, targeting precision, and also the potential backlash such an attack would unleash. Huddleston recalls a "big fight" with General Wald that included him sending two other generals to Mali to brief the Country Team, after which the embassy still said "no." Other officials also recall that "military commanders planned to launch airstrikes against Belmokhtar" (Whitlock 2013a).

General Wald remembers the incident differently: He says that Huddleston "got wind" of an "options paper," one that had four scenarios listed, beginning with doing nothing and moving "all the way to kinetics"—the most extreme being deploying B-52s as had been done in Libya in 1986. But, he says, "we were never going to do that."[47]

In any case, the option of launching an air strike against the training camp run by Mokhtar Belmokhtar was not pursued after Ambassador Huddleston explained the negative consequences.

Other ambassadors told stories of military plans or actions that they stopped. For example, Barbara Bodine recalled:

> The military at one point wanted to do an exercise in Yemen and they were going to storm a beach. In and of itself it wasn't really a problem. I didn't really care, except they were going to do it two days before an election. And the answer is "No." And they said: "But we've had this on the books for a very long time." And I said: "Yes, I know you've been on the books longer than their election. But the election is happening, and we can't have Marines landing on the shores of Yemen two days before an election. It just isn't going to happen." And were they happy about it? No.[48]

In congressional testimony, General Zinni referred to occasions when "Ambassador Bodine requested that we postpone or cancel events, military-to-military events, either in the interest of security or she did not feel the Yeminis [sic] were ready for it yet, or the conditions were [not] right" and he confirmed that CENTCOM had complied with her requests. He averred that the ambassador was not in the chain of command "in the conduct of operations"; but otherwise "anything that goes on in a country, it is with the approval, concurrence and complete visibility to the ambassador" (US Senate 2000).

In another instance, William J. Garvelink, US ambassador to the Democratic Republic of the Congo (2007–10), recalled a disagreement with the military over personnel used to renovate a base in Kisangani. AFRICOM had contracted with some Ugandan nationals to help with water issues, unaware of the intense tensions between Ugandans and Congolese since a conflict in 1999. The Congolese defense minister called the US ambassador to complain.

Garvelink, in turn, phoned Gen. William E. Ward, then the commander of AFRICOM; they agreed that the Ugandans should be pulled out immediately. Both Garvelink and Ward thought the situation had been resolved.

So Garvelink was surprised when the Congolese defense minister called up again the next week and angrily told the ambassador that the Ugandans were still there. Garvelink tracked down General Ward in Washington and recalled the following conversation:

> I said, "General, they are still there." He said, "No, they can't be."
>
> We got hold of a 2-star somewhere [who explained] . . . "You know it's going to cost us an extra million dollars, so we thought [the Ugandans could] stay a couple of weeks and finish it up."
>
> And Ward uploaded: "Didn't you hear what the ambassador said. Get them out. I don't care what it takes. Get them out."
>
> About two days later they were gone.[49]

From Garvelink's perspective, the presence of Ugandan contractors on the military base was such a serious provocation to the Congolese that it was not worth worrying about cost. In his words, "AFRICOM was responsive, except for the guy who was trying to be penny wise and really foolish . . . . It was a mistake. I raised a fuss, and Ward took care of it."

To say that combatant commanders were taking over the diplomatic role of ambassadors, "one would have to identify areas where the military is marching in to do things which the ambassador on the ground thinks are bad ideas"—so observed Ronald E. Neumann, the US ambassador to Afghanistan (2005–07), Bahrain (2001–04), and Algeria (1994–97). But, he added, "it's very, very difficult to reverse an ambassador if he or she really says 'no' to something."[50]

Tensions with SOCOM

Our interviews did uncover a common suspicion toward one combatant command, namely SOCOM. One ambassador said that Special Operations Forces had a "superman" mentality—an attitude that "they know better"; that SOF would have a plan, expecting to be able to act without telling the ambassador or "Big State"; that they had an attitude that they didn't need to run a mission by the State Department or the ambassador because it was a "DoD mission"; their attitude was "this was what we are going to do."[51] Vicki Huddleston (and others we spoke with) agreed with this characterization. As an ambassador who then transitioned into a job as deputy assistant secretary of defense for African affairs between 2009 and 2011, Huddleston was well positioned to observe the SOF operations in Africa. She remarked:

[Geographic] commanders are versed in the area and the procedures. Special Forces have a different mentality. And that mentality is that there are a bunch of bad guys out there and our role is to take care of them. And you [the ambassador] are just getting in the way.[52]

Tensions between State Department diplomats and SOCOM arose out of post–9/11 changes in US policy and institutions and some early transgressions that occurred during the George W. Bush administration. Congress passed the Authorization for the Use of Military Force (AUMF) three days after the 9/11 attack, sanctioning the use of military force against al-Qaeda operatives, and those helping them, anywhere in the world. The United States was officially at "war" with a terrorist group that resided in many different territories. Whereas in the past a war zone was clearly demarcated, now it was undefined. If al-Qaeda were operating in Yemen or Pakistan, then the president was authorized by the US Congress to pursue it even if the US government was not at war with the Yemeni or Pakistani government. As Jennifer Kibbe details in Chapter 11, the Bush administration eventually designated SOCOM, not the CIA, to take the lead role in synchronizing this war against terrorism.

In early 2004, Secretary of Defense Donald Rumsfeld authorized the Joint Special Operations Command (JSOC, a subunit of SOCOM) to attack al-Qaeda in more than a dozen countries outside Afghanistan and Iraq by signing the secret Al Qaeda Network Executive Order (AQN ExOrd) (Ambinder and Grady 2012; Priest and Arkin 2011b, 236; Schmitt and Mazzetti 2008). The Special Operations Command also took on the new role of collecting broad-based intelligence in these hot spots (Shanker and Shane 2006). The scene was now set for conflict between ambassadors, the highest US representative within a country, and the Special Operations Command—now acting on the nation's prioritized mission of counterterrorism as so stated in the nation's 2002, 2006, and 2010 National Security Strategy documents.

Starting in 2003, the Pentagon sent small teams of Special Operations Forces into more than a dozen countries to do reconnaissance (Tyson and Priest 2005, A1; Shanker and Shane 2006). At first, these teams were named Operational Control Elements; the name later changed to Military Liaison Elements (MLEs) (Tyson 2006).

Rust Deming, then ambassador to Tunisia, recalled dealing with the SOF forces sent in for reconnaissance. Soon after 2001 "there was this idea that the area of basically the Sahara desert, including areas of Tunisia, were ungoverned territory, and we needed to go down and take a look and control." He opposed the Special Operations scouting teams because the Tunisians at that time were "in control of their territory and those guys would have lasted about 10 minutes if they went." The Special Operation Command Europe (SOCEUR)

> wanted to set up in the embassies . . . Special Forces cells that would stove pipe—report back to SOCEUR. . . . We killed that as long as I was there, but that was the constant struggle now. [They would say]: "Do we have a deal for you. . . . We can bring in five people. Not even sure [we need your] permission to do it [because it is something we are] doing under Title 10" kind of stuff.[53]

Deming's description captures the wartime attitude of the Special Operations Forces ("Title 10" refers to federal code authorization of the armed forces), the sense that their counterterrorism mission entitled them to act without ambassadorial permission.

In some cases, SOCOM made plans to send—or actually did send—MLEs into a country bypassing the ambassador. For instance, Ambassador Gnehm, then serving in Jordan, learned of a secret plan through his defense attaché (DATT) "to send people out, without anyone knowing, to collect intelligence in Jordan, Bahrain, and Egypt. . . . I was *not* to be told because they were under deep, deep cover."[54]

Even though it put his DATT in an awkward position, Gnehm "couldn't let it just happen." He contacted the ambassadors from Bahrain and Egypt; one had also been told by his defense attaché of the plan; the other had not. The three ambassadors agreed to write to Washington using the same language, saying the teams would need to send a "front-channel country clearance message." In the end, the embassy "got a front channel message asking for clearance for a team. I know the CIA was really furious. Not just State."[55]

One MLE team in Paraguay killed a man who attempted to rob them as they were getting out of a taxi; only then was the ambassador, John Keane, informed that the soldiers were in the country (Mazzetti 2010).

Not surprisingly, the State Department fought against such a blatant violation of a core ambassadorial authority: country clearance. J. Cofer Black, the counterterrorism coordinator at the State Department (who had previously been director of the CIA's Counterterrorism Center), was assigned to be the "point person to try to thwart the Pentagon's initiative" (Tyson and Priest 2005, A1). And the pushback worked. This SOCOM practice of circumventing an ambassador's country clearance authority for scouting operations did not stand. By 2006, spokespersons from the State Department and the Special Operations Command reported that "the Military Liaison Element program was set up so that 'authority is preserved' for the ambassador or the head of the embassy" (Shanker and Shane 2006).[56]

However, suspicion remains. In particular, the ambassador's role when kinetic missions are at play is still perceived to be ambiguous. Ambassador Gillian Milovanovic (Macedonia 2005–08, Mali 2008–11), for example, stated that the "business of whether you [SOCOM] can go and do something in a country without notifying the ambassador is not clear."[57]

> And the very lack of clarity also makes it scary for people and I think is just detrimental ... because then there's a certain sense of "could something be going on" and that's not a healthy situation.[58]

Another high-level State Department official described how usually it is just the ambassador that is briefed about special operations missions: "It doesn't mean everybody else in the embassy is [briefed], probably only she and the DCM know about these missions." And they "don't have to know everything operationally." But it is important not to be surprised "because it's the president [of the country] that could call you up ... and you've got to go up and explain."[59]

Perhaps because of a widespread perception that SOF officials are often dismissive of ambassadorial authority, the commander of SOCOM, William McRaven, made a public campaign of trying to establish trust for his command. Repeatedly in public forums, McRaven made statements that were a variation of the following: "[W]e never go into another country without getting clearance from the Chief of Mission, and the Chief of Mission always has a vote on whether or not the U.S. forces arrive in the nation that he or she is sitting in" (quoted in Feickert 2012, 10–11). SOCOM regularly brought new ambassadors to its headquarters near Tampa, Florida, for a day of briefings, during which the commander would tell them that "we will not do anything in your country without your approval" and if a SOF official steps out of line, "as soon as you tell me about it, I will pull them out and they will be disciplined for any wrong doing."[60] According to one Pentagon official, this was an "institutional statement from the top."[61]

Conclusion

If the question is whether the role of the combatant commander has become so expansive that it fundamentally challenges the traditional role of the ambassador as the principal interlocutor between the US government and a foreign government, then our answer is "No." Ambassadors retain their authority as the highest representative assigned to a particular country. But if the question is whether the combatant commanders and the activities of the COCOMs influence US relations at the country level, in some cases playing an agenda-setting role, or more often, pushing a focus on security issues, then our answer is "Yes." The resource imbalance between the military and the civilian agencies does have implications for the conduct of US diplomatic relations. The militarization of state diplomacy does *not* involve the military leaders taking over policymaking and challenging civilian control; it is a more subtle seeping in of military perspectives, as discussed by Adams and Murray in Chapter 1.

Most ambassadors described the geographic combatant commanders as savvy team players who respected their civilian ambassadorial authority and who visited their posts only infrequently. The relationship is not always harmonious, as seen in the dispute between Vicki Huddleston, the ambassador to Mali, and Gen. Charles Wald, the deputy commander for the European Command. (And there is another prominent example, almost two decades old, of a fight between Gen. Barry McCaffrey, the commander of SOUTHCOM, and Charles Bowers, the ambassador to Bolivia, about who had authority over US military personnel in the country.[62]) Judging from our interviews, however, such a discordant relationship between a commander and ambassador is the exception, not the norm.

The stories we were told suggest that if there is a dispute between the ambassador and the military about an activity within a country, the ambassador usually wins, as did Vicki Huddleston in stopping a missile strike in Mali, as did Barbara Bodine in stopping military exercises at a politically sensitive time in Yemen, and as did William Garvelink in expelling Ugandan contract workers from the Congo. In some cases, though, ambassadors did not assert their authority and acquiesced to military actions that the ambassadors considered ill-conceived. Of course, if a military operation or activity is initiated from or approved by Washington, especially the White House, the ambassador does not have authority to stop it even if she feels it disrupts the diplomatic relationship.[63]

Ambassadors were less accepting of SOCOM. We found both a suspicion among ambassadors regarding SOCOM's commitment to respect ambassadorial authority as well as a public campaign by SOCOM to reassure ambassadors that they do. This tension may be a legacy of post–9/11 policy, when under the direction of Rumsfeld and emboldened by the Global War on Terror, SOCOM initially acted as if the ambassador's chief of mission authority was not a constraint on its activities—that it did not need the permission of the ambassador to enter the country. After an institutional tussle between DoD and State, SOCOM was instructed to abide by the long-established practice and requirement to ask for country clearance for its surveillance teams.

Basic ambassadorial authority has been retained, but at the same time, the vast presence of the US military abroad, and the resources it wields, do affect

US diplomatic relations in more subtle ways. Considering that the ratio of USAID to State to DoD employees deployed abroad is something like 1 to 25 to 600, respectively, it is simply a reality that the military houses enormous capability and becomes an active presence abroad (Adams, Chapter 2). In countries with high strategic importance for the United States, or where the military relationship holds a place of priority for the country's leadership, or where there are ongoing military operations, the ambassador must navigate the spillover of military-to-military relations into broader policy objectives, as did Ambassador Ross Wilson in Turkey. Most subtle, if the monies available to ambassadors for in-country projects come disproportionately from the military, then US activities will be skewed in the direction of the COCOM's priorities. As seen with Ambassador Edward Gnehm's belated vetting of plans for a counterterrorism training facility to be built in Jordan, the availability of resources and the relationship of the combatant commander to the leader of the country can sometimes result in the initiation of major projects outside of the Country Team. In other words, the resource imbalance pushes relationships in some countries in a "security" direction, potentially at the cost of a governance or development orientation.

We conclude with two recommendations to bolster and clarify ambassadorial authority. First, the president's letter, which goes to ambassadors on their appointment, contains generic language about ambassadorial authorities with respect to the military. This language could usefully be made more precise with a view to clarifying the different types of military facilities and deployments over which the chief of mission has authority or about which that individual needs to be kept fully informed. On the military side, the geographic combatant commanders need to receive parallel and compatible guidance so that there is no misunderstanding as to where authority lies and over what aspects of a military program.

Second, the briefing program for outgoing ambassadors (meaning those just leaving for their posts abroad) could be expanded to make sure that ambassadors, most of whom will not have had previous military experience, understand in as great detail as possible the nature of the military programs and activities going on in their country of assignment and their responsibility with respect to each of them. Better training might reduce the instances where ambassadors do not exert their proper authority or manage military presence and activities. This briefing will be particularly important with respect to the capabilities and programs of the Special Operations Command, whose role has been steadily growing in recent years.

But what is needed most is a fundamental shift in congressional and White House priorities—to give diplomacy and development greater resources and foreign policy clout. The Obama administration's "3 Ds" campaign (defense, diplomacy, and development) and then–secretary of state Hillary Clinton's publication of the "Quadrennial Diplomacy and Development Review: Leading through Civilian Power" emphasizing enhanced ambassadorial authority were steps in this direction. But more of a shift of resources needs to occur to address the stark imbalance.

Notes

1. The exception is US Northern Command, which covers the United States, Mexico, Canada, and portions of the Caribbean region.

2. Loftus does not mention the sixth geographic combatant command, which is the US Northern Command, or NORTHCOM.

3. Almost all of the ambassadors we interviewed were career State Department officials, not political appointees. Our pool of interviewees mostly served in countries in SOUTHCOM, CENTCOM, and what is now AFRICOM. We have only a few representatives from PACOM or the big countries in EUCOM. Our analysis also draws upon findings from an investigation done by six of Sen. Richard Lugar's Senate Foreign Relations Committee staff members who interviewed twenty ambassadors in 2006 about their embassies' relationship with DoD (US Senate 2006b).

4. Belote (2004) asked five ambassadors about their perceptions of combatant commanders. He also found that ambassadors held a favorable view of commanders and did not see them as usurping civilian control.

5. There are both geographic and functional unified commands. The missions, responsibilities, and geographic scope of the unified commands are continually reviewed and subject to change.

6. A few combatant commanders do become well known in times of war, such as Gen. Norman Schwarzkopf Jr. during the Persian Gulf War or Gen. David Petraeus during the Iraq War.

7. Ambassadors, however, often have privileged use of defense attaché aircraft in their county of assignment.

8. In some cases, they need State Department concurrence to offer security assistance. See Serafino, Chapter 7.

9. For his part, Zinni translated these instructions into an aspiration to improve the "cooperative mechanisms" of the most prominent regional organization in his AOR, namely the Gulf Cooperation Council (GCC). In order to strengthen the military cohesion and security capabilities of the GCC, Zinni invited leaders from its member countries to a series of technical conferences (with topics such as "a shared computerized early-warning system for biological and chemical weapons attacks") so they could begin working collaboratively (Priest 2003, 80; Zinni and Koltz 2006).

10. Interview by Shoon Murray with Gen. Charles Wald, May 23, 2013.

11. Ibid.

12. Ibid.

13. The capture of Salafist Group for Preaching and Combat (GSPC) leader Abderazak al-Para in 2004.

14. Interview by Shoon Murray with Gen. Charles Wald, May 23, 2013.

15. Ibid.

16. See Oakley and Casey (2007) for a history of the Country Team concept.

17. For some examples of the president's letter of instruction, see "A Generic Letter of Instructions to Chief of Missions," http://transition2008.files.wordpress.com/2007/08/presidential-letter-to-ambassadors.pdf or http://www.state.gov/documents/organization/28466.pdf.

18. Most ambassadors fall within the Foreign Service classes of counselor, minister counselor, or career minister, the equivalent of one-, two-, or three-star general or flag officers. This disparity in rank with the combatant commanders is exacerbated when the ambassador is absent from post, and the embassy is led by the deputy chief of mission, serving in the interim as chargé d'affaires, who is in almost every case junior to the ambassador.

19. Gail McCabe interview with General Ham, August 3, 2011, YouTube.

20. While ambassadors are typically accredited to a single country, there are several cases, usually involving small island nations, where ambassadors have multiple accreditation, such as the ambassadors resident in Barbados and Fiji.

21. Interview by Shoon Murray and Anthony Quainton with Ambassador Barbara Bodine, December 2, 2011.

22. Interview by Shoon Murray and Anthony Quainton with Ambassador Edward W. Gnehm Jr., April 9, 2012.

23. Interview by Shoon Murray with Ambassador Donald Yamamoto, June 26, 2012.

24. There is even a practice whereby the SDO's credentials are presented in a letter of introduction to his counterparts upon his appointment. See US Department of Defense Directive 5105.75, "Department of Defense Operations at US Embassies," December 21, 2007.

25. Interview by Shoon Murray with Ambassador Ross Wilson, June 21, 2012.

26. Ibid.

27. Ibid.

28. Interview by Shoon Murray and Anthony Quainton with Ambassador Barbara Bodine, December 2, 2011.

29. Interview by Shoon Murray with Ambassador Donald Yamamoto, June 26, 2012.

30. Ibid.

31. Conversation with a foreign service officer, June 26, 2012.

32. Interview by Shoon Murray with Ambassador Rust Deming, July 5, 2012.

33. Interview by Shoon Murray and Anthony Quainton with Ambassador Mary Yates, November 8, 2012.

34. Interview by Shoon Murray with Ambassador Linda Jewell, June 27, 2012.

35. Interview by Shoon Murray and Anthony Quainton with Ambassador Edward W. Gnehm Jr., April 9, 2012.

36. Ibid.

37. Ibid.

38. Glain (2011) reports that "Abizaid went around Gnehm by funding the training facility from his own budget, according to a source with intimate knowledge of the matter." Gnehm told us that he got the policy discussions he wanted and supported the project.

39. The ambassador was not identified in the report.

40. According to the GAO (2008, 24) the ambassador in Niger "limited the number of DOD personnel allowed to enter the country" and the ambassador in Chad reportedly "called for a 'strategic pause' in implementing TSCTP (Trans-Sahara Counterterrorism Partnership) activities," stating the need to reassess available embassy personnel to support DoD activities in country.

41. The Section 1206 funding was given to the geographic combatant commanders to train and equip foreign militaries with the goal of enhancing their counterterrorism capabilities. The fund was controversial because it was given to DoD, to be used with the concurrence of the State Department, when historically such programs had been funded through State. The GAO (2007) later found that DoD and State adequately institutionalized this funding such that it could not go forward without the approval of the ambassador.

42. This ambassador asked not to be identified.

43. The Department of Defense spent more than $7 billion for foreign-assistance-related programs in fiscal year 2010 (US Department of Defense 2012d).

44. Interviews by Shoon Murray with Ambassador Vicki Huddleston, July 5 and August 9, 2012.

45. See also Katchadourian 2006.

46. Interview by Shoon Murray with Ambassador Vicki Huddleston, August 9, 2012.

47. Interview by Shoon Murray with Gen. Chuck Wald, May 23, 2013.

48. Interview by Shoon Murray and Anthony Quainton with Ambassador Barbara Bodine, December 2, 2011. See Zinni's Senate testimony about the attack on the USS Cole in Yemen dated October 19, 2000.

49. Interview by Shoon Murray with Ambassador William Garvelink, June 21, 2012.

50. Interview by Shoon Murray and Anthony Quainton with Ambassador Ronald Neumann, June 2011.

51. Interviewee did not want attribution.

52. Interview by Shoon Murray with Ambassador Vicki Huddleston, August 9, 2012.

53. Interview by Shoon Murray with Ambassador Rust Deming, July 5, 2012.

54. Interview by Shoon Murray and Anthony Quainton with Ambassador Edward W. Gnehm Jr., April 9, 2012.

55. Interview by Shoon Murray and Anthony Quainton with Ambassador Edward W. Gnehm Jr., April 9, 2012.

56. A senior State Department official from the Bush administration told Anthony Quainton that the issue of whether special operations teams could come into a country without ambassadorial approval was resolved between Secretary of Defense Donald Rumsfeld and Secretary of State Colin Powell. Interviewee did not want attribution.

57. Interview by Shoon Murray with Ambassador Gillian Milovanovic, August 16, 2012.

58. Ibid.

59. Interviewee did not want attribution.

60. Interview by Shoon Murray with Pentagon officials, May 16, 2013.

61. Ibid.

62. "In a widely remembered incident in 1994," the *Washington Post* reported, "General Barry R. McCaffrey, then chief of SOUTHCOM, circulated a letter asserting his authority over the troops, infuriating the region's ambassadors. Ambassador Charles Bowers in Bolivia was so angry he threatened to expel US troops from Bolivia" (Farah 1998, A1). Several ambassadors that we interviewed also remembered oversteps by General McCaffrey.

63. One illustration of this dynamic was revealed when Ambassador Cameron Munter objected to the CIA's use of drones for signature strikes in Pakistan (i.e., lethal targeting of unknown men based upon suspicious behavior patterns). The question Munter raised was whether the CIA was sensitive enough to diplomatic negotiations and the broader political context when deciding to order a drone strike. After a high-level review in June 2011, the White House

instituted an appeals procedure to give the State Department more of a voice in deciding when and if to strike. If the U.S. ambassador to Pakistan objected to a strike, for example, the CIA director or his deputy would first try to talk through their differences with the ambassador. If the conflict was unresolved, the secretary of state would appeal directly to the CIA director. If they couldn't reach agreement, however, the CIA director retained the final say (Entous, Gorman, Barnes 2011).

Chapter 10

Military Advice for Political Purpose

Sharon K. Weiner

In the United States, the military is expected to stay out of politics. The military can and should provide its professional opinion about what threatens US security, how to prepare to meet those dangers, and the proper strategy and tactics for responding to enemy attack. But questions of social issues, domestic programs, foreign policy, and economic health are supposed to belong exclusively to civilians. This seemingly neat division of labor is, however, complicated by several realities. First, domestic policies often have military implications and vice versa. The same is true for foreign policy. Second, threats and the proper means of meeting them are often so indeterminate that they are a matter for political judgment as much as professional military advice. Third, military advice often has clout in other political domains because of the deference both the public and politicians often give to military leaders. Additionally, when civilian policymakers are divided among themselves, even purely professional military advice can effectively tip the balance of debate in favor of one side because it provides expert support for a position.

The blurry demarcation between civilian and military policy domains means it is often difficult to tell the difference between professional and political military advice. This chapter defines "political" actions by the military, or the "politicization of the military," as advice that either extends into a policy domain that has no direct relevance to professional military activities (for example, voicing a position on social issues) or that is offered with the intention of swaying civilian decision makers who are undecided or divided on a professional military issue.[1] Thus partisan political statements, the expansion of the military into nonmilitary policy, and even military lobbying on professional military issues all constitute political activities.

Although authors sometimes vary in their definitions, there is general agreement that military advice has increasingly strayed beyond the purely military domain, especially since the end of the Cold War. Some argue this shift is due to the identification of a significant majority of the officer corps with positions and values that place them squarely in the Republican party and thus at odds with Democratic policymakers (Feaver and Kohn 2000). In contrast to this partisan explanation, others see the increasing political tone of military advice as the result of a gradual erosion of the norm that military professionalism means being apolitical (Bacevich 1997). Still others see the military as more inclined toward lobbying when senior civilian leaders cross over professional boundaries and try to influence what are seen as military matters (Owens 2011, 53–54). Most of these conclusions, however, are based upon analysis of short-term surveys of military attitudes, discrete periods of civil-military discord, or anecdotal evidence.

In contrast, this chapter argues that the political character of military advice is a function of the organization of the services and, more specifically, the degree to which their corporate identity as "the military" takes primacy over their service-specific roles. This conclusion is based on analysis of newspaper coverage of public statements made by the service chiefs of staff from 1947 to 2009. This data shows that the military has gone through two periods of more intense political activity. The first, from the late 1940s through the 1950s, involved the service chiefs arguing with each other over budget shares and missions. This interservice rivalry was caused by limits on the defense budget but enabled by the relatively equal status the service chiefs enjoyed with respect to each other in the new Department of Defense. In 1986, however, changes to that departmental structure significantly empowered the chairman of the Joint Chiefs of Staff (JCS). As a result, public comments from the military increasingly come in the form of the chairman advocating advice on behalf of the military rather than a specific service. Moreover, this advice has increasingly spread beyond military policy and is often offered during times when civilians are actively debating policy choices and thus constitutes a form of lobbying.

The next section elaborates on the dataset upon which this argument is based. This is followed by an analysis of military comments from 1947 to 2009. Then the dataset is used to examine more closely particular types of military comments over time and discuss their differences. This qualitative analysis shows that since 1947, the service chiefs and particularly the chairmen have used their professional expertise to support and lobby for the president's policy agenda. Since 1986, however, these military leaders have increasingly used their expertise to challenge the president's choices, structure the public debate, and defend the military from charges of mistakes in its operations and misconduct in its treatment of personnel.

The Service Chiefs and the *New York Times*

Although it may be difficult to definitively categorize examples of military advice as either purely professional or political, there is much more agreement about what constitutes the proper channels for conveying military opinion. Military officers are expected to share their personal views, including dissenting with established presidential policy, if requested to do so by civilian authorities, usually the defense secretary but, more importantly, members of Congress. Leaking information, appeals directly to the public, and comments to reporters are generally seen as challenges to civilian authority.[2] In other words, testifying in front of Congress is acceptable; offering policy alternatives to the media or public audiences is not. Thus, under the strictest interpretation of US civil-military relations, military officers should speak to the media only when they are explaining current administration policy or military activities. They should make public speeches only at ceremonial events or other similarly noncontroversial venues. In public, military officers should not offer opinions, contradict the president, or use their clout to provide political support when other civilians question presidential policy choices. For these reasons, active duty military officers have historically been reluctant to engage with the media or to give public lectures.[3]

Because speaking to the media or public directly is usually seen as inappropriate, this chapter uses media coverage of military officers as an indicator of the degree to which the military seeks to offer political advice. More specifically, the chapter looks at the *New York Times* for the period 1947 to 2009, focusing on comments made by any current service chief of staff or the JCS chairman.[4] The dataset consists of articles that reference any comment made by one of these military officers either directly to the media or in a public speech. Also included are editorials written by military officers, and newspaper coverage of pieces written for popular media or policy outlets. Excluded are articles that cover testimony, press releases from the Pentagon, backgrounders, and other comments not directed to a public audience or that cannot be attributed to a particular member of the JCS. The resulting dataset of 1,099 comments has an entry for every *New York Times* article that references a public comment by a member of the JCS; articles that mention more than one member of the JCS have an entry for each member.

Further, each entry in the dataset is coded in two ways. One is whether the JCS member is offering an opinion about only one service, the military overall or defense policy in general, or personal plans or goals. The second coding identifies the main subject of the comment. In cases where comments fall into more than one category, or a military officer addresses more than one issue, the comment is coded according to the predominant theme in the article as presented by the reporter.

The Rise of the Chairman

Figure 10.1 shows the number of comments made by members of the JCS over time. With a median number of fourteen comments per year, the two periods when JCS members have made the most public appeals are 1947–60 and 2001–09. But the data also shows a significant difference in the character of JCS remarks. During the earlier period, the service chiefs were just as likely to comment on a particular service, usually their own, as on an issue pertaining to the military more broadly. By the 2000s, however, the reverse is true and service-specific appeals have given way overwhelmingly to comments about the military overall.

This chapter argues that the transition is explained by the rise of the JCS chairman. Initially, when the services were transferred into one executive-level department in 1947, the Army, Navy, and Air Force had equal status. The National Security Act of 1947 provided for a military chief of staff, but filling the position was optional and left up to the president. Amendments in 1949 to the National Security Act changed this by allowing the president, at his discretion, to appoint a chairman of the JCS, with the advice and consent of the Senate. Although the chairman was also designated as senior in rank to the other service chiefs, he was not allowed a vote in JCS decisions. As a result, the service chiefs continued to enjoy equal status and the chairman had little power to force them to reach consensus on controversial issues. President Harry Truman appointed Army General Omar Bradley as chairman in August 1949, but Bradley was unable to force the services to prioritize overall military needs over service-specific interests. For example, instead of determining which of the services could best provide a nuclear deterrent, each of them argued for its own nuclear weapons, often with little reference to the capabilities of the other services.[5]

It was the continued power of the service chiefs, their open squabbling for dollars and missions, and their willingness to use the media to publicly challenge the president's decisions that led President Eisenhower to increase the clout of the chairman. First, in 1953, Eisenhower used his executive power to modestly reorganize the defense department, including making the chairman responsible for managing the Joint Staff. Each of the service chiefs had a large staff of officers to provide analysis to back up their positions. But, because the

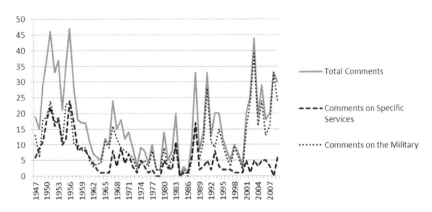

Figure 10.1
Public Comments by Members of the Joint Chiefs of Staff, Per Year, on Service and Military Issues

chairman essentially left his service when he assumed the position of leader of the JCS, he had no comparable resources. The Joint Staff was supposed to fulfill this function. Eisenhower's 1953 reforms proved inadequate, however, and Eisenhower introduced the Defense Reorganization Act of 1958, which Congress passed in July of that year. The act reduced the power of the services by allowing the chairman to vote in JCS decisions, and by giving the secretary of defense more authority to eliminate duplication, assign missions, and administer the services as if they were one collective entity.[6]

The 1958 Act had little practical effect on JCS decision making (Goldberg 1995, 41). Although the chairman had more power, he could not force the services to reach agreement on controversial issues. Nor could he mandate that they approach budget, strategy, or force structure decisions as if the overall military effort was more important than individual service preferences.

Vocal arguments between the services did go down significantly, however. But the reason for the change was not the power of the chairman, it was Robert McNamara. Appointed as secretary of defense in 1961 by President John Kennedy, McNamara found both he and the new president lacked the military expertise to make effective choices between service priorities. To provide a seemingly objective study of military requirements, McNamara introduced systems analysis, and used it to quantify defense problems and then challenge service positions.[7] Because the services still argued with each other, they could not offer unified opposition to McNamara's positions and he was able to prevail in most disputes. This remained the case until the late 1960s, when questions about the Vietnam War called his credibility and judgment into question.

McNamara inadvertently taught the services the value of acting as a corporate body. Indeed, it is under his tenure that the services developed the norm of offering JCS advice only when they could reach consensus (Lovell and Kronenberg 1974, 261). JCS chairman Earle Wheeler, for example, refused to relay JCS split decisions to the secretary of defense (Korb 1976, 116). But this emerging tactic backfired on the military. Although all of the service chiefs opposed the conduct of the war in Vietnam, they disagreed about how the war should be waged. Because they could not agree among themselves, the JCS tended not to question McNamara's conduct of the war, even though they each disagreed with it. The result was a generation of disgruntled junior officers who felt the military had neglected its responsibilities to provide advice to civilian decision makers (McMaster 1998).

The chairman's ability to manage JCS decision making remained weak until 1986 when a series of problems led Congress to impose reform on the military.[8] The Department of Defense Reorganization Act of 1986, also called Goldwater-Nichols in honor of two congressional sponsors, increased the power of the chairman in several ways. First, in place of the JCS, the chairman alone was designated as the principal military adviser to the president, defense secretary, and National Security Council. The chairman is supposed to consult the service chiefs as well as the combatant commanders before offering this advice, and also present any disagreements, but he is also responsible for giving advice even when there is no consensus. Second, to give the chairman resources that were more independent of service influence, he was given more authority over the activities of the Joint Staff, plus made responsible for convening, setting the agenda, and facilitating discussion at JCS meetings. Third, the chairman took on new responsibilities in the areas of strategy, contingency planning, budgetary advice, and doctrine development that used to belong to the JCS and thus tended to reflect an amalgamation of service-specific preferences rather than priorities necessary for the overall defense effort. Last, the law created a vice chairman for the JCS who was senior in rank to the other service chiefs and was to manage the JCS in the absence of the chairman. This ended the practice of the service chiefs delaying controversial decisions until one of them could head a JCS meeting due to the chairman's absence.

The result, as shown in Figure 10.2, has been a significant increase in the chairman's ability to speak for the military. Not only do service-specific comments decline significantly after 1986 (Figure 10.1), comments by individual service chiefs virtually disappear. In their place, the chairman becomes the source of almost all military comment by members of the JCS.

Moreover, the data presented in Figure 10.2 casts doubts on other explanations for the politicization of military advice. The notion that the norm

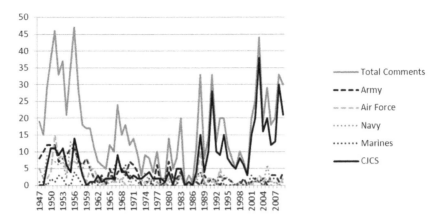

Figure 10.2
Public Comments, Per Year, by Members of the Joint Chiefs of Staff

of military professionalism has gradually eroded over time should lead to a slow but steady increase in comments from either service chiefs or the chairman, or both. Instead, there are periods of increased and decreased activity over time. The more recent claim that links politicization to the alignment of the officer corps with the Republican Party is also not supported. Instead, comments increase during the tenure of Ronald Reagan, decline significantly when Bill Clinton was president, and then increase again under George W. Bush, a trend that seems to have continued under Barack Obama.[9] The data also does not consistently support the claim that the military becomes more political when civilians try and manage what have traditionally been military affairs. During the Vietnam War when the service chiefs were concerned about President Lyndon Johnson's micromanagement of the war, comments increase but the period overall remains one of limited activity.[10] Similarly, comments decline during the early Clinton years when the military resented the administration's efforts to reduce defense budgets, allow gays into the military, and use the military for humanitarian, peacekeeping, and other nontraditional activities.[11]

Political Content

Analysis of JCS comments since 1947 also shows a qualitative shift in the way issues are addressed. Each comment from the *New York Times* was coded according to its main focus: defense budgets, civil-military relations (including social issues and partisan comments pertaining to a particular political party), the organization of defense functions and roles and missions, discipline in the military, foreign policy, structural issues such as housing and bases, specific weapons systems, a current war or deployment, or issues about the end strength of a service or how it acquires personnel. Out of 1,099 comments from 1947 to 2009, most pertain to current wars and deployments (315 comments), followed by foreign policy (224 comments).

A closer look at these two areas, however, shows a qualitative shift in service comments. The service chiefs repeatedly use their positions to support the president, although such comments increase dramatically after 1986. However, since 1986 the service chiefs have also increasingly been willing to use their professional expertise to contradict the president and take a side in ongoing policy debates. First, however, is an analysis of the few instances of comments by service chiefs that are unquestionably political because of the topics they address.

Taboo Topics

Some areas of commentary are off limits to the military because they are inherently unrelated to the military profession. For example, service chiefs should not offer opinions on purely social issues, domestic political contests, or the moral qualities of civilian leaders. But sometimes they do. Although such comments are infrequent, they have increased since 1986.

From 1947 through the mid-1980s, military leaders, usually the chairman, offered a handful of comments on clearly taboo subjects including the appropriateness of racial integration in America, the role of both public education and religious belief in preserving freedom, the permissive nature of society and pop culture, and the ability of the public to accept women in combat.[12] From 1986 onwards, however, there is a shift toward comments about the character of civilian policymakers. For example, in 1987 the chief of the Navy referred to Navy Secretary John Lehman as "not a balanced human being," Chairman William Crowe felt it was appropriate to comment on the moral fiber of Oliver North, and various officers gave their personal opinions of President Clinton.[13] There were also efforts to support civilian leaders in the face of criticism from other parts of the military. Chairman Mullen, for example, spoke in support of Barack Obama, and others commented on Secretary of Defense Donald Rumsfeld.[14] These comments, whether in support of or opposition to an established narrative, are all inappropriate because they use the clout of military expertise in an attempt to influence behaviors and policies that are not related to military effectiveness. Even comments by the chairman in support of controversial civilian leaders, such as reminders to the military that it is inappropriate to make derogatory comments toward the president, are political. This is because they suggest that the traditionally proper level of respect for civilian leadership is not due to the long-established principle of civilian supremacy, but rather derived from respect for the chairman. In other words, soldiers should respect the president as commander in chief, not because the chairman tells them to do so.

Further, the service chiefs have been increasingly willing to write editorials. Because they are expressly intended to convey the writer's opinion on an issue, editorials in civilian media outlets have traditionally been considered inappropriately political. In the *New York Times*, the first one appears in 1973 when Chief of Naval Operations Elmo Zumwalt makes an appeal to continue the draft.[15] This is followed in 1989 by two editorials aimed at maintaining defense spending, a 1990 piece in which Army Chief of Staff Carl Vuono downplays competition with the Marines, and in 1992 the articulation of the Powell doctrine by Chairman Colin Powell.[16]

Talking about the War

Members of the JCS often brief the press on current military operations. Indeed, such remarks are the largest subset of comments. Yet, over time these comments have shifted from support of the war effort to criticism of presidential policy, as well as efforts to engage in political debates about strategy, the level of success, and the nature of the threat.

In the 1940s and 1950s, the main ongoing activities were the occupation of Germany and Japan and the war in Korea. There are general comments that these operations are succeeding. For example, after a 1950 trip to the Korean front, the army chief of staff and the chief of naval operations argue that progress is "very satisfactory" and there is a "general offensive spirit and an air of optimism" among the troops.[17] Individual service chiefs also often praise the performance of their specific service or a particular weapon in Korea. Illustrative is a comment by Army Chief of Staff Lawton Collins who praises the Sherman tank, claiming, "[I]n every single engagement since they arrived, they have knocked out everything the enemy could send at them."[18]

There are only a few instances of comments on active political debates, or which contradict the president. In November 1950, President Truman refused to rule out the use of nuclear weapons in Korea yet the next week Army Chief of Staff Collins tells reporters that tactical nuclear weapons are not necessary.[19] As the war continues, the Air Force uses the performance of their weapons to argue for budget increases and sustained aircraft production. For example, Air Force Chief of Staff Hoyt Vandenberg argues that US strategic bombers are the main deterrent in Korea and therefore their production should continue at the current pace, even after the war.[20] The Air Force and

Marines also bicker over close air support.[21] Perhaps most controversially, Vandenberg tells reporters that the United States is considering bombing targets in Manchuria, one of the policy disagreements that contributed to Truman's firing of Army General Douglas MacArthur.[22] The next day, however, Vandenberg retracted his statement, claiming he was misquoted.[23]

Again in the 1960s and 1970s, most of the comments involve the services praising their own performance, first in the Cuban missile crisis and later in Vietnam. There is little active criticism of presidential policy or an attempt to sway ongoing debates.

Vietnam does, however, bring a few comments from service chiefs that are intended to directly contradict concerns about the military's performance or the conduct of the war. For example, amid concerns about the efficacy of close air support from Army helicopters, Marine Corps Commandant Wallace Greene tells reporters that there are no problems.[24] In contrast to the optimistic prognosis being given by Secretary of Defense Robert McNamara, in 1965 Army Chief of Staff Harold Johnson offers the first service chief comment suggesting that the war may, in fact, last much longer.[25] Although all of the service chiefs shared this sentiment, this claim is not repeated again in the *New York Times* until 1968.

Instead of voicing criticism, beginning in 1964 Chairman Maxwell Taylor increasingly supports the administration's statements that the war is going well, will be over soon, and he begins to appear in joint news conferences with McNamara.[26] Taylor, the other chiefs, and especially the commandant of the Marine Corps offer justifications for the conduct of the war including press censorship, claims about battlefield success, denials of the bombing of North Vietnam, and estimates for troop levels, with which at the time they either disagreed or knew were inaccurate.[27] By 1968, Taylor is repeatedly telling reporters that US strategy is "sound" and that US forces are "unbeatable." His support of the war effort is echoed by Army Chief of Staff William Westmoreland, who by 1969 is supporting the administration's claims that guerrillas in Southeast Asia have been pacified and life is returning to normal. In 1973, Chairman Thomas Moorer argues that a congressionally mandated halt to the bombing of Cambodia is "a big mistake."[28]

By the mid-1980s, however, a new norm is in place. Instead of defending the president, the majority of comments involve the service chiefs defending the military's own operational failures. This trend begins in 1980 when Chairman David Jones supports both President Jimmy Carter and the services, arguing that the failure of the plan to rescue US hostages in Iran could not have been anticipated.[29] Similarly, the military explains that the terrorist attack in 1983 on Marines in Beirut, service coordination problems in the 1983 invasion of Grenada, and the Navy's 1988 downing of an Iranian passenger plane were all unfortunate but not a symptom of underlying problems with communication, intelligence, or coordination.

Two-thirds of the military's comments on ongoing wars and operations happen after 1990. Overwhelmingly, these comments come mostly from the chairman. While some are informational—that is, they provide details of a particular activity—an increasing number defend administration actions but also articulate policy choices. For example, in the first US war against Iraq in 1990–91, Chairman Colin Powell defends administration strategy and casualty estimates, counters rumors that the goal is to remove Iraqi leader Saddam Hussein from power, and gives daily press briefings on the war with Secretary of Defense Richard Cheney. Subsequently, first Powell's and then Chairman John Shalikashvili's comments serve to establish US goals and parameters for the use of military force in Somalia, Haiti, Iraq, and Bosnia even though these have not been clearly articulated by civilian leaders. For example, amid controversy about the mission in Somalia, Powell tells reporters the goal is famine relief but that forces are authorized to defend themselves if attacked.[30] Shalikashvili helps Clinton explain that US troops in Haiti are there only temporarily, to establish order and then will be replaced by UN forces.[31] Chairman Hugh Shelton actively tries to sell Clinton's plan for air strikes in Iraq, arguing both that they are necessary for national security and that Saddam has had more than enough time to comply with UN resolutions.[32]

Similarly, after 2001, members of the JCS give numerous briefings about events and military operations in both the Afghan and Iraq wars. But they also seek to actively structure the way these conflicts are viewed on terms beneficial to the president. For example, in 2002 Chairman Richard Myers explains that major efforts in Afghanistan will be over in six months, makes numerous media appearances making the case for attacking Iraq, supports President Bush's claim that the war in Iraq will last longer than expected but is still on track, and supports what turns out to be false claims about the discovery of biological weapons materials in Iraq.[33] In both wars, when civilians are debating whether to send additional troops, the chairman attempts to prepare Americans for a long but worthwhile war. In 2003, when criticism was especially intense, Myers was so strong in his criticism of antiwar dissent in the media and among retired generals that Secretary of Defense Donald Rumsfeld felt it necessary to remind him that the constitution allows freedom of speech.[34]

Comments by the chairman also defend the conduct of the military. Chairman Myers explains to reporters that detainees are being treated in a humane and culturally appropriate fashion, in spite of internal Pentagon reports that at the time brought this into question, that people being sent to Guantanamo Bay prison are not "Little League Kids" but terrorists, and that troop shifts from Iraq to Afghanistan are appropriate even though there is no civilian consensus on this issue.[35] Chairman Myers also defends his own lack of knowledge about problems of abuse at Abu Ghraib prison, first claiming he did not know and then arguing he asked for the story about the abuse to be delayed due to safety concerns for troops in Iraq.[36]

Later comments question US strategy in both Iraq and Afghanistan, offer alternatives, and weigh in on active political debates. For example, in 2002 Chairman Myers led the charge to switch from combat to nation building in Afghanistan.[37] Similarly, in 2005 he argues insurgency is still a problem in Iraq despite claims of progress.[38] Chairman Peter Pace argues that the Bush administration policy of planting stories in the Iraqi media is misplaced and may be "detrimental to the proper growth of democracy," and that the military was not consulted about the decision to formally dissolve the Iraq military, thus leading to problems restoring order.[39] Various members of the JCS also seek to inform active debates on potential troop surges or cutbacks.[40] In 2006, Chairman Pace explains to reporters that the United States is not winning or losing in Iraq, an assessment that is later endorsed by President Bush as he backs away from claims about "victory."[41] During the 2008 presidential debate, Chairman Mullen sided with President Bush, telling reporters that any timeline for removing US troops from Iraq would be dangerous.[42]

Foreign Policy

The second most common type of comment relates to US foreign policy. Included here are statements about US relations with other countries and international organizations, the role of military force in those relationships and in maintaining US status and power around the globe, other tools of statecraft such as trade or foreign assistance, arms control, and whether or not the United States should use force in a specific situation. In talking about foreign policy, the members of the JCS show a persistent willingness to offer political advice. The content of that advice, however, changes over time, starting off as general support for presidential initiatives from the various service chiefs. By the 1980s, however, comments come mostly from the chairman, who often appeals to policymakers and the public for policies that directly oppose presidential goals or established preferences.

For example, during the 1940s and 1950s, the service chiefs show a consistent willingness to use their clout to support the president, even when presidential policy is actively opposed by members of Congress. In the years after World War II, the service chiefs urge Congress and the public to support the UN, democracy, and constant vigilance against communist aggression. When presidential initiatives to approve NATO, the Marshall Plan, and other post–World War II foreign assistance are bogged down in Congress, the service chiefs make public comments in support of the president. When civilians debate whether the United States should focus on Europe or East Asia, the service chiefs argue predominately for the former in support of first Truman and then Eisenhower. The chiefs also defend President Eisenhower's policies in Korea.

This presidential support tends to come in the form of general statements supporting a "strong defense" or "opposing communism." For example, in 1947 Army Chief of Staff Dwight Eisenhower urged the United States to maintain its military might even after the war because "without the United States, civilization, as we know it, will perish."[43] The first chairman, Omar Bradley, urged organized labor to support Truman's creation of NATO because it is "part of a strategy for lasting peace."[44]

During this time, the chiefs expressed significant opposition to presidential foreign policy only twice. During the mid-1950s, they tried unsuccessfully to convince the president to commit to the defense of nationalist forces on Taiwan, Matsu, and Quemoy. Beginning in the mid-1950s, successive Army chiefs of staff questioned the wisdom of what would become Mutually Assured Destruction (MAD) and instead argued for investing in tactical nuclear weapons and conventional infantry to prepare for "nibbling aggressions."

During the Vietnam era and into the early 1980s, comments from the service chiefs diminish significantly in all areas, including foreign policy. There is general support for fighting communism in Southeast Asia and, even though there are few direct contradictions of statements made by the administration, on occasion a service chief suggests that the war in Vietnam may last longer than anticipated. For example, in 1965 Army Chief of Staff Harold Johnson contradicted the notion that troops would be home soon, stating, "Even if the level and scope of hostilities in Vietnam were to decline, a sudden phase down in our strength would not necessarily follow."[45] Explicit political support for President Carter came in 1977 when Chairman David Jones, speaking on behalf of all of the service chiefs, endorsed the embattled Panama Canal Treaty and pledged military support to help with its ratification, but without mentioning whether the treaty had any military significance.[46]

Starting in the early 1980s, the service chiefs are increasingly willing to express opposition to presidential foreign policy. Moreover, their statements are precise, often drawing clear distinctions between military and civilian opinion on an issue. For example, the service chiefs are united in their opposition to the use of US troops in Central America and in 1988 Chairman William Crowe directly contradicts President Reagan by claiming that a deal to remove Panamanian leader Manuel Noriega is not close, and that Secretary of State George Shultz's policy to remove Noriega by force is not "a viable option."[47] Similarly, the head of the Navy calls into question Reagan's plan for the military to play a role in drug-interdiction efforts, arguing instead "to shut off demand" in the United States.[48] Finally, with the Cold War over, successive chairmen engage in a persistent campaign to convince civilian leaders that the military should not be used for peacekeeping, humanitarian assistance, or in the words of Chairman Colin Powell, that the United States "should not go around saying we are the world's policeman."[49] After the Cold War, the military was so influential in articulating the conditions when it was appropriate to use military force that the policy became known as the Powell Doctrine, and it was advocated by the chairman openly in newspapers, speeches, as well as in an article Powell authored in *Foreign Affairs*.[50] Moreover, this willingness to challenge civilians on the use of force persists after Powell. Chairman Shalikashvili, for example, challenged President Clinton on his plan to send troops to Bosnia, arguing, "I don't think the American public today is sold on that."[51]

Throughout this period and into the 2000s, the chairman continues to openly advocate for some presidential foreign policy initiatives, including efforts to build public support for the use of force in Afghanistan and Iraq. But opposition to the president remains a fixture of military comments. For example, Chairman Richard Myers in a speech at the National Press Club objects to the Bush administration's phrase "war on terrorism" because it encourages the United States to think the military is the only solution to this problem.[52] When Vice President Cheney implicitly warns Iran about possible military action to prevent it from developing nuclear weapons, Chairman Mike Mullen gives an interview explaining this is a "bad idea."[53] Moreover, the chairman increasingly provides an assessment of foreign policy developments around the world including Chinese space launches, Russia's policy toward Georgia, Israel's threats to Iran, and the success of US public diplomacy toward Muslims.

Conclusion

The *New York Times* is but one media outlet. A more complete analysis of trends in military advice would include other newspapers and media sources, as well as statements by other senior military officers in addition to the JCS. For example, future research might include public statements by the combatant commanders or other senior officers in charge of ongoing military operations.

That said, the analysis presented here of comments in the *New York Times* provides a solid indicator of trends that deserve future study and verification. This analysis provides evidence of a clear increase in the willingness of the military to offer advice for political purposes—that is, to offer advice either on nonmilitary matters or with the explicit aim of influencing policy disagreements between civilians. Moreover, the number of such political comments has increased since 1947 but especially since the mid-1980s. Arguably, these trends are due to the development of a corporate identity among the service chiefs that was nascent by the mid-1960s but enabled by changes to the power of the JCS chairman in 1986.

Comments by members of the JCS have been on the rise since the mid-1980s, although by 2010 they had yet to reach the peak of the late 1940s and 1950s, when the services actively argued over budget shares and roles and missions. But the nature of those comments has changed. Largely gone are statements by chiefs in support of their individual service. They have been replaced by opinions about broader military issues that are almost always offered by the chairman. Further, although members of the JCS have consistently used their professional expertise to support and lobby for the president's policy agenda, since the mid-1980s the chairman also uses that expertise to challenge the president's choices and to actively engage in ongoing debates between civilian leaders. In other words, the chairman offers his opinion in an attempt to sway issues of strategy and foreign policy, definitions of national security or wartime success, and the nature of threats that have traditionally belonged to civilians.

Notes

1. This definition is consistent with that offered by Samuel P. Huntington, *The Soldier and the State: The Theory and Politics of Civil-Military Relations* (Huntington 1957), 80–97; and Samuel P. Huntington, "Interservice Competition and the Political Roles of the Armed Services," *American Political Science Review*, vol. 55, no. 1 (March 1961), 40–52. This is not to argue that the military cannot offer its professional military advice but rather that such advice should be offered in testimony, not to reporters or in speeches to the general public.

2. For a good review of the contemporary literature and debates about the military's right to dissent, see Mackubin Thomas Owens, "What Military Officers Need to Know about Civil-Military Relations," (Owens 2012), 67–87.

3. This reluctance has historically extended into retirement, with few retired officers commenting on partisan or policy issues in public. This tendency to avoid the political, however, has changed since the Clinton administration, which used retired military officers to support the administration's policy choices. Since that time, retired officers have been more willing to speak on political matters.

4. The service chiefs and JCS chairman may find it easier to offer comments in defense industry trade publications, the military press, and other media outlets that focus more specifically on military policy. Further, other senior military officers and the combatant commanders may also offer political advice. By focusing on the *New York Times* and the service chiefs and JCS chairman, it is likely that my analysis is based on a small subset of similar comments; as such, it underestimates the degree of politicization.

5. For an example of this dynamic, see David Alan Rosenberg, "The Origins of Overkill: Nuclear Weapons and American Strategy, 1945–1960," (Rosenberg 1983), 3–71.

6. The act deleted a controversial clause that had previously required the secretary to "separately administer" the services.

7. For the political rationale behind systems analysis, see Alain Enthoven and K. Wayne Smith, *How Much Is Enough? Shaping the Defense Program 1961–1969* (Enthoven and Wayne 1971); and William W. Kaufman, *The McNamara Strategy* (New York: Harper & Row, 1964).

8. Especially important were the failed effort to rescue US hostages in Iran, a terrorist attack on Marines serving as part of a peacekeeping operation in Lebanon, and the conduct of the war in Grenada. The inability of the services to cooperate was seen as critical to each of these problems.

9. Preliminary analysis of post-2010 comments in the *New York Times* suggests a continuing increase in comments about the military overall by the JCS chairman.

10. For the persistent dissatisfaction of the service chiefs with Johnson's conduct of the war, see H. R. McMaster, *Dereliction of Duty: Lyndon Johnson, Robert McNamara, The Joint Chiefs of Staff, and the Lies That Led to Vietnam* (McMaster 1998).

11. For an overview of the problems Clinton experienced with the military, see Thomas E. Ricks, "The Widening Gap between Military and Society," (Ricks 1997); and David Halberstam, *War in a Time of Peace: Bush, Clinton, and the Generals* (Halberstam 2001).

12. Excluded here are comments about the military effectiveness of women in combat.

13. See Richard Halloran, "Navy Chief Says Lehman Was Not 'Balanced,'" *New York Times*, April 30, 1987, A24; "Top Brass, Low Key," *New York Times*, March 22, 1988, A30; Eric Schmitt and Thomas Friedman, "Clinton and Powell Discover They Need Each Other," *New York Times*, June 4, 993, A1; and Steven Greenhouse, "Chairman of Joint Chiefs Defends Clinton against Attack by Helms," *New York Times*, November 20, 1994, 1.

14. See Elisabeth Bumiller, "Challenges and Perhaps More Influence for Chairman of Joint Chiefs," *New York Times*, December 16, 2008, A25; and Shane Scott, "Civilians Reign over US Military by Tradition and Design," *New York Times*, April 16, 2006, 18.

15. Elmo R. Zumwalt, "The New Society," *New York Times*, January 14, 1973, 235.

16. See William J. Crowe Jr., "Don't Cut a Winner," *New York Times*, April 10, 1989, A17; Carl E. Vuono, "Five Myths about National Security," *New York Times*, June 18, 1989, E27; Carl E. Vuono, "Army Doesn't Have to Compete with Marines," *New York Times*, January 1, 1990, 24; and Colin L. Powell, "Why Generals Get Nervous," *New York Times*, October 8, 1992, A35.

17. "Optimistic over Korean Situation," *New York Times*, August 26, 1950, 5.

18. "Army Chief Says U.S. Tanks Won Every Battle with Russian Armor," *New York Times*, September 3, 1950, 1.

19. "Gen. Collins Sees No Value for Atom Bomb in Korea," *New York Times*, December 6, 1950, 10.

20. "Vandenberg Fears False Peace Hopes," *New York Times*, July 8, 1951, 11.

21. "Air Support System for Marines Decried," *New York Times*, March 7, 1951, 6.

22. "Vandenberg Hints at Bombing Shift," *New York Times*, November 23, 1951, 3.

23. "Vandenberg Misquoted on Air Dubs in Korea," *New York Times*, November 24, 1951, 3.

24. "Marine Chief Backs Copters in Vietnam," *New York Times*, January 11, 1964, 7.

25. "War for Vietnam May Last 10 Years, Army Chief Says," *New York Times*, January 15, 1965, 3.

26. "Transcript of the McNamara-Taylor News Conference," *New York Times*, May 15, 1964, 12.

27. It is clear, however, that there was significant dissent within the military but still pressure not to contradict civilian leaders. For example, Marine Corps General David Shoup, who went on to be one of the most vocal opponents of the war, waited until he was retired to offer his dissent. In a 1967 radio interview, Shoup argued that President Johnson's claim that Vietnam was vital to US interests was "pure, unadulterated poppycock." See "Gen. Shoup Calls Johnson View on War 'Poppycock,'" *New York Times*, December 19, 1967, 12.

28. "US Aides Predict Phnom Penh Drive," *New York Times*, August 22, 1973, 11.

29. See, for example, "Sand Screens of Copters in Raid Were Removed," *New York Times*, April 30, 1980s, A15.

30. Jane Perlez, "US Role Is Not to Disarm, Aide to Top Somali Insists," *New York Times*, December 6, 1992, 14.

31. Steven Greenhouse, "Restoring Order," *New York Times*, September 19, 1994, A1.

32. John M. Broder, "Clinton Is Sending Bombers and G.I.'s to Persian Gulf," *New York Times*, November 12, 1998, A1.

33. See John F. Burns, "Saying Battle Is Reaching End, US Sends Troops Back to Base," *New York Times*, March 11, 2002, A1; Todd S. Purdum, "Bush Officials Say the Time Has Come for Action on Iraq," *New York Times*, September 9, 2002, A1; Richard W. Stevenson, "Bush, Pleased by Progress, Tries to Lower Expectations," *New York Times*, March 24, 2003, B12; Richard W. Stevenson, "White House Says War Is 'On Track,'" *New York Times*, March 29, 2003, A1; and C. J. Chivers, "With Militant Group Routed, American and Kurdish Forces Hunt for Clues about Al Qaeda," *New York Times*, March 31, 2003, B3.

34. Thom Shanker and John Tierney, "Top-Ranked Officer Denounces Critics of Iraq Campaign," *The New York Times*, April 2, 2003, A1.

35. See, for example, Thom Shanker, "Army Denies Mistreatment of Afghans," *New York Times*, February 11, 2002, A10; Ted Conover, "In the Land of Guantanamo," *New York Times*, June 29 2003, SM40; and Eric Schmitt, "Up to 2,000 Marines to Go to Afghanistan from Gulf," *New York Times*, March 26, 2004, A3.

36. James Risen, "Command Errors Aided Iraq Abuse, Army Has Found," *New York Times*, May 3, 2004, A1.

37. James Dao, "US Shifts Emphasis in Afghanistan to Security and Road Building," November 12, 2002, A14.

38. Eric Schmitt, "US Commanders See Possible Cut in Troops in Iraq," April 11, 2005, A1.

39. Jeff Gerth, Schott Shane, Eric Schmitt, Kirk Semple, and Eric Wong, "US Is Said to Pay to Plant Articles in Iraq Papers," *New York Times*, December 1, 2005, A1; Michael Gordon, "As Policy Decisions Loom, a Code of Silence Is Broken," *New York Times*, April 16, 2006, 18.

40. See, for example, David Sanger and Michael Gordon, "Options Weighted for Surge in G.I.'s to Stabilize Iraq," *New York Times*, December 16, 2006, A1; and Steven Myers and David Clous, "Bush Fights Back on Iraq Debate," *New York Times*, September 1, 2007, A1.

41 Jim Rutenberg, "A New Phrase Enters Washington's War on Words over Iraq," *New York Times*, December 21, 2006, A18.

42. Richard Oppel and Jeff Zeleny, "For Obama, a First Step Is Not a Misstep," *New York Times*, July 22, 2008, A1.

43. Harold B. Hinton, "Eisenhower Bids US Stabilize World," *New York Times*, June 7, 1947, 1.

44. "Bradley Urges Support of Labor for Atlantic Pact and Arms Aid," *New York Times*, November 3, 1949, 11.

45. "Long US Role in Vietnam Is Foreseen by Army Chief," *New York Times*, October 27, 1965, 3.

46. James T. Wooten, "Joint Chiefs Pledge to Help Carter," *New York Times*, August 12, 1977, A6.

47. Elaine Sciolino, "Joint Chiefs' Head Skeptical on Noriega," *New York Times*, May 19, 1988, A3.

48. Richard Halloran, "Top Navy Officer Opposes Drug Role," *New York Times*, July 23, 1988, 10.

49. Andrew Rosenthal, "Military Chief: Man of Action and of Politics," *New York Times*, August 17, 1990, A1.

50. Colin Powell, "US Forces: The Challenges Ahead," *Foreign Affairs*, Winter 1992/93.

51. Eric Schmitt, "A Tough Sell: Sending G.I.'s to Bosnia," *New York Times*, March 10, 1994, A12.

52. Eric Schmitt and Thom Shanker, "New Name for 'War on Terror' Reflects Wider US Campaign," *New York Times*, July 26, 2005, A7.

53. Sheryl Stolberg, "Cheney, Like President, Has a Warning for Iran," *New York Times*, October 22, 2007, A8.

Chapter 11

The Military, the CIA, and America's Shadow Wars

Jennifer D. Kibbe

Introduction

President Barack Obama surprised supporters and critics alike with his ardent support of the shadow wars against terrorism—that is, covert operations in countries where the United States is not at war. While US troops have left Iraq and are (seemingly) on track to leave Afghanistan by the end of 2014, Obama has made it clear that US involvement in the shadow wars is not going to slow down anytime soon. Although he explained in a May 2013 speech that the United States should not define its effort as a "boundless 'global war on terror,'" he went on to describe it as a "series of persistent, targeted efforts to dismantle specific networks of violent extremists that threaten America" (Obama 2013). One week earlier, a senior Pentagon official testifying before the Senate Armed Services Committee gave some indication of the administration's temporally and geographically expansive notion of the continuing shadow wars: The fight against terror is going to go on "at least 10 to 20 [more] years" in places like Yemen, east Africa, and north Africa (US Senate 2013, 19, 37). That open-endedness raises critical questions about who is conducting the shadow wars, where and how they are conducting them, and whether they are subject to adequate oversight and accountability.

Since its creation in 1947, the Central Intelligence Agency (CIA) has been the United States' designated covert operator. Since 9/11 thrust the United States into the "war on terrorism," however, the conduct of the shadow wars has provided some of the clearest evidence of the recent militarization of US foreign policy, in terms of both a militarized counterterrorism policy and the increased involvement of military units in enacting that policy. In the decade since 9/11, the military's Special Operations Forces (SOF) underwent an unprecedented expansion as they competed with the CIA's paramilitary operatives for the prestige and resources that went with leading the fight against the new enemy. Many analysts called attention to the potential for the lack of appropriate congressional oversight of SOF, as opposed to CIA, operations far from a recognized battlefield. That concern notwithstanding, counterterrorism operations continued to evolve in the search for the most effective way of combating the unconventional threat posed by terrorism. The newest phase of the militarization of covert action has been the emergence of hybrid operations that combine the two groups of operators in a way that purportedly maximizes their advantages while minimizing the constraints of each, all the while further blurring the boundaries of oversight and accountability.

This chapter begins by laying out the evolution of the CIA's and then SOF's roles in the post–9/11 shadow wars. The next section explains the legal distinctions between the two, followed by a discussion of the complexity of the congressional oversight mechanisms and the resulting difficulties in conducting effective oversight. Next, the chapter explains the trend toward convergence of CIA and SOF operations and the resulting rise of hybrid or joint operations. The chapter concludes with an examination of the consequences of the militarization of counterterrorism policy.

Central Intelligence Agency

Six days after 9/11, President George W. Bush signed a top-secret presidential finding granting the CIA broad authority to pursue al-Qaeda suspects around the world. That finding laid the basis for the program code-named Greystone (Scahill 2013): dozens of highly classified individual programs that allowed the CIA to maintain secret prisons abroad, capture al-Qaeda suspects and render them to third countries for interrogation, use "enhanced interrogation techniques" that critics have charged amounted to torture, and maintain a fleet of aircraft for moving detainees around. The finding also permitted the CIA to create paramilitary teams to hunt and kill designated individuals anywhere in the world (Priest 2005), although this part apparently never became operational and was ended when CIA Director Leon Panetta pulled the plug in the spring of 2009 (Gorman 2009; Kibbe 2012[1]). The finding was also notable in that it did not require the CIA to return to the president for permission to conduct individual covert actions.

As the United States prepared to go after al-Qaeda and the Taliban in Afghanistan, the CIA also enacted a familiar strategy: establishing, funding, and training its own local proxy militia. It assembled what would become a

3,000-strong army, consisting mostly of Afghans, organized into Counterterrorism Pursuit Teams (CTPTs). These teams "conducted operations designed to kill or capture Taliban insurgents," and went "into tribal areas to pacify and win support" (Woodward 2011, 8). While the CTPTs operated mostly in Afghanistan (and thus within a war zone), they reportedly crossed over into Pakistan on several occasions (Whitlock and Miller 2010; Kibbe 2012).

The best-known facet of the CIA's involvement in offensive operations beyond war zones has been its drone missile attacks in Pakistan and Yemen. The first drone strike targeted Qaed Salim Sinan al-Harethi, a suspect in the 2000 bombing of the USS *Cole*, in Yemen in November 2002. The use of drone attacks was originally quite controversial as Washington had condemned Israel's policy of targeted killing just two months before 9/11. That controversy notwithstanding, the United States began using drone attacks in Pakistan as a solution to the problem of Taliban and al-Qaeda fighters from Afghanistan hiding out in Pakistan's tribal border regions, where Pakistani forces were either unable or unwilling to root them out and where US forces were prohibited from operating on the ground. The drone attacks in Pakistan were used originally against specific "high-value" targets (so-called "personality strikes") selected with the help of the Pakistani government in exchange for access to Pakistani airspace (Mazzetti 2013a). The targeting rules were significantly expanded in mid-2008, however, to include suspected lower-level militants whose names were not known (Cloud 2010; Shane, Mazzetti, and Worth 2010; Entous, Gorman, and Rosenberg 2011). This expanded authority enabled the CIA to conduct "signature strikes," referring to situations where the targets' intelligence signatures (i.e., evidence gathered from signals intercepts, human sources, and aerial surveillance) exhibit patterns of terrorist behavior (Kibbe 2012; Miller 2012).

The United States made another significant policy change at around the same time. Until mid-2008, US policy had been to get Pakistan's consent for strikes, which meant giving advance notice. When the strikes proved less effective than expected, officials running the program suspected that the Pakistanis were warning al-Qaeda and Taliban targets. Eventually, Bush "had enough," and decided that Pakistani officials would get only "'concurrent notification' meaning they learned of a strike as it was underway or, just to be sure, a few minutes *after*" (Woodward 2011).

While these policy and targeting changes led to an increase in drone strikes during Bush's last six months in office, there is no question that Obama increased the pace dramatically. From the Bush administration's high of 36 strikes in Pakistan in 2008, the number rose to 54 in 2009, 122 in 2010, 73 in 2011, and 48 in 2012 (all in Pakistan) (New America Foundation 2013b).[2] Of course, increasingly sophisticated drone technology and better intelligence on the ground also played a role in the increased frequency of drone strikes, not just a different approach in the White House (Miller 2011c). The pace of strikes in Pakistan slowed again in 2011 as a result of the rising tension in the Washington-Islamabad relationship. Since then, the pace has varied with the volatility of the political relationship and, some speculate, slowed overall as a result of a lack of high-value targets (Shane 2013).

Meanwhile, the CIA was also given the green light to conduct personality strikes in Yemen in 2011 (Miller 2011a). In April 2012, Obama expanded the CIA's (and SOF's) targeting in Yemen, allowing the agency to use a type of signature strike, albeit a more limited one than that allowed in Pakistan. The new strikes were allowed against people whose identities did not have to be known and whose names did not have to be on a previously approved "kill list" if there was a clear indication of the presence of an al-Qaeda in the Arabian Peninsula (AQAP) leader or of plotting against the United States (Entous, Gorman, and Barnes 2012; Miller 2012). The CIA had asked for such expanded targeting authority the previous year but Obama had denied it then, leery of being drawn into the growing insurgency against the Yemeni regime. But as AQAP took advantage of the chaotic situation in Yemen and expanded its control into new territory, Obama changed his mind.

Special Operations Forces

In the preparations for war in Afghanistan in late 2001, the CIA's operatives proved able to get on the ground and make contact with the rebels of the Northern Alliance far more deftly than the military's Special Operations Forces. Secretary of Defense Donald Rumsfeld took that lesson to heart and set about building SOF's capacity and authority, ensuring that the Pentagon would never again have to rely on the CIA to accomplish a mission (Kibbe 2004).

Special Operations Forces include units that conduct overt or "white" operations and units that conduct "black" (i.e., classified) operations, including both covert missions (where the sponsor is unacknowledged) and clandestine missions (i.e., tactical secrecy). White special operations units include Army Special Forces (Green Berets), most Ranger units, most of the Navy SEALs (Sea, Air, Land), and numerous aviation, civil affairs, and psychological operations units. These white special operators are largely involved in training selected foreign forces in counterterror, counterinsurgency, and counternarcotics tactics, helping with various civil affairs projects, and disseminating information to foreign audiences through the mass media (Kibbe 2007).

The black operators fall under the Pentagon's Joint Special Operations Command (JSOC), which incorporates the elite units of each service's special operations forces, including the Combat Applications Group (CAG), more widely known as 1st Special Forces Operational Detachment-Delta (Delta Force), Naval Special Warfare Development Group (DEVGRU, or SEAL Team 6), the Air Force's 24th Special Tactics Squadron, and the Army's 160th Special Operations Aviation Regiment and 75th Ranger Regiment. These units (also known as special mission units) specialize in direct action, or "kinetic," operations such as hunting terrorists and rescuing hostages (Kibbe 2007). Since 2003, JSOC has also included the highly classified Mission Support Activity (MSA, which has been previously known as the Intelligence Support Activity, Gray Fox, and Intrepid Spear—its name changes every two years). Inside JSOC, it is known as the Activity or Task Force Orange. It was imported from the Army and intended to be JSOC's clandestine intelligence-gathering organization, although intelligence and military officials have confirmed that the MSA has also conducted direct action missions in Somalia, Pakistan, and several other countries (Ambinder and Grady 2012, 883–907).

By 2012, it was clear that Rumsfeld and his successors, Robert Gates and Leon Panetta, had expanded US Special Operations Command (SOCOM, the formal command under which SOF are organized) substantially. The administration's SOF budget request for FY 2013 was $10.41 billion, roughly three times its 2001 budget, and at close to 63,000 personnel (20,000 of whom are SOF operators), it had almost doubled in size (Feickert 2012, 7; Feickert and Livingston 2010, 7). JSOC itself had tripled in size since 9/11 and acquired "its own intelligence division, its own drones and reconnaissance planes, even its own dedicated satellites" (Priest and Arkin 2011a, A1). While the Pentagon is facing possibly significant budget cuts, those are not likely to come out of the SOF budget. The 2010 Quadrennial Defense Review called for increases in SOF force structure and the plan the Pentagon presented in early 2012 for trimming its budget did as well (Feickert 2010, 6–7; Weisgerber 2012).

Beyond tangible numbers, Rumsfeld also significantly boosted SOCOM's authority and prestige. In early 2004, Rumsfeld signed a secret order, the Al Qaeda Network Execute Order (AQN ExOrd), which gave JSOC broad new authority to conduct offensive strikes against al-Qaeda in fifteen to twenty countries, including Syria, Pakistan, Iran, the Philippines, and Somalia (Ambinder 2011; Scahill 2013). The executive order replaced the previous cumbersome case-by-case approval process with a system of preapprovals for activities permitted in particular countries under various scenarios. For instance, lethal action against al-Qaeda in Iraq and Afghanistan was granted without additional approval, whereas in the Philippines, "JSOC could undertake psychological operations to confuse or trap al-Qaeda operatives, but it needed approval from the White House for lethal action" (Priest and Arkin 2011a). Targets in Somalia needed the approval of the defense secretary;

targets in Pakistan and Syria required that of the president (Kibbe 2007; Schmitt and Mazzetti 2008; Priest and Arkin 2011a).

In 2004, SOCOM's growing role was formalized. After an intensive bureaucratic struggle between the Pentagon and both the CIA and the State Department, President Bush signed the Unified Command Plan 2004, officially designating SOCOM as the "lead combatant commander for planning, synchronizing, and as directed, executing global operations" in the war on terror (US Senate 2006a). Congress then granted SOF the authority, for the first time, to spend money to pay informants, recruit foreign paramilitary fighters, and purchase equipment or other items from foreigners (so-called Section 1208 funds).[3] Previously, only the CIA had been authorized to disburse such funds, meaning that SOF had had to rely on the CIA to provide the funds for various operations (Best and Feickert 2005, 5). Congress initially authorized $25 million to SOCOM; that amount gradually increased to $50 million (Kibbe 2007; Best 2011, 3).

President Obama was initially reluctant to rely on SOF operations in countries outside the war zones until SEAL Team 6 rescued the captain of the *Maersk Alabama* from pirates in the Indian Ocean in April 2009, just three months into his term (Ambinder 2011). The rescue mission demonstrated just how effective JSOC units could be, but it also highlighted some of the bureaucratic impediments in utilizing them when the plan encountered a delay in deploying the SEAL team. Combined with the ongoing terrorist threat, these factors led the Obama administration to enact several significant changes in terms of how JSOC is tasked for missions. Most importantly, JSOC was given standing authority to use whatever military resources it needed anywhere in the world in pursuit of its counterterrorist mission, thereby avoiding sometimes costly delays while the military bureaucracy processed its requests for use of a submarine, for instance, for a particular mission. The leaders of JSOC, Gen. Stanley McChrystal from 2003–08 and VAdm. William McRaven from 2008–11, had been slowly developing this authority for several years; Obama extended it and formalized it into policy during the summer of 2009 (Ambinder 2010; Kibbe 2012).

Another notable change was that regional combatant commanders (such as the commander of Central or Southern Command), as well as the theater commanders in Iraq and Afghanistan, were granted the authority to use SOF personnel, including JSOC, in forming task forces in their regions (rather than only SOCOM having that authority). While JSOC had effectively had a global range since the 2004 AQN ExOrd, the 2009 changes were intended to make efforts to use military capabilities outside of war zones "more systematic and long term" (Mazzetti 2010; Kibbe 2012; Scahill 2013). One former top JSOC commander reportedly described the changes implemented during 2009 in

stark terms: "Obama gave JSOC unprecedented authority to track and kill terrorists, to 'mow the lawn'" (quoted in Ambinder 2011).

As noted above, JSOC has also developed its own drone program, conducting attacks in both Yemen and Somalia (Gorman and Entous 2011; Miller
2011c). Despite Obama's April 2012 expansion of targeting authority in Yemen, some JSOC officials continued to push for even wider targeting authority in both Yemen and Somalia. They saw AQAP and al-Shabaab gaining
strength in those countries and argued that the best way to prevent the terrorist groups from establishing a terror hub in the Horn of Africa was to strike
widely to eliminate lower-level operatives before they and their superiors
could be replaced (Klaidman 2012, 49, 253–54).

JSOC's role in Yemen expanded beyond the drone campaign after new
president Abed Rabbo Mansour Hadi took over from the embattled Ali Abdullah Saleh in February 2012. Hadi allowed members of JSOC into the country,
at first to train Yemeni special operations forces, which gradually evolved into
joint intelligence and targeting missions (Dilanian and Cloud 2012).

Another area of JSOC expansion that highlights a new facet of the militarization issue is that of intelligence gathering. One of JSOC's innovations
in Iraq, which is given considerable credit for turning around the situation
there by 2007, was its fusion of intelligence and operations to create a system
of "network-centered warfare" that enabled units to pursue terrorists and
insurgents more effectively. The head of JSOC, Lt. Gen. Stanley McChrystal
and his chief intelligence officer, Maj. Gen. Michael Flynn, understood that in
order to maximize JSOC's impact, they needed to reduce the amount of time
between the collection of intelligence at the site of raids and the exploitation
of it (so-called "blinks"). By relaxing JSOC's legendary secrecy and inviting
collaboration with various intelligence agencies, they were eventually able to
create interagency teams where the "shooters" were trained in basic detective
skills and could funnel information collected at the scene to intelligence analysts immediately, to be able to develop and pursue further leads more quickly
(Ambinder and Grady 2012, 419–701; Lamb and Munsing 2011; Priest and Arkin 2011b). JSOC also created the JSOC Intelligence Brigade (JIB) as part of
its efforts to analyze raw and finished intelligence for the command's special
mission units (Ambinder and Grady 2012, 985). Within the context of the
wars in Iraq and Afghanistan, this expanded intelligence activity by a military
unit (one that is not a formal member of the Intelligence Community) did not
pose a problem. However, in light of JSOC's spreading operations around the
world, such activity raises important questions about the legal authority under which it is being conducted (see below).

One final indication of JSOC's increasing prominence came with the news
in early 2011 that it had built a new Targeting and Analysis Center (TAAC)

near the Pentagon to help it monitor the increased use of special operations missions against suspected militants around the world. Modeled after the National Counterterrorism Center (NCTC), the TAAC (since renamed for security reasons) combines JSOC's elite special operators with at least a hundred counterterrorism analysts from various intelligence agencies in an effort to speed up information sharing and shorten the time between receiving a piece of intelligence and taking action on it (Dozier 2011). Symbolically and operationally, the new targeting center clearly established JSOC as the lead agency in the counterterrorism battle (Kibbe 2012).

There is every indication that SOCOM and JSOC plan to continue expanding. Since being promoted to commander of SOCOM in August 2011, Adm. McRaven has worked assiduously to develop a global network of special operations forces that entails not just increased flexibility to move his "light, agile" forces around the globe as US conventional military forces retrench, but also building overseas partners' local SOF capacities "so that we can help them take care of their problems so we don't have to end up doing [counterterrorism]" (quoted in Miles 2013; Cloud 2012; Schmitt and Shanker 2013). The stated focus is clearly on expanding the "white" SOF training and liaison missions, but the unstated truth is that, in order for partners' SOF to be able to conduct their own counterterrorism operations, JSOC will also be doing training, and JSOC training missions often have the capability to go operational if "necessary."

Legal Distinctions

Shadow wars raise the fundamental question of whether they are subject to the appropriate level of oversight and accountability, and there are important differences between CIA and SOF operations on these points. Shadow wars fall into the murky realm of covert action, defined in US law as activity that is meant "to influence political, economic, or military conditions abroad, where it is intended that the role of the United States Government will not be apparent or acknowledged publicly."[4]

Covert actions are thus legally distinct from clandestine missions: "clandestine" refers to the tactical secrecy of the operation itself; "covert" refers to the secrecy of its sponsor. The 1991 Intelligence Authorization Act, the governing legislation on covert action, codified two requirements for any covert action: First, there must be a written presidential finding stating that the action is important to US national security, which cannot be issued retroactively; and second, the administration must notify the congressional intelligence committees of the action as soon as possible after the finding has been issued (50 USC 413(b); Kibbe 2004, 2007, 2010b).

Notably, the 1991 Act, written in response to the Reagan administration's use of the National Security Council (NSC) staff to conduct covert action in connection with the Iran-Contra scandal, expressly applied the requirements to "any department, agency, or entity of the United States Government." This would seem to indicate that where SOF are conducting unacknowledged operations in countries with which the United States is not at war, they are in fact acting covertly and should follow the same regulations for presidential findings and congressional notification that the CIA does (Kibbe 2004, 2007, 2012).

However, the law also included a few designated exceptions to the definition of covert action. Most relevant here, "activities the primary purpose of which is to acquire intelligence" and "traditional . . . military activities or routine support to such activities" are deemed not to be covert action and thus do not require a presidential finding or congressional notification. While the act itself does not define "traditional military activities" (TMA), the conference committee report states that the phrase is meant to include actions "preceding and related to hostilities which are either anticipated . . . to involve U.S. military forces, or where such hostilities involving United States military forces are ongoing, and, where the fact of the U.S. role in the overall operation is apparent or to be acknowledged publicly" (US House 1991a; Kibbe 2004, 2007, 2012).

According to the conferees, the determination of whether or not unacknowledged activities are TMA depends "in most cases" upon whether they constitute "routine support" to such an operation. The conferees (referencing the Senate Intelligence Committee's report) considered "routine support" to be unilateral US activities to provide or arrange for logistical or other support for US military forces in the event of a military operation that is intended to be publicly acknowledged (even if that operation ends up not taking place). Examples cited by the Senate committee included caching communications equipment or weapons in an area where such a future military operation is to take place; acquiring property to support an aspect of such an operation; and obtaining currency or documentation for use in such an operation. "Other-than-routine" activities that would constitute covert action if conducted on an unacknowledged basis include recruiting or training foreign nationals to support a future US military operation; organizing foreign nationals to take certain actions during a future US military operation; and targeting public opinion in the country concerned (US Senate 1991; Kibbe 2010b, 2012).

Covert operations conducted by SOF during wartime clearly do not require a presidential finding and congressional notification.[5] For unacknowledged special operations in countries with which the United States is not at war, however, the definition leaves a gray area around the interpretation of the word "anticipated." It is most commonly thought of in the literal sense of "preparing the battlefield," a term the Pentagon has since expanded to "operational preparation of the environment." The legislative history defines "anticipated" as meaning that approval has been given by the president and the secretary of defense "for the activities and for operational planning for hostilities" (US House 1991b; Kibbe 2007, 2012). However, as Robert Chesney points out, it is important to understand what "operational planning" means in the context of the military: "The military has developed a rather elaborate process for the production of operational plans, embodied in a decisionmaking system called the Joint Operation Planning Execution System (JOPES).... [T]he nature of the process is to anticipate circumstances that, though potentially quite unlikely, might foreseeably result in an order from the President to use armed force" (Chesney 2012). In other words, the "operational planning" standard is not restrictive at all. Indeed, during the Bush administration, the Pentagon interpreted that language as including events taking place "years in advance" of any involvement of US military forces (Kibbe 2004).

Critics charged that the Bush administration was shifting ever more covert activity from the CIA to the military in a deliberate strategy to exploit the TMA loophole and evade congressional oversight (Kibbe 2007). As one military intelligence official characterized the Pentagon's view: "Everything can be justified as a military operation versus a [covert] intelligence performed by the CIA, which has to be informed to Congress.... [Pentagon officials] were aware of that and they knew that, and they would exploit it at every turn.... They were preparing the battlefield, which was on all the PowerPoints: 'Preparing the Battlefield'" (quoted in Scahill 2009; Kibbe 2012).

The Bush administration bolstered its broad conception of the TMA exception by using an equally broad interpretation of the congressional Authorization for Use of Military Force (AUMF) adopted in response to the attacks of September 11, 2001. That resolution authorized the president "to use all necessary and appropriate force against those nations, organizations, or persons he determines planned, authorized, committed, or aided the terrorist attacks that occurred on September 11, 2001" (US Senate 2001). Although there has been continued debate about just how broadly the resolution should be interpreted, the Bush administration contended that it grants the president virtually unlimited legal authority as long as he "determines" that a particular target has some connection to al-Qaeda (Kibbe 2004, 2007, 2012).

In response to any lingering questions about its authority to use force post–9/11, the Bush administration argued that the "global war on terror" was just that—a war—and therefore any military action undertaken as part of it was part of the self-defense of the United States, authorized by the president's

Article II commander-in-chief power. This approach made it that much easier to argue that any military act was, therefore, a traditional military activity that did not require a presidential finding or congressional notification (Kibbe 2004, 2007, 2010b, 2012).

For its part, the Obama administration also justified its use of SOF beyond the war zones by invoking the 2001 AUMF and the United States' right of self-defense. Critics have pointed out, however, that some of the administration's terrorist targets, such as AQAP, could not credibly be said to have a connection to 9/11 in any way (DeYoung and Jaffe 2010; Ackerman 2012). The administration's response has been to interpret the AUMF as allowing the targeting of al-Qaeda, Taliban, and "associated forces." Despite continuing criticism about the legality and wisdom of such an interpretation, Congress expressly affirmed the administration's take in Section 1034 in the National Defense Authorization Act for Fiscal Year 2012.[6]

Although the TMA exception to the definition of covert action has received far more attention, JSOC's evolution as an intelligence unit also touches on the intelligence activities exception to the definition of covert action. JSOC can conduct operational, tactical intelligence; however, outside of war zones, it can only conduct it clandestinely, not covertly. While the definition of covert action is more clear-cut in the case of something like a lethal raid, gathering intelligence can itself be considered a covert action if it is intended to affect the conditions in a foreign country and where the US role is intended to remain unacknowledged. Moreover, with the heightened emphasis on decreasing the amount of time between finding intelligence and exploiting it, potentially in kinetic actions, one can begin to see the difficulties raised by JSOC units conducting an increasing amount of intelligence collection over an ever-widening geographical area.

Oversight Complexity

A crucial question raised by the militarization of covert action, therefore, is whether it is subject to sufficient oversight by Congress. One facet of this complex question is simply which congressional committee(s) should be doing the oversight. Legally, the ultimate arbiters of what constitutes covert action are the House and Senate intelligence committees, which exert a potential veto through their control of the intelligence authorization process. However, there are numerous ways their authority is circumscribed. First, if it is a special operations mission, funding authorization in the Senate shifts to the Armed Services Committee (in the House, it remains with the House Permanent Select Committee on Intelligence, or HPSCI, assuming, of course, that it has been disclosed to the committee; since the Pentagon usually defines

SOF missions as traditional military activities, it tends to send its funding requests directly to the armed services committees) (Kibbe 2007, 2012).

Second, because the intelligence budget has always been largely hidden within the defense budget as a matter of national security, the armed services committees have ultimate control over the great majority of the intelligence authorization process in any case, since they must sign off on intelligence authorization bills before they go to the full House and Senate for votes. Third, appropriations for a SOF mission would fall to the defense subcommittees of the House and Senate Appropriations Committees. Finally, appropriations for nearly all intelligence activities are included as a classified section of the defense appropriations bill anyway, meaning that the real control over the intelligence purse also lies with the appropriations defense subcommittees (Kibbe 2010a, 2012).

Beyond the inevitable turf wars that all of this divided jurisdiction creates, the critical question is whether intelligence, and specifically covert action, issues are receiving appropriate congressional oversight. One indication that they are not is that neither the armed services committees nor the appropriations defense subcommittees have the same time or expertise to spend on intelligence matters as the intelligence committees do. In one comparison, in August 2009, the Senate Select Committee on Intelligence (SSCI) had forty-five staffers to analyze the intelligence budget (including covert action issues), whereas the Senate Appropriations Subcommittee on Defense had just five people assigned to intelligence issues, each of whom also had additional responsibilities for other parts of the defense budget (Kibbe 2010a). In addition, Pentagon officials understand the current jurisdictional setup all too well and have effectively cultivated relationships with the armed services committees and appropriations defense subcommittees that help ensure a favorable reception for their interpretation of the TMA exception (Kibbe 2012). Thus, the crux of the problem: As long as the Pentagon is conducting unacknowledged operations far from any recognized war zone but creatively defining them as TMA, and as long as the armed services committees accept that definition, the United States is taking covert action risks that are not subject to scrutiny outside the executive branch.

In his January 2009 nomination hearings to become the director of national intelligence (DNI), Dennis Blair acknowledged some difficulty in distinguishing between covert action and some military operations. In response to a written question from SSCI asking how he differentiated among "covert action, military support operations, and operational preparation of the environment," Blair conceded that "[t]here is often not a bright line between these operations" (US Senate 2009a, 15). Similarly, in answer to the same question as part of his nomination to be CIA director, Panetta admitted that "the line between covert actions under Title 50 and clandestine military operations under Title 10 has blurred," and expressed his concern that although Title 10 operations were "practically identical" to Title 50 ones, the former "may not be subjected to the same oversight" (US Senate 2009b, 15; Kibbe 2012).

It was clear in June 2009 that some members of Congress were becoming fed up with the sense that SOF were conducting some unacknowledged missions that were falling through the oversight cracks. In its report on the Intelligence Authorization Act for FY 2010, HPSCI noted "with concern" that "[i]n categorizing its clandestine activities, DOD frequently labels them as 'Operational Preparation of the Environment' (OPE) to distinguish particular operations as traditional military activities and not as intelligence functions. The Committee observes, though, that overuse of this term has made the distinction all but meaningless" (US House 2009a, 48). HPSCI further complained that "[w]hile the purpose of many such operations is to gather intelligence [meaning those operations are not covert actions], DOD has shown a propensity to apply the OPE label where the slightest nexus of a theoretical, distant military operation might one day exist. Consequently, these activities often escape the scrutiny of the intelligence committees, and the congressional defense committees cannot be expected to exercise oversight outside of their jurisdiction" (Ibid., 49; Kibbe 2012).

Rep. Rush Holt (D-NJ) expressed similar concerns at a HPSCI subcommittee hearing in October 2009:

> There is a lot that one could imagine that is going on in the world these days, whether it be remote killings or assassinations or intelligence collection ... —or other kinds of actions—that fall somewhere between Title 10 and Title 50, depending on who does them and how they are done. It has become practice here on the Hill not to brief some of these activities. It is not clear whether some of those activities are briefed to anyone. But, in any case, they are often not briefed to the Intelligence Committees when I think a reasonable person would say [those activities] are intelligence activities or [that] there are significant intelligence components of the activities. (US House 2009b, 55)

One of the witnesses reinforced Holt's point that although certain operations may appear to be under the intelligence committees' jurisdiction, "because they are considered at least by the Defense Department to be a part of a military operation, they say jurisdiction belongs to the Armed Services Committee. And ... sometimes the Armed Services Committees get notice and sometimes they don't, of what is being done in preparation for a military operation"[7] (Kibbe 2012).

At some point (it is unclear exactly when) the Obama administration did begin briefing the "appropriate" committees on "all lethal action" taken outside of Iraq and Afghanistan (it is also unclear just how extensive that briefing is) (Obama 2013). Those briefings notwithstanding, in March 2012 Congress began to require that the Pentagon provide the armed services committees with quarterly briefings on its counterterrorism operations (Whitlock 2013b). While this step (and, indeed, the Obama administration's briefings) is an improvement, it fails to sufficiently close the existing oversight gaps. First, while it does give the armed services committees a more thorough view of military operations, the measure does nothing to fix the fact that the key overseers of covert action, the intelligence committees, do not have a full view of what the United States is doing covertly around the world. Second, in a major difference from CIA covert actions, the measure does not by law require presidential approval of the military operations. Third, it is doubtful that this reporting requirement includes the military's various categories of "beyond classified" programs. The military has three kinds of Special Access Programs (SAPs) to provide need-to-know and access controls beyond those normally provided by the government's "standard" levels of classified material, that is, confidential, secret, and top secret information. While currently the Defense Department does provide the defense committees with a list of the SAP program names every year (this list of the names alone runs to 300 pages), two other categories ("waived SAPs" and "unacknowledged SAPs") are only reported, in the vaguest terms, to the committee leadership (Priest and Arkin 2011b; Kibbe 2012). While the CIA has a similar program (the Controlled Access Program, or CAP), with similar reporting restrictions, the fact that at least two-thirds of Washington's intelligence programs are under the Defense Department gives some indication of why the continued lack of clarity on SOF programs is a problem (Priest and Arkin 2011b).[8]

The Obama administration reportedly also increased the requirements for White House, NSC, and Pentagon review of JSOC operations outside of war zones (Mazzetti 2010; Ambinder 2010; DeYoung and Jaffe 2010; Ignatius 2011a), efforts that led to the signing of a classified presidential policy guidance (PPG) in May 2013 (Baker 2013). Over a year in the drafting, the PPG ostensibly laid out the guidelines for lethal action outside of war zones, by both CIA and JSOC, including drone strikes and other covert actions. Unfortunately, the president's speech about the guidelines was less than clear on several issues and leaks to reporters yielded different assessments of whether, for example, the PPG actually tightened or loosened drone targeting (Zenko 2013).

The lack of clarity aside, increased scrutiny within the executive branch does not obviate the need for legislative oversight. For one thing, even if there is stricter internal review now, that would not necessarily carry over to a different administration. More importantly, however, the real question is whether there is sufficient review of the procedures and operations by people outside the circle of officials who have a vested interest in the program or the administration. That is the central importance of requiring congressional oversight of covert operations. That is not to say that congressional oversight is always done well or is without its own problems and constraints (Kibbe 2010a; Zegart 2011a), but requiring administration officials to explain and justify their covert action decisions to the legislative branch does increase the chances that potential problems will be raised before it is too late (Kibbe 2012).

There is, of course, a continual balancing act that needs to be maintained between covert operators being able to act quickly on new intelligence and taking the time to conduct due oversight. Critics of strengthening legislative oversight argue that it is too cumbersome and slows down the targeting process, thus handicapping the United States' counterterrorist efforts. But when counterterrorism operations are emphasized to the degree that they have been, it is all the more important to have people outside the inner circle asking tough questions. As we have already seen in Pakistan and Yemen, lethal operations that go wrong can dramatically erode support for the United States among the local population that is, after all, where the battle against terrorism is really being fought (Kibbe 2012).

It is clear that the current law governing covert action and laying out the requirements for congressional notification and oversight needs to be updated. Written in 1991, its authors could not have foreseen how the issue would change in the ensuing twenty years in terms of actors (with the growth of SOF), issues (with the rise of terrorism), and technology (with the advent of drones and advances in intelligence collection).[9] The explanation and guidelines for the TMA exception need to be updated in light of current circumstances with a view to closing what has become a notably wide loophole and enforcing the requirements for covert action more stringently (Kibbe 2012). We should not forget why the covert action legislation was adopted in the first place. As Jack Devine, a former top covert operator for the CIA captured the dilemma, "We got the covert action programs under well-defined rules after we had made mistakes and learned from them. Now, we're coming up with a new model and I'm concerned there are not clear rules" (quoted in Shane, Mazzetti and Worth 2010).

Convergence

So far, this chapter has discussed SOF and CIA operations independently, partly because that is largely how they originally functioned in the aftermath of 9/11 and partly for the sake of clarity. The reality, though, has become a good bit more complex. The CIA faced the aftermath of 9/11 with a greatly reduced paramilitary division, its ranks having been decimated by post–Cold War budget cuts. All of a sudden, it was being asked to smooth the way into Afghanistan and to pursue al-Qaeda and its affiliates around the world. As a result, the agency borrowed or "opconned" (assumed operational control over) members of SOF to help with the workload. Even while Rumsfeld was fighting fierce bureaucratic battles against the CIA to ensure JSOC took the lead in counterterrorism, there were reports of how well CIA and JSOC operators on the ground were working together (Kibbe 2012).

As the "war on terror" expanded, despite some lingering turf battles, their operators and missions became increasingly integrated. In discussing some of the operations that have taken place under the 2004 ExOrd, for instance, senior US officials said some of the military missions have "been conducted in close coordination with the CIA" while in others, "the military commandos acted in support of CIA-directed operations" (Schmitt and Mazzetti 2008). Similarly, the Obama administration's campaign in Yemen was described in June 2011 as being "led by" JSOC and "closely coordinated" with the CIA (Mazzetti 2011; Kibbe 2012).

Much of the bureaucratic tussling was gradually alleviated through the improved personal relationships among the key figures as Gates took over from Rumsfeld at Defense, Gen. Michael Hayden became CIA director, and Gen. James Clapper replaced Stephen Cambone as the under secretary of defense for intelligence. It was also a function of JSOC Commander Lt. Gen. McChrystal's willingness to pursue collaboration with other agencies as part of his drive to maximize the efficiency of battlefield intelligence. In 2009, another close relationship, that between CIA Director Leon Panetta and McChrystal's successor as JSOC commander, VAdm. William McRaven, yielded an unprecedented agreement setting out rules for joint missions (Nakashima and Jaffe 2010; Gorman and Barnes 2011; Ignatius 2011b; Kibbe 2012).

By mid-2011, this new phase of the militarization of US counterterrorism policy, the convergence of CIA and JSOC operators, was "so complete that U.S. officials ranging from congressional staffers to high-ranking CIA officers said they often [found] it difficult to distinguish agency [CIA] from military personnel" (Miller and Tate 2011).

Meanwhile, by 2006 there were indications that policymakers were thinking about how to combine what they saw as the advantages of the two organizations. Michael Vickers, then with the Center for Strategic and Budgetary Assessments but soon to become the assistant secretary of defense for special operations and low-intensity conflict, emphasized in a congressional hearing the "critical" nature of "making full use of authorities in the Global War on

Terror," "particularly the flexible detailing and exploitation of the CIA's Title 50 authority" (US House 2006, 7; Kibbe 2012). Vickers's statement highlights an elusive aspect of the debate over covert action. This chapter has, so far, focused on the domestic legal differences between CIA and JSOC covert action, that is, the more stringent and clear oversight requirements for the former as opposed to the latter. Vickers, though, was referring to the international political differences between the two: the reality that in a situation where a covert operation goes wrong, the diplomatic fallout is likely to be worse if the military is involved than if it is a CIA action. Even though both constitute a violation of sovereignty, most countries have intelligence agencies that conduct espionage and covert action (albeit not at the same rate as the United States), so while there might well be some form of protest about a CIA covert action, most governments accept it as a de facto reality and want to preserve their own room for similar action (Stone 2003). But if US military personnel are caught conducting covert operations in countries where the United States is not at war, such activities could be interpreted as acts of war under international law but, at a minimum, could attract far more negative attention (Kibbe 2004, 2012). It is for precisely this reason that Pakistan's government essentially looks the other way at CIA drone strikes on its territory while refusing to allow JSOC strikes or personnel on the ground.

Thus, by detailing JSOC personnel to the CIA, policymakers could leverage the CIA's wider international room to maneuver to conduct JSOC operations on a more wide-ranging basis, albeit at the cost of having to inform Congress. This "flexible detailing" means that in each situation, the administration can weigh the trade-off between the domestic and international ramifications. Notably, according to all accounts, this was the way the bin Laden raid was conducted on May 2, 2011. It was in all respects a JSOC operation, but was nominally run under the CIA's imprimatur because Pakistan was kept in the dark. One administration official described the bin Laden strike as the "proof of concept" for the administration's new strategy in the fight against terrorism, implying that more such operations will be in the offing (Gorman and Barnes 2011; Kibbe 2012). Sure enough, just five months later, the drone attack that felled the charismatic imam Anwar al-Awlaqi in Yemen was conducted by a combination of JSOC and CIA drones operating under CIA authority. As one journalist described it, Awlaqi's death represented "the latest, and perhaps most literal, illustration to date of the convergence between the CIA and the nation's most elite military units in the counterterrorism fight" (Miller 2011b). There has even been discussion of exploiting the "flexible detailing" of CIA's authority as one of the options being considered for post-pullout Afghanistan: putting JSOC troops in the country under CIA control after 2014 so that both Washington and Kabul can claim that US troops are no longer present (Dozier 2012).

The problem, however, is that if an operation is really just a JSOC raid being run under the CIA's Title 50 authority (a process known as "sheep-dipping" (Mazzetti 2013a), as opposed to a CIA raid run with some help from JSOC personnel), then the distinction between the two begins to blur. And in fact the CIA's authority over the bin Laden raid seems to have been a bit contrived. Even CIA Director Panetta said that although he was formally in charge because the president had chosen to conduct it as a covert operation, "I have to tell you that the real commander was Admiral McRaven because he was on site, and he was actually in charge of the military operation that went in and got bin Laden" (Panetta 2011). Note that Panetta himself describes it as a military operation. The problem with blurring or ignoring the differences between the CIA and JSOC is that the ostensible plausible deniability that is seen as the virtue of CIA operations becomes precariously thin (Kibbe 2012). Moreover, while such detailing could improve oversight (assuming the CIA notifies Congress appropriately), it is unclear whether in such a situation the CIA would have sufficient insight into the operation's planning to be able to brief Congress adequately.

Consequences

Covert action carries political and diplomatic risks, no matter which operators are used, and one major consequence of all this militarization of counterterrorism is that under the present oversight system, only the CIA risks are being evaluated as such since the Pentagon and the armed services committees define military covert action away as TMA. As explained above, though, in some cases the risks could be even worse when covert action is conducted by JSOC. And the recent popularity of "sheep-dipping" raises the question of whether the new types of risks that it raises are being appropriately considered.

In addition to the general foreign policy risks of conducting any covert action in another country, military covert operations raise the additional issue of what would happen to the operatives if something goes wrong. CIA operatives understand from the outset that they will be working covertly and that, should they be captured, they cannot expect any formal protection from either the United States government or international law. Military personnel, however, begin their service under the very different understanding that if they follow all lawful orders, they will receive the protection of the government and the Geneva Conventions if they are captured (Kibbe 2004, 2007,

2010b). But what happens if they are captured on a covert operation? If it is in a country with which the United States is not at war, the Geneva Conventions may not apply. Beyond that, it would depend in part on the particular situation and Washington's relationship with the country in question. The results of capture in Mali would likely differ from those of capture in either Pakistan or Iran. As became evident in the aftermath of the early 2011 arrest of Raymond Davis, even Pakistan, begrudgingly cooperative in the United States' shadow war up to that point, tired of its position and extracted a high price, demanding the expulsion of over three hundred covert operatives in exchange for releasing Davis (Perlez and Khan 2011). Although in this case Davis was a CIA contractor, one can imagine the situation would have been even more sensitive if he had been found to be part of the military (Kibbe 2012). There is, moreover, a related risk to using military covert operators. While they may voluntarily agree to forego their military protections, their use may nonetheless set an undesirable precedent that runs the risk of lessening the protection afforded other US military personnel who are subsequently captured in conventional operations (Kibbe 2004, 2007, 2010b, 2012).

Even when JSOC has at least tacit approval from the relevant government, there are still several reasons for caution. First, governmental approval is moot in some of the failed or failing states where there is no central government to speak of and, while Washington claims it has the right to go after terrorists wherever a country cannot do so itself, that claim is not universally accepted and still leaves the United States open to charges of its military running rampant around the world. Second, several states that have allowed JSOC to operate inside their borders have done so only in secret and have been highly reluctant to admit having done so publicly. Thus, even with a government's assent, if word gets out about JSOC's presence, the United States still runs the risk of negative publicity and alienating various other states, which can reduce its diplomatic leverage on a host of other issues.

Another major consequence of relying so heavily on a militarized counterterrorism policy involves the opportunity costs of doing so, for both JSOC and the CIA. Former SOCOM commander Adm. Eric Olson warned Congress in 2010 that because so much of JSOC's time and resources had been devoted to countering terrorism over the last decade (and to the wars in Iraq and Afghanistan as part of that), its preparation for other types of missions, including counterproliferation of weapons of mass destruction, had been shortchanged (Capaccio 2010). As military analyst Michele Malvesti describes the problem, WMD terrorism is "arguably the gravest threat to U.S. national security," and "[v]irtually no other military component or U.S. department or agency has the ability to conduct the full range of counterproliferation missions or address WMD networks under the unique set of conditions in which SOF have been trained to operate and complete such tasks" (Malvesti 2010).

Others have raised analogous concerns about the CIA. While the agency has the "advantage" of (ostensibly) plausible deniability,[10] some critics, including the President's Intelligence Advisory Board, charge that the agency's embrace of lethal counterterrorist operations has undermined its traditional intelligence mission (Miller 2013a). As evidence, they point to the fact that about 20 percent of CIA analysts are now "targeters," "scanning data for individuals to recruit, arrest or place in the crosshairs of a drone" (Miller and Tate 2011). But that means 20 percent fewer people conducting analysis of broader strategic and political issues. During his CIA director confirmation hearings, John Brennan voiced support for reallocating the agency's mission, describing the degree of CIA's involvement in lethal operations as an "aberration from its traditional role" (quoted in Miller 2013a).

Other critics of the CIA's post–9/11 evolution argue that it now functions in all but name as a military force (via its drone program), but without the public accountability expected of the (conventional) military and without the military's training in abiding by the laws of war (Miller and Tate 2011; Horton 2011; Chesney 2012). In the May 2013 PPG laying out his revised counterterrorism policy, Obama expressed a "preference" for the military to take the lead in the use of force beyond war zones, triggering numerous headlines about a momentous shift of the drone program from CIA to "the military" (Klaidman 2013; Mazzetti and Shane 2013a).

While this would ostensibly obviate the issue of a civilian agency conducting what is in essence a military task (large-scale targeted killing), it could well exacerbate the other problems discussed here. For instance, while many commentators assume that "the military" would be more transparent than the CIA, for the reasons listed above, JSOC operations (which is where the CIA's program would most likely go) could well result in less transparency to Congress and the public. In any case, the CIA's reluctance to cede its authority over its drone program combined with Pakistan's distaste for all things US military led to a (far less public) compromise: that the transition in Pakistan (and also possibly in Yemen, where the two units run parallel drone programs) will happen over some undetermined amount of time (Baker 2013; Mazzetti 2013b; Miller 2013b). Given that Pakistan has so far accounted for approximately 80 percent of the drone strikes, it does not appear that the PPG's "preference" will lead to much tangible change anytime soon.

One final consequence of the increasing militarization of US counterterrorism policy, in terms of both giving military units (namely JSOC) more of a role and in relying largely on force, is neatly summed up by the aphorism, "When all you have is a hammer, everything starts to look like a nail."

Secretary of State Hillary Clinton, although reportedly in favor of drone strikes, also complained about the drones-only approach in Situation Room meetings and told the president there should be more attention paid to the root causes of radicalization (Becker and Shane 2012). Clinton's concerns have been echoed in numerous forums questioning the wisdom and ultimate success of the short-term "Whac-A-Mole™" approach. As even former JSOC commander Gen. McChrystal has noted, "the resentment created by American use of unmanned strikes . . . is much greater than the average American appreciates. They are hated on a visceral level, even by people who've never seen one or seen the effects of one" (Crilly 2013).

A major problem of having relied on a militarized counterterrorism policy for so long, though, is that within both the CIA and JSOC, that approach has become so ingrained in a whole generation of operators that, even with a policy change in Washington, turning that instinct off will be very difficult. As one experienced intelligence professional noted about the CIA, for example, more than half of its work force has joined the agency since 9/11, creating a "huge cultural and generational issue. . . . A lot of the people hired since 9/11 have done nothing but tactical work [i.e., man-hunting and targeted killing] for the past 12 years, and intellectually it's very difficult to go from a tactical approach to seeing things more strategically" (Mark Lowenthal, quoted in Mazzetti 2013b).

Conclusion

President Obama has largely kept his promise to cut dramatically the military's imprint in Iraq and Afghanistan. He has, however, continued the Bush administration's expansion of SOF, in terms of both numbers and authorities. As the terrorist threat has evolved from al-Qaeda central in Afghanistan to a more multipronged, disparate threat emanating from AQAP, al-Shabaab, and various other groups in north and west Africa, it is apparent that Washington intends to continue to combat the threat by training local counterterrorism troops where possible, but with continued kinetic US action, much of it covert, where necessary. It is also apparent that, for the latter, the United States plans to continue using both JSOC and CIA covert operators, often together in hybrid operations. That intention raises significant questions about whether those operations are subject to adequate congressional oversight and held to appropriate standards of accountability. This chapter has shown how US law regarding oversight is woefully in need of updating. Some entity outside the administration should be weighing the costs and benefits of CIA, JSOC, and hybrid covert operations, evaluating not just the risks for US foreign policy, but also for the agencies and operators themselves.

Notes

1. I wish to thank Praeger for granting permission to reproduce portions of text in this chapter that originally appeared in "Covert Action and the Pentagon," from *Strategic Intelligence, Volume 3: Covert Action*, edited by Loch Johnson (Westport, CT: Praeger Security International), 131–44.

2. There have also been 116 total strikes in Yemen from 2009 to March 2013, but it is unclear how many of those are drone strikes as opposed to conventional air strikes (New America Foundation 2013a).

3. Ronald W. Reagan National Defense Authorization Act for Fiscal Year 2005, October 2004.

4. See "Presidential approval and reporting of covert actions," 2012, Title 50 US Code— Section 413B. Covert actions are often referred to as Title 50 actions, referring to the section of the US Code that includes their definition.

5. These military actions are known as Title 10 actions, referring to the US Code section that authorizes (conventional) military activity. Although many use Title 50 and Title 10 as shorthand to refer to CIA and SOF operations, respectively, this is inaccurate as the Title 50 definition does allow for military covert operations.

6. "National Defense Authorization Act for Fiscal Year 2012," 2011 (Public Law 112-81, Sec. 1034 December 31).

7. Britt Snider, in US House 2009b, 55.

8. In May 2013, Rep. Mac Thornberry (R-TX) introduced legislation that would require the Pentagon to provide written, post hoc notification to the armed services committees of any "sensitive military operations" involving lethal force or attempts to capture, whether conducted under Title 10 or Title 50 (Whitlock 2013b). While an encouraging attempt to close the TMA loophole, this measure, even if adopted, would still not address the concerns listed here.

9. A further complicating factor that needs to be accounted for in any updating of the covert action legislation is the increasing role being played by private contractors (Dickinson 2012).

10. This is more true for some types of operations than others. As Kenneth Anderson argues, drone strikes, and who is behind them, are not truly covert but instead are at most deniable (Anderson 2011).

PART III

IMPLICATIONS OF MILITARIZATION

Chapter 12

The State Department

No Longer the Gatekeeper

Edward Marks

After the Second World War, the United States led the world in the reform of global governance. It also articulated and implemented a grand strategy to cope with the bipolar order that the war had brought into being. Confronted at present with a comparable crisis in global governance amid massive shifts in the global distribution of wealth and power, the United States has yet to articulate a vision, lead reform efforts, or reformulate its global strategy. This lapse from leadership reflects changes in the US political system that reinforce a militarized approach to foreign policy and make it difficult, if not impossible, for the United States to formulate strategic initiatives or to implement them through diplomacy and other measures short of war.

—*Chas W. Freeman Jr., "The Incapacitation of US Statecraft and Diplomacy,"*
The Hague Journal of Diplomacy, 2011

"Ministries of Foreign Affairs are no longer the monopolists of foreign affairs," as international relations now include domestic agencies and important nonstate actors as major participants (Rana 2011). Today, ministries of foreign affairs are no longer the exclusive channel for international contacts, as important domestic agencies now have their own direct foreign contacts. Facilitated by modern communications, finance and economic ministries are often the primary power brokers in international affairs, while the continuing role of intrastate as well as interstate violence increasingly makes ministries of defense major players. Further complicating the conduct of international relations has been the rise in importance of nonstate actors: international

companies, nongovernmental organizations, global crime and political networks, and even individuals—all with ready access to public media and the
general population. Nation-states are no longer the only players on the field.

For the United States, the challenges that the State Department faces are
especially profound as it competes bureaucratically and politically with the
world's largest military establishment in the conduct of the nation's foreign
affairs. American uniformed personnel and military establishments are on
the ground throughout the world, requiring a complex network of formal and
informal bilateral and multilateral arrangements. Procuring and managing
these security arrangements has become a major theme of the warp and woof
of American foreign policy.

This change in the State Department's gatekeeper role occurred at the
dawn of the Cold War. Prior to World War II, the State Department led in
times of peace, and the military only in times of war. For example, in World
War II, with President Franklin Delano Roosevelt actively involved as
commander in chief, State essentially withdrew from the national security
arena for most of the war. Secretary of State Cordell Hull described this declining influence in his memoirs:

> During peacetime, the State Department had been responsible, under
> the President, for the conduct of our international relations and also for
> making recommendations regarding movements of our military forces
> abroad. When war came, the Department was no longer connected with
> military operations abroad (Hull 1948).

By tradition, State would resume its central role once the armies demobi-
lized. But the almost immediate emergence of the Cold War and the creation
of a permanent military and security establishment through the National Security Act of 1947 prevented the traditional postwar return to prominence of
the Department of State. The establishment of the National Security Council
(NSC) began a significant alternation in the relationship of the departments
and the White House, an alteration that has only increased over the years as
the NSC staff has expanded into a permanent policy and managerial agency.
Meanwhile, in the atmosphere of the Cold War, the Department of Defense
gradually became *primus inter pares* among departments, in practice if not formally. This time the military did not return to their barracks (Breslin-Smith
and Krieger 2011, 7–8).

Since that time, the Department of State has been involved in a constant
effort to define its role as the concept of "foreign affairs" was replaced by
the broader concept of "national security" in which the role of diplomacy or
the conduct of foreign affairs by governments—State's primary function in
traditional terms—was diminished. One challenge was the permanent, daily

presence of the White House in the conduct of foreign affairs as the NSC staff expanded. Another has been that of adjusting to the now permanent presence and involvement of other agencies, and most especially the Department of Defense, in the day-to-day management of foreign relations. If not the "gate-keeper," then what is the role of the Department of State among a collection of specific interest agencies (e.g., defense, finance, intelligence, commerce), all operating under the overall policy direction of the White House?

This chapter describes how State has not been able to accomplish that re-set and create for itself an appropriate new role in the national security structure, and proposes some reforms that might contribute to that end.

Growth of a Parallel Foreign Policy Structure

While almost all departments and agencies of the federal government, not to mention a few states and even cities, have learned to engage in "foreign affairs," they have pretty much done so within the traditional diplomatic structure of the nation-state system. In particular, their permanent overseas operations are established and operate within American embassies. The military, however, while also continuing to participate in embassies as attachés and military assistance teams, have also created a parallel intergovernmental system.

One of the lessons learned in World War II was the need for better-coordinated military policymaking and implementation. Following observation of the British practice, the United States created the Joint Chiefs of Staff structure and then the first unified military command in the Pacific arena: commander-in-chief, Pacific, or CINCPAC as it was known until it became US Pacific Command (PACOM) in the first decade of the twenty-first century. Over the years of the Cold War, the military unified geographic command system was expanded until—with the creation of Africa Command in 2008—every regional area had its own geographic combatant command (COCOM). In addition, there is a Special Operations Command (SOCOM), which has a global combatant mission. (See Kibbe, Chapter 11, for a discussion of the role of SOCOM after 9/11.) This network of operational bureaucracies constitutes a parallel foreign policy establishment practicing daily bilateral and multilateral diplomacy.

A briefing slide from PACOM, reproduced in Figure 12.1, illustrates the two parallel foreign policy establishments as perceived by some in the military. It is quite telling that the slide highlights how the two foreign policy systems are "only tenuously connected."

The increasingly prominent role played by the COCOMs in American foreign policy grew during the Cold War but did not end with it. The 1986

THE TWO FOREIGN POLICIES OF THE UNITED STATES

1. The one conducted by the administration in Washington.
2. The other conducted by the regional unified commanders.

The two are only tenuously connected.

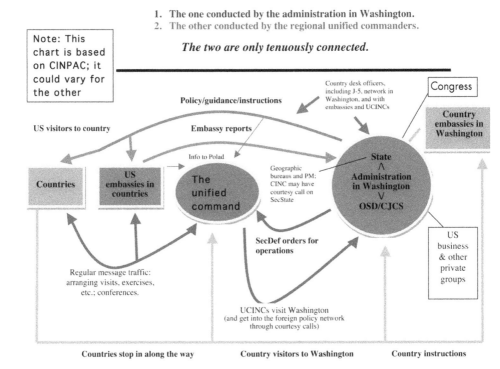

DoD does not instruct embassies; **State does not give orders to UCINCs.**

The problem: How do UCINCs know what the foreign policy is—except through the POLAD?
How do they get instructions on foreign policy matters—say, on China?
(Some might say: "No one knows what the foreign policy is anyway.")
It all unfolds day-by-day, case-by-case, incident-by-incident, though driven mostly by exchanges of visits.

Figure 12.1
A Military Perspective on the Parallel Diplomacy by the Combatant Commands

Source: US Department of Defense, Pacific Command

Goldwater-Nichols reform of the defense community consolidated the geographic commands as operational organizations, and confirmed that US military activity outside US territory was no longer a sporadic activity, confined to wartime, but now a normal activity pursued everywhere in the world. This activist role was then expanded further after the September 11, 2001, attacks with the decision to treat countering the terrorist threat as essentially a military task. The resulting two long-running wars then morphed into military occupations involving counterinsurgency, postconflict reconstruction, nation building, and economic development.

The existence of this dual system means that at any given time in any given country, the US government has two responsible senior representatives: the resident ambassador and the geographic combatant commander. The authority as well as the perspective of the geographic combatant commander is regional as well as bilateral whereas that of an ambassador is essentially local. With the existence of these two parallel "foreign policy" bureaucracies, coordination is heavily dependent on personal relations or high-level coordination in Washington. (See Murray and Quainton, Chapter 9, for an analysis of the relationship between ambassadors and commanders in some detail.)

The process works "pretty well most of the time" but is under increasing pressure due to the prominent operational role of the military services as they have increasingly become the default option for US government action and response. As one political analyst put it: "Over the nearly six decades that separate us from Truman's great moment, the Pentagon has become a far more overwhelming institution . . . it has swallowed up much of what once was intelligence, as it is swallowing up much of what once was diplomacy."[1]

This situation has fostered and been driven by the resource disparity in the federal bureaucracy, a disparity that has grown since 9/11. The wealth of the military services—in money, personnel, and equipment—stems of course from the undeniable resource requirements of war fighting. A number of other problems and challenges—such as natural disaster emergencies, postconflict reconstruction, and nation building—also require the extensive use of resources. Unfortunately, the fact that many of these new missions are essentially nonmilitary tasks does not trump the temptation to use existing Defense Department resources to provide a quick response. That the military may not be the most appropriate organization to perform these tasks is irrelevant; they exist, are available, and can react quickly. Once they are engaged they tend to continue as it is difficult and time consuming to transfer the responsibility to civilian organizations ill-equipped or nonexistent. Bureaucratic as well as political inertia takes over.

The combatant commands have essentially two "bundles" of tasks or portfolios: The first is the obvious mission to plan and fight wars. The other portfolio is composed of military-to-military relations and cooperation with other countries and military forces in "peacetime." These activities—training, military equipment sales, etc.—are generally referred to as "engagement" activities and occupy much of the time, staff, and resources of the COCOM headquarters, especially when they are not managing a war. Justified by an elaborate policy rationale related to potential war planning and fighting, well-funded bi- and multilateral engagement programs often appear to have a make-work character. In any case, well-funded engagement budgets lead to much activity because they can be done, not always because they should be done. Commanders making high-visibility visits during which they announce new or additional security assistance and exchange programs is common. "The military commands, with their forward presence, large planning staffs, and various engagement tools are well equipped for those roles and increasingly welcome them. Today they routinely pursue regional-level engagement by playing host to international security conferences, promoting military-to-military contacts, and providing military presence, training and equipment to improve regional security" (Reveron 2007b; also Reveron, Chapter 4).

Unfortunately, this activity of the geographic commands militates against effective "whole-of-government" programs and therefore coherent foreign policy. First, the "stovepiped" organizational structure and perspective of the federal bureaucracy is an obstacle in itself to a comprehensive interagency approach. Among the federal government stovepipes, the Defense Department stands out for its action-oriented bureaucratic culture and the disparity of resources compared to other agencies. This disparity is reinforced by the unfortunate tendency for our political leadership to consider the military services the default mode in national security. The Defense Department's 1997 Quadrennial Defense Review formally called for this expanded role with a concept called "shape-respond-prepare," which in addition to the capacity to fight and win wars called for "greater emphasis on the continuing need to maintain continuous overseas presence in order to shape the international environment" (US Department of Defense 1997, 1).

When called upon, the Defense Department—with the geographic commands as its agents—responds with alacrity if not always enthusiasm and, in doing so, tends to sweep aside other agencies and departments. This is true even when senior political leadership does not consciously direct a unilateral military approach.

In any case, with the combination of a broad mission, broad discretion, and vast resources, the senior four-star combatant commanders bestride their "areas of responsibilities" like "modern-day pro-consul[s]" (Priest 2003, 70). Compared with the essentially low-key operations of American ambassadors and even senior official visitors from Washington, the highly visible presence of these commanding figures, who tour their areas with extensive entourages, has contributed much to the imbalance in US government official representation. As a Canadian prime minister remarked in a different context, it is difficult and dangerous for a mouse to share a bed with an elephant, even a well-meaning elephant.[2]

In essence, the Department of Defense and its community of geographic combatant commands constitute a separate "foreign affairs" organization that interacts directly with foreign governments at the highest levels in parallel with the Department of State and its embassy structure.

Political Factors Tilting the Balance

Some traditional American political and cultural factors also play roles in the militarization of American foreign policy. American culture has always exhibited a passion for the "man with the gun," from Minutemen to cowboys. During and after World War II, this passion focused on two modern action heroes: the military figure and the spy a la James Bond and Jack Ryan. Popular culture feasted on the heroics of World War II and then extended the obsession into the Cold War years. Movies, books, and then TV were full of heroic adventures, which are always successful through the use of muscles and weapons and, increasingly, technology. John Wayne was the model for the warrior and James Bond for the spy. The movie ends and the villains are defeated. This satisfying result fits well with the traditional American view of war: You fought it, won it, and then went home—as in General MacArthur's insistence that "there is no substitute for victory."

So over the decades from the end of World War II, the American public increasingly came to the view that international problems or challenges can be best met by an energetic use of force. American political leaders come out of this popular culture, are formed by it, and in any case always feel obliged to respond to it. The phrase "Nothing is off the table," threatening the use of direct military power, has become an almost obligatory commitment by American leaders when discussing major international challenges, for instance Iran and its nuclear program.

This popular perspective is not one naturally sympathetic to the ambiguities and time frame of diplomacy. Indeed, the requirements of diplomacy produce impatience and frustration and reinforce the instinct to turn to those demonstrated solvers of problems—the action heroes—and a foreign policy with a marked bias toward military activism. After all, if a given administration cannot really do much about a given problem, it can at least rattle its sword in the media with soldiers marching, planes flying, and ships sailing. A secretary of state getting out of a car or an airplane cannot compete.[3]

Especially after the Korean War, the concept of "national security" took on this tone of "military activism" and focus. In the emotional environment of the early Cold War, exacerbated by the politics of Sen. Joseph McCarthy, many politicians were concerned about being charged with favoring appeasement or anything less than an energetic defense of American interests and the "American Way of Life." The slogan "better dead than red" was seriously adopted in many circles, and helped cultivate military activism. Congress consistently finds defense issues more compelling, even in these days of required budget austerity, and politicians clearly have an interest in associating themselves with patriotism and national strength. The conventional wisdom in Congress is that while voters understand defense spending, international assistance and similar international civilian expenses remain mysterious, wasteful, and somehow irrelevant.

Domestic political constituencies have been another factor in the allocation of department roles in foreign affairs over the years. Departments (and the Congress) keep a careful eye on the interests and advocates of domestic programs and sectors. Every department or agency has a section of the American body politic and economy with a direct collective interest in its mission: from Commerce to Labor to mine safety. That of the Department of Defense is especially prominent, composed as it is of diverse and important elements beginning with the personal interest of service people and veterans and their families and the financial interests of defense suppliers and contractors, all overlaid by identification with strong feelings of patriotism.

Unfortunately, there is one department without a meaningful political constituency: the Department of State. This is not surprising, as State deals in the external aspects of almost all elements of public policy but without a specific, unilateral responsibility for any—except a broad responsibility for representing the country on the international scene. Given this general and undefined responsibility, State inevitably is in the position of brokering compromises between the more focused constituencies and their interests. This is not generally a popular position, and one constantly buffeted by the to-and-fro of politics. (See Adams, Chapter 2, for a detailed comparison of DoD and State Department constituencies.)

In fact, instead of being supported by a domestic constituency, the State Department suffers from a traditional and uniquely American dislike and distrust of foreign affairs and consequently of the department responsible for it. While true of the public in general, it is also prevalent among members of Congress. This is nothing new. Several nineteenth-century commentators noted that the Congress would rather ignore the outside world than recognize it and that therefore, as Presidents McKinley and Roosevelt's Secretary of State John Hay said in his memoirs, the Congress "really seems to think that the State Department has no function but to provide their friends with offices."[4]

Of course State does have, at least theoretically, one important constituent: the president of the United States. State is the one unit of the federal bureaucracy outside of the White House staff that comes closest to sharing the president's comprehensive responsibility and perspective, at least with respect to foreign affairs and national security. State is therefore in theory the implementing instrumentality of the chief executive with respect to overall policy and performance in the foreign policy area. Or at least it once was, and possibly could be again. However the history of the relationship between presidents (and the White House) and State is a rocky one, given the special-interest character of American politics and bureaucracy. Although it may only be a Washington urban legend, John F. Kennedy reportedly asked early in his presidency, and with some asperity, the respected senior diplomat Charles "Chip" Bohlen: "What is wrong with that department of yours, Chip?" and received the reply: "You are, Mr. President, you are."

State's Response

After the end of World War II, Congress made an effort to respond to the new situation concerning the role of State within the new national security structure by first significantly expanding the Foreign Service. Most important was the development of the chief of mission (COM) authority and the accompanying Country Team concept. By 1948, the authority of the resident ambassador had reached a low point with the establishment of essentially independent aid, information, and intelligence organizations and overseas missions. As a Department of State message later put it: "No clear and enforceable guidance existed to coordinate local U.S. policy in countries such as Greece, where three independent U.S. Missions—Diplomatic, Military, and Economic Aid—pursued their own agendas."[5] In 1949, President Herbert Hoover's report to President Harry Truman concluded that ambassadors should have "the ultimate authority overseas with respect to the foreign affairs aspects of program operations" (Simmons 1994).

President Truman made a clear statement of the primary position of the ambassador to Secretary of State Dean Acheson in a 1951 letter: "At the country level, all US representatives to that country must speak and act in a consistent manner. The US Ambassador is the representative of the President of the United States to the country and he is responsible for assuring a coordinated US position" (Simmons 1994). President Dwight Eisenhower took this concept a step further and began the practice of sending individual letters to every ambassador tasking them as chief of mission "to exercise full responsibility for the direction, coordination, and supervision of all Executive branch US offices and personnel," with several exceptions, the most important being that of "personnel under the command of a US area military commander" (Simmons 1994). Thereafter, every president has used the same language in delegating authority to his chiefs of mission.

Congress then codified this chief of mission authority in the Foreign Service Act of 1980 during the Carter administration. The law states:

Under the direction of the President, the chief of mission to a foreign country:

(1) shall have full responsibility for the direction, coordination, and supervision of all Government executive branch employees in that country (except for employees under the command of a United States area military commander) (Public Law 96–465, October 17, 1980).

The Country Team is a logical extension of COM authority. The Country Team is the organizational structure through which COM authority is exercised; it has been organized and operated to behave more like a team than a committee. A specific Country Team is composed of the different organizational representatives who serve under the direction of a specific ambassador (chief of mission) and are subject to that chief of mission's explicitly delegated presidential authority for "integrating executive branch activities within his or her geographic domain." Actually, there still is no statutory or regulatory basis for its composition and functions. However, when Congress enacted the Mutual Security Act of 1951, it essentially conceived the Country Team concept by requiring the president to "assure coordination among representatives of the U.S. Government in each country, under the leadership of the Chief of the United States Diplomatic Mission."[6]

From the beginning there has been some ambiguity in the interpretation of the extent of the executive authority being delegated. Other departments and agencies sometimes dispute what constitutes an applicable COM directive, requiring on-the-ground disagreements to be sent up respective chains of command, ultimately to be resolved when necessary by cabinet-level or presidential authority. This has been especially true with those departments that also conduct extensive foreign operations: the US Agency for International Development, the Department of Defense, and the Central Intelligence Agency.

Chief of mission authority is country specific, provided to ambassadors assigned to a specific country. This complicates any given ambassador's relationship with departments and agencies with regional as well as country-specific responsibilities, especially DoD and its regional combatant commanders, and some intelligence agencies. The ambassadors' relationship with intelligence agencies is also complicated by their concern for protecting sources and methods, the disclosure of which they often claim, through a careful and self-serving interpretation of relevant legislation, lies outside the responsibility of the chief of mission.

The turf question, especially with the Department of Defense and the CIA, has become exacerbated since 9/11 and the inauguration of the "Global War on

Terrorism." There have been problems with aggressive military operations, as for example when members of the "military liaison element" in Paraguay whose presence in the country had not been made known to embassy officials were pulled out of the country after killing an armed robber who had attacked them in 2004. Other deployments were also made without embassy or State Department involvement (Murray and Quainton, Chapter 9). With SOCOM's interest in more "operational flexibility" against terrorists and the dramatic expansion of DoD responsibilities in areas such as postconflict reconstruction, new questions of operational authority are raised.

There has been much commentary over the years on the degree to which the combined chief of mission and Country Team model has actually been successful in managing interagency integration. Most, if not all, observers recognize that there is a gap between a chief of mission's de jure and de facto authority given the tendency of other agency representatives to independently pursue their organization's equities.[7] The Special Inspector General for Iraq Reconstruction, for example, commented in his final report that "agency personnel always report to their department heads in Washington," which will "inevitably exert a countervailing force on interagency coordination" (Special Inspector General for Iraq Reconstruction 2009).

Nevertheless, most observers believe that the chief of mission and Country Team model works well enough most of the time in most embassies. However, this judgment refers essentially to the "tactical" level and to bilateral relations and not to the increasingly "functional," "regional," and "global" character of international relations.

Even with the COM authority and Country Team organization, however, State has lost bureaucratic ground. One reason is the stubborn persistence of the traditional diplomatic culture. Part of the State Department's organizational identity takes the form of the insistence on the centrality of bilateral relations and the role of the resident bilateral embassy. Although this view in fact retains a great degree of validity, changes in the geopolitical environment clearly have diluted it.

State itself has recognized this by greatly expanding the number and role of the geographic bureaus. The geographic bureaus, in turn, have been reinforced and almost submerged by a plethora of so-called functional bureaus— from economic affairs to narcotics, politico-military, human rights, and so on. These bureaus do not have a simple bilateral worldview and are intimately connected with other departments and agencies with similar substantive responsibilities.

Despite these changes, the policy, organizational, and operational inadequacies of the Department of State remain serious and have been outlined in detail in other chapters of this book. However, to some degree this view, widespread among commentators, is an act of blaming the victim. Having been persistently and deliberately sidelined, kept short of resources and influence, and increasingly politicized, the department is then criticized for lacking capability and influence. Unfortunately, the career Foreign Service has adapted to this history by learning to like it, a form of institutional masochism. (For ambassadors, this situation is at least partially compensated for by the personal respect generally accorded to individual ambassadors by their military counterparts.)

So State has come some way along the road to a "whole-of-government" role, and still today no other department, except for the White House itself, has a responsibility for as wide a range of US government interests as does State. The American embassy is arguably the only formal "whole of government" institution in the US government besides the White House. Of course, the State Department shares interest and responsibility for all of these interests with other departments who each, however, have the advantage of focus and constituency support. State is in a sense responsible for managing the traffic flow, but a traffic cop without arrest authority—and no one really likes the traffic cop.

Can a New Balance Be Found?

If all of these factors have indeed produced an imbalance that does not serve our national interests, what can be done about it? A "resetting" of relations and responsibilities between departments will obviously be difficult. Efforts to reorganize are often dismissed as moving around the deck chairs on the Titanic, although this is too easy a criticism as some comparatively minor changes on that ill-fated ship would have made all the difference. Despite natural skepticism about the potential for change, it is worthwhile remembering that the National Security Act of 1947 reconfigured US national security institutions and the Goldwater-Nichols Act of 1986 successfully introduced "jointness" into the military services.

One effort to emphasize the leadership and coordinating role of the State Department was recently launched. The Department of State's first Quadrennial Diplomacy and Development Review (QDDR), subtitled "Leading Through Civilian Power," was released in 2010. The report emphasizes the need to lead the implementation of global civilian operations overseas by empowering and holding accountable chiefs of mission as CEOs of a multiagency effort (US Department of State 2010), although in essence this is merely a restatement of the COM authority contained in the Foreign Service Act. The document emphasizes the role of ambassadors as "whole-of-government" managers of integrated programs.

The QDDR also calls for some internal structural changes to meet new challenges, specifically a new under secretary for economic growth, energy, and the environment; an undersecretary for civilian security, democracy, and human rights; and a new Bureau for Energy Resources and a chief economist. It also calls for the upgrading of existing offices into full bureaus: namely, Counterterrorism and Conflict and Stabilization Operations. These new bureaus continue a historic movement toward the creation of functional bureaus to supplement the old geographic bureaus of the traditional ministry of foreign affairs. Being responsible for specific subjects, for example, economic affairs, and with a global perspective, functional bureaus are inevitably required to work and coordinate with other government departments and agencies with similar missions. Functional bureaus are almost by definition responsible for coordinating US government policy among responsible departments.[8]

But apart from its internal reorganization, the QDDR lacks specificity. Emphasizing the important role of the ambassador does not necessarily make it so, especially since the authority in question has actually been around a long time. Even it if did, a more central management role for ambassadors still leaves a gap at the operational level between the setting of strategic policy by the White House and implementation at the country level.

Three Proposals for Reform

The following three proposals are an attempt to deal with this gap. These proposals are organizational, two concerning the Department of State, the other the Department of Defense.

Mandate Professional Positions

State's current structure and personnel system lacks a clear, firm role for its Foreign Service professionals. As noted in a recent op-ed by three distinguished diplomatic practitioners, we see an

> overwhelming—and growing—presence of political appointees in mid-level and top leadership positions at the State Department. For all their merit, political appointees are short-term officials, subject to partisan, personality-specific pressures. They do not notably contribute to the institution's longer-term vitality, and their ascension creates a system inherently incapable of providing expert, nonpartisan foreign policy advice (Johnson, Neumann, and Pickering 2013).

Even when senior foreign service officers are appointed to senior positions, the process is helter-skelter and highly personalized. There is no place for senior FSOs to serve as professional leaders and role models, in the way the members of the military service chiefs do. The counselor of the Department of State and the director-general of the Foreign Service once played that role, but both positions have long since been downgraded, the latter into a clerical head of personnel (now called Human Resources) and no one today knows quite what the counselor does.

At the political level, on the other hand, there are no institutional arrangements to provide the sort of professional advice analogous to that given by the military chiefs in their area of expertise. The absence of this institutional input means that the longer-term, professional diplomatic perspective is less represented in policymaking.

Correcting this organizational lacuna would be relatively simple organizationally, although extremely difficult politically, as it would require amendment of the Foreign Service Act of 1980. The correction would involve a legislative mandate that the following positions must be filled by career foreign service officers:

- One of the deputy secretaries of state;
- Under secretary for management;
- Counselor of the department;
- Director-general of the foreign service;
- Director of the Foreign Service Institute.

It might also be useful to have the last three positions mandated for fixed terms, analogous to the terms of the office of the members of the Joint Chiefs of Staff.

Importing the Chief of Mission Authority to Washington

The State Department's QDDR aspires to "empower and hold accountable Chiefs of Mission as Chief Executive Officers of interagency missions," in essence repeating what has been the traditional view since the days of President Truman. Another way of putting it is that, under this authority, the ambassador is supposed to perform the role of the chief executive officer of a multi-agency mission. As the QDDR points out, "the best Ambassadors play that role effectively." However, it is no secret that the executive authority of ambassadors as chiefs of mission has often been challenged in the interplay of bureaucratic competition and policy debate. In addition, the managerial expertise of ambassadors as COMs has varied widely with little thought and effort by the department to provide background and training. The clear objective of the

QDDR reforms in this area, therefore, is to turn sometime effectiveness into something more robust and persistent.

Even if successful, however, enhancing the role of ambassadors in the field can only go so far in enhancing the role of the State Department in regional and global policy, and in Washington. As has been pointed out, there are few cross-agency oversight or management authorities between the president/ White House and resident ambassadors with chief of mission authority. The existing COM authority provides a model for how to deal with the challenge of managing multiple department programs working overseas by creating an intermediate management level at the under- or assistant secretary level of the (significantly restructured) Department of State.

The objective would be to strengthen the lines of authority across the stovepipes by "importing" the COM authority back into the headquarters organization of the Department of State, and specifically grant it to what ought to be the key intermediate management level: the regional assistant secretaries (Lamb and Marks 2010). An operational oversight chain of authority would therefore be created running from the president through the secretary of state and assistant secretaries of state, which would oversee and reinforce at each level the integrating role that chiefs of mission are responsible for exercising in their Country Teams.

The thus empowered regional assistant secretaries would provide a middle level in the chain of management to ensure that policy and resources are integrated and coordinated at the policy level and then flow down to Country Teams, rather than going directly through numerous discrete bureaucratic and authority stovepipes. With this authority, the Department of State could provide for integrated management and oversight of all US government civilian and political-military international operations.[9]

Horizontally, an assistant secretary (possibly elevated to the undersecretary level) with COM-type authority would provide a Washington-based mid-level coordinating point for all concerned departments and agencies. Operating as a regional interagency team, the various US government interests and programs could be coordinated at the operational level analogous to the manner in which the Country Team coordinates the various departments at the "tactical" level.

While this arrangement would better integrate military-engagement programs with other government activities, it would not extend to combatant commanders or their assigned forces in combat operations or other "Title 10" missions assigned by the National Command Authority. However, while the combatant commands would continue to prepare and review war plans through their existing military chain of command, the State Department regional assistant secretaries would provide assistance in developing the plans developed at the COCOMs for pre- and postconflict activities to include military-to-military cooperation, liaison arrangements, and humanitarian relief.

Thus, the regional under/assistant secretaries would fulfill the long-expressed desire of the military for an effective civilian counterpart to their geographic commanders. Having the close relationship between the relevant combatant commander and regional assistant secretaries would ensure a strong relationship between peacetime engagement and deterrence and preservation of a stable steady-state situation in the regions.

In sum, the whole Department of State would be reorganized as the Department of Foreign Affairs Coordination, where policy and resource integration directed at the White House or cabinet level would be implemented in a coordinated fashion at the regional under/assistant secretary level, and then at the Country Team level.

Resizing the COCOMs

But reorganizing State would achieve only part of the desired objective. Defense and the military structure also require reorganization. The problematic parallel foreign policy system has arisen with the growth of the post–Goldwater-Nichols combatant command structure. Again to quote Derek Reveron: "[W]hile the State Department is America's lead foreign-policy organization, U.S. military commanders are as much policy entrepreneurs as they are war fighters, and they increasingly fulfill important diplomatic roles" (Reveron 2007b).

The geographic commands have essentially two tasks: war planning and fighting and intragovernment military engagement. Both tasks remain, and will always remain, fundamental responsibilities of the Department of Defense and the military services. However, while the war-planning-and-fighting responsibility is obviously uniquely a duty of the Department of Defense and the military services, the government-to-government military programs no longer can be handled as a discrete military activity. In today's world, US military commanders can no longer be permitted to operate as "policy entrepreneurs" except as part of the overall US government, as part of the total team. The so-called "nexus" of security challenges—terrorism, narcotics, smuggling, international criminal networks, etc.—can no longer be managed as single agency programs but must be integrated into "whole-of-government" programs.

But if the COCOMs as robust bureaucratic organizations contribute to this imbalance, what could replace them, or how could they be reorganized? After all, these responsibilities must be performed in some manner by someone.

Perhaps another way to pose the question is to ask "Could much of the work-load done at the COCOMs be accomplished more efficiently through a division of labor between the Joint Staff and Service headquarters rather than maintaining separate four-star commands?" (Kosloski 2012).

This approach suggests it might be possible to separate the two portfolios: the war-planning-and-fighting mission would stay with the current COCOMs (perhaps downsized some) while the intragovernment military-engagement mission would be reassigned to a unified support organization, located somewhere in the United States but preferably in the Washington, DC, area under the authority of the Joint Staff and in close proximity to the Department of State, USAID, the intelligence community, and other pertinent parts of the US government. Within the Department of Defense this "engagement command" (foreign military sales, foreign military training, etc.) would report directly to the Joint Staff while operating downstream in support of beefed-up military representation in American embassies.

This arrangement would recognize the essentially bilateral character of military engagement programs while providing for greater integration with coherent, overall foreign policy (Marks 2010a). All of the present range of military-engagement activity—from international military education and training to medical and dental teams—would be planned and implemented by military members of our individual embassy Country Teams and would therefore from initiation to completion be an integral part of our overseas operations and relationships. Interagency coordination—"whole of government" operations—would be a more natural result if it were the product of operators in the field and not the product of two distinct higher headquarters.

This approach would be especially effective if the State Department reforms outlined above were implemented. Then coordination of planning would take place at two levels: the operational level in Washington and the tactical level in the Country Team.

In any case, the primary objective is not to remove or diminish the role of the Defense Department in foreign policy making and implementation but to integrate it into the broader "whole-of-government" of the United States by actually moving its "engagement" activities into the broad stream of "engagement" activities of the rest of the foreign policy community.

Conclusion

If the perspective of the State Department as a uniquely "presidential" department is accepted, then the effectiveness of State depends to a large degree on its being used appropriately. The record is mixed. The periods of high and effective usage obviously match the incumbencies of the "great" secretaries of state: people like Dean Acheson, Henry Kissinger, and George Shultz. In each case, the most notable aspect of their success was their relationship with and support of their president. The secretary of state is not an independent actor; the role requires a close supporting partnership with the political principal but these situations are heavily driven by personality. Despite occasional recoveries by especially strong secretaries, the long-term trend has produced the present situation that many feel suffers from an imbalance in our management of foreign affairs, an imbalance that does not serve us well in today's world. This development in itself is not to be regretted. However, pending further developments it leaves the US government in a difficult position vis-à-vis management of its foreign policy obligations. Governments deal with each other across a multiplicity of contacts and subjects, across a bewildering network of department relationships. This cannot be changed; there is no going back to the "gatekeeper" situation. But some order is required.

The Department of Defense reports to the president and then operates a parallel foreign policy system that maintains a separate operational US government relationship with foreign governments. It is true that the Defense Department interacts with the Department of State and other departments at various levels in Washington, and that the deployed COCOMs interact with embassies across the globe. However, this is a coordination relationship between two systems, not an integrated governmental system.

In essence, then, this chapter is proposing three reforms that could better integrate the foreign policy structure of the US government. These changes would facilitate any president who consciously wishes to better utilize the Department of State as an "executive agent" for implementing the strategic policy decisions made in the White House.

The three organizational changes discussed in this chapter—providing a professional institutional mentoring role for the Foreign Service, empowering State to operate as a midlevel implementation chairperson, and shifting a significant amount of COCOM operating authority away from the COCOMs—would inevitably lead to greater integration. Until we go at least some way down these roads, the United States will continue to wrestle with a bifurcated foreign policy bureaucracy. Secretary of State Henry Kissinger once commented that he had no telephone number with which to call Europe. How fortunate the other countries of the world are, then—they have two telephone numbers with which to call Washington.

Notes

1   Tom Engelhardt, "How to Trap a President in a Losing War," Twitter, September 24, 2009.

2. Former Canadian prime minister Pierre Trudeau is attributed as using this metaphor to describe Canada's relationship with the United States. When addressing the Press Club in 1969, he said that "living next to you is in some ways like sleeping with an elephant. No matter how friendly and even-tempered is the beast, if I can call it that, one is affected by every twitch and grunt."

3. The CIA has also been affected by this military activism bias. Created primarily for intelligence gathering and analysis, it has over the years increasingly engaged in quasi- or semimilitary activities, to where today it conducts—only semicovertly—a kinetic air war that parallels a similar effort by the US Air Force.

4. Quoted in *All the Great Prizes: The Life of John Hay from Lincoln to Roosevelt* by John Taliaferro (New York: Simon & Schuster, 2013, 392).

5. "Circular Telegram from the Department of State to All Diplomatic Missions," *Foreign Relations of the United States, 1955–1957, Foreign Aid and Economic Defense Policy*, vol. X, Document 21 (Washington, DC: Government Printing Office, July 24, 1956).

6. Public Law 165 found at www.gpo.gov/fdsys/pkg/STATUTE-65/pdf/STATUTE -65-Pg373.pdf.

7. Robert Oakley and Michael Casey noted that the core problem with Country Team management was that "other agencies often view the Ambassador as the Department [of State's] representative, rather than the President's." For these and other reasons, there remains a significant chasm between the chief of mission's formal authority and his ability to exercise it. See Oakley and Casey 2007.

8. "Presidents Are Breaking the U.S. Foreign Service," By Susan R. Johnson, Ronald E. Newmann, and Thomas R. Pickering, *Washington Post*, April 11, 2013.

9. A fuller discussion of this approach is contained in Marks 2010a.

Chapter 13

Conclusion
Does Mission Creep Matter?

Gordon Adams

This book has explored in depth the "militarization" of US statecraft, a grow-ing civilian/military institutional imbalance that is the result of several trends: 1) a pervasive sense in the policy world that the military is the primary and most effective instrument for defining and pursuing national security aims; 2) a consequent tendency for national security strategy to be defined as mili-tary strategy, for foreign and national security policy decisions to be framed in terms of military issues and capabilities, and for national security to mean military security and action by the uniformed forces; 3) a resulting "mission creep" toward the military instrument of statecraft, especially over the past decade (building on earlier patterns), bringing the military into areas that are not its core competence, which are then institutionalized in and funded through DoD; and 4) the self-fulfilling prophecy that results—the forces be-come the default instrument when a national security problem arises, which in turn further resources and strengthens the military, widening the institu-tional imbalance.

The militarization described in this book takes many forms and covers different areas. There is a difference in emphasis among the chapters about the implications of this trend, but all of them agree that mission creep has occurred. Most point to an acceleration of this trend over the first decade of this century, although its roots are to be found earlier in Cold War history. Most, but not all, of the chapters express concern about this trend and its im-plications for the capabilities and role of the civilian institutions in foreign policy. Most of the chapters suggest possible reforms to the authorities and processes in US foreign policy that might remediate the trend.

Some of the authors argue that mission creep is inevitable and not as harmful as others suggest. The overreliance on the military for noncombat tasks is real, some would argue, but is not the consequence of a military eager to take on these roles. The most important source of this trend, this argument would suggest, is the decisions made by senior policymakers—"the president made me do it."[1] The Defense Department and the military, in this view, do not seek such mission expansion and would happily turn responsibility for such missions as reconstruction over to empowered civilian institutions. However, given that the civilian institutions cannot raise the funds and are not organized or staffed to execute the missions, but they must be performed, the military must be ready to perform them.[2] This view is set out in detail in the Defense Department's 2005 Directive 3000.05, laying out basic doctrinal direction for the military's role in stabilization and reconstruction missions (see Adams and Murray, Chapter 1).

The argument has merit. Presidents respond to crisis or decide to carry out an intervention overseas, and seek the capabilities they need to bring to bear rapidly. The military is a readily available tool for such missions, with an operational culture and a "can do" attitude. It is the institution with surge capacity. The acceleration of "mission creep" over the past decade clearly reflects White House decisions to pursue terrorist organizations around the world, remove the Taliban in Afghanistan, and overthrow Saddam Hussein in Iraq. President Bush asked the military to undertake a leadership role; both he and President Obama have endorsed a global mission for the Special Operations Forces in counterterror, security assistance, and development operations (Feickert 2013).

The reality of such decisions does not necessarily answer the question of whether the military is the best or most appropriate tool for such interventions. As Dobbins (Chapter 3) points out, it is not inevitable that the military take the lead in noncombat operations. The US intervention in the Balkans distributed roles differently than in Iraq, with the State Department taking a lead on reconstruction and governance programs. In the case of Iraq, the Defense Department vigorously asserted a leadership role across the board.[3] And as Dobbins points out, there is a difference between a smaller-scale humanitarian intervention and a larger-scale counterinsurgency. DoD did not expect to encounter social and economic disintegration or an insurgency in Iraq, for which there had been no broader governmentwide planning.

Given the trajectory of the militarization trend, it may appear to be a self-fulfilling prophecy. Repeatedly asked to perform such missions, the military services have become more accustomed and prepared to do them, especially over the first decade of the twenty-first century. Over time, this can lead to the reality that because the military is used, it is prepared; and because it is prepared, it is used.[4] It is clear that some in the military wish to retain and build on the capability to perform such missions, while others argue for a return to more conventional war-fighting capabilities.

This internal argument in the military suggests a second line of argument: the trend is acceptable, even necessary. Some advocates of mission creep argue that it reflects a fundamental change in the nature of conflict in the twenty-first century. US conventional military dominance, in this view, forced adversaries to adopt less direct or "asymmetrical" tactics: insurgency, improvised explosive devices, disruption of governance, and terrorist attacks. From this perspective, traditional conventional war is a thing of the past. Given the realities of globalization, the military must adapt, focusing on such missions as "building partner capacity," counterinsurgency operations, "winning hearts and minds," cultural awareness, diplomacy, and economic development—in short, nation building by the military.[5]

Again, there is some merit to this argument. The adversaries the United States has faced over the past two decades have used asymmetrical tactics. The Gulf War of 1991 was the last conventional force-on-force battle the US military faced, and not a serious confrontation, at that. It is worth asking, however, whether the militarization of US strategy and tactics risks driving the policy train—the "if all you have is a hammer, everything looks like a nail" perspective. The decision to engage overseas may involve something other than an across-the-board military confrontation of asymmetrical adversaries.

Stepping outside the military framework, US engagement may be a question of which conflicts to engage in and which tools are actually most appropriate for the challenges of terrorist organizations and fragile states. This may be the issue senior policymakers need to consider, not a decision to deal with these challenges through military action. The change in the nature of conflict does not resolve the question of how, more broadly, conflict and instability should be addressed and which instruments of statecraft should be used. Military force is only one tool for confronting instability, terrorism, cultural and religious extremism, or weak or failing states. The issue may be less the changing face of war than it is the need to change the face of US statecraft, as this book suggests.

A third critique of the militarization view argues that the source of the trend is in the failure of US foreign policy institutions to adapt to new global challenges. Overreliance on the military tool, from this perspective, is the result of a failure to integrate the foreign policy toolkit more thoroughly. The response to the trend is to integrate the toolkit more effectively—a "whole-of-government" approach—in order to restore the institutional balance.[6] It is hard to argue against the idea that the foreign policy tools ought to be more synergistically linked. A more integrated statecraft might well lead to more effective American leadership, with the full participation of the civilian foreign policy institutions.

It is not clear, however, that a "whole-of-government" solution would correct the imbalance; the size and culture of the military institutions will not change as a result, and will continue to be better funded, better organized, quicker to respond. A whole-of-government solution with an unbalanced toolkit might not counter the "hammer/nail" problem, but lead instead to enrolling the civilian institutions more fully into the pursuit of an agenda, or a target, that continues to be defined from a military perspective. The result could be what William Olson describes:

> Much of the buzz for reform of the "whole-of-government" . . . is heavily influenced by defense experts. Much of the discussion is how the interagency community must be reconstructed in order to complement military programs and efforts, from contingency operations to counterinsurgency to stability operations, all the reforms aiming to make agencies DoD compliant (Olson 2012).[7]

Iraq and Afghanistan could be a case in point. If the civilian foreign policy institutions had been more capable of executing stabilization and reconstruction operations, they could have been smoothly integrated into a military intervention, leading to a different postinvasion outcome. While this may be correct, it is a level below the actual decision to intervene, which was not driven by the goal of stabilization and reconstruction in Iraq, but by the goal of regime change, ostensibly to halt a nuclear and biological weapons program. The whole-of-government demand followed that decision; it did not precede it. The question of how, where, and whether the United States should intervene, with force *or* civilian capacity, remains unanswered by a "whole of government." The policy question is "whole-of-government" for what?

The most compelling critique of the militarization problem is that it is inevitable, from a political and budgetary point of view. State and USAID will just never acquire the resources—budgetary and human—let alone the institutional coherence, planning skills, operational capability, or constituency that will rebalance the toolkit. This is an "if you can't beat 'em, join 'em" point of view. When State lacked the budgetary and fiscal resources to staff reconstruction teams in Iraq (Provincial Reconstruction Teams, or PRTs), for example, the Defense Department, with State support, asked the Congress for a temporary authority permitting DoD to transfer funds to State for such operations (called Section 1207 authority). To cite another example, in 2010, State negotiated with DoD to create a new, highly flexible joint security assistance program—the Global Security Contingency Fund (GSCF), following the same principle: DoD had the resources; State did not (Serafino 2012b). While GSCF is a joint fund, the larger pool of available funding would be provided by DoD. From State's point of view, GSCF allows it to pursue flexible security assistance programs using DoD resources. But the fund gives DoD decision-making authority on issues that once belonged solely to State. And it is not clear that the programs and projects that are funded are choices that State would make if it had control over its own funding for such a program.

The Consequences of the Institutional Imbalance

While some see the militarization trend as inevitable, perhaps benign or even advantageous, there are potentially seriously negative consequences for US foreign and national security policy that are worth examining. First, asking the military to conduct such noncore missions may run a high risk of failure, as they are not core to military competence and unlikely to become so. Failure, such as the lack of sustained democratic governance in Iraq, corruption in Afghanistan, or development and social projects funded and executed by the military that have been abandoned or are unsustainable in both countries, has consequences for the credibility and effectiveness of US foreign policy.[8]

The US military has worked hard to develop the capacity to succeed in these noncore missions. The learning curve has been steep, however, and it seems increasingly clear that the expertise for building sustainable health and education systems, maintainable roads, profitable private enterprise, and stable governance able to direct security forces professionally is not a core competence of the US military.[9] Anderson and Veillette (Chapter 6) have shown how DoD lacks expertise in development, puts a priority on the visibility of its noncombat programs for public information reasons, but not because they are sustainable long-term, and has made cultural missteps. This has not discouraged some in the US military, especially the Special Operations Forces, from seeking to expand the model, as part of what is called "building partner capacity," enhancing the capabilities of security forces in a number of other countries and providing economic, social, and governance assistance. But the questionable results of these efforts in Iraq and Afghanistan risk diminishing the reputation and effectiveness of American statecraft, while the diversion of the military from its core capabilities and missions risks compromising its effectiveness at performing its core missions.[10]

The militarization trend also risks becoming a self-fulfilling prophecy, with long-term consequences for the effectiveness of the civilian agencies. The more the military is asked to substitute for civilian competence, the weaker the civilian tools become, with a consequent further loss of credibility with the Congress and the American public. As William Olson argues, it leads to

> DoD components, who on the one hand increasingly see themselves as the only agency competent to act effectively, regardless of issues; and on the other hand who bemoan other agencies, unwillingness to do their fair share. This has meant years and years of under-investing in the non-military components of national security and foreign policy. Components then blamed for not being prepared to help DoD fight the wars it wants and knows how to fight (Olson 2012).

The most significant negative consequence of the militarization trend for US foreign policy is the increased risk of "blowback." The more the military assumes a central role in US foreign policy, the more it is turned to for non-core missions, the more the international community may come to see US international engagement as wearing a uniform. Encountering the United States in uniform in another country may be fine for the military of that country; it may even be popular for the child helped by a military doctor in a temporary clinic. But it is likely to be less well received by the average citizen or government of another country in most circumstances other than humanitarian and natural disaster relief.[11] The invasions and occupations of Iraq and Afghanistan have not increased the popularity of US foreign policy overseas. The effort to find a headquarters in Africa for the new US Combatant Command—AFRICOM—was rejected by African countries who worried about why, after years of economic assistance programs, the United States suddenly wanted to engage African countries through the military. The headquarters had to be located in Germany, instead.

There is some unease in the State Department about the programs and activities of the Special Forces, AFRICOM, and the US military in Africa.[12] A focus on US security assistance to Africa on counterterror operations risks distorting the training and orientation of African militaries toward the narrow, if important, mission of combating terrorist organizations, undermining the link that should exist between security force assistance and the broader strengthening of governance capabilities in countries with weak governments. This is a subtle point, but it underlines the potential risks in the militarization trend.

Add to this risk the historic reality that for decades the United States has advised well-endowed and powerful militaries in less developed countries that they should remove themselves from politics, social work, and the local economy. The expansion of the US military into noncore missions sends a conflicting message to these militaries—if the US military can be an investor, governance adviser, developer, why not them?

What Is to Be Done?

If the militarization trend is risky for American statecraft, what does this book offer as the corrective? There are steps these chapters recommend to correct the trend. The authors agree there is a need to strengthen the capabilities, authorities, and funding of the civilian institutions in the toolkit, though many of their proposals for reform are embedded in an objective of improving "whole-of-government" operations. Several authors suggest reforms that would expand the authorities of the State Department over a range of foreign policy and national security activities.

In the area of reconstruction assistance, Anderson and Veillette (Chapter 6) would restrict DoD-run development activities to active conflict situations. They see a place for a military role in conflict prevention and conflict resolution, disasters, security sector reform, and HIV/AIDS prevention and treatment. In all these cases, however, they argue that the military should be subordinate to civilian leadership. In the security assistance arena, Serafino (Chapter 7) suggests that all security assistance programs, including those funded and administered solely within the Defense Department, might require State Department concurrence, which would expand State's authority. In addition, she suggests that USAID might be given some oversight over security assistance programs in country, when they include "development-like military activities." Finally, she suggests that State will need additional personnel to oversee these responsibilities.[13]

Dobbins (Chapter 3) is considerably more ambitious for the civilian institutions. Based on his Balkans experience, he proposes new legislation to clarify agency responsibilities for complex operations and urges that authority over all the noncombat elements of complex operations, along with all of the funding, be in the hands of the State Department, with the authority to distribute those funds as appropriate to other agencies, including the Defense Department. USAID, he argues, is an appropriate lead capability for reconstruction operations, under State Department leadership.

Marks would go even further, expanding State Department authority to coordinate policy and operations more broadly. He proposes a reorganization of the entire department into a Department of Foreign Affairs Coordination, which would include regional assistant secretaries with the responsibility for integrated management and oversight of all US government civilian and political-military operations.[14] In this design, he would substantially expand the role of the regional assistant secretaries to coordinate actions in Washington, DC, that would then be transmitted to the country teams (headed by the ambassador) in the field.[15] This would put the regional assistant secretaries on a more equal level with the current authorities of the military's combatant commanders. Within this construct, the regional assistance secretaries would help develop postconflict reconstruction planning with a smaller COCOM.

Many authors recognize that field-level operations are often less conflict-laden than the turf battles that can preoccupy Washington, DC. (Marks Chapter 12) notes that field-level cooperation is often less contentious than DC turf battles. Murray and Quainton (Chapter 9) note that ambassadors generally feel they are not subject to an end-run by the Defense Department or the military (with the exception of the Special Operations Forces) and can halt in-country operations they feel run counter to the broader goals of US foreign policy. They point out, however, that the predominance of resources (people and funding) in the military risks distorting US foreign policy goals in the direction of security sector goals and military relationships. They urge greater precision in the president's instructions to new ambassadors about the terms of their relationships with the combatant commanders, as well as clear guidance to the commanders about that relationship. To increase the weight of ambassadorial authority, they urge better briefings for newly embarking ambassadors about the wide variety of military activities occurring at their post and their own authority and responsibilities in the management of these activities. Indeed, training and education are a common theme of the reforms proposed here. Serafino (Chapter 7) also concedes the evident reality that DoD will have greater resources than State and, until that changes, smaller steps may be needed to improve the working relationship. She points to the importance of training in particular, suggesting that new ambassadors need more preparation for their mission-level responsibilities for security assistance programs. While Carlson (Chapter 8) does not recommend specific training needs in the public diplomacy arena, he does underline the importance of appointing a knowledgeable, experienced person to State's senior public diplomacy position as a way to reinforce State's stature in this arena.

Where work clearly still needs to be done, if the militarization trend is to be slowed, is on how one overcomes the obstacles to such reforms. Whole-of-government recommendations, while valuable in the near term, do not clearly right the balance in the toolkit. The obstacles to doing so are great. Perhaps one of the most important, as Cushman (Chapter 5) makes clear, is the way in which the Congress mirrors the imbalance that exists in the executive branch. As a result, he notes, it has proven unwilling to generate or support reform proposals, constrain the growth of military responsibilities, or provide the resources and systematic oversight the civilian agencies need to strengthen their capabilities and right the imbalance. "Nothing will come of any hope that such a balance might organically emerge from Congress," given the reflection of the institutional imbalances he describes in the congressional committee structure and the incentive structure that drives members of Congress.

The militarization trend is an important new dimension of civil-military relations. It does not reflect a struggle over the control of the state, which was Huntington's concern. Nor is it about a gap between the culture of the military and the culture of American society in general. As the trend continues, it does have implications, however, for the way the agenda of US foreign policy is shaped and the selections of policies and tools policymakers may make to implement those policies. As this book suggests, it has major implications for the way policy is implemented and for the long-term balance between the civilian and military institutions responsible for foreign and national security policy.

These implications go deeper than many of the policy recommendations this book discusses. Should the trend continue, the downside risks are failures in the implementation of American foreign policy, because such missions are not core to the military, a further weakening of the civilian institutions, and ultimately a decline in the international welcome for the US presence.

It is not clear how this trend and the resulting imbalance can be reversed. The weaknesses and failures of the invasions and occupations of Iraq and Afghanistan may slow the trend, but they do not seem to have weakened the development of capabilities at DoD that would make it even more inevitable—Special Operations programs, building partner capacity, AFRICOM, for example. It could be that only a major crisis—a rejection of a leading role for the United States, a negative reaction to US military presence, coups in countries the United States has supported with military programs, a major civilian policy or program failure that leads to a decision to strengthen those institutions—will truly slow the trend. Without such a shock, it seems likely that mission creep will continue and the institutional imbalance will widen.

Notes

1. Dobbins (Chapter 3), for example, suggests that the interagency process should be better prepared for these missions, as they are going to continue, driven by senior policymakers' decisions.

2. Reveron makes this argument both in Chapter 4 and in his 2010 book on security assistance.

3. The decision process leading to the Iraq invasion is discussed in detail in Gordon (2007), Ricks (2007), Woodward (2004), and Diamond (2006).

4. Dobbins argues, however, that the capacities to perform such missions have been created anew with each intervention, with a minimum of lessons learned.

5. This is the gist of the argument in Nagl and Schoomacher (2005). It is also the core of the counterinsurgency doctrine Nagl had a hand in writing, along with Gen. David Petraeus

(US Department of Defense 2006), as well as Army doctrine for stabilization and reconstruction operations (US Army 2009).

6. This is the core of the proposals for a different structure of the US government to cope with the complexities of the new challenges. See Project on National Security Reform (2009) and Center for Strategic and International Studies (2005).

7. Nonetheless, some advocates are impatient to get the job done. For example, Reveron states: "As people continue to search for interagency solutions, the military is not waiting. . . . [T]he military is incorporating civilian functions to ensure that it accomplishes national goals" (Reveron 2010, 181).

8. There is by now enough literature on the failures in Iraq to fill a small library. For reference, see Hodge (2011); the Special Inspector General for Iraq Reconstruction (2013), which underlines many failures while it remains studiously neutral about the overall effort; and more critically, Van Buren, a diplomat involved in the reconstruction effort, who notes, among other critiques, the absence of sustainable projects resulting from the American effort: "By 2010, the Iraqi government had taken on only three hundred of the fifteen hundred reconstruction projects we tried to hand over. The rest have been 'put on the shelf,' because they were too shoddy to continue, didn't meet any existing need, or were incomplete and lacked the documentation, plans, and contracts that the Iraqis would require to finish them" (Van Buren 2011, 69–70). On Afghanistan, see Special Inspector General for Afghanistan Reconstruction (2013), which reported: "While there has been major progress in Afghanistan, SIGAR's work since 2009 has repeatedly identified problems in every area of the reconstruction effort—from inadequate planning, insufficient coordination, and poor execution, to lack of meaningful metrics to measure progress. We have also found delays, cost overruns, and poor construction of infrastructure projects. We have also found US-funded facilities that are not being used for their intended purposes. These problems have resulted in lost opportunities and in incalculable waste, but they have also presented opportunities to learn" (SIGAR 2013, cover letter from the IG).

9. Reveron disagrees: "Fundamentally, foreign service officers are diplomats, not urban planners, contract managers, or town councilors. Although diplomats are civilians, they are not more prepared to rebuild countries than their counterparts in the military" (Reveron 2010, 171). However, this argument does not support the notion that the military has greater competence to perform these missions. The United States is full of public- and private-sector personnel more skilled at urban planning, contract management, and governance than either the diplomats or the military, including the professionals at USAID. Downes argues that "the disproportionate capability and funding of the military instrument has encouraged US leaders to see a tempting utility in military force and methods well beyond the boundaries of conventional effectiveness. This has led to applying military forces where their effectiveness is compromised" (Downes 2010, 381).

10. Kibbe (Chapter 11) argues that such missions have distracted the SOF from pure counterproliferation operations and the intelligence community away from intelligence gathering.

11. Freeman argues that even short of mission creep, overreliance on the military has blowback consequences for the United States: "The United States' focus on the retention of global military dominance answers change not with accommodation or revised strategy but with enhanced war-fighting capabilities. It sends a message of suspicion and hostility to the newly wealthy and powerful and inclines them to respond to perceived US animosity with their own" (Freeman 2011, 430).

12. See Murray and Quainton, Chapter 9.

13. This recommendation is consistent with the 2008 report from the Stimson Center and the American Academy of Diplomacy, which urged an expansion of the number of political-military officers at State to enhance the capabilities of the Bureau of Political-Military Affairs over security assistance (Stimson Center and American Academy of Diplomacy 2008).

14. The concept of a drastically restructured State Department, with similarly broad responsibilities and incorporating other agencies such as USAID, was proposed by the HELP (Helping to Enhance the Livelihood of People around the Globe) Commission, chartered by the Congress, in its 2007 report *The HELP Commission Report on Foreign Assistance Reform*, at http://helpcommission.info/.

15. This authority would clearly need to exclude coordination for combat operations, which are the responsibility of combatant commanders.

References

Ackerman, Bruce. 2012. "President Obama: Don't Go There." *Washington Post,* April 20.

Adams, Gordon. 1981. *The Iron Triangle: The Politics of Defense Contracting.* New Brunswick, NJ: Transaction Press.

———. 2011. "The Office of Management and Budget: The President's Policy Tool." In *The National Security Enterprise: Navigating the Labyrinth,* edited by George Roger George and Harvey Rishikof, 55–78. Washington, DC: Georgetown University Press.

Adams, Gordon, and Cindy Williams. 2010. *Buying National Security: How America Plans and Pays for Its Global Role and Safety at Home.* New York: Routledge.

Adams, Gordon, and Becky Williams. 2011. *A New Way Forward: Rebalancing Security Assistance Programs and Authorities,* April 20. Washington, DC: The Stimson Center. http://www.stimson.org/books-reports/a-new-way-forward-rebalancing-security -assistance-programs-and-authorities/.

Adams, Gordon, Cindy Williams, Rebecca Williams, and Trice Kabundi. 2010. "Buying National Security: The Lopsided Toolkit." *The Will and the Wallet: Budgeting for Foreign Affairs and Diplomacy Blog,* February 26. The Stimson Center. http://thewil landthewallet.squarespace.com/blog/2010/2/26/buying-national-security-the-lop sided-toolkit.html.

Advisory Committee on Transformational Diplomacy. 2008. *Final Report of the State Department in 2025 Working Group.* Washington, DC: Department of State

Ambinder, Marc. 2010. "Obama Gives Commanders Wide Berth for Secret Warfare." *The Atlantic,* May 25. http://www.theatlantic.com/politics/archive/2010/05 /obama-gives-commanders-wide-berth-for-secret-warfare/57202/.

———. 2011. "Then Came 'Geronimo.'" *National Journal,* May 7.

Ambinder, Marc, and D. B. Grady. 2012. *The Command: Deep Inside the President's Secret Army.* New Jersey: John Wiley & Sons, Inc.

Ambrose, Stephen, and Douglas Brinkley. 2010. *Rise to Globalism: American Foreign Policy Since 1938.* New York: Penguin.

Anderson, Kenneth. 2011. "Washington Post Stories on the CIA and JSOC—and My Prediction of Harold Koh's Legacy as Legal Adviser." *OpinioJurisBlog,* September 3. http://opiniojuris.org/2011/09/03/washington-post-stories-on-the-cia-and-jsoc -and-my-prediction-of-harold-kohs-legacy-as-legal-adviser/.

Bacevich, Andrew J. 1997. "The Paradox of Professionalism: Eisenhower, Ridgway, and the Challenge to Civilian Control, 1953–1955." *The Journal of Military History,* 61 (2): 306.

———. 2006. *The New American Militarism: How Americans Are Seduced by War.* New York: Oxford University Press.

———. 2007. "Elusive Bargain: The Pattern of US Civil-Military Relations since World War II." In *The Long War: A New History of US National Security Policy Since World War II,* edited by Andrew Bacevich. New York: Columbia University.

———. 2010. *Washington Rules: America's Path to Permanent War.* New York: Metropolitan Books.

Baker, Peter. 2013. "In Terror Shift, Obama Took Long Path." *New York Times*, May 27.

Becker, Jo, and Scott Shane. 2012. "Secret 'Kill List' Proves a Test of Obama's Principles and Will." *New York Times*, May 29.

Bell, Peter, Scott Bland, and Ryan Morris. 2011. "Toeing the Line: A Historical Look at NJ's Vote Ratings Shows Senate Centrists Are in Decline." *National Journal*, February 25. http://nationaljournal.com/magazine/vote-ratings-senate-centrists-in-decline-20110224.

Belote, Howard D. 2004. "Proconsuls, Pretenders or Professionals? The Political Role of the Regional Combatant Commanders." Institute for National Security Studies. http://www.isn.ethz.ch/isn/Digital-Library/Publications/Detail/?id=100788.

Best, Richard A., Jr. 2011. *Covert Action: Legislative Background and Possible Policy Questions*. Report RL33715, December 27. Washington, DC: Congressional Research Service.

Best, Richard A., Jr., and Andrew Feickert 2005. *Special Operations Forces (SOF) and CIA Paramilitary Operations: Issues for Congress*. Report RS 22017, January 4. Washington, DC: Congressional Research Service.

Bishop, Bill. 2008. *The Big Sort: Why the Clustering of Like-Minded Americans Is Tearing Us Apart*. Boston, MA: Mariner Books.

Bradbury, Mark, and Michael Kleinman. 2009. *Winning Hearts and Minds: Examining the Relationship between Aid and Security in Kenya*. Medford, MA: Feinstein International Center, Tufts University.

Breslin-Smith, Janet, and Clifford R. Krieger. 2011. *The National War College: A History of Strategic Thinking in Peace and War*. National War College Alumni Association, Washington, DC.

Brinkerhoff, Derick. 2011. "State Fragility and Governance: Conflict Mitigation and Subnational Perspectives." *Development Policy Review* 29: no. 2: 131–53.

Brooks, Risa. 2008. *Shaping Strategy: The Civil-Military Politics of Strategic Assessment*. Princeton, NJ: Princeton University Press.

Brownstein, Ronald. 2011. "Pulling Apart." *National Journal*, February 27. http://www.nationaljournal.com/magazine/congress-hits-new-peak-in-polarization-20110224.

Burk, Matthew M. 2012. "Navy Seabees Embrace New Roles While Navigating Budget Cutbacks." *Stars and Stripes*, October 28. http://www.stripes.com/news/navy-s-seabees-embrace-new-roles-while-navigating-budget-cutbacks-1.194949.

Business Executives for National Security. Tooth-to-Tail Commission. 2001. *Call to Action*. Washington, DC: 2001. http://www.bens.org/document.doc?id=30. Based on two papers by Tom Davis, "Framing the Problem of PPBS" and "Changing PPBS," unpublished, 2000.

Capaccio, Tony. 2010. "Top US Commando Says War Demands Hinder Global Hunt for Nuclear Weapons." *Bloomberg*, August 27. http://www.bloomberg.com/news/2010-08-26/top-u-s-commando-says-war-demands-compromising-hunt-for-deadliest-weapons.html.

Center for Army Lessons Learned. 2008. *Commanders' Emergency Response Program Handbook: Tactics, Techniques, and Procedures*, March. No. 08-12.

Center for Strategic and International Studies. 2005. *US Government and Defense Reform for a New Strategic Era, Beyond Goldwater-Nichols*. Phase II Report, July. Washington, DC.

Chesney, Robert. 2012. "Military-Intelligence Convergence and the Law of the Title 10/Title 50 Debate." *Journal of National Security Law and Policy* 5 (2012): 599–600.

Clinton, Hillary Rodham. 2009. "Opening Remarks before the House Foreign Affairs Committee." April 22. http://www.state.gov/secretary/rm/2009a/04/122048.html.

Cloud, David S. 2010. "CIA Drones Have Broader List of Targets." *Los Angeles Times,* May 5.

———. 2012. "Greater Role Sought for Special Forces." *Los Angeles Times,* May 5.

Cobble, W. Eugene, H. H. Gaffney, and Dmitry Gorenburg. 2003. *For the Record: All US Forces' Responses to Situations, 1970–2000,* June. Alexandria, VA: Center for Strategic Studies.

Collier, Paul. 2007. *The Bottom Billion: Why the Poorest Countries Are Failing and What Can Be Done about It.* New York: Oxford University Press.

Crilly, Rob. 2013. "Stanley McChrystal Criticises Reliance on Drones as Strikes Hit Pakistan." *The Telegraph,* January 8.

Cushman, Charles B. Jr. 2006. *An Introduction to the US Congress.* Armonk, NY: ME Sharpe. 157–75.

Davenport, Coral, and Yochi Dreazen. 2011. "The Green Lantern." *National Journal,* May 28.

Davidson, Roger, and Walter Oleszek. 2004. *Congress & Its Members.* Washington DC: CQ Press. Ninth Edition.

Deering, Christopher. 1993. "Decision Making in the Armed Services Committees." In *Congress Resurgent: Foreign and Defense Policy on Capitol Hill*, edited by Randall Ripley and James Lindsay, 155–82. Ann Arbor: University of Michigan.

Defense Science Board. 2008. "Task Force on Strategic Communication," January. http://www.acq.osd.mil/dsb/reports/ADA476331.pdf.

———. 2011. *Report of the Defense Science Board Task Force on Strategic Communications.* Office of the Undersecretary of Defense for Acquisition, Technology, and Logistics, September. Washington, DC.

DeYoung, Karen, and Greg Jaffe. 2010. "US 'Secret War' Expands Globally as Special Operations Forces Take Larger Role." *Washington Post,* June 4.

Diamond, Larry. 2006. *Squandered Victory: The American Occupation and the Bungled Effort to Bring Democracy to Iraq.* New York: Holt.

Dickinson, Laura A. 2012. "Outsourcing Covert Activities." *Journal of National Security Law and Policy* 5(2012): 521–37.

Dilanian, Ken, and David S. Cloud. 2012. "A Deepening Role for the US in Yemen." *Los Angeles Times,* May 17.

Dobbins, James. 2008. *After the Taliban: Nation Building in Afghanistan.* Washington, DC: Potomac Books, Inc.

Dobbins, James, Seth G. Jones, Keith Crane, and Beth Cole DeGrasse. 2007. *The Beginner's Guide to Nation-Building.* Santa Monica, CA: Rand Corporation. http://www.rand.org/pubs/monographs/MG557.

Dobbins, James, Seth G. Jones, Benjamin Runkle, and Siddharth Mohandas. 2009. *Occupying Iraq: A History of the Coalition Provisional Authority.* Santa Monica, CA: Rand Corporation. http://www.rand.org/pubs/monographs/MG847.

Dobbins, James, John G. McGinn, Keith Crane, Seth G. Jones, Rollie Lal, Andrew Rathmell, Rachel M. Swanger, and Anga R. Timilsina. 2003. *America's Role in Nation-Building: From Germany to Iraq.* Santa Monica, CA: Rand Corporation. http://www.rand.org/pubs/monograph_reports/MR1753.

Dorman, Shawn. 2005. *Inside a US Embassy: How the Foreign Service Works for America.* Washington, DC: American Foreign Service Association.

Downes, Cathy. 2010. "Unintentional Militarism: Over-Reliance on Military Methods and Mindsets in US National Security and Its Consequences." *Defense and Security Analysis* 26: no. 4, December.

Dozier, Kimberly. 2011. "Building a Network to Hit Militants." *Associated Press*, January 5.

———. 2012. "CIA Could Control Forces in 'Stan after 2014," *Army Times*, March 3.

Draper, Robert. 2012. "The League of Dangerous Mapmakers." *The Atlantic*, October. http://www.theatlantic.com/magazine/archive/2012/10/the-league-of/309084/.

Drezner, Daniel. 2012. "Why Presidents Love Foreign Affairs." *New York Times Campaign Stops Blog*, September 20. http://campaignstops.blogs.nytimes.com/2012/09/20/why-presidents-love-foreign-affairs/.

Dunlap, Charles J. Jr. 1992. "The Origins of the American Military Coup of 2012." *Parameters* Winter 1992–93: 2–20. http://www.carlisle.army.mil/USAWC/parameters/Articles/1992/1992%20dunlap.pdf.

Eisenhower, Dwight D. 1955. *Letter to Secretary of State John Foster Dulles Regarding Transfer of the Affairs of the Foreign Operations Administration to the Department of State*, April 17. Available through the University of California at Santa Barbara American Presidency Project. http://www.presidency.uscb.edu.

Enthoven, Alain C., and K. Wayne Smith. 2005. *How Much Is Enough? Shaping the Defense Program 1961–1969*. Santa Monica, CA: Rand Corporation. First published 1971 by Harper & Row.

Entous, Adam, Siobhan Gorman, and Julian E. Barnes. 2011. "US Tightens Drone Rules." *Wall Street Journal*, November 4.

———. 2012. "US Relaxes Drone Rules." *Wall Street Journal*, April 26.

Entous, Adam, Siobhan Gorman, and Matthew Rosenberg. 2011. "Drone Attacks Split US Officials." *Wall Street Journal*, June 4.

Epstein, Susan. 2011. *Foreign Aid Reform, National Strategy, and the Quadrennial Review*. Report No. R41173. Washington, DC: Congressional Research Service.

Epstein, Susan, and Marion Leonardo Lawson. 2012. *State, Foreign Operations, and Related Programs, FY2012 Budget and Appropriations*, January. Congressional Research Service, Washington, DC.

Farah, Douglas. 1998. "A Tutor to Every Army in Latin America." *Washington Post*, July 13.

Feaver, Peter D., and Richard H. Kohn. 2000. "The Gap: Soldiers, Civilians and their Mutual Misunderstanding." *The National Interest*, Fall, 29–37.

———, eds. 2001. *Soldiers and Civilians: The Civil-Military Gap and American National Security*. Boston, MA. MIT Press.

Feickert, Andrew. 2010. *US Special Operations Forces (SOF): Background and Issues for Congress*. Report RS21048, January 11. Washington, DC: Congressional Research.

———. 2012. *US Special Operations Forces (SOF): Background and Issues for Congress*. Report RS21048, March 23. Washington, DC: Congressional Research Service.

———. 2013. *US Special Operations Forces (SOF): Background and Issues for Congress*. Report RS21048, February 6. Washington, DC: Congressional Research Service.

Feickert, Andrew, and Thomas K. Livingston. 2010. *US Special Operations Forces (SOF): Background and Issues for Congress*. Report RS21048, March 28. Washington, DC: Congressional Research Service.

Fenno, Richard. 1978. *Home Style: House Members in Their Districts*. Boston: Little, Brown.

Fettweis, Christopher J. 2004. "Militarizing Diplomacy: Warrior-Diplomats and the Foreign Policy Process." In *America's Viceroys: The Military and U.S. Foreign Policy*, edited by Derek Reveron, Chap 3. New York: Palgrave and MacMillan.

Fidler, Stephen. 2013. "In Europe, a Moment of Truth on Defense." *Wall Street Journal*, January 31. http://online.wsj.com/news/articles/SB10001424127887323701904578279619279011920.

Finer, Samuel. 1988. *The Man on Horseback: The Role of the Military in Politics*. Boulder, CO: Westview Press.

Fitzgerald, Paula M. 2003. "CJTF-HOA Medical Team Treats Djiboutians." US Marine Corps, February 1. http://www.hqmc.marines.mil/News/NewsArticleDisplay/tabid/3488/Article/77937/cjtf-hoa-medical-team-treats-djiboutians.aspx.

Fowler, Linda, and Seth Hill. 2006. "Guarding the Guardians: US Senate Oversight of Foreign and Defense Policy, 1947–2004." Paper presented at annual meeting of American Political Science Association, Philadelphia, PA, August 31–September 3.

Freeman, Chas W., Jr. 2011. "The Incapacitation of US Statecraft and Diplomacy." *The Hague Journal of Diplomacy* 6:414.

Gaddis, John Lewis. 1972. *The United States and the Origins of the Cold War*. New York: Columbia University Press.

Gates, Robert. 2007a. "Remarks as Delivered by Secretary of Defense Robert M. Gates." Speech given at Association of the United States Army, October 10. Washington, DC. http://www.defense.gov/speeches/speech.aspx?speechid=1181.

———. 2007b. "Landon Lecture (Kansas State University)." Kansas State University, Manhattan, Kansas, November 26. Reprinted in *Military Review*, January–February 2008.

———. 2008. "US Global Leadership Campaign." Speech, July 15. US Department of State, Washington, DC. http://www.defense.gov/speeches/speech.aspx?speechid=1262.

———. 2009a. "A Balanced Strategy: Reprogramming the Pentagon for a New Age." *Foreign Affairs*, January/February.

———. 2009b. "Policy Guidance of DOD Overseas Humanitarian Assistance Program (HAP)." November 8. Washington, DC.

———. 2010. "Helping Others Defend Themselves: The Future of US Security Assistance." *Foreign Affairs*, May/June.

George, Roger, and Harvey Rishikof, eds. 2011. *The National Security Enterprise: Navigating the Labyrinth*. Washington, DC: Georgetown University Press.

Gerth, Jeff. 2005. "Military Information War Is Vast and Often Secretive." *New York Times*, December 11.

Glain, Stephen. 2011. *State vs. Defense: The Battle to Define America's Empire*. New York: Crown.

Goldberg, Alfred. 1995. "A Brief History of the Organization of the Department of Defense," Washington, DC: Office of the Secretary of Defense Historical Office.

Goldstein, Gordon. 2008. *Lessons in Disaster: McGeorge Bundy and the Path to War in Vietnam*. New York: Henry Holt.

Gordon, Michael R. 2000. "The 2000 Campaign: The Military; Bush Would Stop US Peacekeeping in Balkan Fights." *New York Times*, October 21.

———. 2003. "The Struggle for Iraq: Reconstruction; 101st Airborne Scores Success in Northern Iraq." *New York Times*, September 4.

———. 2007. *Cobra II: The Inside Story of the Invasion and Occupation of Iraq.* New York: Vintage.

———. 2008. "US Army Shifts Focus to Nation-Building." *New York Times,* February 8.

Gordon, Vance, Dave McNichol, and Bryan Jack. 2009. "Revolution, Counter-Revolution, and Evolution: A Brief History of the PPBS." Unpublished manuscript.

Gorman, Siobhan. 2009. "CIA Had Secret Al Qaeda Plan." *Wall Street Journal,* July 13.

Gorman, Siobhan, and Julian E. Barnes. 2011. "Spy, Military Ties Aided bin Laden Raid." *Wall Street Journal,* May 23.

Gorman, Siobhan, and Adam Entous. 2011. "CIA Plans Yemen Drone Strikes." *Wall Street Journal,* June 14.

Government Accountability Office. 2007. *"Section 1206 Security Assistance Program—Findings on Criteria, Coordination, and Implementation."* http://www.gao.gov/new .items/d07416r.pdf.

———. 2008. "Combating Terrorism: Actions Needed to Enhance Implementation of Trans-Sahara Counterterrorism Partnership." GAO-08-860, July. Washington, DC: Government Printing Office.

———. 2009. *Military Operations: Actions Needed to Improve Oversight and Interagency Coordination for the Commander's Emergency Response Program in Afghanistan.* GAO-09-615, May 18. Washington, DC: Government Printing Office.

———. 2010a. "International Security: DOD and State Need to Improve Sustainment Planning and Monitoring and Evaluation for Section 1206 and 1207 Assistance Programs." GAO 10-4312010, April 15. Washington, DC: Government Printing Office.

———. 2010b. DOD Need to Determine the Future of Its Horn of Africa Task Force. GAO-10-504.2010a, April 15. Washington, DC: Government Printing Office.

———. 2010c. *Improved Planning, Training, and Interagency Collaboration Could Strengthen DOD's Efforts in Africa.* GAO-10-794, July 28. Washington, DC: Government Printing Office.

———. 2010d. *Interagency Collaboration Practices and Challenges at DOD's Southern and Africa Commands.* GAO-10-962T, July 28. Washington, DC: Government Printing Office.

———. 2011. *Defense Acquisitions: Further Action Needed to Better Implement Requirements for Conducting Inventory of Service Contract Activities.* GAO 11-192, January. Washington, DC: Government Printing Office.

———. 2012a. *Humanitarian and Development Assistance: Project Evaluations and Better Information Sharing Needed to Manage the Military's Efforts.* GAO-12-359, February 8. Washington DC: Government Printing Office.

———. 2012b. "DOD Financial Management: Improvements Needed in Prompt Payment Monitoring and Reporting." Letter to Sen. Carl Levin. GAO-12-662R, June 26.

Graham, James R., ed. 1993. *Non-Combat Roles for the US Military in the Post Cold War Era.* Washington, DC: National Defense University Press.

Graham-Silverman, Adam. 2009. "The Foreign Aid Crusade: Overdue for a Makeover." *CQ Weekly,* June 8. 1303–04.

Grimmett, Richard. 2012. *Intelligence Authorization Legislation: Status and Challenges.* Report No. R40240. Washington DC: Congressional Research Service.

Groseclose, Tim, and Charles Stewart III. 1998. "The Value of Committee Seats in the House, 1947–91." *American Journal of Political Science,* April 2, 42: 453–74.

Hagel, Chuck. 2004. "A Republican Foreign Policy." *Foreign Affairs* 83 (4): 64–76.

Halberstam, David. 1993. *The Best and the Brightest.* Twentieth-Anniversary Edition. New York: Ballantine Books.

———. 2001. *War in a Time of Peace: Bush, Clinton, and the Generals.* New York: Scribner.

Hammond, Paul. 1961. *Organizing for Defense.* Princeton, NJ: Princeton University Press.

HELP Commission. 2007. *The HELP Commission Report on Foreign Assistance Reform.* HELP Commission.

Herrnson, Paul. 2001. "The Money Maze: Financing Congressional Elections." In *Congress Reconsidered*, edited by Lawrence Dodd and Bruce Oppenheimer. Seventh Edition. Washington, DC: CQ Press.

———. 2012. *Congressional Elections: Campaigning at Home and in Washington.* Sixth Edition. Washington DC: Sage-CQ Press.

Hitch, Charles J. 1965. "Decision-Making for Defense." Gaither Memorial Lectures, University of California. April 5–9.

Hodge, Nathan. 2011. *Armed Humanitarians: The Rise of the Nation Builders.* New York: Bloomsbury.

Horton, Scott. 2011. "The Rizzo Investigation." *Harper's: No Comment Blog,* November 11. http://harpers.org/archive/2011/11/hbc-90008314.

Hull, Cordell. 1948. *The Memoirs of Cordell Hull.* 2 vols. London: Hodder & Stoughton.

Huntington, Samuel. 1957. *The Soldier and the State: The Theory and Politics of Civil-Military Relations.* Cambridge, MA: Belknap Press of Harvard University Press.

Ignatius, David. 2011a. "The Blurring of CIA and Military." *Washington Post*, June 1.

———. 2011b. "Rewriting Rumsfeld's Rules." *Washington Post*, June 3.

Jackall, Robert, and Janice M. Hirota. 2000. *Image Makers: Advertising, Public Relations and the Ethos of Advocacy.* Chicago: University of Chicago Press.

Johnson, Dennis. 2007. *No Place for Amateurs: How Political Consultants Are Reshaping American Democracy.* Second Edition. New York: Routledge.

Johnson, Gregory, Vijaya Ramachandran, and Julie Walz. 2011. "The Commanders Emergency Response Program in Afghanistan: Refining US Military Capabilities in Stability and In-Conflict Development." Center for Global Development Working Paper No. 265, September. http://www.cgdev.org/files/1425397_file_Johnson _Ramachandran_Walz_CERP_FINAL.pdf.

———. 2012. "CERP in Afghanistan: Refining Military Capabilities in Development Activities." *Prism* 3: No. 2: 87–98.

Johnson, Jason. 2012. *Political Consultants and Campaigns: One Day to Sell.* Boulder, CO: Westview Press.

Johnson, Robert David. 2006. *Congress and the Cold War.* New York: Cambridge University Press.

Johnson, Susan R., Ronald E. Neumann, and Thomas R. Pickering. (2013) "Presidents Are Breaking the US Foreign Service." *Washington Post*, April 11.

Joint Special Operations Task Force. 2011. Philippines Fact Sheet, July http://jsotf-p .blogspot.com/2011/09/type-your-summary-here_20.html.

Katchadourian, Raffi. 2006. "Pursuing Terrorists in the Great Desert: The US Military's $500 Million Gamble to Prevent the Next Afghanistan." *Village Voice*, January 17.

Keehan, Mark P., and Gerry Land. 2010. "Teaching Note: Planning, Programming, Budgeting, and Execution (PPBE) Process." February. Washington, DC: Defense Acquisition University. https://learn.test.dau.mil/CourseWare/802510/1/M8/JobAids /PPBE.pdf.

Kelly, John F. 2013. "Posture Statement of General John F. Kelly, United States Marine Corps Commander, United States Southern Command before the 113th Congress Senate Armed Services Committee." http://www.southcom.mil/newsroom/Documents/SOUTHCOM%202013%20Posture%20Statement%20FINAL%20SASC.pdf.

Kibbe, Jennifer D. 2004. "The Rise of the Shadow Warriors." *Foreign Affairs* 83 (March/April 2004): 106.

_____. 2007. "Covert Action and the Pentagon." In *Strategic Intelligence, Volume 3: CovertAction*, edited by Loch Johnson, 131–44. Westport, CT: Praeger Security International.

———. 2010a. "Congressional Oversight of Intelligence: Is the Solution Part of the Problem?" *Intelligence and National Security* 25 (February): 30.

———. 2010b. "Covert Action, Pentagon-style." In *The Oxford Handbook on National Security Intelligence*, edited by Loch Johnson, 569–86. New York: Oxford University.

———. 2012. "Conducting Shadow Wars." *Journal of National Security Law & Policy* 5 (2): 373–92. Washington, DC: Georgetown Law Center.

Kilcullen, David. 2007. "New Paradigms for 21st Century." *Small Wars Journal*, June 23. http://smallwarsjournal.com/blog/new-paradigms-for-21st-century-conflict.

———. 2009. "Balanced Response: A National Security Strategy for the Protracted Struggle against Extremism." In *Beyond Bullets*, edited by Alice E. Hunt, Kristin M. Lord, John A. Nagl, and Seth D. Rosen. Center for a New American Security. http://www.cnas.org/files/documents/publications/LordNaglRosen_Beyond%20Bullets%20Edited%20Volume_June09_0.pdf.

King, Kay. 2010. *Congress and National Security*, Council Special Report No. 58, November. New York: Council on Foreign Relations, 6–7.

Klaidman, Daniel. 2012. *Kill or Capture: The War on Terror and the Soul of the Obama Presidency*. New York: Houghton Mifflin Harcourt.

———. 2013. "No More Drones for CIA." *Daily Beast*, March 19. http://www.thedailybeast.com/articles/2013/03/19/exclusive-no-more-drones-for-cia.html.

Klein, Ezra. 2012. "The President Will Do What Congress Lets Him Do." *Washington PostWonkblog*, June 12. http://www.washingtonpost.com/blogs/ezra-klein/post/the-president-will-do-what-congress-lets-him-do/2012/06/12/gJQAgjm7XV_blog.html.

Koger, Gregory. 2010. *Filibustering: A Political History of Obstruction in the House and Senate*. Chicago: University of Chicago Press.

Kohn, Richard. 2002. "The Erosion of Civilian Control of the Military in the United States Today." *Naval War College Review* LV: No. 3.

———. 2009. "The Danger of Militarization in an Endless 'War' on Terrorism." *Journal of Military History* 73: No.1.

Korb, Lawrence. 1976. *The Joint Chiefs of Staff: The First Twenty-Five Years*. Bloomington: Indiana University Press.

Kosloski, Robert P. 2012. "Letter to the Editor." *Joint Forces Quarterly*. Issue 64 (1st Quarter).

Krasner, Stephen D., and Carlos Pascual. 2005. "Addressing State Failure." *Foreign Affairs* 8 (4).

Krehbiel, Keith. 1991. *Information and Legislative Organization*. Ann Arbor: University of Michigan.

LaFeber, Walter. 1973. *American, Russia and the Cold War*. New York: McGraw Hill.

Lamb, Christopher J., and Edward Marks. 2010. "Chief of Mission Authority as a Model for National Security Integration." INSS Strategic Perspectives 2. National Defense University: Washington, DC.

Lamb, Christopher J., and Evan Munsing. 2011. *Secret Weapon: High-Value Target Teams as an Organizational Innovation*. Washington, DC: National Defense University.

Lee, Jessica, and Maureen Farrell. 2011. "Civil-Military Operations in Kenya's Rift Valley." *Prism* 2: No. 2: March, 159–61.

Lindsay, James M., and Randall B. Ripley. 1993. *Congress Resurgent: Foreign and Defense Policy on Capitol Hill*. Ann Arbor: University of Michigan Press.

Locher, James. 2004. *Victory on the Potomac: The Goldwater-Nichols Act Unifies the Pentagon*. College Station: Texas A & M University Press.

Loftus, Gerald. 2007. "Expeditionary Sidekicks? The Military-Diplomatic Dynamic." *Avuncular America blog*. http://avuncularamerican.typepad.com/blog/2007/12/eating-the-seed.html.

Lovell, John P., and Philip S. Kronenberg, eds. 1974. *New Civil-Military Relations: The Agonies of Adjustment to Post-Vietnam Realities*. New Brunswick, NJ: Transaction Books.

Maddow, Rachel. 2012. *Drift: The Unmooring of American Military Power*. New York: Crown.

Maltzman, Forrest. 1997. *Competing Principals: Committees, Parties, and the Organization of Congress*. Ann Arbor: University of Michigan, 165–66.

Malvesti, Michele J. 2010. "To Serve the Nation: US Special Operations Forces in an Era of Persistent Conflict." Center for a New American Security. http://www.cnas.org/files/documents/publications/CNAS_To%20Serve%20the%20Nation_Malvesti.pdf.

Mann, Thomas, and Norman Ornstein. 2006. *The Broken Branch: How Congress Is Failing America and How to Get It Back on Track*. New York: Oxford University Press.

———. 2012. *It's Even Worse Than It Looks: How the American Constitutional System Collided with the New Politics of Extremism*. New York: Basic Books.

Marks, Edward. 2010a. "The Next Generation Department of State Project." *Foreign Service Journal*, 87 (5): 29–33.

———. 2010b. "Rethinking the Geographic Combatant Commands." *InterAgency Journal*, 1(1): 19–23. http://thesimonscenter.org/wp-content/uploads/2010/11/IAJ-1-1-pg19-23.pdf.

Mayhew, David. 1974. *Congress: The Electoral Connection*. New Haven, CT: Yale University Press.

Mazzetti, Mark. 2006. "Military Role in US Embassies Creates Strains, Report Says," *New York Times*, December 20.

———. 2010. "US Is Said to Expand Secret Actions in Mideast." *New York Times*, May 24.

———. 2011. "US Is Intensifying a Secret Campaign of Yemen Airstrikes." *New York Times*, June 8.

———. 2013a. *The Way of the Knife: The CIA, a Secret Army, and a War at the Ends of the Earth*. New York: Penguin.

———. 2013b. "New Terror Strategy Shifts CIA Focus Back to Spying." *New York Times*, May 23.

Mazzetti, Mark, and Scott Shane. 2013. "As New Drone Policy Is Weighed, Few Practical Effects Are Seen." *New York Times*, March 21.

McCormick, James. 1993. "Decision Making in the Foreign Affairs and Foreign Relations Committees." In *Congress Resurgent: Foreign and Defense Policy on Capitol Hill*, edited by Randall Ripley and James Lindsay, 115–54. Ann Arbor: University of Michigan.

McMaster, H. R. 1998. *Dereliction of Duty: Lyndon Johnson, Robert McNamara, the Joint Chiefs of Staff, and the Lies That Led to Vietnam*. New York: Harper Collins.

Meckstroth, Margee. 2010. *Please, Sir, May I Have Some More?: Congress, the Military Services, and the Unfunded Requirements Process*. MA Thesis, Georgetown University Security Studies program.

Miles, Donna. 2013. "McRaven Sets Future Course for Special Ops Command." *Defense.Gov*, May 22. http://www.defense.gov/news/newsarticle.aspx?id=120113.

Miller, Greg. 2006. "US Seeks to Rein in Its Military Spy Teams." *Los Angeles Times*, December 18.

———. 2011a. "CIA Will Direct Yemen Drones." *Washington Post*, June 14.

———. 2011b. "Joint Strike Is Latest Example of CIA-Military Convergence." *Washington Post*, October 1.

———. 2011c. "Under Obama, A Drone Network." *Washington Post*, December 28.

———. 2012. "US Drone Campaign in Yemen Expanded." *Washington Post*, April 26.

———. 2013a. "Secret Report Raises Alarms on Intelligence Blind Spots Because of AQ Focus." *Washington Post*, March 20.

———. 2013b. "Obama's New Drone Policy Leaves Room for CIA Role." *Washington Post*, May 25.

Miller, Greg, and Julie Tate. 2011. "CIA Shifts Focus to Killing Targets." *Washington Post*, September 1.

Milner, Helen, and Dustin Tingley. 2010. "The Political Economy of US Foreign Aid: American Legislators and the Domestic Politics of Aid." *Economics & Politics*, 22: 200–32.

Modernizing Foreign Assistance Network. 2008. *New Day, New Way: US Foreign Assistance for the 21st Century*. Washington, DC: Center for Global Development.

Morgan, Matthew J., ed. 2009. *The Impact of 9/11 on the Media, Arts, and Entertainment: The Day That Changed Everything*. New York: Palgrave MacMillian.

Nagl, John, and Peter Schoomacher. 2005. *Learning to Eat Soup with a Knife: Counterinsurgency Lessons from Malaya and Vietnam*. Chicago: University of Chicago Press.

Nakamura, Kennon H. 2009. *US Public Diplomacy: Background and Current Issues*. Congressional Research Service, December 18.

Nakashima, Ellen. 2012. "Pentagon Seeks More Powers for Cyberdefense." *Washington Post*, August 10.

Nakashima, Ellen, and Greg Jaffe. 2010. "Clapper Is Front-Runner for Intelligence Post." *Washington Post*, May 22.

New America Foundation. 2013a. "Obama's Covert War in Yemen: Recent Strikes." http://yemendrones.newamerica.net/.

———. 2013b. "Analysis: Pakistan Drone Strikes." natsec.newamerica.net/drones /pakistan/analysis.

Newport, Frank. 2012. "Congress' Job Approval at New Low of 10%; Republicans and Democrats equally negative." *GallupPolitics*, February 8. http://www.gallup.com /poll/152528/Congress-Job-Approval-New-Low.aspx?ref=image.

Nielsen, Suzanne C., and Don M. Snider, eds. 2009. *American Civil-Military Relations: The Soldier and the State in a New Era*. Baltimore: Johns Hopkins Press.

Nye, Joseph. 2004. *Soft Power: The Means to Success in World Politics.* Cambridge, MA: Public Affairs.

Oakley, Robert B., and Michael Casey, Jr. 2007. "The Country Team: Restructuring America's First Line of Engagement." Strategic Forum No. 227. Institute for National Strategic Studies, National Defense University.

Obama, Barack. 2009. "Remarks by the President on a New Beginning." Speech. Egypt: Cairo University, June 4. The White House, http://www.whitehouse.gov /the_press_office/Remarks-by-the-President-at-Cairo-University-6-04-09/.

———. 2013. "Remarks by the President at the National Defense University." Speech. Washington, DC: National Defense University, May 23 http://www.whitehouse.gov /the-press-office/2013/05/23/remarks-president-national-defense-university.

Office of Personnel Management. 2012. "Total Government Employment Since 1962." Table. http://www.opm.gov/policy-data-oversight/data-analysis-documen tation/federal-employment-reports/historical-tables/total-government-employ ment-since-1962.

Olson, William J. 2012. "The Slow Motion Coup: Militarization and the Implications of Eisenhower's Prescience." *Small Wars Journal,* August 11. http://smallwarsjour nal.com/jrnl/art/the-slow-motion-coup-militarization-and-the-implications-of -eisenhower%E2%80%99s-prescience.

Ornstein, Norman, Thomas Mann, and Michael Malbin. 2008. "Vital Statistics on Congress," Tables 6-1, 6-2, 6-4. 124–25, 127. Washington, DC: Brookings Institution.

Owens, Mackubin Thomas. 2011. *US Civil-Military Relations after 9/11: Renegotiating the Civil-Military Bargain.* New York: Continuum.

———. 2012. "What Military Officers Need to Know about Civil-Military Relations." *Naval War College Review* 65 (2): 67–87.

Page, Benjamin I., and Marshall M. Bouton. 2006. *The Foreign Policy Disconnect: What Americans Want from Our Leaders but Don't Get.* Chicago: University of Chicago Press.

Panetta, Leon. 2011. Interview with Leon Panetta. *PBS Newshour,* WETA-TV 26, May 3.

Perlez, Jane, and Ismail Khan. 2011. "Pakistan Tells US It Must Sharply Cut CIA Activities." *New York Times,* April 11.

Perlmutter, Amos. 1977. *The Military and Politics in Modern Times.* New Haven, CT: Yale University Press.

Pincus, Walter. 2011a. "Pentagon Cancer Research Budget Comes under Scrutiny." *Washington Post,* March 13.

———. 2011b. "Lawmakers Slash Budget for Defense Department's Information Ops." *Washington Post,* June 22.

Ploch, Lauren. 2011. *Africa Command: US Strategic Interests and the Role of the US Military in Africa.* Congressional Research Service, July 22.

Poole, Keith, and Howard Rosenthal. 2012. "The Polarization of the Congressional Parties." http://voteview.com/political_polarization.asp.

Priest, Dana. 2000. "A Four-Star Foreign Policy? US Commanders Wield Rising Clout, Autonomy." *Washington Post,* September 28.

———. 2003. *The Mission: Waging War and Keeping Peace with America's Military.* New York: W. W. Norton and Company.

———. 2005. "Covert CIA Program Withstands New Furor." *Washington Post,* December 30.

Priest, Dana, and William Arkin. 2011a. "Stealth Missions." *Washington Post,* September 4.

———. 2011b. *Top Secret America: The Rise of the New American Security State.* New York: Little Brown and Company.

Project on National Security Reform. 2009. "Forging a New Shield." Center for the Study of the Presidency & Congress, May. Washington, DC.

Rana, Kishan S. 2011. *21st Century Diplomacy.* London: Continuum International Publishing Company.

Ray, Charles. 2009. "Defining Lines of Authority." *Armed Forces Journal,* February. http://www.armedforcesjournal.com/2009/02/3875360.

Redente, Jennifer. 2008. "New Engineers Drilling Wells in Djibouti." *US Army,* January 2. http://www.army.mil/article/6819/new-engineers-drilling-wells-in-djibouti/.

Rennack, Dianne, Lisa Mages, and Susan Chesser. 2011. *Foreign Operations Appropriations: General Provisions.* Report No. R40557. Washington, DC: Congressional Research Service.

Reveron, Derek S., ed. 2004. *America's Viceroys: The US Military and Foreign Policy.* New York: Palgrave MacMillan.

———. 2007a. "Shaping and Military Diplomacy." Paper presented at the 2007 Annual Meeting of the American Political Science Association, August 30–September 2.

———. 2007b. "The Military and US Foreign Policy." *The Chronicle Review,* December 21.

———. 2010. *Exporting Security: International Cooperation, Security Cooperation, and the Changing Face of the US Military.* Washington, DC: Georgetown University Press.

Rice, Condoleezza. 2008. "Remarks at the Civilian Response Corps Rollout." Speech. US Department of State, July 16. Washington DC.

Ricks, Thomas E. 1997. "The Widening Gap between Military and Society." *The Atlantic Magazine,* July.

———. 2007. *Fiasco: The American Military Adventure in Iraq, 2003–05.* New York: Penguin.

Rife, Lt. Col. Rickey L. 1998. "Defense Is from Mars; State Is from Venus." Army War College Strategy Research Project, Carlisle: Army War College.

Ripley, Randall, and Grace Franklin. 1990. *Congress, the Bureaucracy, and Public Policy.* Fifth Edition. Pacific Grove, CA: Brooks/Cole.

Rosenberg, David Alan. 1983. "The Origins of Overkill: Nuclear Weapons and American Strategy, 1945–1960." *International Security,* vol. 7, no. 4 (Spring), 3–71.

Rubin, Barry. 1985. *Secrets of State: The State Department and the Struggle Over US Foreign Policy.* New York: Oxford University Press.

Rumbaugh, Russell, and Mathew Leatherman. 2012. "The Pentagon as Pitchman: Perception and Reality of Public Diplomacy." Stimson Center, September.

Rundquist, Barry, and Thomas Carsey. 2002. *Congress and Defense Spending: The Distributive Politics of Military Procurement.* Norman, OK: Red River Books, University of Oklahoma Press.

Scahill, Jeremy. 2009. "The Secret US War in Pakistan." *The Nation,* December 7.

———. 2013. *Dirty Wars: The World Is a Battlefield.* New York: Nation.

Schake, Kori. 2012. *State of Disrepair: Fixing the Culture and Practices of the State Department.* Palo Alto, CA: Hoover Institution Press.

Schelling, Tom. 1968. "PPBS and Foreign Affairs." *The Public Interest* No.11: Spring.

Schmitt, Eric, and Mark Mazzetti. 2008. "Secret Order Lets US Raid Al Qaeda." *New York Times,* November 9.

———. 2013. "A Commander Seeks to Chart a New Path for Special Operations." *New York Times,* May 2.

Serafino, Nina M. 2011a. *Security Assistance Reform:"Section 1206" Background and Issues for Congress*. Report RS22855, February 11. Washington, DC: Congressional Research Service.

———. 2011b. *Department of Defense "Section 1207" Security and Stabilization Assistance: Background and Congressional Concerns, FY2006–FY2010*. March 3. Congressional Research Service.

———. 2012a. "Building Civilian Interagency Capacity for Missions Abroad: Key Proposals and Issues for Congress." January 23. Washington, DC: Congressional Research Service.

———. 2012b. "Global Security Contingency Fund: Summary and Issue Overview." R42641, August 1. Washington, DC: Congressional Research Service.

———. 2012c. *Peacekeeping, Stabilization and Conflict Transitions: Background and Congressional Action on the Civilian Response/Reserve Corps and other Civilian Stabilization and Reconstruction Capabilities*. RL32862, October 2. Washington, DC: Congressional Research Service.

Serafino, Nina M., Dale, Catherine Dale, Richard F. Grimmett, Rhoda Margesson, John Rollins, Tiaji Salaam-Blyther, Curt Tarnoff, Amy F. Woolf, Liana Sun Wyler, and Steve Bowman. 2008. *The Department of Defense Role in Foreign Assistance: Background, Major Issues, and Options for Congress*. August 25. Washington, DC: Congressional Research Service.

Shane, Scott. 2013. "Debate Aside, Number of Drone Strikes Drops Sharply." *New York Times*, May 21.

Shane, Scott, Mark Mazzetti, and Robert F. Worth. 2010. "Secret Assault on Terrorism Widens on Two Continents." *New York Times*, August 14.

Shanker, Thom. 2009. "Top Officer Urges Limit on Mission of Military." *New York Times*, January 13.

Shanker, Thom, and Scott Shane. 2006. "Elite Troops Get Expanded Role on Intelligence," *New York Times*, March 8.

Simmons, Barry K. 1994. "Executing US Foreign Policy through the Country Team Concept." *Air Force Law Review* 37 (1994).

Sinclair, Barbara. 2006. *Party Wars: Polarization and the Politics of National Policy Making*. Norman, OK: University of Oklahoma Press.

Smith, Steven, and Christopher Deering. 1990. *Committees in Congress*. Second Edition. 87, 101. Washington, DC: Congressional Quarterly.

Somaliland Times. 2003. "Guelleh Visits CJTF-HOA Commander." May 7. http://somalilandtimes.net/2003/68/6817.shtml.

Special Inspector General for Afghanistan Reconstruction. 2011. *Commander's Emergency Response Program in Laghman Province Provided Some Benefits, but Oversight Weaknesses and Sustainment Concerns Led to Questionable Outcomes and Potential Waste*. SIGAR Audit 11-7, January 27. Washington, DC: Government Printing Office.

———. 2013. *Quarterly Report to the United States Congress*. January 30. Washington, DC: Government Printing Office.

Special Inspector General for Iraq Reconstruction. 2006. *Management of the Commander's Emergency Response Program (CERP) for Fiscal Year 2005*. SIGIR 05-025, January 23. Washington DC: Government Printing Office.

———. 2009. *Hard Lessons: The Iraq Reconstruction Experience*. Washington, DC: Government Printing Office.

———. 2013. *Learning from Iraq: A Final Report from the Special Inspector General for Iraq Reconstruction*. March. Washington, DC: Government Printing Office.

Steinberg, Donald. 2012. "An Interview with Donald Steinberg." *PRISM* 3, no. 2: 157–63.

Stewart III, Charles. 2012. "The Value of Committee Assignments in Congress Since 1994." Midwest Political Science Association. MIT Political Science Department Research Paper 2012-7, April 6. http://ssrn.com/abstract=2035632.

Stimson Center/American Academy of Diplomacy. 2008. *A Foreign Affairs Budget for the Future.* Washington, DC: Stimson Center.

Stone, Col. Kathryn. 2003. *"All Necessary Means"—Employing CIA Operatives in a War- fighting Role Alongside Special Operations Forces.* July 4. US Army War College Strat- egy Research Project.

Strickler, Ted. 1985. "The US Foreign Service: A Fit of Crisis or a Crisis of Fit." March. Research Report, National War College.

Theriault, Sean. 2008. *Party Polarization in Congress.* New York, NY: Cambridge Uni- versity Press.

Tremlett, Giles. 2004. "US Sends Special Forces into North Africa." *The Guardian,* March 14.

Tyson, Ann Scott. 2006. "Rumsfeld Approved Military's Most Ambitious Secret Plan on Terror." *Washington Post,* April 23.

Tyson, Ann Scott, and Dana Priest. 2005. "Pentagon Seeking Leeway Overseas; Opera- tions Could Bypass Envoys." *Washington Post,* February 24.

Ungar, David. 2012. *The Emergency State: America's Pursuit of Absolute Security at All Costs.* New York, NY: Penguin.

US Africa Command. 2009. "HIV/AIDS Prevention Program Fact Sheet." May.

———. 2011. Public Affairs Office. "Fact Sheet: United States Africa Command." http://www.africom.mil/getArticle.asp?art=1644.

———. 2012a. "Combined Joint Task Force—Horn of Africa." Fact Sheet, January 31. http://www.hoa.africom.mil/pdfFiles/Fact%20Sheet.pdf.

———. 2012b. "Pandemic Response Program." Fact Sheet, January. Stuttgart, Germany.

U.S Agency for International Development. 2011. "South Sudan Transition Strategy 2011–2013." June. http://pdf.usaid.gov/pdf_docs/PDACR770.pdf.

US Army. 2007. *US Army–US Marine Corps Counterinsurgency Field Manual*, Signalman Publishing.

———. 2009. *Stability Operations Field Manual.* FM 3-07. Washington, DC: US Army.

US Congress. 2001. "Authorization for Use of Military Force." Joint Resolution. Public Law 107-40.

US Department of Defense. 1997. "Report of the Quadrennial Defense Review (QDR)." http://www.dod.mil/pubs/qdr/toc.html.

———. 2005a. "Military Support for Stability, Security, Transition, and Reconstruction (SASTR) Operations." DoD Directive 3000.05. http://www.fas.org/irp/doddir/dod /d3000_05.pdf.

———. 2005b. "Quadrennial Defense Review (QDR) Strategic Communication Road- map. QDR, Strategic Communication Roadmap 2006." http://www.defense.gov /pubs/pdfs/QDRRoadmap20060925a.pdf.

———. 2006. "Quadrennial Defense Review Report." February 6. http://www.defense .gov/qdr/report/Report20060203.pdf.

———. 2008. "DoD Policy and Responsibilities Relating to Security Cooperation." DoD Directive 5132.03, October 24. http://www.dtic.mil/whs/directives/corres /pdf/513203p.pdf.

———. 2010a. "Quadrennial Defense Review (QDR)." http://www.defense.gov/qdr /images/QDR_as_of_12Feb10_1000.pdf.

———. 2010b. "Joint Publication 1-02: Department of Defense Dictionary of Military and Associated Terms," Joint Chiefs of Staff, as amended through April 15, 2013. http://www.dtic.mil/doctrine/new_pubs/jp1_02.pdf.

———. 2011. Personnel and Procurement Statistics. "Active Duty Military Personnel Strengths by Regional Area and by Country (309A)." September 30. http://siadapp .dmdc.osd.mil/personnel/MILITARY/history/hst1109.pdf.

———. 2012a. *Base Structure Report, Fiscal Year 2012 Baseline.* http://www.acq.osd.mil /ie/download/bsr/BSR2012Baseline.pdf.

———. 2012b. *National Defense Budget Estimates for FY 2013.* March. http://comptroller .defense.gov/defbudget/fy2013/FY13_Green_Book.pdf.

———. 2012c. *Sustaining US Global Leadership: Priorities for 21st Century Defense.* January.

———. 2012d. *Section 1209 and Section 1203 (b) Report to Congress on Foreign-Assistance Related Programs for Fiscal Years 2008, 2009, and 2010.* April. http://justf.org/files /primarydocs/1204_1209_rept.pdf.

———. 2014. "Quadrennial Defense Review (QDR)."

US Department of Energy. 2003. Office of the Inspector General, Office of Audit Services. *Audit Report: National Nuclear Security Administration's Planning, Programming, Budgeting, and Evaluation Process.* DOE/IG 1604, August.

US Department of State. 2007. "FY 2007–2012 Department of State and USAID Strategic Plan." http://www.state.gov/s/d/rm/rls/dosstrat/2007/html/82982.htm.

———. 2009. "Report of Inspection: The Bureau of African Affairs." August. http://oig .state.gov/documents/organization/127270.pdf.

———. 2010. "Quadrennial Diplomacy and Development Review: Leading through Civilian Power." www.state.gov/s/dmr/qddr/.

US Department of State and the Broadcasting Board of Governors. Office of the Inspector General. 2010. "Report of Inspection: Embassy Addis Ababa, Ethiopia." Report number ISP-1-10-51A. http://oig.state.gov/documents/organization/143590 .pdf.

US House. 1959. *US Foreign Aid: Its Purposes, Scope, Administration, and Related Information*, House Document No. 116, Washington, DC: Government Printing Office.

———. 1991. *Joint Explanatory Statement of the Committee of Conference* (H.R. 1455). July 25.

———. 2006. *Assessing US Special Operations Command's Missions and Roles: Hearing before the Subcommittee on Terrorism, Unconventional Threats and Capabilities Subcommittee of the House Committee on Armed Services, US House of Representatives.* 109th Cong., 2d Sess., June 29.

———. 2009a. *Intelligence Authorization Act for Fiscal year 2010 (accompanying H.R. 2701) (H. Rept. 111-186),* June 26.

———. 2009b. *Legal Perspectives on Congressional Notification: Hearing of the Subcommittee on Intelligence Community Management of the Permanent Select Committee on Intelligence, US House of Representatives.* 111th Cong., 1st. Sess., October 22.

———. 2009c. House Conference Report on the Supplemental Appropriations Act, 2009, H. Rept. 111-185.

———. 2009d. *House Report 111-230—Department of Defense Appropriations Bill, 2010.* July 24. Washington, DC: Government Printing Office.

US Joint Chiefs of Staff. 2011. *The National Military Strategy of the United States.* Washington, DC: Government Printing Office.

US Library of Congress."Bills Introduced, 111th Congress." http://thomas.loc.gov/home/bills_res.html.

———. *Status of Appropriations Bills, FY 1998 through 2013.* Tables. http://thomas.loc.gov/home/approp/app13.html.

US National Security Council. 1950. "United States Objectives and Programs for National Security." NSC 68. http://www.fas.org/irp/offdocs/nsc-hst/nsc-68.htm.

US Senate. 1991. Senate Select Committee on Intelligence. *Authorizing Appropriations for Fiscal Year 1991 for the Intelligence Activities of the U.S. Government (Accompanying S. 1325)* (S. Rept. 102-85), June 19.

———. 1998. Budget Committee. *International Affairs: Activities of Domestic Agencies: Statement of Benjamin F. Nelson, Director, International Relations and Trade Issues, National Security and International Affairs Division, General Accounting Office.* GAO/T-NSIAD-98-174, June 4.

———. 2000. Committee on Armed Services. "Statement of Anthony C. Zinni, Commander in Chief, US Central Command." February 29.

———. 2006a. Armed Services Committee Subcommittee on Emerging Threats and Capabilities. 109th Cong. 2. *Statement Given by Vice Admiral Eric T. Olson, US Navy Deputy Commander United States Special Operations Command 2006.* US Senate, April 6. http://www.dod.mil/dodgc/olc/docs/TestOlson060405.pdf.

———. 2006b. Committee on Foreign Relations. "Embassies as Command Posts in the Anti-Terror Campaign." United States Senate, December 15. http://pdf.usaid.gov/pdf_docs/PCAAB569.pdf.

———. 2007. 107th Cong., 115 Stat. 224. 2001. *Authorization for Use of Military Force.* US Senate Joint Resolution.

———. 2008. Committee on Foreign Relations."*Defining the Military's Role towards Foreign Policy.*" July 31. http://www.foreign.senate.gov/imo/media/doc/BidenStatement080731p.pdf.

———. 2009a. Senate Select Committee on Intelligence. *Questions for the Record for Admiral Dennis Blair upon Nomination to Be Director of National Intelligence, Select Committee on Intelligence.* January 22.

———. 2009b. Select Committee on Intelligence. *Questions for the Record, Nomination of the Honorable Leon E. Panetta to be Director, Central Intelligence Agency.* http://intelligence.senate.gov/090205/panetta_post.pdf.

———. 2012a. Report accompanying S. 3254, National Defense Authorization Act for 2013, S. Rpt. 112-173, 235, June 4. http://thomas.loc.gov/cgi-bin/cpquery/?&sid=cp112fDBZZ&r_n=sr173.112&dbname=cp112&&sel=TOC_822124&.

———. 2012b. *Arthur Vandenburg: A Featured Biography.* http://www.senate.gov/artandhistory/history/common/generic/Featured_Bio_Vandenberg.htm.

———. 2013. Committee on Armed Services. *Hearing to Receive Testimony on the Law of Armed Conflict, the Use of Military Forces, and the 2001 Authorization for Use of Military Force.* May 16.

Van Buren, Peter. 2011. *We Meant Well: How I Helped Lose the Battle for the Hearts and Minds of the Iraqi People.* New York: Metropolitan Books/Henry Holt.

Ward, Justin Matthew. 2008. "Cultivating Capacity-Building in the Caucasus." July 21. http://www.army.mil/article/11028/.

Watson, Cynthia A. 2010.*Combatant Commands: Origins, Structures and Engagements.* Praeger Security International.

Weisgerber, Marcus. 2012. "Spec Ops to Grow as Pentagon Budget Shrinks." *Army Times*, February 7.

White House. 1997. A *National Security Strategy for a New Century*. May. http://nssar chive.us/NSSR/1997.pdf.

———. 2002. *The National Security Strategy of the United States of America*. September. http://nssarchive.us/NSSR/2002.pdf.

———. 2005. National Policy on Management of Interagency Efforts Concerning Reconstruction and Stabilization. National Security Presidential Directive 44, December 7. www.fas.org/irp/offdocs/nspd/nspd-44.pdf.

Whitlock, Craig. 2013a. "US Counterterrorism Efforts in Africa Defined by a Decade of Missteps." *Washington Post*, February 4.

———. 2013b. "Lawmaker Wants Military to Promptly Alert Congress about Drone Strikes." *Washington Post*, May 8.

Whitlock, Craig, and Greg Miller. 2010. "US Covert Paramilitary Presence in Afghanistan Much Larger Than Thought." *Washington Post*, September 22.

Whittaker, Alan G., Frederick C. Smith, and Elizabeth McKune. 2011. *The National Security Policy Process: The National Security Council and Interagency System*. Research Report, August 15. Washington, DC: Industrial College of the Armed Forces, National Defense University. http://www.ndu.edu/icaf/outreach/publications/nspp /docs/icaf-nsc-policy-process-report-08-2011.pdf.

Woodward, Bob. 2003. *Bush at War*. New York: Simon and Schuster.

———. 2004. *Plan of Attack: The Definitive Account of the Decision to Invade Iraq*. New York: Simon and Schuster.

———. 2007. *State of Denial: Bush at War, Part III*. New York: Simon and Schuster.

———. 2010. *Obama's Wars*. New York: Simon and Schuster.

Zegart, Amy. 2011a. "The Domestic Politics of Irrational Intelligence Oversight." *Political Science Quarterly*, 126: 1–25.

———. 2011b. *Eyes on Spies: Congress and the United States Intelligence Community*. Stanford, CA: Hoover Institution.

Zenko, Micah. 2013. "Confront and Confuse." *Foreign Policy* May 28. http://www.foreign policy.com/articles/2013/05/28/confront_and_confuse_obama_drone_speech.

Zinni, Tony, and Tony Koltz. 2006. *The Battle for Peace: A Frontline Vision of America's Power and Purpose*. New York: Palgrave Macmillan.

Contributors

Gordon Adams, a professor at the School of International Service at American University, Washington, DC, has published widely on defense and national security policy, the defense policy process, and national security budgets. He is extensively consulted by the nation's media for comment on US national security policy and is a regular columnist for *Foreign Policy*'s online website. From 1993 to 1997, he was associate director for national security and international affairs at the White House Office of Management and Budget. He was founder and director of the Defense Budget Project for the ten years preceding his government service. His most recent book is *Buying National Security: How America Plans and Pays for Its Global Role and Safety at Home* (with Cindy Williams, 2009), a unique study of how foreign policy and national security budgets are made across all relevant agencies. He received his Ph.D. from Columbia University.

G. William Anderson is an independent consultant on international development, foreign assistance, and national security and a professor of practice in Virginia Tech University's School of Public and International Affairs. He has worked on development, national security, and related public policy issues for over thirty-five years in the Congress as legislative director for a former chairman of the House Foreign Operations Appropriations Subcommittee, as a senior foreign officer in the US Agency for International Development, and as a private consultant. He has been USAID representative to the European Union in Brussels and senior development adviser at the US European and African Commands in Stuttgart, Germany, USAID mission director to Eritrea during the Eritrea-Ethiopia Border War, and as director of USAID's Office of East and South Asia in its Asia Near East Bureau. Anderson holds a Master's in Public Affairs (M.P.A.) degree from Princeton University's Woodrow Wilson School of Public and International Affairs and is a distinguished graduate of the Industrial College of the Armed Forces (part of the National Defense University).

Brian E. Carlson is an experienced public diplomacy specialist and a former career minister in the Foreign Service, and currently represents the international audience analysis firm InterMedia Research Institute on strategic communication matters. From 2006 to 2010, he was the State Department's liaison with the Department of Defense on strategic communication and public diplomacy. He worked on interagency collaboration projects under the direction of three under secretaries of state for public diplomacy and public affairs and was awarded the Joint Meritorious Civilian Service Award by the chairman of the Joint Chiefs of Staff in May 2010. Carlson served thirty-six years in the Foreign Service, including as the ambassador to the Republic of Latvia from 2001 to 2005.

Charles B. Cushman Jr. is a senior fellow at Georgetown University's Government Affairs Institute. Previously, he spent a decade at the Graduate School of Political Management at George Washington University, where he taught courses on political history, politics and public policy, national security policymaking, and Congress's roles in defense policy. Cushman is the author of *An Introduction to the US Congress*

(2005) and a forthcoming book on Congress and national security policymaking. He is a graduate of West Point and served nine years in the US Army as an armor officer, commanding troops in Germany and at Fort Knox, Kentucky, and completing his service as an instructor in the Department of Social Sciences at West Point. He holds a Ph.D. in political science from the University of North Carolina at Chapel Hill. He has been a lobbyist working to advance peace in the Middle East, and was defense and foreign affairs legislative assistant to Rep. David Price (D-NC) in the 105th Congress.

James F. Dobbins was appointed as the State Department's special representative for Afghanistan and Pakistan in May 2013. Prior to his appointment, he directed RAND's International Security and Defense Policy Center. He has held State Department and White House posts including assistant secretary of state for Europe, special assistant to the president for the Western Hemisphere, special adviser to the president and secretary of state for the Balkans, and ambassador to the European Community. He has handled a variety of crisis management assignments as the Clinton administration's special envoy for Somalia, Haiti, Bosnia, and Kosovo, and the Bush administration's first special envoy for Afghanistan. He is lead author of the three-volume *RAND History of Nation Building* and *Occupying Iraq: A History of the Coalition Provisional Authority*. In the wake of Sept 11, 2001, Dobbins was designated as the Bush administration's representative to the Afghan opposition. Dobbins helped organize and then represent the United States at the Bonn Conference, where a new Afghan government was formed. On December 16, 2001, he raised the flag over the newly reopened US Embassy. Dobbins graduated from the Georgetown School of Foreign Service and served three years in the US Navy.

Jennifer Kibbe is an associate professor of government at Franklin & Marshall College, where she focuses on US foreign policy and intelligence. Before returning to graduate school at UCLA, she worked on South African politics for a number of years at the Investor Responsibility Research Center in Washington, DC. Kibbe has written numerous articles on US foreign policy and intelligence, including "The Rise of the Shadow Warriors" in *Foreign Affairs* and "Covert Action and the Pentagon" in *Intelligence and National Security*. She received her Ph.D. in political science from UCLA and had a two-year postdoctoral fellowship at The Brookings Institution.

Edward Marks is currently the Washington director of the Simons Center for the Study of Interagency Cooperation at Ft. Leavenworth, Kansas. He is a retired senior Foreign Service officer, and he has held senior positions that include deputy coordinator for counterterrorism in the Department of State from 1982 to 1985, ambassador to Guinea-Bissau and Cape Verde, and deputy US representative to the Economic and Social Council of the UN. He was recalled to active duty in 2002 to serve as the first State Department representative in the Joint Inter-Agency Coordination Group on Counterterrorism (JIACG-CT) at the US Pacific Command. He was a distinguished visiting fellow at the Center for Strategic and International Studies, a visiting senior fellow at the Institute for National and Strategic Studies of the National Defense University, and is currently a distinguished senior fellow at George Mason University and a founding trustee of the Command and General Staff College (Ft. Leavenworth) Foundation. He is a graduate of the University of Michigan (BA), the University of Oklahoma (MA), and the National War College, and has published extensively on terrorism, interagency coordination, and related subjects.

Shoon Murray is an associate professor at the School of International Service at American University and served as director of the US Foreign Policy Master's Program between 2008 and 2014. She is the author of *Anchors against Change: American Opinion Leaders' Beliefs after the Cold War*, which investigated the tenacity of "enemy images" and how much American leaders' attitudes changed in response to dramatic international events. Her most recent book is *The Terror Authorization: History and Politics of the 2001 AUMF*. She received her Ph.D. from Yale University.

Anthony Quainton is a distinguished diplomat-in-residence at American University's School of International Service. He teaches diplomatic practice and public diplomacy, as well as US foreign policy toward the Middle East and Latin America. Prior to teaching, Quainton spent a career in the Foreign Service, including serving as US ambassador to the Central African Republic, Nicaragua, Kuwait, and Peru. He also served as assistant secretary of state for diplomatic security from 1992 to 1995.

Derek Reveron is a professor of national security affairs and the EMC Informationist Chair at the US Naval War College in Newport, Rhode Island, and a faculty affiliate at the Belfer Center for Science and International Affairs at Harvard University. Reveron specializes in strategy development, nonstate security challenges, intelligence, and US defense policy. He has authored or edited seven books, including *Exporting Security: International Engagement, Security Cooperation, and the Changing Face of the U.S. Military*; *Cyberspace and National Security*; and *Human Security in a Borderless World*. As a serving officer in the navy reserves, he has served in navy and joint units to include the National Military Command Center, NATO's Supreme Headquarters Allied Powers Europe, and NATO Training Mission-Afghanistan. During graduate school, he formulated, implemented, and evaluated democracy promotion programs for Heartland International. He received a diploma from the Naval War College, an MA in political science, and a Ph.D. in public policy analysis from the University of Illinois at Chicago.

Nina M. Serafino is a specialist in international security affairs with the Congressional Research Service (CRS). She began her career at CRS in 1981 as an analyst in Latin American affairs, working on the conflicts and peace processes in Central America. After serving four years as head of the Asia/Latin America section of CRS's Foreign Affairs Division, Serafino assumed her current position in 1993, working on US military operations other than war, in particular, peacekeeping. Subsequently, her work expanded to issues related to the use of force, stabilization, and reconstruction missions, security assistance, and interagency reform. Prior to joining CRS, Serafino worked as a journalist in New England, Argentina, and Chile. She holds a master's degree in international affairs from Columbia University. The views expressed in her chapter are those of the author, and do not represent a position of the Congressional Research Service or of the Library of Congress.

Connie Veillette is an independent consultant on development and foreign assistance issues, and an adjunct professor at George Washington University. She spent a thirty-year career in and around Congress as chief of staff to a senior member of the House Appropriations Committee, a specialist in foreign assistance at the Congressional Research Service, and as senior professional staff at the Senate Foreign Relations Committee. From 2010 to 2012, she led the Rethinking US Foreign Assistance Program at the Center for Global Development. She holds an M.A. in Latin American studies and a Ph.D. in comparative foreign politics from George Washington University.

Sharon Weiner is an associate professor at the School of International Service at American University and director of the school's Ph.D. program. Weiner's research interests include US national security policy and institutions, organizational politics, nonproliferation, and civil-military relations. Her book *Our Own Worst Enemy? Institutional Interests and the Proliferation of Nuclear Weapons Expertise* evaluates US–Russian cooperative nonproliferation programs and the role that organizational and partisan politics played in their success after the fall of the Soviet Union. She received her Ph.D. from the Massachusetts Institute of Technology.

Index